The
Sacred Books of the East

translated
by various Oriental scholars
and edited by

F. Max Müller

Vol. XXXIX

The Texts of Taoism

Translated by James Legge

in two parts
Part I

The Tao Te Ching of Lao Tzŭ

The Writings of Chuang Tzŭ

(Books I-XVII)

Dover Publications, Inc.
New York   New York

For bibliographic ease and accuracy the Wade-Giles Romanization of Chinese has been adopted for the title page and cover of this book. Within the text, however, the original transliteration has been retained.

This new Dover edition, first published in 1962, is an unabridged and unaltered republication of the work first published by the Oxford University Press in 1891. *The Texts of Tâoism,* Part I, is Volume XXXIX of "The Sacred Books of the East," and Part II is Volume XL of the same series.

Standard Book Number: 486-20990-3
Library of Congress Catalog Card Number: 62-53181

Manufactured in the United States of America
Dover Publications, Inc.
180 Varick Street
New York, N.Y. 10014

CONTENTS.

THE TÂO TEH *K*ING.

THE WRITINGS OF *K*WANG-3ZE.

INTRODUCTION.

CORRIGENDUM ET ADDENDUM.

On page 58, for the third and fourth sentences of the explanatory note to Chapter XIV, substitute the following :—It was but an interesting fancy of the ingenious writer, and the elaborate endeavour of Victor von Strauss to support it in 1870 has failed to make me think more favourably of it.

Dr. Edkins, in an article in the China Review for July and August, 1884, takes a different view of the chapter. He reads the monosyllables Î, Hî, and Wei according to his view of the old names of the Chinese characters, and calls them Âi, Kâi, and Mâi, considering them to be representative of one or three names of God. He says:—'I am inclined to find here marks of the presence of Babylonian thought . . . . We have not the original words for the first trinity of the Babylonian religion. They are in the Assyrian or Semitic form Anu, Bel, Nuah. In Accadian they were Ilu, Enu, Hia. Of these Ilu was the supreme God, source of Chaos, in Chinese Hwun tun or Hwun lun. In this chaos all forms were confounded as is the case with the Tâoist chaos. Bel or Enu is the word which separates the elements of chaos. Nuah or Hia is the light of God which penetrates the universe, and maintains the order established by the word. It was this Trinity of God, in the language of some intermediate nation, which Lâo-tsze appears to have had in view in the various passages where he speaks of the original principle of the universe in a triple form.'

This reading of our chapter is not more satisfactory to me than that of Rémusat ; and I am content, in my interpretation of it, to abide by the aids of Chinese dictionaries and commentators of reputation who have made it their study.

PREFACE.

In the Preface to the third volume of these 'Sacred Books of the East' (1879), I stated that I proposed giving in due course, in order to exhibit the System of Tâoism, translations of the Tâo Teh *K*ing by Lâo-ʒze (sixth century B.C.), the Writings of *K*wang-ʒze (between the middle of the fourth and third centuries B.C.), and the Treatise of 'Actions and their Retributions' (of our eleventh century) ; and perhaps also of one or more of the other characteristic Productions of the System.

The two volumes now submitted to the reader are a fulfilment of the promise made so long ago. They contain versions of the Three Works which were specified, and, in addition, as Appendixes, four other shorter Treatises of Tâoism ; Analyses of several of the Books of *K*wang-ʒze by Lin Hsî-*k*ung ; a list of the stories which form so important a part of those Books ; two Essays by two of the greatest Scholars of China, written the one in A.D. 586 and illustrating the Tâoistic beliefs of that age, and the other in A.D. 1078 and dealing with the four Books of *K*wang-ʒze, whose genuineness is frequently called in question. The concluding Index is confined very much to Proper Names. For Subjects the reader is referred to the Tables of Contents, the Introduction to the Books of *K*wang-ʒze (vol. xxxix, pp. 127–163), and the Introductory Notes to the various Appendixes.

The Treatise of Actions and their Retributions exhibits to us the Tâoism of the eleventh century in its moral or ethical aspects ; in the two earlier Works we see it rather as a philosophical speculation than as a religion in the ordinary sense of that term. It was not till after the introduction of Buddhism into China in our first century that Tâoism began to organise itself as a

Religion, having its monasteries and nunneries, its images
and rituals. While it did so, it maintained the superstitions peculiar to itself :—some, like the cultivation of the
Tâo as a rule of life favourable to longevity, come down
from the earliest times, and others which grew up
during the decay of the Kâu dynasty, and subsequently
blossomed;—now in Mystical Speculation; now in the
pursuits of Alchemy; now in the search for the pills of
Immortality and the Elixir vitae; now in Astrological
fancies; now in visions of Spirits and in Magical arts to
control them; and finally in the terrors of its Purgatory
and everlasting Hell. Its phases have been continually
changing, and at present it attracts our notice more as a
degraded adjunct of Buddhism than as a development of
the speculations of Lâo-ȝze and Kwang-ȝze. Up to its con-
tact with Buddhism, it subsisted as an opposition to the
Confucian system, which, while admitting the existence and
rule of the Supreme Being, bases its teachings on the study
of man's nature and the enforcement of the duties binding
on all men from the moral and social principles of their
constitution.

It is only during the present century that the Texts
of Tâoism have begun to receive the attention which
they deserve. Christianity was introduced into China
by Nestorian missionaries in the seventh century; and
from the Hsî-an monument, which was erected by
their successors in 781, nearly 150 years after their first
entrance, we perceive that they were as familiar with the
books of Lâo-ȝze and Kwang-ȝze as with the Confucian
literature of the empire, but that monument is the only
memorial of them that remains. In the thirteenth century
the Roman Catholic Church sent its earliest missionaries
to China, but we hardly know anything of their literary
labours.

The great Romish missions which continue to the present
day began towards the end of the sixteenth century; and
there exists now in the India Office a translation of the
Tâo Teh King in Latin, which was brought to England

by a Mr. Matthew Raper, and presented by him to the Royal Society, of which he was a Fellow, on January 10th, 1788. The manuscript is in excellent preservation, but we do not know by whom the version was made. It was presented, as stated in the Introduction, p. 12, to Mr. Raper by P. de Grammont, 'Missionarius Apostolicus, ex-Jesuita.' The chief object of the translator or translators was to show that 'the Mysteries of the Most Holy Trinity and of the Incarnate God were anciently known to the Chinese nation.' The version as a whole is of little value. The reader will find, on pp. 115, 116, its explanation of Lâo's seventy-second chapter;—the first morsel of it that has appeared in print.

Protestant missions to China commenced in 1807; but it was not till 1868 that the Rev. Dr. Chalmers, a member of one of them, published his 'Speculations on Metaphysics, Polity, and Morality of "The Old Philosopher," Lao-Tsze.' Meanwhile, Abel Rémusat had aroused the curiosity of scholars throughout Europe, in 1823, by his 'Memoir on the Life and Opinions of Lâo-Tseu, a Chinese Philosopher of the sixth century before our era, who professed the opinions commonly attributed to Pythagoras, to Plato, and to their disciples.' Rémusat was followed by one who had received from him his first lessons in Chinese, and had become a truly great Chinese scholar,—the late Stanislas Julien. He published in 1842 'a complete translation for the first time of this memorable Work, which is regarded with reason as the most profound, the most abstract, and the most difficult of all Chinese Literature.' Dr. Chalmers's translation was also complete, but his comments, whether original or from Chinese sources, were much fewer than those supplied by Julien. Two years later, two German versions of the Treatise were published at Leipzig;—by Reinhold von Plänckner and Victor von Strauss, differing much from each other, but both marked by originality and ability.

I undertook myself, as stated above, in 1879 to translate for 'The Sacred Books of the East' the Texts of Tâoism which appear in these volumes; and, as I could find time from my labours on 'The Texts of Confucianism,' I had written out more than one version of Lâo's work by the end of 1880. Though not satisfied with the result, I felt justified in exhibiting my general views of it in an article in the British Quarterly Review of July, 1883.

In 1884 Mr. F. H. Balfour published at Shanghai a version of 'Taoist Texts, Ethical, Political, and Speculative.' His Texts were ten in all, the Tâo Teh King being the first and longest of them. His version of this differed in many points from all previous versions; and Mr. H. A. Giles, of H. M.'s Consular Service in China, vehemently assailed it and also Dr. Chalmers's translation, in the China Review for March and April, 1886. Mr. Giles, indeed, occasionally launched a shaft also at Julien and myself; but his main object in his article was to discredit the genuineness and authenticity of the Tâo Teh King itself. 'The work,' he says, 'is undoubtedly a forgery. It contains, indeed, much that Lâo Tzŭ did say, but more that he did not.' I replied, so far as was necessary, to Mr. Giles in the same Review for January and February, 1888; and a brief summary of my reply is given in the second chapter of the Introduction in this volume. My confidence has never been shaken for a moment in the Tâo Teh King as a genuine relic of Lâo-ȝze, one of the most original minds of the Chinese race.

In preparing the version now published, I have used:—

First, 'The Complete Works of the Ten Philosophers;'— a Sû-ᵏâu reprint in 1804 of the best editions of the Philosophers, nearly all belonging more or less to the Tâoist school, included in it. It is a fine specimen of Chinese printing, clear and accurate. The Treatise of Lâo-ȝze of course occupies the first place, as edited by Kwei Yû-kwang (better known as Kwei ᵏăn-shan) of the Ming dynasty. The Text and Commentary are those of Ho-shang Kung (Introd., p. 7), along with the division of the whole into Parts and eighty-one chapters, and the titles of the several chapters, all attributed to him. Along the top of the page, there is a large collection of notes from celebrated commentators and writers down to the editor himself.

Second, the Text and Commentary of Wang Pî (called also Fû-sze), who died A.D. 249, at the early age of twenty-four. See Introduction, p. 8.

Third, 'Helps (lit. Wings) to Lâo-ʒze;' by ꝫiâo Hung (called also Zâo-hâu), and prefaced by him in 1587. This is what Julien calls 'the most extensive and most important contribution to the understanding of Lâo-ʒze, which we yet possess.' Its contents are selected from the ablest writings on the Treatise from Han Fei (Introd., p. 5) downwards, closing in many chapters with the notes made by the compiler himself in the course of his studies. Altogether the book sets before us the substance of the views of sixty-four writers on our short King. Julien took the trouble to analyse the list of them, and found it composed of three emperors, twenty professed Tâoists, seven Buddhists, and thirty-four Confucianists or members of the Literati. He says, 'These last constantly explain Lâo-ʒze according to the ideas peculiar to the School of Confucius, at the risk of misrepresenting him, and with the express intention of throttling his system;' then adding, 'The commentaries written in such a spirit have no interest for persons who wish to enter fully into the thought of Lâo-ʒze, and obtain a just idea of his doctrine. I have thought it useless, therefore, to specify the names of such commentaries and their authors.'

I have quoted these sentences of Julien, because of a charge brought by Mr. Balfour, in a prefatory note to his own version of the Tâo Teh King, against him and other translators. 'One prime defect,' he says, though with some hesitation, 'lies at the root of every translation that has been published hitherto; and this is, that not one seems to have been based solely and entirely on commentaries furnished by members of the Tâoist school. The Confucian element enters largely into all; and here, I think, an injustice has been done to Lâo-ʒze. To a Confucianist the Tâoist system is in every sense of the word a heresy, and a commentator holding this opinion is surely not the best expositor. It is as a Grammarian rather than as a Philosopher that a member of the Jû Chiâ deals with the Tâo Teh King; he gives the sense of a passage according to the syntactical construction rather than according to the genius of the philosophy itself; and in attempting to explain the text by his own canons, instead of by the canons of Tâoism, he mistakes the superficial and apparently obvious meaning for the hidden and esoteric interpretation.'

Mr. Balfour will hardly repeat his charge of imperfect or erroneous interpretation against Julien; and I believe that it is equally undeserved by most, if not all, of the other translators against whom it is directed. He himself adopted as his guide the 'Explanations of the Tâo Teh King,' current as the work of Lü Yen (called also Lü 3û, Lü Tung-pin, and Lü Khun-yang), a Tâoist of the eighth century. Through Mr. Balfour's kindness I have had an opportunity of examining this edition of Lâo's Treatise; and I am compelled to agree with the very unfavourable judgment on it pronounced by Mr. Giles as both 'spurious' and 'ridiculous.' All that we are told of Lü Yen is very suspicious; much of it evidently false. The editions of our little book ascribed to him are many. I have for more than twenty years possessed one with the title of 'The Meaning of the Tâo Teh King Explained by the TRUE Man of Khun-yang,' being a reprint of 1690, and as different as possible from the work patronised by Mr. Balfour.

Fourth, the Thâi Shang Hwun Hsüan Tâo Teh Kăn King,—a work of the present dynasty, published at Shanghai, but when produced I do not know. It is certainly of the Lü 3û type, and is worth purchasing as one of the finest specimens of block-printing. It professes to be the production of 'The Immortals of the Eight Grottoes,' each of whom is styled 'a Divine Ruler (Tî Kün).' The eighty-one chapters are equally divided for commentary among them, excepting that 'the Divine Ruler, the Universal Refiner,' has the last eleven assigned to him. The Text is everywhere broken up into short clauses, which are explained in

a very few characters by 'God, the True Helper,' the same,
I suppose, who is also styled, 'The Divine Ruler, the True
Helper,' and comments at length on chapters 31 to 40.
I mention these particulars as an illustration of how the
ancient Tâoism has become polytheistic and absurd. The
name 'God, the True Helper,' is a title, I imagine, given to
Lü 3û. With all this nonsense, the composite commentary is
a good one, the work, evidently, of one hand. One of several
recommendatory Prefaces is ascribed to Wân *Kh*ang, the
god of Literature ; and he specially praises the work, as
'explaining the meaning by examination of the Text.'

Fifth, a 'Collection of the Most Important Treatises of
the Tâoist Fathers (Tâo 3û *K*ăn *K*wan *K*î Yâo).' This
was reprinted in 1877 at *Kh*ang-*k*âu in *K*iang-sû ; beginning with the Tâo Teh *K*ing, and ending with the Kan
Ying Phien. Between these there are fourteen other
Treatises, mostly short, five of them being among Mr. Balfour's 'Tâoist Texts.' The Collection was edited by a Lû
Yü ; and the Commentary selected by him, in all but the
last Treatise, was by a Lî Hsî-yüeh, who appears to have
been a recluse in a monastery on a mountain in the department of Pâo-ning, Sze-*kh*wan, if, indeed, what is said of
him be not entirely fabulous.

Sixth, the Commentary on the Tâo Teh *K*ing, by
Wû *Kh*ăng (A.D. 1249–1333) of Lin *Kh*wan. This has
been of the highest service to me. Wû *Kh*ăng was the
greatest of the Yüan scholars. He is one of the Literati
quoted from occasionally by 3iâo Hung in his 'Wings ;'
but by no means so extensively as Julien supposes (Observations Détachées, p. xli). My own copy of his work is in
the 12th Section of the large Collection of the 'Yüeh-yâ
Hall,' published in 1853. Writing of Wû *Kh*ăng in 1865
(Proleg. to the Shû, p. 36), I said that he was 'a bold
thinker and a daring critic, handling his text with a freedom
which I had not seen in any other Chinese scholar.' The
subsequent study of his writings has confirmed me in this
opinion of him. Perhaps he might be characterised as an
independent, rather than as a bold, thinker, and the daring

of his criticism must not be supposed to be without caution. (See Introd., p. 9.)

The Writings of _K_wang-₃ze have been studied by foreigners still less than the Treatise of Lâo-₃ze. When I undertook in 1879 to translate them, no version of them had been published. In 1881, however, there appeared at Shanghai Mr. Balfour's 'The Divine Classic of Nan-hua (Introd., pp. 11, 12), being the Works of Chuang Tsze, Tâoist Philosopher.' It was a 'bold' undertaking in Mr. Balfour thus to commence his translations of Chinese Books with one of the most difficult of them. I fancy that he was himself convinced of this, and that his undertaking had been 'too bold,' by the criticism to which his work was subjected in the China Review by Mr. Giles. Nevertheless, it was no small achievement to be the first to endeavour to lift up the veil from _K_wang-₃ze. Even a first translation, though imperfect, is not without benefit to others who come after, and are able to do better. In preparing the draft of my own version, which draft was finished in April, 1887, I made frequent reference to the volume of Mr. Balfour.

Having exposed the errors of Mr. Balfour, Mr. Giles proceeded to make a version of his own, which was published last year in London, with the title of ' CHUANG TZǓ, Mystic, Moralist, and Social Reformer.' It was not, however, till I was well through with the revision of my draft version, that I supplied myself with a copy of his volume. I did not doubt that Mr. Giles's translation would be well and tersely done, and I preferred to do my own work independently and without the help which he would have afforded me. In carrying my sheets through the press, I have often paused over my rendering of a passage to compare it with his ; and I have pleasure in acknowledging the merits of his version. The careful and competent reader will see and form his own judgment on passages and points where we differ.

Before describing the editions of _K_wang-₃ze which I

have consulted, I must not omit to mention Professor Gabelentz's 'Treatise on the Speech or Style of *K*wang-ʒze,' as 'a Contribution to Chinese Grammar,' published at Leipzig in 1888. It has been a satisfaction to me to find myself on almost every point of usage in agreement with the views of so able a Chinese scholar.

The works which I employed in preparing my version have been :—

First, 'The True *K*ing of Nan-hwâ,' in 'The Complete Works of the Ten Philosophers,' which has been described above. The Commentary which it supplies is that of Kwo Hsiang (Introd., pp. 9, 10), with 'The Sounds and Meanings of the Characters' from Lû Teh Ming's 'Explanations of the Terms and Phrases of the Classics,' of our seventh century. As in the case of the Tâo Teh *K*ing, the Ming editor has introduced at the top of his pages a selection of comments and notes from a great variety of scholars down to his own time.

Second, 'Helps (Wings) to *K*wang-ʒze by Ȝiâo Hung,'— a kindred work to the one with a similar title on Lâo-ʒze; by the same author, and prefaced by him in 1588. The two works are constructed on the same lines. Ȝiâo draws his materials from forty-eight authorities, from Kwo Hsiang to himself. He divides the several Books also into paragraphs, more or fewer according to their length, and the variety of subjects in them; and my version follows him in this lead with little or no change. He has two concluding Books; the one containing a collation of various readings, and the other a collection of articles on the history and genius of *K*wang-ʒze, and different passages of his Text.

Third, the *K*wang-ʒze Hsüeh or '*K*wang-ʒze made like Snow,' equivalent to our '*K*wang-ʒze Elucidated;' by a Lû Shû-*k*ih of Canton province, written in 1796. The different Books are preceded by a short summary of their subject-matter. The work goes far to fulfil the promise of its title.

Fourth, *K*wang-ʒze Yin, meaning 'The Train of

Thought in *K*wang-*z*ze Traced in its Phraseology.' My copy is a reprint, in 1880, of the Commentary of Lin Hsî-*k*ung, who lived from the Ming into the present dynasty, under the editorship of a Lû *K*hû-wang of *K*iang-sû province. The style is clear and elegant, but rather more concise than that of the preceding work. It leaves out the four disputed Books (XXVIII to XXXI); but all the others are followed by an elaborate discussion of their scope and plan.

Fifth, 'The Nan-hwâ Classic of *K*wang-*z*ze Explained,' published in 1621, by a Hsüan Ying or *z*ung (宣 穎, 宣 頴; the name is printed throughout the book, now in one of these ways, now in the other), called also Mâu-kung. The commentary is carefully executed and ingenious; but my copy of the book is so incorrectly printed that it can only be used with caution. Mr. Balfour appears to have made his version mainly from the same edition of the work; and some of his grossest errors pointed out by Mr. Giles arose from his accepting without question the misprints of his authority.

Sixth, 'Independent Views of *K*wang-*z*ze (莊 子 獨 見);'—by Hû Wăn-ying, published in 1751. Occasionally, the writer pauses over a passage, which, he thinks, has defied all preceding students, and suggests the right explanation of it, or leaves it as inexplicable.

It only remains for me to refer to the Repertories of 'Elegant Extracts,' called by the Chinese K û W ă n, which abound in their literature, and where the masterpieces of composition are elucidated with more or less of critical detail and paraphrase. I have consulted nearly a dozen of these collections, and would mention my indebtedness especially to that called Mêi *Kh*wan, which discusses passages from twelve of *K*wang-*z*ze's books.

When consulting the editions of Lin Hsî-*k*ung and Lû Shû-*k*ih, the reader is surprised by the frequency with which they refer to the 'old explanations' as 'incomplete and unsatisfactory,' often as 'absurd,' or 'ridiculous,' and he finds on examination that they do not so express themselves without reason. He is soon convinced that the translation of *K*wang-ʒze calls for the exercise of one's individual judgment, and the employment of every method akin to the critical processes by which the meaning in the books of other languages is determined. It was the perception of this which made me prepare in the first place a draft version to familiarise myself with the peculiar style and eccentric thought of the author.

From *K*wang-ʒze to the Tractate of 'Actions and their Retributions' the transition is great. Translation in the latter case is as easy as it is difficult in the former. It was Rémusat who in 1816 called attention to the Kan Ying Phien in Europe, as he did to the Tâo Teh *K*ing seven years later, and he translated the Text of it with a few Notes and Illustrative Anecdotes. In 1828 Klaproth published a translation of it from the Man-châu version; and in 1830 a translation in English appeared in the Canton Register, a newspaper published at Macao. In 1828 Julien published what has since been the standard version of it; with an immense amount of additional matter under the title—'Le Livre Des Récompenses et Des Peines, en Chinois et en Français; Accompagné de quatre cent Légendes, Anecdotes et Histoires, qui font connaître les Doctrines, les Croyances et les Mœurs de la Secte des Tâo-ssé.'

In writing out my own version I have had before me :—

First, 'The Thâi Shang Kan Ying Phien, with Plates and the Description of them;' a popular edition, as profusely furnished with anecdotes and stories as Julien's original, and all pictorially illustrated. The notes, comments, and corresponding sentences from the Confucian Classics are also abundant.

Second, 'The Thâi Shang Kan Ying Phien, with explanations collected from the Classics and Histories;'— a Cantonese reprint of an edition prepared in the *K*hien-lûng reign by a Hsiâ *K*iû-hsiâ.

Third, the edition in the Collection of Tâoist Texts described above on p. xvii; by Hsü Hsiû-teh. It is decidedly Tâoistic; but without stories or pictures.

Fourth, 'The Thâi Shang Kan Ying Phien *K*û;' by Hui Tung, of the present dynasty. The Work follows the Commentary of Wû *Kh*ăng on the Tâo Teh *K*ing in the Collection of the Yüeh-yâ Hall. The preface of the author is dated in 1749. The Commentary, he tells us, was written in consequence of a vow, when his mother was ill, and he was praying for her recovery. It contains many extracts from Ko Hung (Introduction, p. 5, note), to whom he always refers by his nom de plume of Pao-phoh 3ze, or 'Maintainer of Simplicity.' He considers indeed this Tractate to have originated from him.

I have thus set forth all that is necessary to be said here by way of preface. For various information about the Treatises comprised in the Appendixes, the reader is referred to the preliminary notes, which precede the translation of most of them. I have often sorely missed the presence of a competent native scholar who would have assisted me in the quest of references, and in talking over difficult passages. Such a helper would have saved me much time; but the result, I think, would scarcely have appeared in any great alteration of my versions.

J. L.

OXFORD,
December 20, 1890.

THE TEXTS OF TÂOISM.

INTRODUCTION.

CHAPTER I.

WAS TÂOISM OLDER THAN LÂO-ƷZE?

1. In writing the preface to the third volume of these
Sacred Books of the East in 1879, I referred to Lâo-ɉze as
'the acknowledged founder' of the system of Tâoism. Prolonged study and research, however, have brought me to
the conclusion that there was a Tâoism earlier than his;
and that before he wrote his Tâo Teh *King*, the principles taught in it had been promulgated, and the ordering
of human conduct and government flowing from them
inculcated.

For more than a thousand years 'the Three Religions'
Three Religions
in China. has been a stereotyped phrase in China,
meaning what we call Confucianism, Tâoism,
and Buddhism. The phrase itself simply means 'the
Three Teachings,' or systems of instruction, leaving the
subject-matter of each 'Teaching' to be learned by inquiry.
Of the three, Buddhism is of course the most recent, having
been introduced into China only in the first century of our
Christian era. Both the others were indigenous to the
country, and are traceable to a much greater antiquity, so
that it is a question to which the earlier origin should be
assigned. The years of Confucius's life lay between B.C.
551 and 478; but his own acknowledgment that he was
'a transmitter and not a maker,' and the testimony of his
grandson, that 'he handed down the doctrines of Yâo and
Shun (B.C. 2300), and elegantly displayed the regulations

of Wân and Wû (B. C. 1200), taking them as his model,' are well known.

2. Lâo-ʒze's birth is said, in the most likely account of it, to have taken place in the third year of king Ting of the Ḵâu dynasty, (B. C.) 604. He was thus rather more than fifty years older than Confucius. The two men seem to have met more than once, and I am inclined to think that the name of Lâo-ʒze, as the designation of the other, arose from Confucius's styling him to his disciples 'The Old Philosopher.' They met as Heads of different schools or schemes of thought; but did not touch, so far as we know, on the comparative antiquity of their views. It is a peculiarity of the Tâo Teh Ḵing that any historical element in

Peculiarity of the Tâo Teh Ḵing. it is of the vaguest nature possible, and in all its chapters there is not a single proper name. Yet there are some references to earlier sages whose words the author was copying out, and to 'sentence-makers' whose maxims he was introducing to illustrate his own sentiments[1]. In the most distant antiquity he saw a happy society in which his highest ideas of the Tâo were realised, and in the seventeenth chapter he tells us that in the earliest times the people did not know that there were their rulers, and when those rulers were most successful in dealing with them, simply said, 'We are what we are of ourselves.' Evidently, men existed to Lâo-ʒze at first in a condition of happy innocence,—in what we must call a paradisiacal state, according to his idea of what such a state was likely to be.

When we turn from the treatise of Lâo-ʒze to the writings of Ḵwang-ʒze, the greatest of his followers, we are

---

[1] The sixth chapter of Lâo's treatise, that about 'the Spirit of the Valley,' is referred to in Lieh-ʒze (I, 1ᵇ), as being from Hwang Tî, from which the commentator Tû Tâo-ḵien (about A. D. 1300) takes occasion to say: 'From which we know that Lâo-ʒze was accustomed to quote in his treatise passages from earlier records,—as when he refers to the remarks of "some sage," of "some ancient," of "the sentence-makers," and of "some writer on war." In all these cases he is clearly introducing the words of earlier wise men. The case is like that of Confucius when he said, "I am a transmitter and not a maker," &c.' Found in Ȝiâo Hung, in loc.

not left in doubt as to his belief in an early state of paradisiacal Tâoism. Hwang Tî, the first year of whose reign is placed in B.C. 2697, is often introduced as a seeker of the Tâo, and is occasionally condemned as having been one of the first to disturb its rule in men's minds and break up 'the State of Perfect Unity.' He mentions several sovereigns of whom we can hardly find a trace in the records of history as having ruled in the primeval period, and gives us more than one description of the condition of the world during that happy time [1].

I do not think that Kwang-ȝze had any historical evidence for the statements which he makes about those early days, the men who flourished in them, and their ways. His narratives are for the most part fictions, in which the names and incidents are of his own devising. They are no more true as matters of fact than the accounts of the characters in Bunyan's Pilgrim's Progress are true, with reference to any particular individuals; but as these last are grandly true of myriads of minds in different ages, so may we read in Kwang-ȝze's stories the thoughts of Tâoistic men beyond the restrictions of place and time. He believed that those thoughts were as old as the men to whom he attributed them. I find in his belief a ground for believing myself that to Tâoism, as well as to Confucianism, we ought to attribute a much earlier origin than the famous men whose names they bear. Perhaps they did not differ so much at first as they came afterwards to do in the hands of Confucius and Lâo-ȝze, both great thinkers, the one more of a moralist, and the other more of a metaphysician. When and how, if they were ever more akin than they came to be, their divergence took place, are difficult questions on which it may be well to make some remarks after we have tried to set forth the most important principles of Tâoism.

Those principles have to be learned from the treatise of Lâo-ȝze and the writings of Kwang-ȝze. We can hardly

---

[1] See in Books IX, X, and XII.

say that the Tâoism taught in them is the Tâoism now current in China, or that has been current in it for many centuries; but in an inquiry into the nature and origin of religions these are the authorities that must be consulted for Tâoism, and whose evidence must be accepted. The treatise, 'Actions and the Responses to them,' will show one of the phases of it at a much later period.

CHAPTER II.

THE TEXTS OF THE TÂO TEH *K*ING AND *K*WANG-ȜZE SHÛ, AS REGARDS THEIR AUTHENTICITY AND GENUINENESS, AND THE ARRANGEMENT OF THEM.

I. 1. I will now state briefly, first, the grounds on which I accept the Tâo Teh *K*ing as a genuine production of the age to which it has been assigned, and the truth of its authorship by Lâo-ȝze to whom it has been ascribed. It would not have been necessary a few years ago to write as if these points could be called in question, but in 1886 Mr. Herbert A. Giles, of Her Majesty's Consular Service in China, and one of the ablest Chinese scholars living, vehemently called them in question in an article in the China Review for the months of March and April. His strictures have been replied to, and I am not going to revive here the controversy which they produced, but only to state a portion of the evidence which satisfies my own mind on the two points just mentioned.

2. It has been said above that the year B. C. 604 was, probably, that of Lâo-ȝze's birth. The year of his death is not recorded. Sze-mâ *K*hien, the first great Chinese his-

The evidence of Sze-mâ *K*hien, the historian. torian, who died in about B. C. 85, commences his 'Biographies' with a short account of Lâo-ȝze. He tells us that the philosopher had been a curator of the Royal Library of *K*âu, and that, mourning over the decadence of the dynasty, he wished to withdraw from the world, and proceeded to the pass or defile of Hsien-ku [1],

---

[1] In the present district of Ling-pâo, Shan *K*âu, province of Ho-nan.

leading from China to the west. There he was recognised
by the warden of the pass, Yin Hsî (often called Kwan
Yin), himself a well-known Tâoist, who insisted on his
leaving him a writing before he went into seclusion.
Lâo-jze then wrote his views on 'The Tâo and its Characteristics,' in two parts or sections, containing more than
5000 characters, gave the manuscript to the warden, and
went his way[1]; 'nor is it known where he died.' This
account is strange enough, and we need not wonder that it
was by and by embellished with many marvels. It contains, however, the definite statements that Lâo-jze wrote
the Tâo Teh King in two parts, and consisting of more
than 5000 characters. And that Khien was himself well
acquainted with the treatise is apparent from his quotations
from it, with, in almost every case, the specification of the
author. He thus adduces part of the first chapter, and
a large portion of the last chapter but one. His brief
references also to Lâo-jze and his writings are numerous.

3. But between Lâo-jze and Sze-mâ Khien there were
many Tâoist writers whose works remain. I may specify

Lieh-jze, Han
Fei-jze, and
other Tâoist
authors.

of them Lieh-jze (assuming that his chapters,
though not composed in their present form by
him, may yet be accepted as fair specimens
of his teaching); Kwang-jze (of the fourth
century B.C. We find him refusing to accept high office
from king Wei of Khû, B.C. 339–299); Han Fei, a voluminous author, who died by his own hand in B.C. 230; and
Liû An, a scion of the Imperial House of Han, king of
Hwâi-nan, and better known to us as Hwâi-nan 3ze, who
also died by his own hand in B.C. 122. In the books of all
these men we find quotations of many passages that are in
our treatise. They are expressly said to be, many of them,
quotations from Lâo-jze; Han Fei several times all but

---

[1] In an ordinary Student's Manual I find a note with reference to this incident
to which it may be worth while to give a place here :—The warden, it is said,
set before Lâo-jze a dish of tea ; and this was the origin of the custom of tea-
drinking between host and guest (see the 幼學故事尋源,
ch. 7, on Food and Drink).

shows the book beneath his eyes. To show how numerous
the quotations by Han Fei and Liû An are, let it be borne
in mind that the Tâo Teh King has come down to us as
divided into eighty-one short chapters ; and that the whole
of it is shorter than the shortest of our Gospels. Of the
eighty-one chapters, either the whole or portions of seventy-
one are found in those two writers. There are other authors
not so decidedly Tâoistic, in whom we find quotations from
the little book. These quotations are in general wonderfully
correct. Various readings indeed there are ; but if we were
sure that the writers did trust to memory, their differences
would only prove that copies of the text had been multiplied
from the very first.

In passing on from quotations to the complete text, I will
Evidence of Pan clinch the assertion that K*h*ien was well
     Kû.   acquainted with our treatise, by a passage
from the History of the Former Han Dynasty (B.C. 206–
A.D. 24), which was begun to be compiled by Pan Kû, who
died however in 92, and left a portion to be completed by his
sister, the famous Pan K*â*o. The thirty-second chapter of
his Biographies is devoted to Sze-mâ K*h*ien, and towards
the end it is said that 'on the subject of the Great Tâo he
preferred Hwang and Lâo to the six King.' 'Hwang and
Lâo' must there be the writings of Hwang-Tî and Lâo-ʒze.
The association of the two names also illustrates the antiquity claimed for Tâoism, and the subject of note 1, p. 2.

4. We go on from quotations to complete texts, and turn,
first, to the catalogue of the Imperial Library of Han, as
compiled by Liû Hsin, not later than the commencement of
our Christian era. There are entered in it Tâoist works by
Catalogue of the thirty-seven different authors, containing in all
Imperial Library 993 chapters or sections (phien). Î Yin, the
    of Han.   premier of K*h*ăng Thang (B.C. 1766), heads
the list with fifty-one sections. There are in it four editions
of Lâo-ʒze's work with commentaries :—by a Mr. Lin, in
four sections ; a Mr. Fû, in thirty-seven sections ; a Mr.
Hsü, in six sections ; and by Liû Hsiang, Hsin's own
father, in four sections. All these four works have since
perished, but there they were in the Imperial Library before

our era began. *K*wang-ȝze is in the same list in fifty-two books or sections, the greater part of which have happily escaped the devouring tooth of time.

We turn now to the twentieth chapter of *K*hien's Biographies, in which he gives an account of Yo Î, the scion of a distinguished family, and who himself played a famous part, both as a politician and military leader, and became prince of Wang-*k*û under the kingdom of *K*âo in B.C. 279. Among his descendants was a Yo *K*hăn, who learned in *K*hî 'the words,' that is, the Tâoistic writings 'of Hwang-Tî and Lâo-ȝze from an old man who lived on the Ho-side.' The origin of this old man was not known, but Yo *K*hăn taught what he learned from him to a Mr. Ko, who again became preceptor to Ȝhâo Ȝhan, the chief minister of *K*hî, and afterwards of the new dynasty of Han, dying in B.C. 190.

5. Referring now to the catalogue of the Imperial Library of the dynasty of Sui (A.D. 589–618), we find that The catalogue it contained many editions of Lâo's treatise of the Sui dynasty. with commentaries. The first mentioned is 'The Tâo Teh *K*ing,' with the commentary of the old man of the Ho-side, in the time of the emperor Wăn of Han (B.C. 179–142). It is added in a note that the dynasty of Liang (A.D. 502–556) had possessed the edition of 'the old man of the Ho-side, of the time of the Warring States; but that with some other texts and commentaries it had disappeared.' I find it difficult to believe that there had been two old men of the Ho-side [1], both teachers of Tâoism and commentators on our *K*ing, but I am willing to content myself with the more recent work, and accept the copy that has been current—say from B.C. 150, when Sze-mâ *K*hien could have been little more than a boy. Tâoism was a favourite study with many of the Han emperors and their ladies. Hwâi-nan Ȝze, of whose many quotations from

---

[1] The earlier old man of the Ho-side is styled in Chinese 河上丈人; the other 河上公; but the designations have the same meaning. Some critical objections to the genuineness of the latter's commentary on the ground of the style are without foundation.

the text of Lâo I have spoken, was an uncle of the emperor Wăn. To the emperor King (B.C. 156–143), the son of Wăn, there is attributed the designation of Lâo's treatise as a King, a work of standard authority. At the beginning of his reign, we are told, some one was commending to him four works, among which were those of Lâo-ʒze and Kwang-ʒze. Deeming that the work of Hwang-ʒze and Lâo-ʒze was of a deeper character than the others, he ordered that it should be called a King, established a board for the study of Tâoism, and issued an edict that the book should be learned and recited at court, and throughout the country[1]. Thenceforth it was so styled. We find Hwang-fû Mî (A.D. 215–282) referring to it as the Tâo Teh King.

The second place in the Sui catalogue is given to the text and commentary of Wang Pî or Wang Fû-sze, an *The work of Wang Pî.* extraordinary scholar who died in A.D. 249, at the early age of twenty-four. This work has always been much prized. It was its text which Lû Teh-ming used in his 'Explanation of the Terms and Phrases of the Classics,' in the seventh century. Among the editions of it which I possess is that printed in 1794 with the imperial moveable metal types.

I need not speak of editions or commentaries subsequent to Wang Pî's. They soon begin to be many, and are only not so numerous as those of the Confucian Classics.

6. All the editions of the book are divided into two *Divisions into parts, chapters; and number of characters in the text.* parts, the former called Tâo, and the latter Teh, meaning the Qualities or Characteristics of the Tâo, but this distinction of subjects is by no means uniformly adhered to.

I referred already to the division of the whole into eighty-one short chapters (37 + 44), which is by common tradition attributed to Ho-shang Kung, or 'The old man of the Ho-side.' Another very early commentator, called Yen Ʒun or Yen Kün-phing, made a division into seventy-two chapters (40 + 32), under the influence, no doubt, of some

---

[1] See Ʒiâo Hung's Wings or Helps, ch. v, p. 11ᵃ.

mystical considerations. His predecessor, perhaps, had no better reason for his eighty-one; but the names of his chapters were, for the most part, happily chosen, and have been preserved. Wû *Kh*ăng arranged the two parts in sixty-seven chapters (31 + 36). It is a mistake, however, to suppose, as even Mr. Wylie with all his general accuracy did[1], that Wû 'curtails the ordinary text to some extent.' He does not curtail, but only re-arranges according to his fashion, uniting some of Ho-shang Kung's chapters in one, and sometimes altering the order of their clauses.

Sze-mâ *Kh*ien tells us that, as the treatise came from Lâo-jze, it contained more than 5000 characters; that is, as one critic says, 'more than 5000 and fewer than 6000.' Ho-shang Kung's text has 5350, and one copy 5590; Wang Pî's, 5683, and one copy 5610. Two other early texts have been counted, giving 5720 and 5635 characters respectively. The brevity arises from the terse conciseness of the style, owing mainly to the absence of the embellishment of particles, which forms so striking a peculiarity in the composition of Mencius and *K*wang-jze.

In passing on to speak, secondly and more briefly, of the far more voluminous writings of *K*wang-jze, I may say that I do not know of any other book of so ancient a date as the Tâo Teh *K*ing, of which the authenticity of the origin and genuineness of the text can claim to be so well substantiated.

II. 7. In the catalogue of the Han Library we have the entry of '*K*wang-jze in fifty-two books or sections.' By The Books of *K*wang-jze. the time of the Sui dynasty, the editions of his work amounted to nearly a score. The earliest commentary that has come down to us goes by the name of Kwo Hsiang's. He was an officer and scholar of the 3in dynasty, who died about the year 312. Another officer, also of 3in, called Hsiang Hsiû, of rather an earlier date, had undertaken the same task, but left it incomplete; and his manuscripts coming (not, as it appears, by

---

[1] Notes on Chinese Literature, p. 173.

any fraud) into Kwo's hands, he altered and completed them as suited his own views, and then gave them to the public. In the short account of Kwo, given in the twentieth chapter of the Biographies of the Ȝin history, it is said that several tens of commentators had laboured unsatisfactorily on Kwang's writings before Hsiang Hsiû took them in hand. As the joint result of the labours of the two men, however, we have only thirty-three of the fifty-two sections mentioned in the Han catalogue. It is in vain that I have tried to discover how and when the other nineteen sections were lost. In one of the earliest commentaries on the Tâo Teh King, that by Yen Ȝun, we have several quotations from Kwang-ȝze which bear evidently the stamp of his handiwork, and are not in the current Books; but they would not altogether make up a single section. We have only to be thankful that so large a proportion of the original work has been preserved. Sû Shih (Ȝze-kan, and Tung-pho), it is well known, called in question the genuineness of Books 28 to 31 [1]. Books 15 and 16 have also been challenged, and a paragraph here and there in one or other of the Books. The various readings, according to a collation given by Ȝiâo Hung, are few.

8. There can be no doubt that the Books of Kwang-ȝze were hailed by all the friends of Tâoism. It has been

Importance to Tâoism of the Books of Kwang-ȝze.

mentioned above that the names 'Hwang-Tî' and 'Lâo-ȝze' were associated together as denoting the masters of Tâoism, and the phrase, 'the words of Hwang-Tî and Lâo-ȝze,' came to be no more than a name for the Tâo Teh King. Gradually the two names were contracted into 'Hwang Lâo,' as in the passage quoted on p. 6 from Pan Kû. After the Han dynasty, the name Hwang gave place to Kwang, and the names Lâo Kwang, and, sometimes inverted, Kwang Lâo, were employed to denote the system or the texts of Tâoism. In the account, for instance, of Kî

---

[1] A brother of Shih, Sû Keh (Ȝze-yû and Ying-pin), wrote a remarkable commentary on the Tâo Teh King; but it was Shih who first discredited those four Books, in his Inscription for the temple of Kwang-ȝze, prepared in 1078.

Khang, in the nineteenth chapter of the Biographies of Ꝫin, we have a typical Tâoist brought before us. When grown up, 'he loved Lâo and *K*wang;' and a visitor, to produce the most favourable impression on him, says, ' Lâo-ꝫze and *K*wang *K*âu are my masters.'

9. The thirty-three Books of *K*wang-ꝫze are divided into three Parts, called Nêi, or 'the Inner;' Wâi, or 'the Outer;' and Ꝫâ, 'the Miscellaneous.' The first Part com-

Division of the Books into three Parts. prises seven Books; the second, fifteen; and the third, eleven. ' Inner' may be understood as equivalent to esoteric or More Important. The titles of the several Books are significant, and each expresses the subject or theme of its Book. They are believed to have been prefixed by *K*wang-ꝫze himself, and that no alteration could be made in the composition but for the worse. ' Outer ' is understood in the sense of supplementary or subsidiary. The fifteen Books so called are 'Wings' to the previous seven. Their titles were not given by the author, and are not significant of the Tâoistic truth which all the paragraphs unite, or should unite, in illustrating; they are merely some name or phrase taken from the commencement of the first paragraph in each Book,—like the names of the Books of the Confucian Analects, or of the Hebrew Pentateuch. The fixing them originally is generally supposed to have been the work of Kwo Hsiang. The eleven Miscellaneous Books are also supplementary to those of the first Part, and it is not easy to see why a difference was made between them and the fifteen that precede.

10. *K*wang-ꝫze's writings have long been current under the name of Nan Hwa *K*ăn *K*ing. He was a native of

The general title of *K*wang-ꝫze's works. the duchy of Sung, born in what was then called the district of Măng, and belonged to the state or kingdom of Liang or Wei. As he grew up, he filled some official post in the city of Ꝫhî-yüan,—the site of which it is not easy to determine with certainty. In A.D. 742, the name of his birth-place was changed (but only for a time) to Nan-hwa, and an imperial order was issued that *K*wang-ꝫze should thenceforth be styled 'The True Man of Nan-hwa,' and his Book, 'The True Book of Nan-hwa[1].' To be 'a True Man' is the highest Tâoistic achievement of a man, and our author thus canonised communicates his glory to his Book.

CHAPTER III.

WHAT IS THE MEANING OF THE NAME TÂO? AND THE CHIEF POINTS OF BELIEF IN TÂOISM.

1. The first translation of the Tâo Teh *K*ing into a Western language was executed in Latin by some of the Meaning of the Roman Catholic missionaries, and a copy of name Tâo. it was brought to England by a Mr. Matthew Raper, F. R. S., and presented by him to the Society at a meeting on the 10th January, 1788,—being the gift to him of P. Jos. de Grammont, 'Missionarius Apostolicus, ex-Jesuita.' In this version Tâo is taken in the sense of Ratio, or the Supreme Reason of the Divine Being, the Creator and Governor.

M. Abel Rémusat, the first Professor of Chinese in Paris, does not seem to have been aware of the existence of the above version in London, but his attention was attracted to Lâo's treatise about 1820, and, in 1823, he wrote of the character Tâo, 'Ce mot me semble ne pas pouvoir être bien traduit, si ce n'est par le mot λόγος dans le triple sens de souverain Être, de raison, et de parole.'

Rémusat's successor in the chair of Chinese, the late Stanislas Julien, published in 1842 a translation of the whole treatise. Having concluded from an examination of it, and the earliest Tâoist writers, such as *K*wang-ȝze, Ho-kwan Ȝze, and Ho-shang Kung, that the Tâo was devoid of action, of thought, of judgment, and of intelligence, he concluded that it was impossible to understand by it 'the Primordial Reason, or the Sublime Intelligence which created, and which governs the world,' and to

---

[1] See the Khang-hsî Thesaurus (佩文韻府), under 華.

this he subjoined the following note:—'Quelque étrange que puisse paraître cette idée de Lâo-ʒze, elle n'est pas sans exemple dans l'histoire de la philosophie. Le mot n a t u r e n'a-t-il pas été employé par certains philosophes, que la religion et la raison condamnent, pour désigner une c a u s e p r e m i è r e, également dépourvue de pensée et d'intelligence?' Julien himself did not doubt that Lâo's idea of the character was that it primarily and properly meant 'a w a y,' and hence he translated the title T â o T e h *K*ing by ' L e L i v r e d e l a V o i e e t d e l a V e r t u,' transferring at the same time the name Tâo to the text of his version.

The first English writer who endeavoured to give a distinct account of Tâoism was the late Archdeacon Hardwick, while he held the office of Christian Advocate in the University of Cambridge. In his 'Christ and other Masters' (vol. ii, p. 67), when treating of the religions of China, he says, ' I feel disposed to argue that the centre of the system founded by Lâo-ʒze had been awarded to some energy or power resembling the "Nature" of modern speculators. The indefinite expression T â o was adopted to denominate an abstract cause, or the initial principle of life an der, to which worshippers were able to assign the attrib es of immateriality, eternity, immensity, invisibility.'

It was, probably, Julien's reference in his note to the use of the term n a t u r e, which suggested to Hardwick his analogy between Lâo-ʒze's T â o, and 'the Nature of modern speculation.' Canon Farrar has said, 'We have long personified under the name of Nature the sum total of God's laws as observed in the physical world ; and now the n o t i o n of Nature as a distinct, living, independent entity seems to be ineradicable alike from our literature and our systems of philosophy[1].' But it seems to me that this metaphorical or mythological use of the word n a t u r e for the Cause and Ruler of it, implies the previous notion of Him, that is, of God, in the mind. Does not this clearly appear in the words of Seneca ?—'Vis illum (h. e. Jovem Deum) naturam

---

[1] Language and Languages, pp. 184, 185.

vocare, non peccabis:—hic est ex quo nata sunt omnia, cujus spiritu vivimus [1].'

In his translation of the Works of *K*wang-ȝze in 1881, Mr. Balfour adopted Nature as the ordinary rendering of the Chinese Tâo. He says, 'When the word is translated Way, it means the Way of Nature,— her processes, her methods, and her laws; when translated Reason, it is the same as lî,—the power that works in all created things, producing, preserving, and life-giving,—the intelligent principle of the world; when translated Doctrine, it refers to the True doctrine respecting the laws and mysteries of Nature.' He calls attention also to the point that 'he uses NATURE in the sense of Natura naturans, while the Chinese expression wan wû (= all things) denotes Natura naturata.' But this really comes to the metaphorical use of nature which has been touched upon above. It can claim as its patrons great names like those of Aquinas, Giordano Bruno, and Spinoza, but I have never been able to see that its barbarous phraseology makes it more than a figure of speech [2].

The term Nature, however, is so handy, and often fits so appropriately into a version, that if Tâo had ever such a signification I should not hesitate to employ it as freely as Mr. Balfour has done; but as it has not that signification, to try to put a non-natural meaning into it, only perplexes the mind, and obscures the idea of Lâo-ȝze.

Mr. Balfour himself says (p. xviii), 'The primary signification of Tâo is simply "road."' Beyond question this meaning underlies the use of it by the great master of Tâoism and by *K*wang-ȝze [3]. Let the reader refer to the version of the twenty-fifth chapter of Lâo's treatise, and to

---

[1] Natur. Quaest. lib. II, cap. xlv.

[2] Martineau's 'Types of Ethical Theory,' I, p. 286, and his whole 'Conjectural History of Spinoza's Thought.'

[3] 道 is equivalent to the Greek ἡ ὁδός, the way. Where this name for the Christian system occurs in our Revised Version of the New Testament in the Acts of the Apostles, the literal rendering is adhered to, Way being printed with a capital W. See Acts ix. 2; xix. 9, 23; xxii. 4; xxiv. 14, 22.

the notes subjoined to it.   There T âo appears as the spontaneously operating cause of all movement in the phenomena of the universe ; and the nearest the writer can come
to a name for it is ' the Great T âo.'   Having established this
name, he subsequently uses it repeatedly; see chh. xxxiv
and liii.   In the third paragraph of his twentieth chapter,
_K_wang-ʒze uses a synonymous phrase instead of Lâo's
' Great T âo,' calling it the 'Great T h û,' about which there
can be no dispute, as meaning ' the Great Path,' ' Way,'
or ' Course [1].'   In the last paragraph of his twenty-fifth
Book, _K_wang-ʒze again sets forth the metaphorical origin
of the name T âo.   ' T âo,' he says, ' cannot be regarded as
having a positive existence ; existences cannot be regarded
as non-existent.   The name T âo is a metaphor used for
the purpose of description.   To say that it exercises some
causation, or that it does nothing, is speaking of it from the
phase of a thing ;—how can such language serve as a designation of it in its greatness?   If words were sufficient
for the purpose, we might in a day's time exhaust the subject of the T âo.   Words not being sufficient, we may talk
about it the whole day, and the subject of discourse will
only have been a thing.   T âo is the extreme to which
things conduct us.   Neither speech nor silence is sufficient
to convey the notion of it.   When we neither speak nor
refrain from speech, our speculations about it reach their
highest point.'

The T âo therefore is a phenomenon; not a positive
being, but a mode of being.   Lâo's idea of it may become
plainer as we proceed to other points of his system.   In
the meantime, the best way of dealing with it in translating
is to transfer it to the version, instead of trying to introduce
an English equivalent for it.

2. Next in importance to T âo is the name T h i e n, meaning at first the vaulted sky or the open firmament of heaven.
In the Confucian Classics, and in the speech of the Chinese

---

[1] 大塗.   The Khang-hsî dictionary defines t h û by l û, road or way.
Medhurst gives ' road.' Unfortunately, both Morrison and Williams overlooked
this definition of the character. Giles has also a note in l o c., showing how this
synonym settles the original meaning of T âo in the sense of ' r o a d.'

people, this name is used metaphorically as it is by our-
 selves for the Supreme Being, with reference especially to His will and rule. So it was that the idea of God arose among the Chinese fathers; so it was that they proceeded to fashion a name for God, calling Him Tî, and Shang Tî, 'the Ruler,' and 'the Supreme Ruler.' The Tâoist fathers found this among their people; but in their idea of the Tâo they had already a Supreme Concept which superseded the necessity of any other. The name Tî for God only occurs once in the Tâo Teh *King*; in the well-known passage of the fourth chapter, where, speaking of the Tâo, Lâo-ȝze says, 'I do not know whose Son it is; it might seem to be before God.'

Nor is the name Thien very common. We have the phrase, 'Heaven and Earth,' used for the two great con-stituents of the kosmos, owing their origin to the Tâo, and also for a sort of binomial power, acting in harmony with the Tâo, covering, protecting, nurturing, and maturing all things. Never once is Thien used in the sense of God, the Supreme Being. In its peculiarly Tâoistic employment, it is more an adjective than a noun. 'The Tâo of Heaven' means the Tâo that is Heavenly, the course that is quiet and undemonstrative, that is free from motive and effort, such as is seen in the processes of nature, grandly pro-ceeding and successful without any striving or crying. The Tâo of man, not dominated by this Tâo, is contrary to it, and shows will, purpose, and effort, till, submitting to it, it becomes 'the Tâo or Way of the Sages,' which in all its action has no striving.

The characteristics both of Heaven and man are dealt with more fully by *K*wang than by Lâo. In the conclusion of his eleventh Book, for instance, he says:—'What do we mean by Tâo? There is the Tâo (or Way) of Heaven, and there is the Tâo of man. Acting without action, and yet attracting all honour, is the Way of Heaven. Doing and being embarrassed thereby is the Way of man. The Way of Heaven should play the part of lord; the Way of man, the part of minister. The two are far apart, and should be distinguished from each other.'

In his next Book (par. 2), *K*wang-ȝze tells us what he intends by 'Heaven:'—'Acting without action,—this is what is called Heaven.' Heaven thus takes its law from the Tâo. 'The oldest sages and sovereigns attained to do the same,'—it was for all men to aim at the same achievement. As they were successful, 'vacancy, stillness, placidity, tastelessness, quietude, silence, and non-action' would be found to be their characteristics, and they would go on to the perfection of the Tâo[1].

The employment of Thien by the Confucianists, as of Heaven by ourselves, must be distinguished therefore from the Tâoistic use of the name to denote the quiet but mighty influence of the impersonal Tâo; and to translate it by 'God' only obscures the meaning of the Tâoist writers. This has been done by Mr. Giles in his version of *K*wang-ȝze, which is otherwise for the most part so good. Everywhere on his pages there appears the great name 'God;'—a blot on his translation more painful to my eyes and ears than the use of 'Nature' for Tâo by Mr. Balfour. I know that Mr. Giles's plan in translating is to use strictly English equivalents for all kinds of Chinese terms[2]. The plan is good where there are in the two languages such strict equivalents; but in the case before us there is no ground for its application. The exact English equivalent for the Chinese thien is our heaven. The Confucianists often used thien metaphorically for the personal Being whom they denominated Tî (God) and Shang Tî (the Supreme God), and a translator may occasionally, in working on books of Confucian literature, employ our name God for it. But neither Lâo nor *K*wang ever attached anything like our idea of God to it; and when one, in working on books of early Tâoist literature, translates thien by God, such a rendering must fail to produce in an English reader a correct apprehension of the meaning.

There is also in *K*wang-ȝze a peculiar usage of the name Thien. He applies it to the Beings whom he introduces as

[1] The Tâo Teh *K*ing, ch. 25, and *K*wang-ȝze, XIII, par. 1.
[2] See 'Strange Stories from a Chinese Studio,' vol. i, p. 1, note 2.

Peculiar usage
of Thien in
*K*wang-ʒze.
Masters of the Tâo, generally with mystical appellations in order to set forth his own views. Two instances from Book XI will suffice in illustration of this. In par. 4, Hwang-Tî does reverence to his instructor Kwang *Kh*ăng-ʒze [1], saying, 'In Kwang *Kh*ăng-ʒze we have an example of what is called Heaven,' which Mr. Giles renders 'Kwang *Kh*ăng Ʒze is surely God.' In par. 5, again, the mystical Yûn-*k*iang is made to say to the equally fabulous and mystical Hung-mung, 'O Heaven, have you forgotten me?' and, farther on, 'O Heaven, you have conferred on me (the knowledge of) your operation, and revealed to me the mystery of it;' in both which passages Mr. Giles renders thien by 'your Holiness.'

Mr. Giles's own
idea of the
meaning of the
name 'God' as
the equivalent of
Thien.
But Mr. Giles seems to agree with me that the old Tâoists had no idea of a personal God, when they wrote of Thien or Heaven. On his sixty-eighth page, near the beginning of Book VI, we meet with the following sentence, having every appearance of being translated from the Chinese text:—'God is a principle which exists by virtue of its own intrinsicality, and operates without self-manifestation.' By an inadvertence he has introduced his own definition of 'God' as if it were *K*wang-ʒze's; and though I can find no characters in the text of which I can suppose that he intends it to be the translation, it is valuable as helping us to understand the meaning to be attached to the Great Name in his volume.

The relation of
the Tâo to Tî.
I have referred above (p. 16) to the only passage in Lâo's treatise, where he uses the name Tî or God in its highest sense, saying that 'the Tâo might seem to have been before Him.' He might well say so, for in his first chapter he describes the Tâo, '(conceived of as) having no name, as the Originator of heaven and

---

[1] Kwang *Kh*ăng-ʒze heads the list of characters in Ko Hung's 'History of Spirit-like Immortals (神 仙 傳),' written in our fourth century. 'He was,' it is said, 'an Immortal of old, who lives on the hill of M'ung-thung in a grotto of rocks.'

earth, and (conceived of as) having a name, as the Mother of all things.' The reader will also find the same predicates of the Tâo at greater length in his fifty-first chapter.

The character Tî is also of rare occurrence in *K*wang-ʓze, excepting as applied to the five ancient Tîs. In Bk. III, par. 4, and in one other place, we find it indicating the Supreme Being, but the usage is ascribed to the ancients. In Bk. XV, par. 3, in a description of the human SPIRIT, its name is said to be 'Thung Tî,' which Mr. Giles renders 'Of God;' Mr. Balfour, 'One with God;' while my own version is 'The Divinity in Man.' In Bk. XII, par. 6, we have the expression 'the place of God;' in Mr. Giles, 'the kingdom of God;' in Mr. Balfour, 'the home of God.' In this and the former instance, the character seems to be used with the ancient meaning which had entered into the folk-lore of the people. But in Bk. VI, par. 7, there is a passage which shows clearly the relative position of Tâo and Tî in the Tâoistic system; and having called attention to it, I will go on to other points. Let the reader mark well the follow-ing predicates of the Tâo:—'Before there were heaven and earth, from of old, there It was, securely existing. From It came the mysterious existence of spirits; from It the mysterious existence of Tî (God). It produced heaven, It produced earth[1].' This says more than the utterance of Lâo,—that 'the Tâo seemed to be before God;'—does it not say that Tâo was before God, and that He was what He is by virtue of Its operation?

3. Among the various personal names given to the Tâo are those of ʒâo Hwâ, 'Maker and Trans-former,' and ʒâo Wû *K*ê, 'Maker of things.' Instances of both these names are found in Bk. VI, parr. 9, 10. 'Creator' and 'God' have both been employed for them; but there is no idea of Creation in Tâoism.

No idea of Crea-tion proper in Tâoism.

Again and again *K*wang-ʓze entertains the question of

---

[1] For this sentence we find in Mr. Balfour :—'Spirits of the dead, receiving It, become divine; the very gods themselves owe their divinity to its influence; and by it both Heaven and Earth were produced.' The version of it by Mr. Giles is too condensed :—'Spiritual beings drew their spirituality there-from, while the universe became what we see it now.'

how it was at the first beginning of things. Different views
are stated. In Bk. II, par. 4, he says:—'Among the men
of old their knowledge reached the extreme point. What
was that extreme point?

'Some held that at first there was not anything. This
is the extreme point,—the utmost limit to which nothing
can be added.

'A second class held that there was something, but without any responsive recognition of it (on the part of man).

'A third class held that there was such recognition, but
there had not begun to be any expression of different
opinions about it. It was through the definite expression
of different opinions about it that there ensued injury to
the (doctrine of the) Tâo[1].'

The first of these three views was that which Kwang-ʓze
himself preferred. The most condensed expression of it is
given in Bk. XII, par. 8:—' In the Grand Beginning of all
things there was nothing in all the vacancy of space; there
was nothing that could be named[2]. It was in this state
that there arose the first existence; the first existence, but
still without bodily shape. From this things could be produced, (receiving) what we call their several characters.
That which had no bodily shape was divided, and then
without intermission there was what we call the process of
conferring. (The two processes) continued to operate, and
things were produced. As they were completed, there
appeared the distinguishing lines of each, which we call the
bodily shape. That shape was the body preserving in it
the spirit, and each had its peculiar manifestation which
we call its nature.'

Such was the genesis of things; the formation of heaven

---

[1] Compare also Bk. XXII, parr. 7, 8, and XXIII, par. 10.

[2] Mr. Balfour had given for this sentence:—' In the beginning of all things
there was not even nothing. There were no names; these arose afterwards.'
In his critique on Mr. Balfour's version in 1882, Mr. Giles proposed :—' At the
beginning of all things there was nothing; but this nothing had no name.' He
now in his own version gives for it, ' At the beginning of the beginning, even
nothing did not exist. Then came the period of the nameless;'—an improve-
ment, certainly, on the other; but which can hardly be accepted as the correct
version of the text.

and earth and all that in them is, under the guidance of the Tâo. It was an evolution and not a creation. How the Tâo itself came,—I do not say into existence, but into operation,—neither Lâo nor *K*wang ever thought of saying anything about. We have seen that it is nothing material[1]. It acted spontaneously of itself. Its sudden appearance in the field of non-existence, Producer, Transformer, Beautifier, surpasses my comprehension. To Lâo it seemed to be before God. I am compelled to accept the existence of God, as the ultimate Fact, bowing before it with reverence, and not attempting to explain it, the one mystery, the sole mystery of the universe.

4. 'The bodily shape was the body preserving in it the spirit, and each had its peculiar manifestation which we call its nature.' So it is said in the passage quoted above from *K*wang-ʒze's twelfth Book, and the language shows

Man is composed of body and spirit.

how Tâoism, in a loose and indefinite way, considered man to be composed of body and spirit, associated together, yet not necessarily dependent on each other. Little is found bearing on this tenet in the Tâo Teh *K*ing. The concluding sentence of ch. 33, 'He who dies and yet does not perish, has longevity,' is of doubtful acceptation. More pertinent is the description of life as 'a coming forth,' and of death as 'an entering[2];' but *K*wang-ʒze expounds more fully, though after all unsatisfactorily, the teaching of their system on the subject.

At the conclusion of his third Book, writing of the death of Lâo-ʒze, he says, 'When the master came, it was at the proper time; when he went away, it was the simple sequence (of his coming). Quiet acquiescence in what happens at its proper time, and quietly submitting (to its sequence), afford no occasion for grief or for joy. The ancients described (death) as the loosening of the cord on which God suspended (the life). What we can point to are the faggots that have been consumed; but the fire is transmitted elsewhere, and we know not that it is over and ended.'

---

[1] The Tâo Teh *K*ing, ch. 14; et al.   [2] Ch. 50.

It is, however, in connexion with the death of his own wife, as related in the eighteenth Book, that his views most fully—I do not say 'clearly'—appear. We are told that when that event took place, his friend Huî-ʒze went to condole with him, and found him squatted on the ground, drumming on the vessel (of ice), and singing. His friend said to him, 'When a wife has lived with her husband, brought up children, and then dies in her old age, not to wail for her is enough. When you go on to drum on the vessel and sing, is it not an excessive (and strange) demonstration?' Kwang-ʒze replied, 'It is not so. When she first died, was it possible for me to be singular, and not affected by the event? But I reflected on the commencement of her being, when she had not yet been born to life. Not only had she no life, but she had no bodily form. Not only had she no bodily form, but she had no breath. Suddenly in this chaotic condition there ensued a change, and there was breath; another change, and there was the bodily form; a further change, and she was born to life; a change now again, and she is dead. The relation between those changes is like the procession of the four seasons,—spring, autumn, winter, and summer. There she lies with her face up, sleeping in the Great Chamber[1]; and if I were to fall sobbing and going on to wail for her, I should think I did not understand what was appointed for all. I therefore restrained myself.'

The next paragraph of the same Book contains another story about two ancient men, both deformed, who, when looking at the graves on Kwăn-lun, begin to feel in their own frames the symptoms of approaching dissolution. One says to the other, 'Do you dread it?' and gets the reply, 'No. Why should I dread it? Life is a borrowed thing. The living frame thus borrowed is but so much dust. Life and death are like day and night.'

In every birth, it would thus appear, there is, somehow, a repetition of what it is said, as we have seen, took place at 'the Grand Beginning of all things,' when out of the

---

[1] That is, between heaven and earth.

primal nothingness, the Tâo somehow appeared, and there was developed through its operation the world of things,— material things and the material body of man, which enshrines or enshrouds an immaterial spirit. This returns to the Tâo that gave it, and may be regarded indeed as that Tâo operating in the body during the time of life, and in due time receives a new embodiment.

In these notions of Tâoism there was a preparation for the appreciation by its followers of the Buddhistic system when it came to be introduced into the country, and which forms a close connexion between the two at the present day, Tâoism itself constantly becoming less definite and influential on the minds of the Chinese people. The Book which tells us of the death of Kwang-3ze's wife concludes with a narrative about Lieh-3ze and an old bleached skull[1], and to this is appended a passage about the metamorphoses of things, ending with the statement that ' the panther produces the horse, and the horse the man, who then again enters into the great machinery (of evolution), from which all things come forth (at birth) and into which they re-enter (at death).' Such representations need not be characterised.

5. Kû Hsî, ' the prince of Literature,' described the main object of Tâoism to be ' the preservation of the breath of life;' and Liû Mî, probably of our thirteenth century[2], in his ' Dispassionate Comparison of the Three Religions,' declares that ' its chief achievement is the prolongation of longevity.' Such is the account of Tâoism ordinarily given by Confucian and Buddhist writers, but our authorities, Lâo and Kwang, hardly bear out this representation of it as true of their time. There are chapters of the Tâo Teh King which

The Tâo as promotive of longevity.

---

[1] Quoted in the Amplification of the Sixteen Precepts or Maxims of the second emperor of the present dynasty by his son. The words are from Dr. Milne's version of ' the Sacred Edict,' p. 137.

[2] In his Index to the Tripi3aka, Mr. Bunyio Nanjio (p. 359) assigns Liû Mî and his work to the Yüan dynasty. In a copy of the work in my possession they are assigned to that of Sung. The author, no doubt, lived under both dynasties,—from the Sung into the Yüan.

presuppose a peculiar management of the breath, but the
treatise is singularly free from anything to justify what Mr.
Balfour well calls 'the antics of the Kung-fû, or system of
mystic and recondite calisthenics[1].' Lâo insists, however,
on the Tâo as conducive to long life, and in *K*wang-ɜze we
have references to it as a discipline of longevity, though
even he mentions rather with disapproval 'those who kept
blowing and breathing with open mouth, inhaling and
exhaling the breath, expelling the old and taking in new;
passing their time like the (dormant) bear, and stretching
and twisting (their necks) like birds.' He says that 'all
this simply shows their desire for longevity, and is what
the scholars who manage the breath, and men who nourish
the body and wish to live as long as Phăng-ɜû, are fond of
doing[2].' My own opinion is that the methods of the Tâo
were first cultivated for the sake of the longevity which
they were thought to promote, and that Lâo, discoun-
tenancing such a use of them, endeavoured to give the
doctrine a higher character; and this view is favoured by
passages in *K*wang-ɜze. In the seventh paragraph, for
instance, of his Book VI, speaking of parties who had obtained the Tâo, he begins with a prehistoric sovereign, who
'got it and by it adjusted heaven and earth.' Among his
other instances is Phăng-ɜû, who got it in the time of Shun,
and lived on to the time of the five leading princes of *K*âu,
—a longevity of more than 1800 years, greater than that
ascribed to Methuselah! In the paragraph that follows
there appears a Nü Yü, who is addressed by another famous
Tâoist in the words, 'You are old, Sir, while your complexion is like that of a child;—how is it so?' and the
reply is, 'I became acquainted with the Tâo.'

I will adduce only one more passage of *K*wang. In his
eleventh Book, and the fourth paragraph, he tells us of
interviews between Hwang-Tî, in the nineteenth year of his
reign, which would be B. C. 2679, and his instructor Kwang
*Kh*ăng-ɜze. The Tâoist sage is not readily prevailed on

[1] See note on p. 187 of his *K*wang-ɜze.
[2] See Bk. XV, par. 1.

to unfold the treasures of his knowledge to the sovereign, but at last his reluctance is overcome, and he says to him, 'Come, and I will tell you about the Perfect Tâo. Its essence is surrounded with the deepest obscurity; its highest reach is in darkness and silence. There is nothing to be seen, nothing to be heard. When it holds the spirit in its arms in stillness, then the bodily form will of itself become correct. You must be still, you must be pure; not subjecting your body to toil, not agitating your vital force :—then you may live for long. When your eyes see nothing, your ears hear nothing, and your mind knows nothing, your spirit will keep your body, and the body will live long. Watch over what is within you; shut up the avenues that connect you with what is external;—much knowledge is pernicious. I will proceed with you to the summit of the Grand Brilliance, where we come to the bright and expanding (element); I will enter with you the gate of the dark and depressing element. There heaven and earth have their Controllers; there the Yin and Yang have their Repositories. Watch over and keep your body, and all things will of themselves give it vigour. I maintain the (original) unity (of these elements). In this way I have cultivated myself for 1200 years, and my bodily form knows no decay.' Add 1200 to 2679, and we obtain 3879 as the year B.C. of Kwang *Kh*ăng-ȝze's birth!

6. Lâo-ȝze describes some other and kindred results of cultivating the Tâo in terms which are sufficiently startling, and which it is difficult to accept. In his fiftieth chapter he says, 'He who is skilful in managing his life travels on land without having to shun rhinoceros or tiger, and enters a host without having to avoid buff coat or sharp weapon. The rhinoceros finds no place in him into which to thrust its horn, nor the tiger a place in which to fix its claws, nor the weapon a place to admit its point. And for what reason? Because there is in him no place of death.' To the same effect he says in his fifty-fifth chapter, 'He who has in himself abundantly the attributes (of the Tâo) is like an infant. Poisonous

Startling results of the Tâo.

insects will not sting him ; fierce beasts will not seize him ;
birds of prey will not strike him.'

Such assertions startle us by their contrariety to our
observation and experience, but so does most of the teaching
of Tâoism. What can seem more absurd than the declara-
tion that ' the Tâo does nothing, and so there is nothing
that it does not do?' And yet this is one of the fundamental
axioms of the system. The thirty-seventh chapter, which
enunciates it, goes on to say, ' If princes and kings were
able to maintain (the Tâo), all things would of themselves
be transformed by them.' This principle, if we can call it
so, is generalised in the fortieth, one of the shortest chapters,
and partly in rhyme :—

> ' The movement of the Tâo
> By contraries proceeds ;
> And weakness marks the course
> Of Tâo's mighty deeds.

All things under heaven sprang from it as existing (and
named) ; that existence sprang from it as non-existent
(and not named).'

Ho-shang Kung, or whoever gave their names to the
chapters of the Tâo Teh King, styles this fortieth chapter
' Dispensing with the use (of means).' If the wish to use
means arise in the mind, the nature of the Tâo as ' the
Nameless Simplicity' has been vitiated ; and this nature
is celebrated in lines like those just quoted :—

> ' Simplicity without a name
> Is free from all external aim.
> With no desire, at rest and still,
> All things go right, as of their will.'

I do not cull any passages from Kwang-ʒze to illustrate
these points. In his eleventh Book his subject is Government by 'Let-a-be and the exercise of Forbearance.'

7. This Tâo ruled men at first, and then the world was
in a paradisiacal state. Neither of our authorities tells us
The paradisiacal how long this condition lasted, but as Lâo
state.   observes in his eighteenth chapter, 'the Tâo
ceased to be observed.' Kwang-ʒze, however, gives us

more than one description of what he considered the paradisiacal state was.   He calls it 'the age of Perfect Virtue.'
In the thirteenth paragraph of his twelfth Book he says,
'In this age, they attached no value to wisdom, nor employed
men of ability.   Superiors were (but) as the higher branches
of a tree ; and the people were like the deer of the wild.
They were upright and correct, without knowing that to
be so was Righteousness ; they loved one another, without
knowing that to do so was Benevolence ; they were honest
and leal-hearted, without knowing that it was Loyalty ;
they fulfilled their engagements, without knowing that to
do so was Good Faith ; in their movements they employed
the services of one another, without thinking that they were
conferring or receiving any gift.   Therefore their actions
left no trace, and there was no record of their affairs.'

Again, in the fourth paragraph of his tenth Book, address-
ing an imaginary interlocutor, he says, 'Are you, Sir, unacquainted with the age of Perfect Virtue ?'   He then gives
the names of twelve sovereigns who ruled in it, of the
greater number of whom we have no other means of knowing anything, and goes on :—'In their times the people used
knotted cords in carrying on their business.   They thought
their (simple) food pleasant, and their (plain) clothing
beautiful.   They were happy in their (simple) manners,
and felt at rest in their (poor) dwellings.   (The people of)
neighbouring states might be able to descry one another ;
the voices of their cocks and dogs might be heard from
one to the other ; they might not die till they were old ;
and yet all their life they would have no communication
together.   In those times perfect good order prevailed.'

One other description of the primeval state is still more
interesting.   It is in the second paragraph of Bk. IX :—
'The people had their regular and constant nature :—they
wove and made themselves clothes ; they tilled the ground
and got food.   This was their common faculty.   They were
all one in this, and did not form themselves into separate
classes ; so were they constituted and left to their natural
tendencies.   Therefore in the age of Perfect Virtue men
walked along with slow and grave step, and with their

looks steadily directed forwards. On the hills there were no footpaths nor excavated passages; on the lakes there were no boats nor dams. All creatures lived in companies, and their places of settlement were made near to one another. Birds and beasts multiplied to flocks and herds; the grass and trees grew luxuriant and long. The birds and beasts might be led about without feeling the constraint; the nest of the magpie might be climbed to, and peeped into. Yes, in the age of Perfect Virtue, men lived in common with birds and beasts, and were on terms of equality with all creatures, as forming one family;—how could they know among themselves the distinctions of superior men and small men? Equally without knowledge, they did not leave the path of their natural virtue; equally free from desires, they were in the state of pure simplicity. In that pure simplicity, their nature was what it ought to be.'

Such were the earliest Chinese of whom Kwang-ȝze could venture to give any account. If ever their ancestors had been in a ruder or savage condition, it must have been at a much antecedent time. These had long passed out of such a state; they were tillers of the ground, and acquainted with the use of the loom. They lived in happy relations with one another, and in kindly harmony with the tribes of inferior creatures. But there is not the slightest allusion to any sentiment of piety as animating them individually, or to any ceremony of religion as observed by them in common. This surely is a remarkable feature in their condition. I call attention to it, but I do not dwell upon it.

8. But by the time of Lâo and Kwang the cultivation of the Tâo had fallen into disuse. The simplicity of life which it demanded, with its freedom from all disturbing speculation and action, was no longer to be found in individuals or in government. It was the general decay of manners and of social order which unsettled the mind of Lâo, made him resign his position as a curator of the Royal Library, and determine to withdraw from China and hide himself

The decay of the Tâo before the growth of knowledge.

among the rude peoples beyond it. The cause of the deterioration of the Tâo and of all the evils of the nation was attributed to the ever-growing pursuit of knowledge, and of what we call the arts of culture. It had commenced very long before;—in the time of Hwang-Tî, *K*wang says in one place[1]; and in another he carries it still higher to Sui-zǎn and Fu-hsî[2]. There had been indeed, all along the line of history, a groping for the rules of life, as indicated by the constitution of man's nature. The results were embodied in the ancient literature which was the lifelong study of Confucius. He had gathered up that literature; he recognised the nature of man as the gift of Heaven or God. The monitions of God as given in the convictions of man's mind supplied him with a Tâo or Path of duty very different from the Tâo or Mysterious Way of Lâo. All this was gall and wormwood to the dreaming librarian or brooding recluse, and made him say, 'If we could renounce our sageness and discard our wisdom, it would be better for the people a hundredfold. If we could renounce our benevolence and discard our righteousness, the people would again become filial and kindly. If we could renounce our artful contrivances and discard our (scheming for) gain, there would be no thieves nor robbers[3].'

We can laugh at this. Tâoism was wrong in its opposition to the increase of knowledge. Man exists under a law of progress. In pursuing it there are demanded discretion and justice. Moral ends must rule over material ends, and advance in virtue be ranked higher than advance in science. So have good and evil, truth and error, to fight out the battle on the field of the world, and in all the range of time; but there is no standing still for the individual or for society. Even Confucius taught his countrymen to set too high a value on the examples of antiquity. The school of Lâo-ʒze fixing themselves in an unknown region beyond antiquity,—a prehistoric time between 'the Grand Beginning of all things' out of nothing, and the unknown commencement of societies of men,—has made no advance

---

[1] Bk. XI, par. 5. [2] Bk. XVI, par. 2.
[3] Tâo Teh *K*ing, ch. 19.

but rather retrograded, and is represented by the still more degenerate Tâoism of the present day.

There is a short parabolic story of *K*wang-ȝze, intended to represent the antagonism between Tâoism and knowledge, which has always struck me as curious. The last paragraph of his seventh Book is this :—' The Ruler (or god T î) of the Southern Ocean was S h û (that is, Heedless); the Ruler of the Northern Ocean was H û (that is, Hasty); and the Ruler of the Centre was H w u n-t u n (that is, Chaos). Shû and Hû were continually meeting in the land of H w u n-t u n, who treated them very well. They consulted together how they might repay his kindness, and said, "Men have all seven orifices for the purposes of seeing, hearing, eating, and breathing, while this (poor) Ruler alone has not one. Let us try and make them for him." Accordingly they dug one orifice in him every day ; and at the end of seven days Chaos died.'

So it was that Chaos passed away before Light. So did the nameless Simplicity of the T â o disappear before Knowledge. But it was better that the C h a o s should give place to the K o s m o s. 'Heedless' and 'Hasty' did a good deed.

9. I have thus set forth eight characteristics of the Tâoistic system, having respect mostly to what is peculiar and mystical in it. I will now conclude my exhibition of it by

The practical lessons of Lâo-ȝze.

bringing together under one head the practical lessons of its author for men individually, and for the administration of government. The praise of whatever excellence these possess belongs to Lâo himself : *K*wang-ȝze devotes himself mainly to the illustration of the abstruse and difficult points.

First, it does not surprise us that in his rules for individual man, Lâo should place H u m i l i t y in the foremost place. A favourite illustration with him of the T â o is water. In his

Humility.

eighth chapter he says :—' The highest excellence is like that of water. The excellence of water appears in its benefiting all things, and in its occupying, without striving to the contrary, the low ground which all men dislike. Hence (its way) is near to that of the Tâo.' To the same effect in the seventy-eighth chapter:—'There is nothing in the world more soft and weak than water, and yet for attacking things that are firm and strong there is nothing that can take precedence of it. Every one in the world knows that the soft overcomes the hard, and the weak the strong; but no one is able to carry it out in practice.'

In his sixty-seventh chapter Lâo associates with Humility two other virtues, and calls them his three Precious Things or Jewels. They are Gentleness, Economy, and Shrinking from taking precedence of others. 'With that Gentleness,' he says, 'I can be bold; with that Economy I can be liberal; Shrinking from taking precedence of others, I can become a vessel of the highest honour.'

Lâo's three Jewels.

And in his sixty-third chapter, he rises to a still loftier height of morality. He says, '(It is the way of the Tâo) to act without (thinking of) acting, to conduct affairs without (feeling) the trouble of them; to taste without discerning any flavour, to consider the small as great, and the few as many, and to recompense injury with kindness.'

Rendering good for evil.

Here is the grand Christian precept, 'Render to no man evil for evil. If thine enemy hunger, feed him; if he thirst, give him drink. Be not overcome with evil, but overcome evil with good.' We know that the maxim made some noise in its author's lifetime; that the disciples of Confucius consulted him about it, and that he was unable to receive it[1]. It comes in with less important matters by virtue of the Tâoistic 'rule of contraries.' I have been surprised to find what little reference to it I have met with in the course of my Chinese reading. I do not think that *K*wang-ʒze takes notice of it to illustrate it after his fashion. There, however, it is in the Tâo Teh *K*ing. The fruit of it has yet to be developed.

Second, Lâo laid down the same rule for the policy of the state as for the life of the individual. He says in his sixty-first chapter, 'What makes a state great is its being like a low-lying, down-flowing stream;—it becomes the

---

[1] Confucian Analects, XIV, 36.

centre to which tend all (the small states) under heaven.'
He then uses an illustration which will produce a smile :—
'Take the case of all females. The female always overcomes the male by her stillness. Stillness may be considered (a sort of) abasement.' Resuming his subject, he
adds, 'Thus it is that a great state, by condescending to
small states, gains them for itself; and that small states,
by abasing themselves to a great state, win it over to them.
In the one case the abasement tends to gaining adherents;
in the other case, to procuring favour. The great state
only wishes to unite men together and nourish them; a
small state only wishes to be received by, and to serve,
the other. Each gets what it desires, but the great state
must learn to abase itself.'

'All very well in theory,' some one will exclaim, 'but,
the world has not seen it yet reduced to practice.' So it is.
The fact is deplorable. No one saw the misery arising
from it, and exposed its unreasonableness more unsparingly,
than *K*wang-ʒze. But it was all in vain in his time, as it
has been in all the centuries that have since rolled their
course. Philosophy, philanthropy, and religion have still
to toil on, 'faint, yet pursuing,' believing that the time will
yet come when humility and love shall secure the reign of
peace and good will among the nations of men.

While enjoining humility, Lâo protested against war.
In his thirty-first chapter he says, 'Arms, however beautiful, are instruments of evil omen ; hateful, it may be said,
to all creatures. They who have the Tâo do not like to
employ them.' Perhaps in his sixty-ninth chapter he allows
defensive war, but he adds, 'There is no calamity greater
than that of lightly engaging in war. To do that is near
losing the gentleness which is so precious. Thus it is that
when weapons are (actually) crossed, he who deplores the
(situation) conquers.'

There are some other points in the practical lessons of
Tâoism to which I should like to call the attention of the
reader, but I must refer him for them to the chapters of
the Tâo Teh *K*ing, and the Books of *K*wang-ʒze. Its
salient features have been set forth somewhat fully. Not-

withstanding the scorn poured so freely on Confucius by
*K*wang-ȝze and other Tâoist writers, he proved in the
course of time too strong for Lâo as the teacher of their
people. The entrance of Buddhism, moreover, into the
country in our first century, was very injurious to Tâoism,
which still exists, but is only the shadow of its former self.
It is tolerated by the government, but not patronised as it
was when emperors and empresses seemed to think more
of it than of Confucianism. It is by the spread of knowledge, which it has always opposed, that its overthrow and
disappearance will be brought about ere long.

CHAPTER IV.

Accounts of Lâo-ȝze and *K*wang-ȝze given by Sze-mâ *K*ḥien.

It seems desirable, before passing from Lâo and
*K*wang in this Introduction, to give a place in it to
what is said about them by Sze-mâ *K*ḥien. I have
said that not a single proper name occurs in the Tâo
Teh *K*ing. There is hardly an historical allusion in it.
Only one chapter, the twentieth, has somewhat of an
autobiographical character. It tells us, however, of no
incidents of his life. He appears alone in the world through
his cultivation of the Tâo, melancholy and misunderstood,
yet binding that Tâo more closely to his bosom.

The Books of *K*wang-ȝze are of a different nature,
abounding in pictures of Tâoist life, in anecdotes and
narratives, graphic, argumentative, often satirical. But
they are not historical. Confucius and many of his disciples, Lâo and members of his school, heroes and sages
of antiquity, and men of his own day, move across his
pages; but the incidents in connexion with which they
are introduced are probably fictitious, and devised by him
'to point his moral or adorn his tale.' His names of
individuals and places are often like those of Bunyan in
his Pilgrim's Progress or his Holy War, emblematic
of their characters and the doctrines which he employs

them to illustrate. He often comes on the stage himself, and there is an air of verisimilitude in his descriptions, possibly also a certain amount of fact about them; but we cannot appeal to them as historical testimony. It is only to Sze-mâ *Kh*ien that we can go for this; he always writes in the spirit of an historian; but what he has to tell us of the two men is not much.

And first, as to his account of Lâo-ȝze. When he wrote, about the beginning of the first century B.C., the Tâoist master was already known as Lâo-ȝze. *Kh*ien, however, tells us that his surname was Lî, and his name *R*, meaning 'Ear,' which gave place after his death to Tan, meaning 'Long-eared,' from which we may conclude that he was named from some peculiarity in the form of his ears. He was a native of the state of *Kh*û, which had then extended far beyond its original limits, and his birth-place was in the present province of Ho-nan or of An-hui. He was a curator in the Royal Library; and when Confucius visited the capital in the year B.C. 517, the two men met. *Kh*ien says that Confucius's visit to Lo-yang was that he might question Lâo on the subject of ceremonies. He might have other objects in mind as well; but however that was, the two met. Lî said to Khung, 'The men about whom you talk are dead, and their bones are mouldered to dust; only their words are left. Moreover, when the superior man gets his opportunity, he mounts aloft; but when the time is against him, he is carried along by the force of circumstances [1]. I have heard that a good merchant, though he have rich treasures safely stored, appears as if he were poor; and that the superior man, though his virtue be complete, is yet to outward seeming stupid. Put away your proud air and many desires, your insinuating habit and wild will. They are of no advantage to you;—this is all I have to tell you.' Confucius is made to say to his disciples after the interview: ' I know how

---

[1] Julien translates this by 'il erre à l'aventure.' In 1861 I rendered it, 'He moves as if his feet were entangled.' To one critic it suggests the idea of a bundle or wisp of brushwood rolled about over the ground by the wind.

birds can fly, fishes swim, and animals run. But the
runner may be snared, the swimmer hooked, and the
flyer shot by the arrow. But there is the dragon:—I
cannot tell how he mounts on the wind through the clouds,
and rises to heaven. To-day I have seen Lâo-ʒze, and can
only compare him to the dragon.'

In this speech of Confucius we have, I believe, the origin
of the name Lâo-ʒze, as applied to the master of Tâoism.
Its meaning is 'The Old Philosopher,' or 'The Old Gentleman [1].' Confucius might well so style Lî R. At the
time of this interview he was himself in his thirty-fifth
year, and the other was in his eighty-eighth. Khien adds,
'Lâo-ʒze cultivated the Tâo and its attributes, the chief
aim of his studies being how to keep himself concealed
and remain unknown. He continued to reside at (the
capital of) Kâu, but after a long time, seeing the decay
of the dynasty, he left it and went away to the barrier-
gate, leading out of the kingdom on the north-west.
Yin Hsî, the warden of the gate, said to him, "You are
about to withdraw yourself out of sight. Let me insist
on your (first) composing for me a book." On this, Lâo-ʒze
wrote a book in two parts, setting forth his views on the
Tâo and its attributes, in more than 5000 characters. He
then went away, and it is not known where he died. He
was a superior man, who liked to keep himself unknown.'

Khien finally traces Lâo's descendants down to the first
century B.C., and concludes by saying, 'Those who attach
themselves to the doctrine of Lâo-ʒze condemn that of
the Literati, and the Literati on their part condemn Lâo-
ʒze, verifying the saying, "Parties whose principles are
different cannot take counsel together." Lî R taught that
by doing nothing others are as a matter of course trans-

---

[1] The characters may mean 'the old boy,' and so understood have given rise
to various fabulous legends; that his mother had carried him in her womb for
seventy-two years (some say, for eighty-one), and that when born the child had
the white hair of an old man. Julien has translated the fabulous legend of
Ko Hung of our fourth century about him. By that time the legends of
Buddhism about Sâkyamuni had become current in China, and were copied and
applied to Lâo-ʒze by his followers. Looking at the meaning of the two names,
I am surprised no one has characterized Lâo-ʒze as the Chinese Seneca.

formed, and that rectification in the same way ensues from being pure and still.'

This morsel is all that we have of historical narrative about Lâo-ʒze. The account of the writing of the Tâo Teh King at the request of the warden of the barrier-gate has a doubtful and legendary appearance. Otherwise, the record is free from anything to raise suspicion about it. It says nothing about previous existences of Lâo, and nothing of his travelling to the west, and learning there the doctrines which are embodied in his work. He goes through the pass out of the domain of Kâu, and died no one knowing where.

It is difficult, however, to reconcile this last statement with a narrative in the end of Kwang-ʒze's third Book. There we see Lâo-ʒze dead, and a crowd of mourners wailing round the corpse, and giving extraordinary demonstrations of grief, which offend a disciple of a higher order, who has gone to the house to offer his condolences on the occasion. But for the peculiar nature of most of Kwang's narratives, we should say, in opposition to Khien, that the place and time of Lâo's death were well known. Possibly, however, Kwang-ʒze may have invented the whole story, to give him the opportunity of setting forth what, according to his ideal of it, the life of a Tâoist master should be, and how even Lâo-ʒze himself fell short of it.

Second, Khien's account of Kwang-ʒze is still more brief. He was a native, he tells us, of the territory of Măng, which belonged to the kingdom of Liang or Wei, and held an office, he does not say what, in the city of Khî-yüan. Kwang was thus of the same part of China as Lâo-ʒze, and probably grew up familiar with all his speculations and lessons. He lived during the reigns of the kings Hui of Liang, Hsüan of Khî, and Wei of Khû. We cannot be wrong therefore in assigning his period to the latter half of the third, and earlier part of the fourth century B.C. He was thus a contemporary of Mencius. They visited at the same courts, and yet neither ever mentions the other. They were the two ablest debaters of their day, and fond of exposing what they deemed heresy. But it would only be a matter of useless speculation to try to account for their never having come into argumentative collision.

K*h*ien says : ' *K*wang had made himself well acquainted with all the literature of his time, but preferred the views of Lâo-ʒze, and ranked himself among his followers, so that of the more than ten myriads of characters contained in his published writings the greater part are occupied with metaphorical illustrations of Lâo's doctrines. He made " The Old Fisherman," " The Robber *K*ih," and " The Cutting open Satchels," to satirize and expose the disciples of Confucius, and clearly exhibit the sentiments of Lâo. Such names and characters as " Wei-lêi Hsü " and " Khang-sang ʒze " are fictitious, and the pieces where they occur are not to be understood as narratives of real events [1].

' But *K*wang was an admirable writer and skilful composer, and by his instances and truthful descriptions hit and exposed the Mohists and Literati. The ablest scholars of his day could not escape his satire nor reply to it, while he allowed and enjoyed himself with his sparkling, dashing style ; and thus it was that the greatest men, even kings and princes, could not use him for their purposes.

' King Wei of *K*hû, having heard of the ability of *K*wang *K*âu, sent messengers with large gifts to bring him to his court, and promising also that he would make him his chief minister. *K*wang-ʒze, however, only laughed and said to them, " A thousand ounces of silver are a great gain to me, and to be a high noble and minister is a most honourable position. But have you not seen the victim-ox for the border sacrifice ? It is carefully fed for several years, and robed with rich embroidery that it may be fit to enter the Grand Temple. When the time comes for it to do so, it would prefer to be a little pig, but it cannot get to be so. Go away quickly, and do not soil me with your presence.

---

[1] Khang-sang ʒze is evidently the Kăng-sang *K*hû of *K*wang's Book XXIII. Wei-lêi Hsü is supposed by Sze-mâ *K*äng of the Thang dynasty, who called himself the Lesser Sze-mâ, to be the name of a Book ; one, in that case, of the lost books of *K*wang. But as we find the ' Hill of Wei-lêi ' mentioned in Bk. XXIII as the scene of Kăng-sang *K*hû's Tâoistic labours and success, I suppose that *K*hien's reference is to that. The names are quoted by him from memory, or might be insisted on as instances of different readings.

I had rather amuse and enjoy myself in the midst of a filthy ditch than be subject to the rules and restrictions in the court of a sovereign. I have determined never to take office, but prefer the enjoyment of my own free will."'

*Kh*ien concludes his account of *K*wang-ʒze with the above story, condensed by him, probably, from two of *K*wang's own narratives, in par. 11 of Bk. XVII, and 13 of XXXII, to the injury of them both. Paragraph 14 of XXXII brings before us one of the last scenes of *K*wang-ʒze's life, and we may doubt whether it should be received as from his own pencil. It is interesting in itself, however, and I introduce it here : ' When *K*wang-ʒze was about to die, his disciples signified their wish to give him a grand burial. " I shall have heaven and earth," he said, " for my coffin and its shell ; the sun and moon for my two round symbols of jade ; the stars and constellations for my pearls and jewels ;— will not the provisions for my interment be complete ? What would you add to them ? " The disciples replied, "We are afraid that the crows and kites will eat our master." *K*wang-ʒze rejoined, "Above, the crows and kites will eat me ; below, the mole-crickets and ants will eat me ; to take from those and give to these would only show your partiality."'

Such were among the last words of *K*wang-ʒze. His end was not so impressive as that of Confucius ; but it was in keeping with the general magniloquence and strong assertion of independence that marked all his course.

CHAPTER V.

ON THE TRACTATE OF ACTIONS AND THEIR RETRIBUTIONS.

1. The contrast is great between the style of the Tâo Teh *K*ing and the Books of *K*wang-ʒze and that of the

Peculiar style and nature of the Kan Ying Phien.

Kan Ying Phien, a translation of which is now submitted as a specimen of the Texts of Tâoism. The works of Lâo and *K*wang stand alone in the literature of the system. What it was before Lâo cannot be ascertained, and in his chapters it comes before us not as a religion, but as a subject of philosophical speculation, together with some practical applications of it insisted on by Lâo himself. The brilliant pages of *K*wang-ȝze contain little more than his ingenious defence of his master's speculations, and an aggregate of illustrative narratives sparkling with the charms of his composition, but in themselves for the most part unbelievable, often grotesque and absurd. This treatise, on the other hand, is more of what we understand by a sermon or popular tract. It eschews all difficult discussion, and sets forth a variety of traits of character and actions which are good, and a still greater variety of others which are bad, exhorting to the cultivation and performance of the former, and warning against the latter. It describes at the outset the machinery to secure the record of men's doings, and the infliction of the certain retribution, and concludes with insisting on the wisdom of repentance and reformation. At the same time it does not carry its idea of retribution beyond death, but declares that if the reward or punishment is not completed in the present life, the remainder will be received by the posterity of the good-doer and of the offender.

A place is given to the treatise among the Texts of Tâoism in ' The Sacred Books of the East,' because of its popularity in China. ' The various editions of it,' as observed by Mr. Wylie, ' are innumerable ; it has appeared from time to time in almost every conceivable size, shape, and style of execution. Many commentaries have been written upon it, and it is frequently published with a collection of several hundred anecdotes, along with pictorial illustrations, to illustrate every paragraph seriatim. It is deemed a great act of merit to aid by voluntary contribution towards the gratuitous distribution of this work[1].'

2. The author of the treatise is not known, but, as Mr. Wylie also observes, it appears to have been written during

The origin of the treatise. the Sung dynasty. The earliest mention of it which I have met with is in the continua-

---

[1] Notes on Chinese Literature, p. 179.

tion of Ma-twan Lin's encyclopedic work by Wang *Kh*î, first published in 1586, the fourteenth year of the fourteenth emperor of the Ming dynasty. In Wang's supplement to his predecessor's account of Tâoist works, the sixth notice is of 'a commentary on the Thâi Shang Kan Ying Phien by a Lî *Kh*ang-ling,' and immediately before it is a commentary on the short but well-known Yin Fû *K*ing by a Lû Tien, who lived 1042–1102. Immediately after it other works of the eleventh century are mentioned. To that same century therefore we may reasonably refer the origin of the Kan Ying Phien.

As to the meaning of the title, the only difficulty is with the two commencing characters Thâi Shang. Julien left *The meaning of* them untranslated, with the note, however, *the title.* that they were 'l'abréviation de Thâi Shang Lâo *K*ün, expression honorifique par laquelle les Tâo-sze désignent Lâo-ʒze, le fondateur de leur secte[1].' This is the interpretation commonly given of the phrase, and it is hardly worth while to indicate any doubt of its correctness; but if the characters were taken, as I believe they were, from the beginning of the seventeenth chapter of the Tâo Teh *K*ing, I should prefer to understand them of the highest and oldest form of the Tâoistic teaching[2].

3. I quoted on page 13 the view of Hardwick, the Christian Advocate of Cambridge, that 'the indefinite expression

---

[1] See 'Le Livre des Récompense et des Peines en Chinois et en François' (London, 1835).

[2] The designation of Lâo-ʒze as Thâi Shang Lâo *K*ün originated probably in the Thang dynasty. It is on record that in 666 Kâo ʒung, the third emperor, went to Lâo-ʒze's temple at Po *K*âu (the place of Lâo's birth, and still called by the same name, in the department of Făng-yang in An-hui), and conferred on him the title of Thâi Shang Yüan Yüan Hwang Tî, 'The Great God, the Mysterious Originator, the Most High.' 'Then,' says Mayers, Manual, p. 113, 'for the first time he was ranked among the gods as " Great Supreme, the Emperor (or Imperial God) of the Dark First Cause."' The whole entry is 至亳州尊老君爲太上元 (or 玄) 元皇帝. Later on, in 1014, we find *K*ăn ʒung, the fourth Sung emperor, also visiting Po *K*âu, and in Lâo's temple, which has by this time become ' the Palace of Grand Purity,' enlarging his title to Thâi Shang Lâo *K*ün Hwun Yüan Shang Teh Hwang Tî, 'The Most High, the Ruler Lâo, the Great God of Grand Virtue at the Chaotic Origin.' But such titles are not easily translated.

Tâo was adopted to denominate an abstract Cause, or
Was the old　the initial principle of life and order, to
Tâoism a religion? which worshippers were able to assign
the attributes of immateriality, eternity, immensity, invisibility.' His selection of the term worshippers in this
passage was unfortunate. Neither Lâo nor *K*wang says
anything about the worship of the Tâo, about priests or
monks, about temples or rituals. How could they do so,
seeing that Tâo was not to them the name of a personal
Being, nor 'Heaven' a metaphorical term equivalent to the
Confucian Tî, 'Ruler,' or Shang Tî, 'Supreme Ruler.'
With this agnosticism as to God, and their belief that by
a certain management and discipline of the breath life
might be prolonged indefinitely, I do not see how anything of an organised religion was possible for the old
Tâoists.

The Tâoist proclivities of the founder of the *K*/*h*in dynasty are well known. If his life had been prolonged, and
the dynasty become consolidated, there might have arisen
such a religion in connexion with Tâoism, for we have a
record that he, as head of the Empire, had eight spirits[1]
to which he offered sacrifices. *K*/*h*in, however, soon passed
away; what remained in permanency from it was only the
abolition of the feudal kingdom.

4. We cannot here attempt to relate in detail the rise
and growth of the *K*ang family in which the headship of
Tâoism has been hereditary since our first Christian century, with the exception of one not very long interruption.
The family of　One of the earliest members of it, *K*ang
*K*ang.　Liang, must have been born not long after
the death of *K*wang-ʒze, for he joined the party of Liû

---

[1] The eight spirits were:—1. The Lord of Heaven; 2. The Lord of Earth;
3. The Lord of War; 4. The Lord of the Yang operation; 5. The Lord of the
Yin operation; 6. The Lord of the Moon; 7. The Lord of the Sun; and
8. The Lord of the Four Seasons. See Mayers's C. R. Manual, pp. 327, 328.
His authority is the sixth of Sze-mâ *K*/*h*ien's monographs. *K*/*h*ien seems to say
that the worship of these spirits could be traced to Thâi Kung, one of the
principal ministers of kings Wăn and Wû at the rise of the *K*âu dynasty in the
twelfth century B.C., and to whom in the list of Tâoist writings in the Imperial
Library of Han, no fewer than 237 phien are ascribed.

Pang, the founder of the dynasty of Han, in B.C. 208, and by his wisdom and bravery contributed greatly to his success over the adherents of *Kh*in, and other contenders for the sovereignty of the empire. Abandoning then a political career, he spent the latter years of his life in a vain quest for the elixir of life.

Among Liang's descendants in our first century was a *K*ang Tâo-ling, who, eschewing a career in the service of the state, devoted himself to the pursuits of alchemy, and at last succeeded in compounding the grand elixir or pill, and at the age of 123 was released from the trammels of the mortal body, and entered on the enjoyment of immortality, leaving to his descendants his books, talismans and charms, his sword, mighty against spirits, and his seal. Tâo-ling stands out, in Tâoist accounts, as the first patriarch of the system, with the title of Thien Shih, 'Master or Preceptor of Heaven.' 'Hsüan Ʒung of the Thang dynasty in 748, confirmed the dignity and title in the family; and in 1016 the Sung emperor *K*ăn Ʒung invested its representative with large tracts of land near the Lung-hû mountain in *K*iang-hsî. The present patriarch—for I suppose the same man is still alive—made a journey from his residence not many years ago, and was interviewed by several foreigners in Shanghai. The succession is said to be perpetuated by the transmigration of the soul of *K*ang Tâo-ling into some infant or youthful member of the family; whose heirship is supernaturally revealed as soon as the miracle is effected[1].

This superstitious notion shows the influence of Buddhism on Tâoism. It has been seen from the eighteenth of the Books of *K*wang-ʒze what affinities there were between Tâoism and the Indian system; and there can be no doubt that the introduction of the latter into China did more than anything else to affect the development of the Tâoistic system. As early as the time of Confucius there were recluses in the country, men who had withdrawn from the world, disgusted with its

Influence of Buddhism on Tâoism.

---

[1] See Mayers's C. R. Manual, Part I, article 35.

vanities and in despair from its disorders. Lâo would appear to have himself contemplated this course. When their representatives of our early centuries saw the Buddhists among them with their images, monasteries, and nunneries, their ritual and discipline, they proceeded to organise themselves after a similar fashion. They built monasteries and nunneries, framed images, composed liturgies, and adopted a peculiar mode of tying up their hair. The 'Three Precious Ones' of Buddhism, emblematic to the initiated of Intelligence personified in Buddha, the Law, and the Community or Church, but to the mass of the worshippers merely three great idols, styled by them Buddha Past, Present, and To Come: these appeared in Tâoism as the 'Three Pure Ones,' also represented by three great images, each of which receives the title of 'His Celestial Eminence,' and is styled the 'Most High God (Shang Tî).' The first of them is a deification of Chaos, the second, of Lâo-ȝze, and the third of I know not whom or what; perhaps of the Tâo.

But those Three Pure Ones have been very much cast into the shade, as the objects of popular worship and veneration, by Yü Hwang Tî or Yü Hwang Shang Tî. This personage appears to have been a member of the 𝘒ang clan, held to be a magician and venerated from the time of the Thang dynasty, but deified in 1116 by the Sung emperor Hui ȝung at the instigation of a charlatan Lin Ling-sû, a renegade Buddhist monk. He is the god in the court of heaven to whom the spirits of the body and of the hearth in our treatise proceed at stated times to report for approval or condemnation the conduct of men.

Since the first publication of the Kan Ying Phien, the tenets of Buddhism have been still further adopted by the teachers of Tâoism, and shaped to suit the nature of their own system. I have observed that the idea of retribution in our treatise does not go beyond the present life; but the manifestoes of Tâoism of more recent times are much occupied with descriptions of the courts of purgatory and threatenings of the everlasting misery of hell to those whom their sufferings in those courts

fail to wean from their wickedness. Those manifestoes are
published by the mercy of Yü Hwang Shang Tî that
men and women may be led to repent of their faults and
make atonement for their crimes. They emanate from the
temples of the tutelary deities[1] which are found throughout
the empire, and especially in the walled cities, and are
under the charge of Tâoist monks. A visitor to one of the
larger of these temples may not only see the pictures of
the purgatorial courts and other forms of the modern
superstitions, but he will find also astrologers, diviners,
geomancers, physiognomists, et id genus omne, plying
their trades or waiting to be asked to do so, and he will
wonder how it has been possible to affiliate such things
with the teachings of Lâo-ʒze.

Other manifestoes of a milder form, and more like our
tractate, are also continually being issued as from one or
other of what are called the state gods, whose temples are
all in the charge of the same monks. In the approximation which has thus been going on of Tâoism to Buddhism,
the requirement of celibacy was long resisted by the professors of the former; but recent editions of the Penal
Code[2] contain sundry regulations framed to enforce celibacy, to bind the monks and nuns of both systems to the
observance of the Confucian maxims concerning filial piety,
and the sacrificial worship of the dead ; and also to restrict
the multiplication of monasteries and nunneries. Neither
Lâo nor *K*wang was a celibate or recommended celibacy.
The present patriarch, as a married man, would seem to be
able still to resist the law.

---

[1] Called *Kh*ăng Hwang Miâo, 'Wall and Moat Temples,' Palladia of
the city.

[2] See Dr. Eitel's third edition of his 'Three Lectures on Buddhism,' pp.
36–45 (Hongkong: Lane, Crawford & Co., 1884). The edition of the Penal
Code to which he refers is of 1879.

THE TÂO TEH *K*ING,

OR

THE TÂO
AND ITS CHARACTERISTICS.

THE TÂO TEH KING.

PART I.

Ch. 1. 1. The Tâo that can be trodden is not the
enduring and unchanging Tâo. The name that can
be named is not the enduring and unchanging name.

2. (Conceived of as) having no name, it is the
Originator of heaven and earth; (conceived of as)
having a name, it is the Mother of all things.

3. Always without desire we must be found,
   If its deep mystery we would sound;
   But if desire always within us be,
   Its outer fringe is all that we shall see.

4. Under these two aspects, it is really the same;
but as development takes place, it receives the different names. Together we call them the Mystery.
Where the Mystery is the deepest is the gate of all
that is subtle and wonderful.

體道, 'Embodying the Tâo.' The author sets forth,
as well as the difficulty of his subject would allow him, the
nature of the Tâo in itself, and its manifestation. To
understand the Tâo one must be partaker of its nature.

Par. 3 suggests the words of the apostle John, ' He that
loveth not knoweth not God; for God is love.' Both the
Tâo, Lâo-ȝze's ideal in the absolute, and its Teh, or operation, are comprehended in this chapter, the latter being the
Tâo with the name, the Mother of all things. See pages 12,
13 in the Introduction on the translation of the term Tâo.

2. 1. All in the world know the beauty of the
beautiful, and in doing this they have (the idea of)

what ugliness is; they all know the skill of the skilful, and in doing this they have (the idea of) what
the want of skill is.

2. So it is that existence and non-existence give
birth the one to (the idea of) the other; that difficulty and ease produce the one (the idea of) the
other; that length and shortness fashion out the one
the figure of the other; that (the ideas of) height
and lowness arise from the contrast of the one with
the other; that the musical notes and tones become
harmonious through the relation of one with another;
and that being before and behind give the idea of
one following another.

3. Therefore the sage manages affairs without
doing anything, and conveys his instructions without
the use of speech.

4. All things spring up, and there is not one
which declines to show itself; they grow, and there
is no claim made for their ownership; they go
through their processes, and there is no expecta-
tion (of a reward for the results). The work is
accomplished, and there is no resting in it (as an
achievement).

The work is done, but how no one can see;
'Tis this that makes the power not cease to be.

養身, 'The Nourishment of the Person.' But many of
Ho-shang Kung's titles are more appropriate than this.

The chapter starts with instances of the antinomies,
which suggest to the mind each of them the existence of its
corresponding opposite; and the author finds in them an
analogy to the 'contraries' which characterize the operation
of the Tâo, as stated in chapter 40. He then proceeds to
describe the action of the sage in par. 3 as in accordance
with this law of contraries; and, in par. 4, that of heaven

and earth, or what we may call nature, in the processes of the vegetable world.

Par. 2 should be rhymed, but I could not succeed to my satisfaction in the endeavour to rhyme it. Every one who can read Chinese will see that the first four members rhyme. The last two rhyme also, the concluding 隨 being pronounced so;—see the Khang-hsî dictionary in voc.

3. 1. Not to value and employ men of superior ability is the way to keep the people from rivalry among themselves; not to prize articles which are difficult to procure is the way to keep them from becoming thieves; not to show them what is likely to excite their desires is the way to keep their minds from disorder.

2. Therefore the sage, in the exercise of his government, empties their minds, fills their bellies, weakens their wills, and strengthens their bones.

3. He constantly (tries to) keep them without knowledge and without desire, and where there are those who have knowledge, to keep them from presuming to act (on it). When there is this abstinence from action, good order is universal.

安民, 'Keeping the People at Rest.' The object of the chapter is to show that government according to the Tâo is unfavourable to the spread of knowledge among the people, and would keep them rather in the state of primitive simplicity and ignorance, thereby securing their restfulness and universal good order. Such is the uniform teaching of Lâo-ʒze and his great follower Kwang-ʒze, and of all Tâoist writers.

4. 1. The Tâo is (like) the emptiness of a vessel; and in our employment of it we must be on our guard against all fulness. How deep and unfa-

thomable it is, as if it were the Honoured Ancestor of all things!

2. We should blunt our sharp points, and unravel the complications of things; we should attèmper our brightness, and bring ourselves into agreement with the obscurity of others. How pure and still the Tâo is, as if it would ever so continue!

3. I do not know whose son it is. It might appear to have been before God.

無 源, 'The Fountainless.' There is nothing before the Tâo; it might seem to have been before God. And yet there is no demonstration by it of its presence and operation. It is like the emptiness of a vessel. The second character = 冲 = 盅;—see Khang-hsî on the latter. The practical lesson is, that in following the Tâo we must try to be like it.

5. 1. Heaven and earth do not act from (the impulse of) any wish to be benevolent; they deal with all things as the dogs of grass are dealt with. The sages do not act from (any wish to be) benevolent; they deal with the people as the dogs of grass are dealt with.

2. May not the space between heaven and earth be compared to a bellows?

'Tis emptied, yet it loses not its power;
'Tis moved again, and sends forth air the more.
Much speech to swift exhaustion lead we see;
Your inner being guard, and keep it free.

虛 用, 'The Use of Emptiness.' Quiet and unceasing is the operation of the Tâo, and effective is the rule of the sage in accordance with it.

The grass-dogs in par. 1 were made of straw tied up in the shape of dogs, and used in praying for rain; and afterwards, when the sacrifice was over, were thrown aside and left uncared for. Heaven and earth and the sages dealt so with all things and with the people ; but the illustration does not seem a happy one. Both *K*wang-ʒze and Hwâi-nan mention the grass-dogs. See especially the former, XIV, 25 a, b. In that Book there is fully developed the meaning of this chapter. The illustration in par. 2 is better. The Chinese bellows is different to look at from ours, but the principle is the same in the construction of both. The par. concludes in a way that lends some countenance to the later Tâoism's dealing with the breath.

6. The valley spirit dies not, aye the same ;
The female mystery thus do we name.
Its gate, from which at first they issued forth,
Is called the root from which grew heaven and
    earth.
Long and unbroken does its power remain,
Used gently, and without the touch of pain.

成 象, 'The Completion of Material Forms.' This title rightly expresses the import of this enigmatical chapter; but there is a foundation laid in it for the development of the later Tâoism, which occupies itself with the prolongation of life by the management of the breath (氣) or vital force.

'The valley' is used metaphorically as a symbol of 'emptiness' or 'vacancy ;' and 'the spirit of the valley' is the something invisible, yet almost personal, belonging to the Tâo, which constitutes the T e h (德) in the name of our *K*ing. 'The spirit of the valley' has come to be a name for the activity of the Tâo in all the realm of its operation. 'The female mystery' is the Tâo with a name of chapter 1, which is 'the Mother of all things.' All living beings have a father and mother. The processes of generation and production can hardly be imaged by us but by a recognition of this fact; and so Lâo-ʒze thought of the existing realm of nature—of life—as coming through an evolution (not a creation) from the primal air or breath, dividing into two, and thence appearing in the forms of things, material and immaterial. The chapter is found in Lieh-ʒze (I, 1 b) quoted by him from a book of Hwang-Tî; and here Lâo-ʒze has appropriated it, and made it his own. See the Introduction, p. 2.

7. 1. Heaven is long-enduring and earth continues long. The reason why heaven and earth are able to endure and continue thus long is because they do not live of, or for, themselves. This is how they are able to continue and endure.

2. Therefore the sage puts his own person last, and yet it is found in the foremost place; he treats his person as if it were foreign to him, and yet that person is preserved. Is it not because he has no personal and private ends, that therefore such ends are realised?

韜 光, ‘Sheathing the Light.’ The chapter teaches that one’s best good is realised by not thinking of it, or seeking for it. Heaven and earth afford a pattern to the sage, and the sage affords a pattern to all men.

8. 1. The highest excellence is like (that of) water. The excellence of water appears in its benefiting all things, and in its occupying, without striving (to the contrary), the low place which all men dislike. Hence (its way) is near to (that of) the Tâo.

2. The excellence of a residence is in (the suitability of) the place; that of the mind is in abysmal stillness; that of associations is in their being with the virtuous; that of government is in its securing good order; that of (the conduct of) affairs is in its ability; and that of (the initiation of) any movement is in its timeliness.

3. And when (one with the highest excellence) does not wrangle (about his low position), no one finds fault with him.

易 性, 'The Placid and Contented Nature.' Water, as an illustration of the way of the Tâo, is repeatedly employed by Lâo-₃ze.

The various forms of what is excellent in par. 2 are brought forward to set forth the more, by contrast, the excellence of the humility indicated in the acceptance of the lower place without striving to the contrary.

9. 1. It is better to leave a vessel unfilled, than to attempt to carry it when it is full. If you keep feeling a point that has been sharpened, the point cannot long preserve its sharpness.

2. When gold and jade fill the hall, their possessor cannot keep them safe. When wealth and honours lead to arrogancy, this brings its evil on itself. When the work is done, and one's name is becoming distinguished, to withdraw into obscurity is the way of Heaven.

運 夷; but I cannot give a satisfactory rendering of this title. The teaching of the chapter is, that fulness and complacency in success are contrary to the Tâo.

The first clauses of the two sentences in par. 1, 持 而 盈 之, 揣 而 銳 之 = 盈 而 持 之, 銳 而 揣 之, are instances of the 'inverted' style not uncommon in the oldest composition. 'The way of Heaven' = 'the Heavenly Tâo' exemplified by man.

10. 1. When the intelligent and animal souls are held together in one embrace, they can be kept from separating. When one gives undivided attention to the (vital) breath, and brings it to the utmost degree of pliancy, he can become as a (tender)

babe. When he has cleansed away the most mysterious sights (of his imagination), he can become without a flaw.

2. In loving the people and ruling the state, cannot he proceed without any (purpose of) action ? In the opening and shutting of his gates of heaven, cannot he do so as a female bird ? While his intelligence reaches in every direction, cannot he (appear to) be without knowledge ?

3. (The Tâo) produces (all things) and nourishes them; it produces them and does not claim them as its own; it does all, and yet does not boast of it; it presides over all, and yet does not control them. This is what is called 'The mysterious Quality' (of the Tâo).

能爲, 'Possibilities.' This chapter is one of the most difficult to understand and translate in the whole work. Even Kû Hsî was not able to explain the first member satisfactorily. The text of that member seems well supported; but I am persuaded the first clause of it is somehow corrupt.

The whole seems to tell what can be accomplished by one who is possessed of the Tâo. In par. 3 he appears free from all self-consciousness in what he does, and of all self-satisfaction in the results of his doing. The other two paragraphs seem to speak of what he can do under the guidance of the Tâo for himself and for others. He can by his management of his vital breath bring his body to the state of Tâoistic perfection, and keep his intelligent and animal souls from being separated, and he can rule men without purpose and effort. 'The gates of heaven' in par. 2 is a Tâoistic phrase for the nostrils as the organ of the breath;—see the commentary of Ho-shang Kung.

11. The thirty spokes unite in the one nave; but it is on the empty space (for the axle), that the

use of the wheel depends. Clay is fashioned into vessels; but it is on their empty hollowness, that their use depends. The door and windows are cut out (from the walls) to form an apartment; but it is on the empty space (within), that its use depends. Therefore, what has a (positive) existence serves for profitable adaptation, and what has not that for (actual) usefulness.

無 用, 'The Use of what has no Substantive Existence.' The three illustrations serve to set forth the freedom of the Tâo from all pre-occupation and purpose, and the use of what seems useless.

12. 1. Colour's five hues from th' eyes their sight
        will take;
Music's five notes the ears as deaf can make;
The flavours five deprive the mouth of taste;
The chariot course, and the wild hunting waste
Make mad the mind; and objects rare and strange,
Sought for, men's conduct will to evil change.

2. Therefore the sage seeks to satisfy (the craving of) the belly, and not the (insatiable longing of the) eyes. He puts from him the latter, and prefers to seek the former.

檢 欲, 'The Repression of the Desires.' Government in accordance with the Tâo seeks to withdraw men from the attractions of what is external and pleasant to the senses and imagination, and to maintain the primitive simplicity of men's ways and manners. Compare chap. 2. The five colours are Black, Red, Green or Blue, White, and Yellow; the five notes are those of the imperfect Chinese musical scale, our G, A, B, D, E; the five tastes are Salt, Bitter, Sour, Acrid, and Sweet. I am not sure that Wang Pî has caught exactly the author's idea in the contrast between satisfying the belly

and satisfying the eyes; but what he says is ingenious :
'In satisfying the belly one nourishes himself; in gratifying
the eyes he makes a slave of himself.'

13. 1. Favour and disgrace would seem equally
to be feared; honour and great calamity, to be regarded as personal conditions (of the same kind).

2. What is meant by speaking thus of favour and
disgrace? Disgrace is being in a low position
(after the enjoyment of favour). The getting that
(favour) leads to the apprehension (of losing it), and
the losing it leads to the fear of (still greater calamity) :—this is what is meant by saying that favour
and disgrace would seem equally to be feared.

And what is meant by saying that honour and
great calamity are to be (similarly) regarded as personal conditions? What makes me liable to great
calamity is my having the body (which I call myself);
if I had not the body, what great calamity could
come to me?

3. Therefore he who would administer the kingdom, honouring it as he honours his own person,
may be employed to govern it, and he who would
administer it with the love which he bears to his
own person may be entrusted with it.

厭恥, 'Loathing Shame.' The chapter is difficult to
construe, and some disciples of *K*û Hsî had to ask him to
explain it as in the case of ch. 10. His remarks on it are
not to my mind satisfactory. Its object seems to be to
show that the cultivation of the person according to the
Tâo, is the best qualification for the highest offices, even
for the government of the world. Par. 3 is found in
*K*wang-ʒze (XI, 18 b) in a connexion which suggests this
view of the chapter. It may be observed, however, that in
him the position of the verbal characters in the two clauses

of the paragraph is the reverse of that in the text of Ho-shang Kung, so that we can hardly accept the distinction of meaning of the two characters given in his commentary, but must take them as synonyms. Professor Gabelentz gives the following version of *K*wang-ǵze: 'Darum, gebraucht er seine Person achtsam in der Verwaltung des Reiches, so mag man ihm die Reichsgewalt anvertrauen ; . . . liebend (schonend) . . . übertragen.'

14. 1. We look at it, and we do not see it, and we name it 'the Equable.' We listen to it, and we do not hear it, and we name it 'the Inaudible.' We try to grasp it, and do not get hold of it, and we name it 'the Subtle.' With these three qualities, it cannot be made the subject of description ; and hence we blend them together and obtain The One.

2. Its upper part is not bright, and its lower part is not obscure. Ceaseless in its action, it yet cannot be named, and then it again returns and becomes nothing. This is called the Form of the Formless, and the Semblance of the Invisible ; this is called the Fleeting and Indeterminable.

3. We meet it and do not see its Front ; we follow it, and do not see its Back. When we can lay hold of the Tâo of old to direct the things of the present day, and are able to know it as it was of old in the beginning, this is called (unwinding) the clue of Tâo.

贊玄, 'The Manifestation of the Mystery.' The subject of par. 1 is the Tâo, but the Tâo in its operation, and not the primal conception of it, as entirely distinct from things, which rises before the mind in the second paragraph. The Chinese characters which I have translated 'the Equable,' 'the Inaudible,' and 'the Subtle,' are now pronounced Î, Hî, and Wei, and in 1823 Rémusat fancied that they were intended to give the Hebrew tetragrammaton יהוה which he thought had come to Lâo-ʒze somehow from the West, or been found by him there.   It was a mere fancy or dream ; and still more so is the recent attempt to revive the notion by Victor von Strauss in 1870, and Dr. Edkins in 1884.   The idea of the latter is specially strange, maintaining, as he does, that we should read the characters according to their old sounds.   Lâo-ʒze has not in the chapter a personal Being before his mind, but the procedure of his mysterious Tâo, the course according to which the visible phenomena take place, incognisable by human sense and capable of only approximate description by terms appropriate to what is within the domain of sense. See the Introduction, pp. 14, 15.

15. 1. The skilful masters (of the Tâo) in old times, with a subtle and exquisite penetration, comprehended its mysteries, and were deep (also) so as to elude men's knowledge. As they were thus beyond men's knowledge, I will make an effort to describe of what sort they appeared to be.

2. Shrinking looked they like those who wade through a stream in winter ; irresolute like those who are afraid of all around them ; grave like a guest (in awe of his host) ; evanescent like ice that is melting away ; unpretentious like wood that has not been fashioned into anything ; vacant like a valley, and dull like muddy water.

3. Who can (make) the muddy water (clear) ? Let it be still, and it will gradually become clear. Who can secure the condition of rest ? Let movement go on, and the condition of rest will gradually arise.

4. They who preserve this method of the Tâo do not wish to be full (of themselves). It is through their not being full of themselves that they can

afford to seem worn and not appear new and complete.

顯 德, 'The Exhibition of the Quality,' that is, of the Tâo, which has been set forth in the preceding chapter. Its practical outcome is here described in the masters of it of old, who in their own weakness were yet strong in it, and in their humility were mighty to be co-workers with it for the good of the world.

The variety of the readings in par. 4 is considerable, but not so as to affect the meaning. This par. is found in Hwâi-nan (XII, 23 a) with an unimportant variation. From the illustration to which it is subjoined he understood the fulness, evidently as in ch. 9, as being that of a vessel filled to overflowing. Both here and there such fulness is used metaphorically of a man overfull of himself; and then Lâo-ȝze slides into another metaphor, that of a worn-out garment. The text of par. 3 has been variously tampered with. I omit the 人 of the current copies, after the example of the editors of the great recension of the Yung-lo period (A.D. 1403–1424) of the Ming dynasty.

16. 1. The (state of) vacancy should be brought to the utmost degree, and that of stillness guarded with unwearying vigour. All things alike go through their processes of activity, and (then) we see them return (to their original state). When things (in the vegetable world) have displayed their luxuriant growth, we see each of them return to its root. This returning to their root is what we call the state of stillness; and that stillness may be called a reporting that they have fulfilled their appointed end.

2. The report of that fulfilment is the regular, un-changing rule. To know that unchanging rule is to be intelligent; not to know it leads to wild movements and evil issues. The knowledge of that unchanging rule produces a (grand) capacity and forbearance, and

that capacity and forbearance lead to a community
(of feeling with all things). From this community of
feeling comes a kingliness of character; and he who
is king-like goes on to be heaven-like. In that like-
ness to heaven he possesses the Tâo. Possessed
of the Tâo, he endures long; and to the end of his
bodily life, is exempt from all danger of decay.

歸根, 'Returning to the Root.' The chapter exhibits
the operation of the Tâo in nature, in man, and in government; an operation silent, but all-powerful; unaccompanied
with any demonstration of its presence, but great in its
results.

An officer receives a charge or commission from his
superior (受命); when he reports the execution of it
he is said 復命. So all animate things, including men,
receive their charge from the Tâo as to their life, and when
they have fulfilled it they are represented as reporting that
fulfilment; and the fulfilment and report are described as
their unchanging rule, so that they are the Tâo's impassive instruments, having no will or purpose of their own,—according
to Lâo-ȝze's formula of 'doing nothing and yet doing all
things (無爲而無不爲).'

The getting to possess the Tâo, or to be an embodiment
of it, follows the becoming Heaven or Heaven-like; and this
is in accordance with the saying in the fourth chapter that
'the Tâo might seem to have been before God.' But, in
Kwang-ȝze especially, we often find the full possessor and
displayer of the Tâo spoken of as 'Heaven.' The last sentence, that he who has come to the full possession of the Tâo
is exempt from all danger of decay, is generally illustrated by
a reference to the utterances in ch. 50; as if Lâo-ȝze did indeed
see in the Tâo a preservative against death.

17. 1. In the highest antiquity, (the people) did
not know that there were (their rulers). In the
next age they loved them and praised them. In the

next they feared them ; in the next they despised them. Thus it was that when faith (in the Tâo) was deficient (in the rulers) a want of faith in them ensued (in the people).

2. How irresolute did those (earliest rulers) appear, showing (by their reticence) the importance which they set upon their words! Their work was done and their undertakings were successful, while the people all said, 'We are as we are, of ourselves!'

淳 風, 'The Unadulterated Influence.' The influence is that of the Tâo, as seen in the earliest and paradisiacal times. The two chapters that follow are closely connected with this, showing how the silent, passionless influence of the Tâo was gradually and injuriously superseded by 'the wisdom of the world,' in the conduct of government. In the first sentence there is a small various reading of 不 for 下, but it does not affect the meaning of the passage. The first clause of par. 2 gives some difficulty; 其 貴 言, 'they made their words valuable or precious,' i.e. 'they seldom spake;' cp. 1 Sam. iii. 1.

18. 1. When the Great Tâo (Way or Method) ceased to be observed, benevolence and righteousness came into vogue. (Then) appeared wisdom and shrewdness, and there ensued great hypocrisy.

2. When harmony no longer prevailed throughout the six kinships, filial sons found their manifestation ; when the states and clans fell into disorder, loyal ministers appeared.

俗 薄, 'The Decay of Manners.' A sequel to the preceding chapter, and showing also how the general decay of manners afforded opportunity for the display of certain virtues by individuals. Observe 'the Great Tâo,' occurring here for the first time as the designation of 'the Tâo.'

19. 1. If we could renounce our sageness and discard our wisdom, it would be better for the people a hundredfold.   If we could renounce our benevolence and discard our righteousness, the people would again become filial and kindly.   If we could renounce our artful contrivances and discard our (scheming for) gain, there would be no thieves nor robbers.

2. Those three methods (of government)
Thought olden ways in elegance did fail
And made these names their want of worth to veil;
But simple views, and courses plain and true
Would selfish ends and many lusts eschew.

還淳, 'Returning to the Unadulterated Influence.' The chapter desires a return to the simplicity of the Tâo, and shows how superior the result would be to that of the more developed systems of morals and government which had superseded it.   It is closely connected with the two chapters that precede.   Lâo-ʒze's call for the renunciation of the methods of the sages and rulers in lieu of his fancied paradisiacal state is repeated ad nauseam by Kwang-ʒze.

20. 1. When we renounce learning we have no troubles.
The (ready) 'yes,' and (flattering) 'yea ;'—
Small is the difference they display.
But mark their issues, good and ill ;—
What space the gulf between shall fill ?
What all men fear is indeed to be feared ; but how wide and without end is the range of questions (asking to be discussed) !

2. The multitude of men look satisfied and pleased; as if enjoying a full banquet, as if mounted on a tower in spring.   I alone seem listless and still, my desires having as yet given no indication of their

presence. I am like an infant which has not yet smiled. I look dejected and forlorn, as if I had no home to go to. The multitude of men all have enough and to spare. I alone seem to have lost everything. My mind is that of a stupid man; I am in a state of chaos.

Ordinary men look bright and intelligent, while I alone seem to be benighted. They look full of discrimination, while I alone am dull and confused. I seem to be carried about as on the sea, drifting as if I had nowhere to rest. All men have their spheres of action, while I alone seem dull and incapable, like a rude borderer. (Thus) I alone am different from other men, but I value the nursing-mother (the Tâo).

異 俗, 'Being Different from Ordinary Men.' The chapter sets forth the difference to external appearance which the pursuit and observance of the Tâo produces between its votaries and others; and Lâo-ʒze speaks in it as himself an example of the former. In the last three chapters he has been advocating the cause of the Tâo against the learning and philosophy of the other school of thinkers in the country. Here he appears as having renounced learning, and found an end to the troubles and anxieties of his own mind; but at the expense of being misconceived and misrepresented by others. Hence the chapter has an autobiographical character.

Having stated the fact following the renunciation of learning, he proceeds to dwell upon the troubles of learning in the rest of par. 1. Until the votary of learning knows everything, he has no rest. But the instances which he adduces of this are not striking nor easily understood. I cannot throw any light on the four lines about the 'yes' and the 'yea.'

Confucius (Ana. XVI, viii) specifies three things of which the superior man stands in awe; and these and others of

a similar nature may have been the things which Lâo-ʒze
had in his mind. The nursing-mother at the end is, no
doubt, the Tâo in operation, 'with a name,' as in ch. 1;
'the mysterious virtue' of chapters 51 and 52.

> 21. The grandest forms of active force
>   From Tâo come, their only source.
>   Who can of Tâo the nature tell?
>   Our sight it flies, our touch as well.
>   Eluding sight, eluding touch,
>   The forms of things all in it crouch;
>   Eluding touch, eluding sight,
>   There are their semblances, all right.
>   Profound it is, dark and obscure;
>   Things' essences all there endure.
>   Those essences the truth enfold
>   Of what, when seen, shall then be told.
>   Now it is so; 'twas so of old.
>   Its name—what passes not away;
>   So, in their beautiful array,
>   Things form and never know decay.

How know I that it is so with all the beauties of
existing things? By this (nature of the Tâo).

虛 心, 'The Empty Heart.' But I fail to see the
applicability of the title. The subject of the chapter is the
Tâo in its operation. This is the significance of the 德
in the first clause or line, and to render it by 'virtue,' as
Julien and Chalmers do, only serves to hide the meaning.
Julien, however, says that 'the virtue is that of the Tâo;
and he is right in taking 從, the last character of the
second line, as having the sense of 'from,' 'the source
from,' and not, as Chalmers does, in the sense of 'following.'

Lâo-ʒze's mind is occupied with a very difficult subject—
to describe the production of material forms by the Tâo;
how or from what, he does not say. What I have rendered
'semblances,' Julien 'les images,' and Chalmers 'forms,'

seems, as the latter says, in some way to correspond to the 'Eternal Ideas' of Plato in the Divine Mind.   But Lâo-ʒze had no idea of 'personality' in the Tâo.

22. 1. The partial becomes complete; the crooked, straight; the empty, full; the worn out, new.   He whose (desires) are few gets them ; he whose (desires) are many goes astray.

2. Therefore the sage holds in his embrace the one thing (of humility), and manifests it to all the world.   He is free from self-display, and therefore he shines ; from self-assertion, and therefore he is distinguished ; from self-boasting, and therefore his merit is acknowledged; from self-complacency, and therefore he acquires superiority.   It is because he is thus free from striving that therefore no one in the world is able to strive with him.

3. That saying of the ancients that 'the partial becomes complete' was not vainly spoken :—all real completion is comprehended under it.

益 謙, 'The Increase granted to Humility.'   This title rightly expresses the subject-matter of the chapter.   I cannot translate the first clause otherwise than I have done.   It was an old saying, which Lâo-ʒze found and adopted.   Whether it was intended to embrace all the cases which are mentioned may be questioned, but he employs it so as to make it do so.

'The emptiness' which becomes full is literally the hollowness of a cavity in the ground which is sure to be filled by overflowing water ;—see Mencius, IV, ii, 18.   'The worn out' is explained by the withered foliage of a tree, which comes out new and fresh in the next spring.   I have taken the first sentence of par. 2 as Wû *Kh*ăng does ;—see his commentary in loc.

23. 1. Abstaining from speech marks him who is obeying the spontaneity of his nature.   A violent

wind does not last for a whole morning; a sudden rain does not last for the whole day. To whom is it that these (two) things are owing? To Heaven and Earth. If Heaven and Earth cannot make such (spasmodic) actings last long, how much less can man!

2. Therefore when one is making the Tâo his business, those who are also pursuing it, agree with him in it, and those who are making the manifestation of its course their object agree with him in that; while even those who are failing in both these things agree with him where they fail.

3. Hence, those with whom he agrees as to the Tâo have the happiness of attaining to it; those with whom he agrees as to its manifestation have the happiness of attaining to it; and those with whom he agrees in their failure have also the happiness of attaining (to the Tâo). (But) when there is not faith sufficient (on his part), a want of faith (in him) ensues (on the part of the others).

虛無, 'Absolute Vacancy.' This, I think, is the meaning of the title, 'Emptiness and Nothingness,' an entire conformity to the Tâo in him who professes to be directed by it. Such an one will be omnipotent in his influence in all others. The Tâo in him will restrain all (spasmodic) loquacity. Those who are described in par. 2 as 'failing' are not to be thought of as bad men, men given up, as Julien has it, au crime. They are simply ordinary men, who have failed in their study of the Tâo and practice of it, but are won to truth and virtue by the man whom the author has in mind. As we might expect, however, the mention of such men has much embarrassed the commentators.

Compare the concluding sentence with the one at the end of par. 1 in ch. 17.

24. He who stands on his tiptoes does not stand firm ; he who stretches his legs does not walk (easily). (So), he who displays himself does not shine; he who asserts his own views is not distinguished ; he who vaunts himself does not find his merit acknowledged; he who is self-conceited has no superiority allowed to him. Such conditions, viewed from the standpoint of the Tâo, are like remnants of food, or a tumour on the body, which all dislike. Hence those who pursue (the course) of the Tâo do not adopt and allow them.

苦 恩, 'Painful Graciousness.' The chapter should be so designated. This concludes the subject of the two previous chapters,—pursuing the course, the course of the unemotional Tâo without vain effort or display.

The remnants of food were not used as sacrificial offerings ;—see the Lî Kî (vol. xxvii, p. 82). In what I have rendered by 'a tumour attached to the body,' the 行 is probably, by a mistake, for 形 ;—see a quotation by Wû Khăng from Sze-mâ Khien. 'Which all dislike' is, literally, 'Things are likely to dislike them,' the ' things ' being ' spirits and men,' as Wû explains the term.

25. 1. There was something undefined and complete, coming into existence before Heaven and Earth. How still it was and formless, standing alone, and undergoing no change, reaching everywhere and in no danger (of being exhausted) ! It may be regarded as the Mother of all things.

2. I do not know its name, and I give it the designation of the Tâo (the Way or Course). Making an effort (further) to give it a name I call it The Great.

3. Great, it passes on (in constant flow). Passing

on, it becomes remote. Having become remote, it
returns. Therefore the Tâo is great; Heaven is
great; Earth is great; and the (sage) king is also
great. In the universe there are four that are great,
and the (sage) king is one of them.

4. Man takes his law from the Earth; the Earth
takes its law from Heaven; Heaven takes its law
from the Tâo. The law of the Tâo is its being
what it is.

象 玄, 'Representations of the Mystery.' In this
chapter Lâo approaches very near to give an answer to the
question as to what the Tâo is, and yet leaves the reader
disappointed. He commences by calling it 'a thing (物);'
but that term does not necessitate our regarding it as 'material.' We have seen in the preceding chapter that it is
used to signify 'spirits and men.' Nor does his going on
to speak of it as 'chaotic (混 成)' necessarily lead us to
conceive it as made up of the 'material elements of things;'
we have the same term applied in ch. 14 to the three immaterial constituents there said to be blended in the idea
of it.

'He does not know its name,' and he designates it by the
term denoting a course or way (Tâo, 道), and indicating
the phenomenal attribute, the method in which all phenomena come before our observation, in their development or
evolution. And to distinguish it from all other methods of
evolution, he would call it 'the Great Method,' and so he
employs that combination as its name in ch. 18 and elsewhere; but it cannot be said that this name has fully
maintained itself in the writings of his followers. But
understood thus, he here says, as in ch. 1, that it is 'the
Mother of all things.' And yet, when he says that 'it
was before Heaven and Earth were produced,' he comes
very near his affirmations in chapters 1 and 4, that 'the
nameless Tâo was the beginning (or originating cause) of
Heaven and Earth,' and 'might seem to have been before

God.' Was he groping after God if haply he might find
Him? I think he was, and he gets so far as to conceive of
Him as 'the Uncaused Cause,' but comes short of the idea
of His personality. The other subordinate causes which
he mentions all get their force or power from the Tâo, but
after all the Tâo is simply a spontaneity, evolving from
itself, and not acting from a personal will, consciously in
the direction of its own wisdom and love. 'Who can by
searching find out God? Who can find out the Almighty
to perfection?'

The predicate of the Tâo in the chapter, most perplexing
to myself, is 'It returns,' in par. 3. 'It flows away, far
away, and comes back;'—are not the three statements
together equal to 'It is everywhere?'

26. 1. Gravity is the root of lightness; stillness,
the ruler of movement.

2. Therefore a wise prince, marching the whole
day, does not go far from his baggage waggons.
Although he may have brilliant prospects to look at,
he quietly remains (in his proper place), indifferent
to them. How should the lord of a myriad chariots
carry himself lightly before the kingdom? If he
do act lightly, he has lost his root (of gravity); if
he proceed to active movement, he will lose his
throne.

重德, 'The Quality of Gravity.' Gravity and stillness
are both attributes of the Tâo; and he who cultivates it
must not give way to lightness of mind, or hasty action.

The rule for a leader not to separate from his baggage
waggons is simply the necessity of adhering to gravity.
I have adopted from Han Fei the reading of 'the wise
prince' for 'the sage,' which is found in Ho-shang Kung;
and later on the reading of 'has lost his root' for his
'loses his ministers,' though the latter is found also in
Han Fei.

27. 1. The skilful traveller leaves no traces of his wheels or footsteps; the skilful speaker says nothing that can be found fault with or blamed; the skilful reckoner uses no tallies; the skilful closer needs no bolts or bars, while to open what he has shut will be impossible; the skilful binder uses no strings or knots, while to unloose what he has bound will be impossible. In the same way the sage is always skilful at saving men, and so he does not cast away any man; he is always skilful at saving things, and so he does not cast away anything. This is called 'Hiding the light of his procedure.'

2. Therefore the man of skill is a master (to be looked up to) by him who has not the skill; and he who has not the skill is the helper of (the reputation of) him who has the skill. If the one did not honour his master, and the other did not rejoice in his helper, an (observer), though intelligent, might greatly err about them. This is called 'The utmost degree of mystery.'

巧 用, 'Dexterity in Using,' that is, in the application of the Tâo. This is the substance of the chapter, celebrating the effective but invisible operation of the Tâo, and the impartial exercise of it for the benefit of all men and all things.

I have given the most natural construction of the two characters at the end of par. 1, the only possible construction of them, so far as I can see, suitable to the context. The action of the Tâo (non-acting and yet all-efficient) and that of the sage in accordance with it, are veiled by their nature from the sight of ordinary men.

It is more difficult to catch the scope and point of par. 2. If there were not the conditions described in it, it would be hard for even an intelligent onlooker to distinguish between the man who had the skill and the man without it, between him who possessed the Tâo, and him who had it not, which would be strange indeed.

28. 1. Who knows his manhood's strength,
Yet still his female feebleness maintains;
As to one channel flow the many drains,
All come to him, yea, all beneath the sky.
Thus he the constant excellence retains;—
The simple child again, free from all stains.

Who knows how white attracts,
Yet always keeps himself within black's shade,
The pattern of humility displayed,
Displayed in view of all beneath the sky;
He in the unchanging excellence arrayed,
Endless return to man's first state has made.

Who knows how glory shines,
Yet loves disgrace, nor e'er for it is pale;
Behold his presence in a spacious vale,
To which men come from all beneath the sky.
The unchanging excellence completes its tale;
The simple infant man in him we hail.

2. The unwrought material, when divided and distributed, forms vessels. The sage, when employed, becomes the Head of all the Officers (of government); and in his greatest regulations he employs no violent measures.

反樸, 'Returning to Simplicity.' The chapter sets forth humility and simplicity, an artless freedom from all purpose, as characteristic of the man of Tâo, such as he was in the primeval time. 'The sage' in par. 2 may be 'the Son of Heaven,'—the Head of all rule in the kingdom, or the feudal lord in a state.

29. 1. If any one should wish to get the kingdom for himself, and to effect this by what he does, I see

that he will not succeed. The kingdom is a spirit-like thing, and cannot be got by active doing. He who would so win it destroys it; he who would hold it in his grasp loses it.

2. The course and nature of things is such that
> What was in front is now behind;
> What warmed anon we freezing find.
> Strength is of weakness oft the spoil;
> The store in ruins mocks our toil.

Hence the sage puts away excessive effort, extravagance, and easy indulgence.

無 爲, 'Taking no Action.' All efforts made with a purpose are sure to fail. The nature of the Tâo necessitates their doing so, and the uncertainty of things and events teaches the same lesson.

That the kingdom or throne is a 'spirit-like vessel' has become a common enough saying among the Chinese. Julien has, 'L'Empire est comme un vase divin;' but I always shrink from translating 神 by 'divine.' Its English analogue is 'spirit,' and the idea in the text is based on the immunity of spirit from all material law, and the uncertain issue of attempts to deal with it according to ordinary methods. Wû Khǎng takes the phrase as equivalent to 'superintended by spirits,' which is as inadmissible as Julien's 'divin.' The Tâo forbids action with a personal purpose, and all such action is sure to fail in the greatest things as well as in the least.

30. 1. He who would assist a lord of men in harmony with the Tâo will not assert his mastery in the kingdom by force of arms. Such a course is sure to meet with its proper return.

2. Wherever a host is stationed, briars and thorns spring up. In the sequence of great armies there are sure to be bad years.

3. A skilful (commander) strikes a decisive blow, and stops. He does not dare (by continuing his operations) to assert and complete his mastery. He will strike the blow, but will be on his guard against being vain or boastful or arrogant in consequence of it. He strikes it as a matter of necessity; he strikes it, but not from a wish for mastery.

4. When things have attained their strong maturity they become old. This may be said to be not in accordance with the Tâo : and what is not in accordance with it soon comes to an end.

偃 武, 'A Caveat against War.' War is contrary to the spirit of the Tâo, and, as being so, is productive of misery, and leads to early ruin. It is only permissible in a case of necessity, and even then its spirit and tendencies must be guarded against.

In translating 果 by 'striking a decisive blow,' I have, no doubt, followed Julien's 'frapper un coup décisif.' The same 果 occurs six times in par. 3, followed by 而, and 3iâo Hung says that in all but the first instance the 而 should be taken as equivalent to 於, so that we should have to translate, 'He is determined against being vain,' &c. But there is no necessity for such a construction of 而.

'Weakness' and not 'strength' is the character of the Tâo ; hence the lesson in par. 4.

31. 1. Now arms, however beautiful, are instruments of evil omen, hateful, it may be said, to all creatures. Therefore they who have the Tâo do not like to employ them.

2. The superior man ordinarily considers the left hand the most honourable place, but in time of war the right hand. Those sharp weapons are instruments of evil omen, and not the instruments of the

superior man;—he uses them only on the compul-
sion of necessity. Calm and repose are what he
prizes; victory (by force of arms) is to him undesir-
able. To consider this desirable would be to delight
in the slaughter of men; and he who delights in the
slaughter of men cannot get his will in the kingdom.

3. On occasions of festivity to be on the left hand
is the prized position; on occasions of mourning, the
right hand. The second in command of the army
has his place on the left; the general commanding
in chief has his on the right;—his place, that is, is
assigned to him as in the rites of mourning. He
who has killed multitudes of men should weep for
them with the bitterest grief; and the victor in battle
has his place (rightly) according to those rites.

偃 武, 'Stilling War.' The chapter continues the subject
of the preceding. The imperially-appointed editors of
Wang Pî's Text and Commentary (1765) say that from
the beginning of par. 2 to the end, there is the appearance
of text and commentary being mixed together; but they
make no alteration in the text as it is found in Ho-shang
Kung, and in all other ancient copies.

The concluding sentence will suggest to some readers the
words of the Duke of Wellington, that to gain a battle was
the saddest thing next to losing it.

32. 1. The Tâo, considered as unchanging, has
no name.

2. Though in its primordial simplicity it may be
small, the whole world dares not deal with (one
embodying) it as a minister. If a feudal prince or
the king could guard and hold it, all would spontaneously submit themselves to him.

3. Heaven and Earth (under its guidance) unite
together and send down the sweet dew, which, with-

out the directions of men, reaches equally everywhere as of its own accord.

4. As soon as it proceeds to action, it has a name. When it once has that name, (men) can know to rest in it. When they know to rest in it, they can be free from all risk of failure and error.

5. The relation of the Tâo to all the world is like that of the great rivers and seas to the streams from the valleys.

聖 德. Chalmers translates this by 'sagely virtue.' But I cannot adopt that rendering, and find it difficult to supply a better. The 'virtue' is evidently the Attribute of the Tâo come out from the condition of the Absolute, and capable of being named. In the former state it has no name; in the latter, it has. Par. 1 and the commencement of par. 4 must both be explained from ch. 1.

The 'primordial simplicity' in par. 2 is the Tâo in its simplest conception, alone, and by itself, and the 始 制 in par. 4 is that Tâo come forth into operation and become Teh, the Teh which affords a law for men. From this to the end of the paragraph is very obscure. I have translated from the text of Wang Pî. The text of Ho-shang Kung is different, and he comments upon it as it stands, but to me it is inexplicable.

33. 1. He who knows other men is discerning; he who knows himself is intelligent. He who overcomes others is strong; he who overcomes himself is mighty. He who is satisfied with his lot is rich; he who goes on acting with energy has a (firm) will.

2. He who does not fail in the requirements of his position, continues long; he who dies and yet does not perish, has longevity.

辨 德, 'Discriminating between (different) Attributes.' The teaching of the chapter is that the possession of the

Tâo confers the various attributes which are here most distinguished. It has been objected to it that elsewhere the
Tâo is represented as associated with dulness and not
intelligence, and with weakness and not with strength.
But these seem to be qualities viewed from without, and
acting on what is beyond itself. Inwardly, its qualities
are the very opposite, and its action has the effect of
enlightening what is dark, and overcoming what is strong.

More interesting are the predicates in par. 2. 3iâo Hung
gives the comment on it of the Indian monk, Kumâragîva,
'one of the four suns of Buddhism,' and who went to China
in A.D. 401: 'To be alive and yet not alive may well be
called long; to die and yet not be dead may well be
called longevity.' He also gives the views of Lû Năng-
shih (A.D. 1042–1102) that the freedom from change of
Lieh-3ze, from death of *K*wang-3ze, and from extinction of
the Buddhists, have all the same meaning as the concluding
saying of Lâo-3ze here; that the human body is like the
covering of the caterpillar or the skin of the snake; that
we occupy it but for a passing sojourn. No doubt, Lâo-3ze
believed in another life for the individual after the present.
Many passages in *K*wang-3ze indicate the same faith.

34. 1. All-pervading is the Great Tâo! It may
be found on the left hand and on the right.

2. All things depend on it for their production,
which it gives to them, not one refusing obedience
to it. When its work is accomplished, it does not
claim the name of having done it. It clothes all
things as with a garment, and makes no assumption
of being their lord;—it may be named in the smallest
things. All things return (to their root and disappear), and do not know that it is it which presides
over their doing so;—it may be named in the
greatest things.

3. Hence the sage is able (in the same way) to
accomplish his great achievements. It is through

his not making himself great that he can accomplish them.

任 成, 'The Task of Achievement.' The subject is the greatness of what the Tâo, called here by Lâo's own name for it in ch. 25, does; and the unconscious simplicity with which it does it; and then the achievements of the sage who is permeated by the Tâo. Par. 2 is descriptive of the influence of the Tâo in the vegetable world. The statements and expressions are much akin to those in parts of chapters 2, 10, and 51, and for Ho-shang Kung's difficult reading of 不 名 有 some copies give 而 不 居, as in chapter 2.

35. 1. To him who holds in his hands the Great Image (of the invisible Tâo), the whole world repairs. Men resort to him, and receive no hurt, but (find) rest, peace, and the feeling of ease.

2. Music and dainties will make the passing guest stop (for a time). But though the Tâo as it comes from the mouth, seems insipid and has no flavour, though it seems not worth being looked at or listened to, the use of it is inexhaustible.

仁 德, 'The Attribute of Benevolence.' But there seems little appropriateness in this title. The subject of the chapter is the inexhaustible efficacy of the Tâo for the good of the world.

The Great Image (of the invisible Tâo) is a name for the Tâo in its operation; as in chapters 14 and 41. He who embodies this in his government will be a centre of attraction for all the world. Or the 天 下 往 may be taken as a predicate of the holder of the Great Image: —'If he go all under heaven teaching the Tâo.' Both constructions are maintained by commentators of note. In par. 2 the attraction of the Tâo is contrasted with that of ordinary pleasures and gratifications.

36. 1. When one is about to take an inspiration, he is sure to make a (previous) expiration ; when he is going to weaken another, he will first strengthen him ; when he is going to overthrow another, he will first have raised him up ; when he is going to despoil another, he will first have made gifts to him :—this is called 'Hiding the light (of his procedure).'

2. The soft overcomes the hard ; and the weak the strong.

3. Fishes should not be taken from the deep ; instruments for the profit of a state should not be shown to the people.

微 明, 'Minimising the Light ;' equivalent, as Wû *K͟h*ăng has pointed out, to the 襲 明 of ch. 27.

The gist of the chapter is to be sought in the second paragraph, where we have two instances of the action of the Tâo by contraries, supposed always to be for good.

But there is a difficulty in seeing the applicability to this of the cases mentioned in par. 1. The first case, indeed, is merely a natural phenomenon, having no moral character ; but the others, as they have been illustrated from historical incidents, by Han Fei and others at least, belong to schemes of selfish and unprincipled ambitious strategy, which it would be injurious to Lâo-ȝze to suppose that he intended.

Par. 3 is the most frequently quoted of all the passages in our *K*ing, unless it be the first part of ch. 1. Fishes taken from the deep, and brought into shallow water, can be easily taken or killed ; that is plain enough. 'The sharp instruments of a state' are not its 'weapons of war,' nor its 'treasures,' nor its 'instruments of government,' that is, its rewards and punishments, though this last is the interpretation often put on them, and sustained by a foolish reference to an incident, real or coined, in the history of the dukedom of Sung. The lî *k͟h*î are 'contrivances for gain,' machines, and other methods to increase the wealth of a state, but, according to the principles of Lâo-ȝze, really injurious to it. These should not be shown to the people, whom the Tâoistic system would keep in a state of primitive simplicity and ignorance. This interpretation is in accordance with the meaning of the characters, and with the general teaching of Tâoism. In no other way can I explain the paragraph so as to justify the place undoubtedly belonging to it in the system.

37. 1. The Tâo in its regular course does nothing (for the sake of doing it), and so there is nothing which it does not do.

2. If princes and kings were able to maintain it, all things would of themselves be transformed by them.

3. If this transformation became to me an object of desire, I would express the desire by the nameless simplicity.

> Simplicity without a name
> Is free from all external aim.
> With no desire, at rest and still,
> All things go right as of their will.

爲 政, 'The Exercise of Government.' This exercise should be according to the Tâo, doing without doing, governing without government.

The subject of the third paragraph is a feudal prince or the king, and he is spoken of in the first person, to give more vividness to the style, unless the 吾, 'I,' may, possibly, be understood of Lâo-ʒze himself personating one of them.

PART II.

38. 1. (Those who) possessed in highest degree the attributes (of the Tâo) did not (seek) to show them, and therefore they possessed them (in fullest measure). (Those who) possessed in a lower degree those attributes (sought how) not to lose them, and therefore they did not possess them (in fullest measure).

2. (Those who) possessed in the highest degree those attributes did nothing (with a purpose), and had no need to do anything. (Those who) possessed them in a lower degree were (always) doing, and had need to be so doing.

3. (Those who) possessed the highest benevolence were (always seeking) to carry it out, and had no need to be doing so. (Those who) possessed the highest righteousness were (always seeking) to carry it out, and had need to be so doing.

4. (Those who) possessed the highest (sense of) propriety were (always seeking) to show it, and when men did not respond to it, they bared the arm and marched up to them.

5. Thus it was that when the Tâo was lost, its attributes appeared; when its attributes were lost, benevolence appeared; when benevolence was lost, righteousness appeared; and when righteousness was lost, the proprieties appeared.

6. Now propriety is the attenuated form of leal-heartedness and good faith, and is also the commencement of disorder; swift apprehension is

(only) a flower of the Tâo, and is the beginning of stupidity.

7. Thus it is that the Great man abides by what is solid, and eschews what is flimsy ; dwells with the fruit and not with the flower.   It is thus that he puts away the one and makes choice of the other.

論 德, 'About the Attributes;' of Tâo, that is.   It is not easy to render teh here by any other English term than 'virtue,' and yet there would be a danger of its thus misleading us in the interpretation of the chapter.

The 'virtue' is the activity or operation of the Tâo, which is supposed to have come out of its absoluteness. Even Han Fei so defines it here,—'Teh is the meritorious work of the Tâo.'

In par. 5 we evidently have a résumé of the preceding paragraphs, and, as it is historical, I translate them in the past tense; though what took place on the early stage of the world may also be said to go on taking place in the experience of every individual.   With some considerable hesitation I have given the subjects in those paragraphs in the concrete, in deference to the authority of Ho-shang Kung and most other commentators.   The former says, 'By "the highest teh" is to be understood the rulers of the greatest antiquity, without name or designation, whose virtue was great, and could not be surpassed.'   Most ingenious, and in accordance with the Tâoistic system, is the manner in which Wû Khăng construes the passage, and I am surprised that it has not been generally accepted. By 'the higher teh' he understands 'the Tâo,' that which is prior to and above the Teh (上 德 者, 在 德 之 上, 道 也); by 'the lower teh,' benevolence, that which is after and below the Teh; by 'the higher benevolence,' the Teh which is above benevolence; by 'the higher righteousness,' the benevolence which is above righteousness; and by 'the higher propriety,' the righteousness which is above propriety.   Certainly in the summation of these four paragraphs which we have in the fifth, the

subjects of them would appear to have been in the mind
of Lâo-ʒze as thus defined by Wû.

In the remainder of the chapter he goes on to speak
depreciatingly of ceremonies and knowledge, so that the
whole chapter must be understood as descriptive of the
process of decay and deterioration from the early time in
which the Tâo and its attributes swayed the societies
of men.

39. 1. The things which from of old have got
the One (the Tâo) are—

> Heaven which by it is bright and pure ;
> Earth rendered thereby firm and sure ;
> Spirits with powers by it supplied ;
> Valleys kept full throughout their void ;
> All creatures which through it do live ;
> Princes and kings who from it get
> The model which to all they give.

All these are the results of the One (Tâo).

2. If heaven were not thus pure, it soon would
   rend ;
If earth were not thus sure, 'twould break and
   bend ;
Without these powers, the spirits soon would fail ;
If not so filled, the drought would parch each vale ;
Without that life, creatures would pass away ;
Princes and kings, without that moral sway,
Howeve: grand and high, would all decay.

3. Thus it is that dignity finds its (firm) root in
its (previous) meanness, and what is lofty finds its
stability in the lowness (from which it rises). Hence
princes and kings call themselves 'Orphans,' 'Men
of small virtue,' and as 'Carriages without a nave.'
Is not this an acknowledgment that in their considering themselves mean they see the foundation of

their dignity? So it is that in the enumeration of
the different parts of a carriage we do not come on
what makes it answer the ends of a carriage. They
do not wish to show themselves elegant-looking as
jade, but (prefer) to be coarse-looking as an (ordinary)
stone.

法 本, 'The Origin of the Law.' In this title there is
a reference to the Law given to all things by the Tâo, as
described in the conclusion of chapter 25. And the Tâo
affords that law by its passionless, undemonstrative nature,
through which in its spontaneity, doing nothing for the sake
of doing, it yet does all things.

The difficulty of translation is in the third paragraph.
The way in which princes and kings speak depreciàtingly
of themselves is adduced as illustrating how they have indeed got the spirit of the Tâo; and I accept the last
epithet as given by Ho shang Kung, 'naveless' (轂),
instead of 穀 (= 'the unworthy'), which is found in Wang
Pî, and has been adopted by nearly all subsequent editors.
To see its appropriateness here, we have only to refer back
to chapter 11, where the thirty spokes, and the nave, empty
to receive the axle, are spoken of, and it is shown how the
usefulness of the carriage is derived from that emptiness of
the nave. This also enables us to give a fair and consistent
explanation of the difficult clause which follows, in which
also I have followed the text of Ho-shang Kung. For his
車, Wang Pî has 輿, which also is found in a quotation of
it by Hwâi-nan 3ze; but this need not affect the meaning.
In the translation of the clause we are assisted by a somewhat similar illustration about a horse in the twenty-fifth
of *K*wang-ȝze's Books, par. 10.

> 40. 1. The movement of the Tâo
>   By contraries proceeds;
>   And weakness marks the course
>   Of Tâo's mighty deeds.

2. All things under heaven sprang from It as existing (and named); that existence sprang from It as non-existent (and not named).

去用, 'Dispensing with the Use (of Means);'—with their use, that is, as it appears to us. The subject of the brief chapter is the action of the Tâo by contraries, leading to a result the opposite of what existed previously, and by means which might seem calculated to produce a contrary result.

In translating par. 2 I have followed 3iâo Hung, who finds the key to it in ch. 1. Having a name, the Tâo is 'the Mother of all things;' having no name, it is 'the Originator of Heaven and Earth.' But here is the teaching of Lâo-ʒze:—'If Tâo seems to be before God,' Tâo itself sprang from nothing.

41. 1. Scholars of the highest class, when they hear about the Tâo, earnestly carry it into practice. Scholars of the middle class, when they have heard about it, seem now to keep it and now to lose it. Scholars of the lowest class, when they have heard about it, laugh greatly at it. If it were not (thus) laughed at, it would not be fit to be the Tâo.

2. Therefore the sentence-makers have thus expressed themselves :—

'The Tâo, when brightest seen, seems light to lack;
Who progress in it makes, seems drawing back;
Its even way is like a rugged track.
Its highest virtue from the vale doth rise;
Its greatest beauty seems to offend the eyes;
And he has most whose lot the least supplies.
Its firmest virtue seems but poor and low;
Its solid truth seems change to undergo;
Its largest square doth yet no corner show;
A vessel great, it is the slowest made;

Loud is its sound, but never word it said;
A semblance great, the shadow of a shade.'

3. The Tâo is hidden, and has no name; but it is the Tâo which is skilful at imparting (to all things what they need) and making them complete.

同異, 'Sameness and Difference.' The chapter is a sequel of the preceding, and may be taken as an illustration of the Tâo's proceeding by contraries.

Who the sentence-makers were whose sayings are quoted we cannot tell, but it would have been strange if Lâo-ʒze had not had a large store of such sentences at his command. The fifth and sixth of those employed by him here are found in Lieh-ʒze (II, 15 a), spoken by Lâo in reproving Yang Kû, and in VII, 3 a, that heretic appears quoting an utterance of the same kind, with the words, ' according to an old saying (古語有之).'

42. 1. The Tâo produced One; One produced Two; Two produced Three; Three produced All things. All things leave behind them the Obscurity (out of which they have come), and go forward to embrace the Brightness (into which they have emerged), while they are harmonised by the Breath of Vacancy.

2. What men dislike is to be orphans, to have little virtue, to be as carriages without naves; and yet these are the designations which kings and princes use for themselves. So it is that some things are increased by being diminished, and others are diminished by being increased.

3. What other men (thus) teach, I also teach. The violent and strong do not die their natural death. I will make this the basis of my teaching.

道化, ' The Transformations of the Tâo.' In par. 2 we

have the case of the depreciating epithets given to themselves by kings and princes, which we found before in
ch. 39, and a similar lesson is drawn from it. Such depre-
ciation leads to exaltation, and the contrary course of self-
exaltation leads to abasement. This latter case is stated
emphatically in par. 3, and Lâo-ȝze says that it was the
basis of his teaching. So far therefore we have in this
chapter a repetition of the lesson that 'the movement of
the Tâo is by contraries,' and that its weakness is the sure
precursor of strength. But the connexion between this
lesson and what he says in par. 1 it is difficult to trace. Up
to this time at least it has baffled myself. The passage
seems to give us a cosmogony. 'The Tâo produced One.'
We have already seen that the Tâo is 'The One.' Are we
to understand here that the Tâo and the One were one and
the same? In this case what would be the significance of
the 生 ('produced')?—that the Tâo which had been previously 'non-existent' now became 'existent,' or capable of
being named? This seems to be the view of Sze-mâ
Kwang (A. D. 1009–1086).

   The most singular form which this view assumes is in
one of the treatises on our *King*, attributed to the Tâoist
patriarch Lü (呂 祖 道 德 經 解), that 'the One is
Heaven, which was formed by the congealing of the Tâo.'
According to another treatise, also assigned to the same Lü
(道 德 眞 經 合 解), the One was 'the primordial ether;'
the Two, 'the separation of that into its Yin and Yang
constituents;' and the Three, 'the production of heaven,
earth, and·man by these.' In quoting the paragraph Hwâi-
nan ȝze omits 道 生 一, and commences with 一 生 二,
and his glossarist, Kâo Yû, makes out the One to be the
Tâo, the Two to be Spiritual Intelligences (神 明), and
the Three to be the Harmonising Breath. From the
mention of the Yin and Yang that follows, I believe that
Lâo-ȝze intended by the Two these two qualities or elements in the primordial ether, which would be 'the One.'
I dare not hazard a guess as to what 'the Three' were.

43. 1. The softest thing in the world dashes against and overcomes the hardest ; that which has no (substantial) existence enters where there is no crevice.   I know hereby what advantage belongs to doing nothing (with a purpose).

2. There are few in the world who attain to the teaching without words, and the advantage arising from non-action.

偏用, 'The Universal Use (of the action in weakness of the Tâo).'   The chapter takes us back to the lines of ch. 40, that

'Weakness marks the course
Of Tâo's mighty deeds.'

By 'the softest thing in the world' it is agreed that we are to understand 'water,' which will wear away the hardest rocks.   'Dashing against and overcoming' is a metaphor taken from hunting.   Ho-shang Kung says that 'what has no existence' is the Tâo ; it is better to understand by it the unsubstantial air (氣) which penetrates everywhere, we cannot see how.

Compare par. 2 with ch. 2, par. 3.

44. 1. Or fame or life,
    Which do you hold more dear ?
Or life or wealth,
    To which would you adhere ?
Keep life and lose those other things ;
Keep them and lose your life:—which
        brings
    Sorrow and pain more near ?

2. Thus we may see,
    Who cleaves to fame
    Rejects what is more great ;
Who loves large stores
    Gives up the richer state.

3. Who is content
Needs fear no shame.
Who knows to stop
Incurs no blame.
From danger free
Long live shall he.

立 戒, 'Cautions.' The chapter warns men to let nothing
come into competition with the value which they set on the
Tâo. The Tâo is not named, indeed, but the idea of it
was evidently in the writer's mind.

The whole chapter rhymes after a somewhat peculiar
fashion ; familiar enough, however, to one who is acquainted
with the old rhymes of the Book of Poetry.

45. 1. Who thinks his great achievements poor
Shall find his vigour long endure.
Of greatest fulness, deemed a void,
Exhaustion ne'er shall stem the tide.
Do thou what's straight still crooked deem ;
Thy greatest art still stupid seem,
And eloquence a stammering scream.

2. Constant action overcomes cold; being still
overcomes heat. Purity and stillness give the
correct law to all under heaven.

洪 德, 'Great or Overflowing Virtue.' The chapter is
another illustration of the working of the Tâo by contraries.

According to Wû Khăng, the action which overcomes
cold is that of the Yang element in the developing primordial ether ; and the stillness which overcomes heat is that
of the contrary Yin element. These may have been in
Lâo-ʒze's mind, but the statements are so simple as hardly
to need any comment. Wû further says that the purity
and stillness are descriptive of the condition of non-action.

46. 1. When the Tâo prevails in the world, they
send back their swift horses to (draw) the dung-carts.

When the T â o is disregarded in the world, the war-horses breed in the border lands.

2. There is no guilt greater than to sanction ambition; no calamity greater than to be discontented with one's lot; no fault greater than the wish to be getting. Therefore the sufficiency of contentment is an enduring and unchanging sufficiency.

儉 欲, 'The Moderating of Desire or Ambition.' The chapter shows how the practice of the T â o must conduce to contentment and happiness.

In translating par. 1 I have, after Wû *K̲h̲*ăng, admitted a 車 after the 糞, his chief authority for doing so being that it is so found in a poetical piece by *K*ang Hăng (A. D. 78–139). *K*û Hsî also adopted this reading (朱 子 大 全, XVIII, 7 a). In par. 2 Han Ying has a tempting variation of 多 欲 for 可 欲, but I have not adopted it because the same phrase occurs elsewhere.

47. 1. Without going outside his door, one understands (all that takes place) under the sky; without looking out from his window, one sees the T â o of Heaven. The farther that one goes out (from himself), the less he knows.

2. Therefore the sages got their knowledge without travelling; gave their (right) names to things without seeing them; and accomplished their ends without any purpose of doing so.

鑒 遠, 'Surveying what is Far-off.' The chapter is a lesson to men to judge of things according to their internal conviction of similar things in their own experience. Short as the chapter is, it is somewhat mystical. The phrase, 'The T â o' or way of Heaven, occurs in it for the first time; and it is difficult to lay down its precise meaning. Lâo-ᚼze would seem to teach that man is a microcosm; and that, if

he understand the movements of his own mind, he can
understand the movements of all other minds. There are
various readings, of which it is not necessary to speak.
.I have translated par. 2 in the past tense, and perhaps
the first should also be translated so. Most of it is found
in Han Ying, preceded by ' formerly ' or ' anciently.'

48. 1. He who devotes himself to learning (seeks)
from day to day to increase (his knowledge) ; he who
devotes himself to the Tâo (seeks) from day to day
to diminish (his doing).

2. He diminishes it and again diminishes it, till
he arrives at doing nothing (on purpose). Having
arrived at this point of non-action, there is nothing
which he does not do.

3. He who gets as his own all under heaven does
so by giving himself no trouble (with that end). If
one take trouble (with that end), he is not equal to
getting as his own all under heaven.

忘 知, ' Forgetting Knowledge ; '—the contrast between
Learning and the Tâo. It is only by the Tâo that the
world can be won.

Ƹiâo Hung commences his quotations of commentary on
this chapter with the following from Kumâragîva on the
second par. :—' He carries on the process of diminishing
till there is nothing coarse about him which is not put
away. He puts it away till he has forgotten all that was bad
in it. He then puts away all that is fine about him. He
does so till he has forgotten all that was good in it. But
the bad was wrong, and the good is right. Having diminished the wrong, and also diminished the right, the process
is carried on till they are both forgotten. Passion and
desire are both cut off; and his virtue and the Tâo are in
such union that he does nothing ; but though he does
nothing, he allows all things to do their own doing, and all
things are done.' Such is a Buddhistic view of the passage,
not very intelligible, and which I do not endorse.

In a passage in the 'Narratives of the School' (Bk. IX, Art. 2), we have a Confucian view of the passage :—' Let perspicacity, intelligence, shrewdness, and wisdom be guarded by stupidity, and the service of the possessor will affect the whole world ; let them be guarded by complaisance, and his daring and strength will shake the age ; let them be guarded by timidity, and his wealth will be all within the four seas ; let them be guarded by humility, and there will be what we call the method of " diminishing it, and diminishing it again." '   But neither do I endorse this.

My own view of the scope of the chapter has been given above in a few words.   The greater part of it is found in Kwang-jze.

49. 1. The sage has no invariable mind of his own ; he makes the mind of the people his mind.

2. To those who are good (to me), I am good ; and to those who are not good (to me), I am also good ;—and thus (all) get to be good.   To those who are sincere (with me), I am sincere ; and to those who are not sincere (with me), I am also sincere ;—and thus (all) get to be sincere.

3. The sage has in the world an appearance of indecision, and keeps his mind in a state of indifference to all.   The people all keep their eyes and ears directed to him, and he deals with them all as his children.

任德, ' The Quality of Indulgence.'   The chapter shows how that quality enters largely into the dealing of the sage with other men, and exercises over them a transforming influence, dominated as it is in him by the Tâo.

My version of par. 1 is taken from Dr. Chalmers.   A good commentary on it was given by the last emperor but one of the earlier of the two great Sung dynasties, in the period A. D. 1111–1117 :—' The mind of the sage is free from preoccupation and able to receive ; still, and able to respond.'

In par. 2 I adopt the reading of 得 (' to get ') instead of

the more common 德 ('virtue' or 'quality'). There is a passage in Han Ying (IX, 3 b, 4 a), the style of which, most readers will probably agree with me in thinking, was moulded on the text before us, though nothing is said of any connexion between it and the saying of Lâo-ꝫze. I must regard it as a sequel to the conversation between Confucius and some of his disciples about the principle (Lâo's principle) that 'Injury should be recompensed with Kindness,' as recorded in the Con. Ana., XIV, 36. We read :—' Ʒze-lû said, " When men are good to me, I will also be good to them ; when they are not good to me, I will also be not good to them." Ʒze-kung said, " When men are good to me, I will also be good to them ; when they are not good to me, I will simply lead them on, forwards it may be or backwards." Yen Hui said, " When men are good to me, I will also be good to them ; when they are not good to me, I will still be good to them." The views of the three disciples being thus different, they referred the point to the Master, who said, " The words of Ʒze-lû are such as might be expected among the (wild tribes of) the Man and the Mo ; those of Ʒze-kung, such as might be expected among friends ; those of Hui, such as might be expected among relatives and near connexions." ' This is all. The Master was still far from Lâo-ꝫze's standpoint, and that of his own favourite disciple, Yen Hui.

50. 1. Men come forth and live ; they enter (again) and die.

2. Of every ten three are ministers of life (to themselves) ; and three are ministers of death.

3. There are also three in every ten whose aim is to live, but whose movements tend to the land (or place) of death. And for what reason ? Because of their excessive endeavours to perpetuate life.

4. But I have heard that he who is skilful in managing the life entrusted to him for a time travels on the land without having to shun rhinoceros or

tiger, and enters a host without having to avoid buff coat or sharp weapon. The rhinoceros finds no place in him into which to thrust its horn, nor the tiger a place in which to fix its claws, nor the weapon a place to admit its point. And for what reason? Because there is in him no place of death.

貴生, 'The Value set on Life.' The chapter sets forth the Tâo as an antidote against decay and death.

In par. 1 life is presented to us as intermediate between two non-existences. The words will suggest to many readers those in Job i. 21.

In pars. 2 and 3 I translate the characters 十 有 三 by 'three in ten,' instead of by 'thirteen,' as Julien and other translators have done. The characters are susceptible of either translation according to the tone in which we read the 有. They were construed as I have done by Wang Pî; and many of the best commentators have followed in his wake. 'The ministers of life to themselves' would be those who eschewed all things, both internal and external, tending to injure health; 'the ministers of death,' those who pursued courses likely to cause disease and shorten life; the third three would be those who thought that by mysterious and abnormal courses they could prolong life, but only injured it. Those three classes being thus disposed of, there remains only one in ten rightly using the Tâo, and he is spoken of in the next paragraph.

This par. 4 is easy of translation, and the various readings in it are unimportant, differing in this respect from those in par. 3. But the aim of the author in it is not clear. In ascribing such effects to the possession of the Tâo, is he 'trifling,' as Dr. Chalmers thinks? or indulging the play of his poetical fancy? or simply saying that the Tâoist will keep himself out of danger?

51. 1. All things are produced by the Tâo, and nourished by its outflowing operation. They receive their forms according to the nature of each, and are

completed according to the circumstances of their condition. Therefore all things without exception honour the Tâo, and exalt its outflowing operation.

2. This honouring of the Tâo and exalting of its operation is not the result of any ordination, but always a spontaneous tribute.

3. Thus it is that the Tâo produces (all things), nourishes them, brings them to their full growth, nurses them, completes them, matures them, maintains them, and overspreads them.

4. It produces them and makes no claim to the possession of them; it carries them through their processes and does not vaunt its ability in doing so; it brings them to maturity and exercises no control over them;—this is called its mysterious operation.

養德, 'The Operation (of the Tâo) in Nourishing Things.' The subject of the chapter is the quiet passionless operation of the Tâo in nature, in the production and nourishing of things throughout the seasons of the year;— a theme dwelt on by Lâo-ʒze, in II, 4, X, 3, and other places.

The Tâo is the subject of all the predicates in par. 1, and what seem the subjects in all but the first member should be construed adverbially.

On par. 2 Wû *Khăng* says that the honour of the Son of Heaven is derived from his appointment by God, and that then the nobility of the feudal princes is derived from him; but in the honour given to the Tâo and the nobility ascribed to its operation, we are not to think of any external ordination. There is a strange reading of two of the members of par. 3 in Wang Pî, viz. 亭之毒之 for 成之熟之. This is quoted and predicated of 'Heaven,' in the Nestorian Monument of Hsî-an in the eighth century.

52. 1. (The Tâo) which originated all under the sky is to be considered as the mother of them all.

2. When the mother is found, we know what her children should be.　When one knows that he is his mother's child, and proceeds to guard (the qualities of) the mother that belong to him, to the end of his life he will be free from all peril.

3. Let him keep his mouth closed, and shut up the portals (of his nostrils), and all his life he will be exempt from laborious exertion.　Let him keep his mouth open, and (spend his breath) in the promotion of his affairs, and all his life there will be no safety for him.

4. The perception of what is small is (the secret of) clear-sightedness ; the guarding of what is soft and tender is (the secret of) strength.

5. Who uses well his light,
　　Reverting to its (source so) bright,
　　Will from his body ward all blight,
　　And hides the unchanging from men's sight.

歸 元, 'Returning to the Source.'　The meaning of the chapter is obscure, and the commentators give little help in determining it.　As in the preceding chapter, Lâo-ʒze treats of the operation of the Tâo on material things, he seems in this to go on to the operation of it in man, or how he, with his higher nature, should ever be maintaining it in himself.

For the understanding of paragraph 1 we must refer to the first chapter of the treatise, where the Tâo, 'having no name,' appears as ' the Beginning' or ' First Cause' of the world, and then, 'having a name,' as its 'Mother.'　It is the same thing or concept in both of its phases, the ideal or absolute, and the manifestation of it in its passionless doings.　The old Jesuit translators render this par. by ' Mundus principium et causam suam habet in Divino 有, seu actione Divinae sapientiae quae dici potest ejus mater.' So far I may assume that they agreed with me in understanding that the subject of the par. was the Tâo.

Par. 2 lays down the law of life for man thus derived from the T â o. The last clause of it is given by the same translators as equivalent to ' Unde fit ut post mortem nihil ei timendum sit,'—a meaning which the characters will not bear. But from that clause, and the next par., I am obliged to conclude that even in Lâo-3ze's mind there was the germ of the sublimation of the material frame which issued in the asceticism and life-preserving arts of the later Tâoism.

Par. 3 seems to indicate the method of 'guarding the mother in man,' by watching over the breath, the proto-plastic ' one ' of ch. 42, the ethereal matter out of which all material things were formed. The organs of this breath in man are the mouth and nostrils (nothing else should be understood here by 兌 and 門 ;—see the explanations of the former in the last par. of the fifth of the appendixes to the Yî in vol. xvi, p. 432); and the management of the breath is the mystery of the esoteric Buddhism and Tâoism.

In par. 4 ' The guarding what is soft ' is derived from the use of ' the soft lips ' in hiding and preserving the hard and strong teeth.

Par. 5 gives the gist of the chapter :—Man's always keeping before him the ideal of the T â o, and, without purpose, simply doing whatever he finds to do ; T â o-like and powerful in all his sphere of action.

I have followed the reading of the last character but one, which is given by 3iâo Hung instead of that found in Ho-shang Kung and Wang Pî.

53. 1. If I were suddenly to become known, and (put into a position to) conduct (a government) according to the Great T â o, what I should be most afraid of would be a boastful display.

2. The great T â o (or way) is very level and easy ; but people love the by-ways.

3. Their court(-yards and buildings) shall be well kept, but their fields shall be ill-cultivated, and their granaries very empty. They shall wear elegant and

ornamented robes, carry a sharp sword at their girdle, pamper themselves in eating and drinking, and have a superabundance of property and wealth;—such (princes) may be called robbers and boasters.   This is contrary to the Tâo surely!

益 證, 'Increase of Evidence.'   The chapter contrasts government by the Tâo with that conducted in a spirit of ostentation and by oppression.

In the 'I' of paragraph 1 does Lâo-ȝze speak of himself? I think he does. Wû *Kh*ăng understands it of 'any man,' i.e. any one in the exercise of government ;—which is possible. What is peculiar to my version is the pregnant meaning given to 有 知, common enough in the mouth of Confucius.   I have adopted it here because of a passage in Liû Hsiang's Shwo-wăn (XX, 13 b), where Lâo-ȝze is made to say ' Excessive is the difficulty of practising the Tâo at the present time,' adding that the princes of his age would not receive it from him.   On the ' Great Tâo,' see chapters 25, 34, et al.   From the twentieth book of Han Fei (12 b and 13 a) I conclude that he had the whole of this chapter in his copy of our *K*ing, but he broke it up, after his fashion, into fragmentary utterances, confused and confounding. He gives also some remarkable various readings, one of which (拏, instead of Ho-shang Kung and Wang Pî's 夸, character 48) is now generally adopted.   The passage is quoted in the Khang-hsî dictionary under 拏 with this reading.

54. 1. What (Tâo's) skilful planter plants
        Can never be uptorn ;
    What his skilful arms enfold,
        From him can ne'er be borne.
    Sons shall bring in lengthening line,
    Sacrifices to his shrine.

    2. Tâo when nursed within one's self,
        His vigour will make true ;

And where the family it rules
    What riches will accrue!
The neighbourhood where it prevails
    In thriving will abound;
And when 'tis seen throughout the state,
    Good fortune will be found.
Employ it the kingdom o'er,
    And men thrive all around.

3. In this way the effect will be seen in the person,
by the observation of different cases; in the family;
in the neighbourhood; in the state; and in the
kingdom.

4. How do I know that this effect is sure to
hold thus all under the sky? By this (method of
observation).

修 觀, 'The Cultivation (of the Tâo), and the Observation (of its Effects).' The sentiment of the first paragraph
is found in the twenty-seventh and other previous chapters,—that the noiseless and imperceptible acting of the
Tâo is irresistible in its influence; and this runs through
to the end of the chapter with the additional appeal to the
influence of its effects. The introduction of the subject of
sacrifices, a religious rite, though not presented to the
Highest Object, will strike the reader as peculiar in our
King.

The Teh mentioned five times in par. 2 is the 'virtue'
of the Tâo embodied in the individual, and extending from
him in all the spheres of his occupation, and is explained
differently by Han Fei according to its application; and
his example I have to some extent followed.

The force of pars. 3 and 4 is well given by Ho-shang
Kung. On the first clause he says, 'Take the person of
one who cultivates the Tâo, and compare it with that of
one who does not cultivate it;—which is in a state of decay?
and which is in a state of preservation?'

55. 1. He who has in himself abundantly the attributes (of the Tâo) is like an infant. Poisonous insects will not sting him; fierce beasts will not seize him; birds of prey will not strike him.

2. (The infant's) bones are weak and its sinews soft, but yet its grasp is firm. It knows not yet the union of male and female, and yet its virile member may be excited;—showing the perfection of its physical essence. All day long it will cry without its throat becoming hoarse;—showing the harmony (in its constitution).

3. To him by whom this harmony is known,
(The secret of) the unchanging (Tâo) is shown,
And in the knowledge wisdom finds its throne.
All life-increasing arts to evil turn;
Where the mind makes the vital breath to burn,
(False) is the strength, (and o'er it we should mourn.)

4. When things have become strong, they (then) become old, which may be said to be contrary to the Tâo. Whatever is contrary to the Tâo soon ends.

玄 符, 'The Mysterious Charm;' meaning, apparently, the entire passivity of the Tâo.

With pars. 1 and 2, compare what is said about the infant in chapters 10 and 20, and about the immunity from dangers such as here described of the disciple of the Tâo in ch. 50. My 'evil' in the second triplet of par. 3 has been translated by 'felicity;' but a reference to the Khang-hsî dictionary will show that the meaning which I give to 祥 is well authorised. It is the only meaning allowable here. The third and fourth 曰 in this par. appear in Ho-shang Kung's text as 日, and he comments on the clauses accord-

ingly; but 日 is now the received reading. Some light
is thrown on this paragraph and the next by an apocryphal
conversation attributed to Lâo-ʒze in Liû Hsiang's Shwo-
wǎn, X, 4 a.

56. 1. He who knows (the Tâo) does not (care
to) speak (about it); he who is (ever ready to) speak
about it does not know it.

2. He (who knows it) will keep his mouth shut
and close the portals (of his nostrils). He will
blunt his sharp points and unravel the complications
of things; he will attemper his brightness, and bring
himself into agreement with the obscurity (of others).
This is called ' the Mysterious Agreement.'

3. (Such an one) cannot be treated familiarly or
distantly; he is beyond all consideration of profit or
injury; of nobility or meanness :—he is the noblest
man under heaven.

玄 德, ' The Mysterious Excellence.' The chapter gives
us a picture of the man of Tâo, humble and retiring, oblivious of himself and of other men, the noblest man under
heaven.

Par. 1 is found in Kwang-ʒze (XIII, 20 b), not expressly
mentioned, as taken from Lâo-ʒze, but at the end of a string
of sentiments, ascribed to ' the Master,' some of them, like
the two clauses here, no doubt belonging to him, and the
others, probably Kwang-ʒze's own.

Par. 2 is all found in chapters 4 and 52, excepting the
short clause in the conclusion.

57. 1. A state may be ruled by (measures of)
correction; weapons of war may be used with crafty
dexterity; (but) the kingdom is made one's own
(only) by freedom from action and purpose.

2. How do I know that it is so? By these

facts :—In the kingdom the multiplication of prohibi-
tive enactments increases the poverty of the people ;
the more implements to add to their profit that the
people have, the greater disorder is there in the
state and clan ; the more acts of crafty dexterity
that men possess, the more do strange contrivances
appear ; the more display there is of legislation,
the more thieves and robbers there are.

3. Therefore a sage has said, ' I will do nothing
(of purpose), and the people will be transformed of
themselves ; I will be fond of keeping still, and the
people will of themselves become correct.   I will
take no trouble about it, and the people will of
themselves become rich ; I will manifest no ambition, and the people will of themselves attain to the
primitive simplicity.'

淳 風, ' The Genuine Influence.' The chapter shows
how government by the Tâo is alone effective, and of universal application ; contrasting it with the failure of other
methods.

After the ' weapons of war' in par. 1, one is tempted to
take ' the sharp implements' in par. 2 as such weapons, but
the meaning which I finally adopted, especially after studying
chapters 36 and 80, seems more consonant with Lâo-ʒze's
scheme of thought.   In the last member of the same par.,
IIo-shang Kung has the strange reading of 法 物, and uses
it in his commentary ; but the better text of 法 令 is found
both in Hwâi-nan and Sze-mâ *Kh*ien, and in Wang Pî.

We do not know if the writer were quoting any particular sage in par. 3, or referring generally to the sages of
the past ;—men like the ' sentence-makers' of ch. 41.

58. 1. The government that seems the most un-
        wise,
        Oft goodness to the people best supplies ;

That which is meddling, touching everything,
Will work but ill, and disappointment bring.
Misery!—happiness is to be found by its side!
Happiness!—misery lurks beneath it! Who knows
what either will come to in the end?

2. Shall we then dispense with correction? The
(method of) correction shall by a turn become distortion, and the good in it shall by a turn become
evil. The delusion of the people (on this point) has
indeed subsisted for a long time.

3. Therefore the sage is (like) a square which cuts
no one (with its angles); (like) a corner which injures
no one (with its sharpness). He is straightforward,
but allows himself no license; he is bright, but does
not dazzle.

順 化, 'Transformation according to Circumstances;'
but this title does not throw light on the meaning of the
chapter; nor are we helped to an understanding of it by
Han Fei, with his additions and comments (XI, 3 b, 4 b),
nor by Hwâi-nan with his illustrations (XII, 21 a, b). The
difficulty of it is increased by its being separated from the
preceding chapter of which it is really the sequel. It contrasts still further government by the Tâo, with that by
the method of correction. The sage is the same in both
chapters, his character and government both marked by
the opposites or contraries which distinguish the procedure
of the Tâo, as stated in ch. 40.

59. 1. For regulating the human (in our constitution) and rendering the (proper) service to the
heavenly, there is nothing like moderation.

2. It is only by this moderation that there is
effected an early return (to man's normal state).
That early return is what I call the repeated accumulation of the attributes (of the Tâo). With that

repeated accumulation of those attributes, there comes the subjugation (of every obstacle to such return). Of this subjugation we know not what shall be the limit; and when one knows not what the limit shall be, he may be the ruler of a state.

3. He who possesses the mother of the state may continue long. His case is like that (of the plant) of which we say that its roots are deep and its flower stalks firm:—this is the way to secure that its enduring life shall long be seen.

守道, 'Guarding the Tâo.' The chapter shows how it is the guarding of the Tâo that ensures a continuance of long life, with vigour and success. The abuse of it and other passages in our King helped on, I must believe, the later Tâoist dreams about the elixir vitae and life-preserving pills. The whole of it, with one or two various readings, is found in Han Fei (VI, 4 b–6 a), who speaks twice in his comments of 'The Book.'

Par. 1 has been translated, 'In governing men and in serving Heaven, there is nothing like moderation.' But by 'Heaven' there is not intended 'the blue sky' above us, nor any personal Power above it, but the Tâo embodied in our constitution, the Heavenly element in our nature. The 'moderation' is the opposite of what we call 'living fast,' 'burning the candle at both ends.'

In par. 2 I must read 復, instead of the more common 服. I find it in Lû Teh-ming, and that it is not a misprint in him appears from his subjoining that it is pronounced like 服. Its meaning is the same as in 復歸 其明 in ch. 52, par. 5. Teh is not 'virtue' in our common meaning of the term, but 'the attributes of the Tâo,' as almost always with Lâo-ʒze.

In par. 3 'the mother of the state' is the Tâo as in ch. 1, and especially in ch. 52, par. 1.

60. 1. Governing a great state is like cooking small fish.

2. Let the kingdom be governed according to the
Tâo, and the manes of the departed will not manifest their spiritual energy.   It is not that those
manes have not that spiritual energy, but it will not
be employed to hurt men.   It is not that it could not
hurt men, but neither does the ruling sage hurt them.

3. When these two do not injuriously affect each
other, their good influences converge in the virtue
(of the Tâo).

居 位, 'Occupying the Throne;' occupying it, that is,
according to the Tâo, noiselessly and purposelessly, so
that the people enjoy their lives, free from all molestation
seen and unseen.

Par. 1. That is, in the most quiet and easy manner. The
whole of the chapter is given and commented on by Han
Fei (VI, 6a–7b); but very unsatisfactorily.

The more one thinks and reads about the rest of the
chapter, the more does he agree with the words of Julien :—
'It presents the frequent recurrence of the same characters,
and appears as insignificant as it is unintelligible, if we give
to the Chinese characters their ordinary meaning.'—The
reader will observe that we have here the second mention
of spirits (the manes; Chalmers, 'the ghosts;' Julien, les
démons).   See ch. 39.

Whatever Lâo-ƶze meant to teach in par. 2, he laid in it
a foundation for the superstition of the later and present
Tâoism about the spirits of the dead ;—such as appeared
a few years ago in the 'tail-cutting' scare.

61. 1. What makes a great state is its being (like)
a low-lying, down-flowing (stream) ;—it becomes the
centre to which tend (all the small states) under
heaven.

2. (To illustrate from) the case of all females :—the
female always overcomes the male by her stillness.
Stillness may be considered (a sort of) abasement.

3. Thus it is that a great state, by condescending to small states, gains them for itself; and that small states, by abasing themselves to a great state, win it over to them. In the one case the abasement leads to gaining adherents, in the other case to procuring favour.

4. The great state only wishes to unite men together and nourish them; a small state only wishes to be received by, and to serve, the other. Each gets what it desires, but the great state must learn to abase itself.

謙德, 'The Attribute of Humility;'—a favourite theme with Lâo-ʒze; and the illustration of it from the low-lying stream to which smaller streams flow is also a favourite subject with him. The language can hardly but recall the words of a greater than Lâo-ʒze:—'He that humbleth himself shall be exalted.'

62. 1. Tâo has of all things the most honoured
        place.
    No treasures give good men so rich a grace;
    Bad men it guards, and doth their ill efface.

2. (Its) admirable words can purchase honour; (its) admirable deeds can raise their performer above others. Even men who are not good are not abandoned by it.

3. Therefore when the sovereign occupies his place as the Son of Heaven, and he has appointed his three ducal ministers, though (a prince) were to send in a round symbol-of-rank large enough to fill both the hands, and that as the precursor of the team of horses (in the court-yard), such an offering would not be equal to (a lesson of) this Tâo, which one might present on his knees.

4. Why was it that the ancients prized this Tâo

so much ? Was it not because it could be got by
seeking for it, and the guilty could escape (from the
stain of their guilt) by it ? This is the reason why
all under heaven consider it the most valuable thing.

為道, 'Practising the Tâo.' 貴道, 'The value set
on the Tâo,' would have been a more appropriate title.
The chapter sets forth that value in various manifestations
of it.

Par. 1. For the meaning of 奧, see Confucian Analects,
III, ch. 13.

Par. 2. I am obliged to adopt the reading of the first
sentence of this paragraph given by Hwâi-nan, 美言可
以市尊, 美行可以加人;—see especially his
quotation of it in XVIII, 10 a, as from a superior man,
I have not found his reading anywhere else.

Par. 3 is not easily translated, or explained. See the
rules on presenting offerings at the court of a ruler or the
king, in vol. xxvii of the 'Sacred Books of the East,' p. 84,
note 3, and also a narrative in the 3o Kwan under the
thirty-third year of duke Hsî.

63. 1. (It is the way of the Tâo) to act without
(thinking of) acting ; to conduct affairs without (feeling the) trouble of them ; to taste without discerning
any flavour ; to consider what is small as great, and
a few as many ; and to recompense injury with
kindness.

2. (The master of it) anticipates things that are
difficult while they are easy, and does things that
would become great while they are small. All difficult things in the world are sure to arise from a
previous state in which they were easy, and all
great things from one in which they were small.
Therefore the sage, while he never does what is
great, is able on that account to accomplish the
greatest things.

3. He who lightly promises is sure to keep but little faith; he who is continually thinking things easy is sure to find them difficult. Therefore the sage sees difficulty even in what seems easy, and so never has any difficulties.

思 始, 'Thinking in the Beginning.' The former of these two characters is commonly misprinted 恩, and this has led Chalmers to mistranslate them by 'The Beginning of Grace.' The chapter sets forth the passionless method of the Tâo, and how the sage accordingly accomplishes his objects easily by forestalling in his measures all difficulties. In par. 1 the clauses are indicative, and not imperative, and therefore we have to supplement the text in translating in some such way, as I have done. They give us a cluster of aphorisms illustrating the procedure of the Tâo 'by contraries,' and conclude with one, which is the chief glory of Lâo-ᵹze's teaching, though I must think that its value is somewhat diminished by the method in which he reaches it. It has not the prominence in the later teaching of Tâoist writers which we should expect, nor is it found (so far as I know) in *K*wang-ᵹze, Han Fei, or Hwâi-nan. It is quoted, however, twice by Liû Hsiang;—see my note on par. 2 of ch. 49.

It follows from the whole chapter that the Tâoistic 'doing nothing' was not an absolute quiescence and inaction, but had a method in it.

64. 1. That which is at rest is easily kept hold of; before a thing has given indications of its presence, it is easy to take measures against it; that which is brittle is easily broken; that which is very small is easily dispersed. Action should be taken before a thing has made its appearance; order should be secured before disorder has begun.

2. The tree which fills the arms grew from the tiniest sprout; the tower of nine storeys rose from a

(small) heap of earth; the journey of a thousand lî commenced with a single step.

3. He who acts (with an ulterior purpose) does harm; he who takes hold of a thing (in the same way) loses his hold. The sage does not act (so), and therefore does no harm; he does not lay hold (so), and therefore does not lose his hold. (But) people in their conduct of affairs are constantly ruining them when they are on the eve of success. If they were careful at the end, as (they should be) at the beginning, they would not so ruin them.

4. Therefore the sage desires what (other men) do not desire, and does not prize things difficult to get; he learns what (other men) do not learn, and turns back to what the multitude of men have passed by. Thus he helps the natural development of all things, and does not dare to act (with an ulterior purpose of his own).

守微, 'Guarding the Minute.' The chapter is a continuation and enlargement of the last. Wû Khăng, indeed, unites the two, blending them together with some ingenious transpositions and omissions, which it is not necessary to discuss. Compare the first part of par. 3 with the last part of par. 1, ch. 29.

65. 1. The ancients who showed their skill in practising the Tâo did so, not to enlighten the people, but rather to make them simple and ignorant.

2. The difficulty in governing the people arises from their having much knowledge. He who (tries to) govern a state by his wisdom is a scourge to it; while he who does not (try to) do so is a blessing.

3. He who knows these two things finds in them also his model and rule. Ability to know this

model and rule constitutes what we call the mysterious excellence (of a governor).   Deep and far-reaching is such mysterious excellence, showing indeed its possessor as opposite to others, but leading them to a great conformity to him.

淳德, 'Pure, unmixed Excellence.' The chapter shows the powerful and beneficent influence of the Tâo in government, in contrast with the applications and contrivances of human wisdom.   Compare ch. 19.   My 'simple and ignorant' is taken from Julien.   More literally the translation would be 'to make them stupid.'   My 'scourge' in par. 2 is also after Julien's 'fléau.'

66. 1. That whereby the rivers and seas are able to receive the homage and tribute of all the valley streams, is their skill in being lower than they ;—it is thus that they are the kings of them all.   So it is that the sage (ruler), wishing to be above men, puts himself by his words below them, and, wishing to be before them, places his person behind them.

2. In this way though he has his place above them, men do not feel his weight, nor though he has his place before them, do they feel it an injury to them.

3. Therefore all in the world delight to exalt him and do not weary of him.   Because he does not strive, no one finds it possible to strive with him.

後已, 'Putting one's self Last.'   The subject is the power of the Tâo, by its display of humility in attracting men.   The subject and the way in which it is illustrated are frequent themes in the King.   See chapters 8, 22, 39, 42, 61, et al.

The last sentence of par. 3 is found also in ch. 22.   There seem to be no quotations from the chapter in Han Fei or Hwâi-nan ; but Wû Khăng quotes passages from Tung

*K*ung-shû (of the second century B.C.), and Yang Hsiung (B.C. 53–A.D. 18), which seem to show that the phraseology of it was familiar to them. The former says:—'When one places himself in his qualities below others, his person is above them; when he places them behind those of others, his person is before them;' the other, 'Men exalt him who humbles himself below them; and give the precedence to him who puts himself behind them.'

67. 1. All the world says that, while my Tâo is great, it yet appears to be inferior (to other systems of teaching). Now it is just its greatness that makes it seem to be inferior. If it were like any other (system), for long would its smallness have been known!

2. But I have three precious things which I prize and hold fast. The first is gentleness; the second is economy; and the third is shrinking from taking precedence of others.

3. With that gentleness I can be bold; with that economy I can be liberal; shrinking from taking precedence of others, I can become a vessel of the highest honour. Now-a-days they give up gentleness and are all for being bold; economy, and are all for being liberal; the hindmost place, and seek only to be foremost;—(of all which the end is) death.

4. Gentleness is sure to be victorious even in battle, and firmly to maintain its ground. Heaven will save its possessor, by his (very) gentleness protecting him.

三 寶, 'The Three Precious Things.' This title is taken from par. 2, and suggests to us how the early framer of these titles intended to express by them the subject-matter of their several chapters. The three things are the three distinguishing qualities of the possessor of the Tâo, the

three great moral qualities appearing in its followers, the
qualities, we may venture to say, of the Tâo itself. The
same phrase is now the common designation of Buddhism
in China,—the Tri-ratna or Ratna-traya, 'the Precious
Buddha,' 'the Precious Law,' and 'the Precious Priesthood
(or rather Monkhood) or Church;' appearing also in the
'Tri-sara*n*a,' or 'formula of the Three Refuges,' what Dr.
Eitel calls 'the most primitive formula fidei of the early
Buddhists, introduced before Southern and Northern Buddhism separated.' I will not introduce the question of
whether Buddhism borrowed this designation from Tâoism,
after its entrance into China. It is in Buddhism the formula
of a peculiar Church or Religion; in Tâoism a rule for the
character, or the conduct which the Tâo demands from all
men. 'My Tâo' in par. 1 is the reading of Wang Pî;
Ho-shang Kung's text is simply 我. Wang Pî's reading
is now generally adopted.

The concluding sentiment of the chapter is equivalent to
the saying of Mencius (VII, ii, IV, 2), 'If the ruler of a
state love benevolence, he will have no enemy under heaven.'
'Heaven' is equivalent to 'the Tâo,' the course of events,—
Providence, as we should say.

> 68. He who in (Tâo's) wars has skill
>   Assumes no martial port;
>   He who fights with most good will
>   To rage makes no resort.
>   He who vanquishes yet still
>   Keeps from his foes apart;
>   He whose hests men most fulfil
>   Yet humbly plies his art.
>
>   Thus we say, ' He ne'er contends,
>   And therein is his might.'
>   Thus we say, ' Men's wills he bends,
>   That they with him unite.'
>   Thus we say, ' Like Heaven's his ends,
>   No sage of old more bright.'

配 天, 'Matching Heaven.' The chapter describes the work of the practiser of the Tâo as accomplished like that of Heaven, without striving or crying. He appears under the figure of a mailed warrior (士) of the ancient chariot. The chapter is a sequel of the preceding, and is joined on to it by Wû *Kh*ăng, as is also the next.

69. 1. A master of the art of war has said, 'I do not dare to be the host (to commence the war); I prefer to be the guest (to act on the defensive). I do not dare to advance an inch; I prefer to retire a foot.' This is called marshalling the ranks where there are no ranks; baring the arms (to fight) where there are no arms to bare; grasping the weapon where there is no weapon to grasp; advancing against the enemy where there is no enemy.

2. There is no calamity greater than lightly engaging in war. To do that is near losing (the gentleness) which is so precious. Thus it is that when opposing weapons are (actually) crossed, he who deplores (the situation) conquers.

玄 用, 'The Use of the Mysterious (Tâo).' Such seems to be the meaning of the title. The chapter teaches that, if war were carried on, or rather avoided, according to the Tâo, the result would be success. Lâo-ʒze's own statements appear as so many paradoxes. They are examples of the procedure of the Tâo by 'contraries,' or opposites.

We do not know who the master of the military art referred to was. Perhaps the author only adopted the style of quotation to express his own sentiments.

70. 1. My words are very easy to know, and very easy to practise; but there is no one in the world who is able to know and able to practise them.

2. There is an originating and all-comprehending

(principle) in my words, and an authoritative law for the things (which I enforce). It is because they do not know these, that men do not know me.

3. They who know me are few, and I am on that account (the more) to be prized. It is thus that the sage wears (a poor garb of) hair cloth, while he carries his (signet of) jade in his bosom.

知 難, 'The Difficulty of being (rightly) Known.' The Tâo comprehends and rules all Lâo-ʒze's teaching, as the members of a clan were all in the loins of their first father (宗), and continue to look up to him; and the people of a state are all under the direction of their ruler; yet the philosopher had to complain of not being known. Lâo-ʒze's principle and rule or ruler was the Tâo. His utterance here is very important. Compare the words of Confucius in the Analects, XIV, ch. 37, et al.

Par. 2 is twice quoted by Hwâi-nan, though his text is not quite the same in both cases.

71. 1. To know and yet (think) we do not know is the highest (attainment); not to know (and yet think) we do know is a disease.

2. It is simply by being pained at (the thought of) having this disease that we are preserved from it. The sage has not the disease. He knows the pain that would be inseparable from it, and therefore he does not have it.

知 病, 'The Disease of Knowing.' Here, again, we have the Tâo working 'by contraries,'—in the matter of knowledge. Compare par. 1 with Confucius's account of what knowledge is in the Analects, II, ch. 17. The par. 1 is found in one place in Hwâi-nan, lengthened out by the addition of particles; but the variation is unimportant. In another place, however, he seems to have had the correct text before him.

Par. 2 is in Han Fei also lengthened out, but with an

important variation (不 病 for 病 病), and I cannot construe his text. His 不 is probably a transcriber's error.

72. 1. When the people do not fear what they ought to fear, that which is their great dread will come on them.

2. Let them not thoughtlessly indulge themselves in their ordinary life ; let them not act as if weary of what that life depends on.

3. It is by avoiding such indulgence that such weariness does not arise.

4. Therefore the sage knows (these things) of himself, but does not parade (his knowledge) ; loves, but does not (appear to set a) value on, himself. And thus he puts the latter alternative away and makes choice of the former.

愛 已, 'Loving one's Self.' This title is taken from the expression in par. 4 ; and the object of the chapter seems to be to show how such loving should be manifested, and to enforce the lesson by the example of the 'sage,' the true master of the Tâo.

In par. 1 'the great dread' is death, and the things which ought to be feared and may be feared, are the indulgences of the appetites and passions, which, if not eschewed, tend to shorten life and accelerate the approach of death.

Pars. 2 and 3 are supplementary to 1. For 狹, the second character of Ho-shang Kung's text in par. 2, Wang Pî reads 狎, which has the same name as the other ; and according to the Khang-hsî dictionary, the two characters are interchangeable. I have also followed Wû Khăng in adopting 狎 for the former of the two 厭 in par. 3. Wû adopted this reading from a commentator Liû of Lü-ling. It gives a good meaning, and is supported by the structure of other sentences made on similar lines.

In par. 4 'the sage' must be 'the ruler who is a sage,' a master of the Tâo, 'the king' of ch. 25. He 'loves himself,' i. e. his life, and takes the right measures to prolong his life, but without any demonstration that he is doing so.

The above is, I conceive, the correct explanation of the chapter; but as to the Chinese critics and foreign translators of it, it may be said, 'Quot homines, tot sententiae.' In illustration of this I venture to subjoin what is found on it in the old version of the Jesuit missionaries, which has not been previously printed :—

Prima explicatio juxta interpretes.

1. Populus, ubi jam principis iram non timet, nihil non audet ut jugum excutiat, resque communis ad extremum discrimen adducitur.

2. Ambitio principis non faciat terram angustiorem, et vectigalium magnitudine alendo populo insufficientem ; numquam populus patriae pertaesus alias terras quaeret.

3. Vitae si non taedet, neque patrii soli taedebit.

4. Quare sanctus sibi semper attentus potentiam suam non ostentat.

5. Quia vere se amat, non se pretiosum facit ; vel quia sibi recte consulit non se talem aestimat cujus felicitati et honori infelices populi unice servire debeant, immo potius eum se reputat qui populorum felicitati totum se debeat impendere.

6. Ergo illud resecat, istud amplectitur.

Alia explicatio.

1. Populus si non ita timet principis majestatem, sed facile ad eum accedit, majestas non minuitur, immo ad summum pervenit.

2. Vectigalibus terra si non opprimitur, suâ quisque contentus alias terras non quaeret, si se non vexari populus experitur.

3. Vitae si non taedet, nec patrii soli taedebit.

4. Quare sanctus majestatis fastum non affectat, immo similem se caeteris ostendit.

5. Sibi recte consulens, populorum amans, non se pretiosum et inaccessibilem facit.

6. Quidquid ergo timorem incutere potest, hoc evitat; quod amorem conciliat et benignitatem, se demonstrat hoc eligi et ultro amplectitur.

73. 1. He whose boldness appears in his daring (to do wrong, in defiance of the laws) is put to death; he whose boldness appears in his not daring (to do so) lives on. Of these two cases the one appears to be advantageous, and the other to be injurious. But

When Heaven's anger smites a man,
Who the cause shall truly scan?.

On this account the sage feels a difficulty (as to what to do in the former case).

2. It is the way of Heaven not to strive, and yet it skilfully overcomes; not to speak, and yet it is skilful in (obtaining) a reply; does not call, and yet men come to it of themselves. Its demonstrations are quiet, and yet its plans are skilful and effective. The meshes of the net of Heaven are large; far apart, but letting nothing escape.

任爲, 'Allowing Men to take their Course.' The chapter teaches that rulers should not be hasty to punish, especially by the infliction of death. Though they may seem to err in leniency, yet Heaven does not allow offenders to escape.

While Heaven hates the ill-doer, yet we must not always conclude from Its judgments that every one who suffers from them is an ill-doer; and the two lines which rhyme, and illustrate this point, are equivalent to the sentiment in our Old Book, 'Clouds and darkness are round about Him.' They are ascribed to Lâo-ʒze by Lieh-ʒze (VI, 7 a); but, it has been said, that they are quoted by him 'in an entirely different connexion.' But the same text in two different sermons may be said to be in different connexions. In Lieh-ʒze and our *K*ing the lines have the same meaning, and substantially the same application. Indeed *K*ang *K*an, of our fourth century, the commentator of Lieh-ʒze, quotes the comment of Wang Pî on this passage, condensing it into, 'Who can know the mind of Heaven? Only the sage can do so.'

74. 1. The people do not fear death; to what purpose is it to (try to) frighten them with death? If the people were always in awe of death, and I could always seize those who do wrong, and put them to death, who would dare to do wrong?

2. There is always One who presides over the infliction of death. He who would inflict death in the room of him who so presides over it may be described as hewing wood instead of a great carpenter. Seldom is it that he who undertakes the hewing, instead of the great carpenter, does not cut his own hands!

制 惑, 'Restraining Delusion.' The chapter sets forth the inefficiency of capital punishment, and warns rulers against the infliction of it. Who is it that superintends the infliction of death? The answer of Ho-shang Kung is very clear:—'It is Heaven, which, dwelling on high and ruling all beneath, takes note of the transgressions of men.' There is a slight variation in the readings of the second sentence of par. 2 in the texts of Ho-shang Kung and Wang Pî, and the reading adopted by ʒiâo Hung differs a little from them both; but the meaning is the same in them all.

This chapter and the next are rightly joined on to the preceding by Wû *K*hăng.

75. 1. The people suffer from famine because of the multitude of taxes consumed by their superiors. It is through this that they suffer famine.

2. The people are difficult to govern because of the (excessive) agency of their superiors (in governing them). It is through this that they are difficult to govern.

3. The people make light of dying because of the greatness of their labours in seeking for the means of living. It is this which makes them think light of dying. Thus it is that to leave the subject of living altogether out of view is better than to set a high value on it.

貪 損, 'How Greediness Injures.' The want of the nothing-doing Tâo leads to the multiplication of exactions by the government, and to the misery of the people, so as to make them think lightly of death. The chapter is a warning for both rulers and people.

It is not easy to determine whether rulers, or people, or both, are intended in the concluding sentence of par. 2.

76. 1. Man at his birth is supple and weak; at his death, firm and strong. (So it is with) all things. Trees and plants, in their early growth, are soft and brittle; at their death, dry and withered.

2. Thus it is that firmness and strength are the concomitants of death; softness and weakness, the concomitants of life.

3. Hence he who (relies on) the strength of his forces does not conquer; and a tree which is strong will fill the out-stretched arms, (and thereby invites the feller.)

4. Therefore the place of what is firm and strong is below, and that of what is soft and weak is above.

戒 强, 'A Warning against (trusting in) Strength.' To trust in one's force is contrary to the Tâo, whose strength is more in weakness and humility.

In par. 1 the two characters which I have rendered by

'(so it is with) all things' are found in the texts of both
Ho-shang Kung and Wang Pî, but Wû Khăng and Ȝiâo
Hung both reject them.   I should also have neglected
them, but they are also found in Liû Hsiang's Shwo Wăn
(X, 4 a), with all the rest of pars. 1 and 2, as from Lâo-ȝze.
They are an anakoluthon, such as is elsewhere found in
our King; e.g. 天 下 之 牝 in ch. 21, par. 2.

The 'above' and 'below' in par. 4 seem to be merely
a play on the words, as capable of meaning 'more and less
honourable.'

77. 1. May not the Way (or Tâo) of Heaven be
compared to the (method of) bending a bow?   The
(part of the bow) which was high is brought low,
and what was low is raised up.   (So Heaven) diminishes where there is superabundance, and supple-
ments where there is deficiency.

2. It is the Way of Heaven to diminish superabundance, and to supplement deficiency.   It is not
so with the way of man.   He takes away from those
who have not enough to add to his own superabundance.

3. Who can take his own superabundance and
therewith serve all under heaven?   Only he who is
in possession of the Tâo!

4. Therefore the (ruling) sage acts without claiming the results as his; he achieves his merit and
does not rest (arrogantly) in it :—he does not wish
to display his superiority.

天 道, 'The Way of Heaven;' but the chapter contrasts
that way, unselfish and magnanimous, with the way of
man, selfish and contracted, and illustrates the point by the
method of stringing a bow.   This must be seen as it is
done in China fully to understand the illustration.   I have
known great athletes in this country tasked to the utmost

of their strength to adjust and bend a large Chinese bow from Peking.

The 'sage' of par. 4 is the 'King' of ch. 25. Compare what is said of him with ch. 2, par. 4, et al.

78. 1. There is nothing in the world more soft and weak than water, and yet for attacking things that are firm and strong there is nothing that can take precedence of it;—for there is nothing (so effectual) for which it can be changed.

2. Every one in the world knows that the soft overcomes the hard, and the weak the strong, but no one is able to carry it out in practice.

3. Therefore a sage has said,

' He who accepts his state's reproach,
      Is hailed therefore its altars' lord;
To him who bears men's direful woes
      They all the name of King accord.'

4. Words that are strictly true seem to be para-doxical.

任 信, 'Things to be Believed.' It is difficult to give a short and appropriate translation of this title. The chapter shows how the most unlikely results follow from action according to the Tâo.

Par. 1. Water was Lâo-ȝze's favourite emblem of the Tâo. Compare chapters 8, 66, et al.

Par. 2. Compare ch. 36, par. 2.

Par. 3. Of course we do not know who the sage was from whom Lâo-ȝze got the lines of this paragraph. They may suggest to some readers the lines of Burns, as they have done to me :—

' The honest man, though e'er so poor,
      Is king o' men for a' that.'

But the Tâoist of Lâo-ȝze is a higher ideal than Burns's honest man.

Par. 4 is separated from this chapter, and made to begin the next by Wû *Kh*ăng.

79. 1. When a reconciliation is effected (between two parties) after a great animosity, there is sure to be a grudge remaining (in the mind of the one who was wrong).   And how can this be beneficial (to the other)?

2. Therefore (to guard against this), the sage keeps the left-hand portion of the record of the engagement, and does not insist on the (speedy) fulfilment of it by the other party. (So), he who has the attributes (of the Tâo) regards (only) the conditions of the engagement, while he who has not those attributes regards only the conditions favourable to himself.

3. In the Way of Heaven, there is no partiality of love ; it is always on the side of the good man.

任 契, 'Adherence to Bond or Covenant.' The chapter shows, but by no means clearly, how he who holds fast to the Tâo will be better off in the end than he who will rather try to secure his own interests.

Par. 1 presents us with a case which the statements of the chapter are intended to meet :—two disputants, one good, and the other bad ; the latter, though apparently reconciled, still retaining a grudge, and ready to wreak his dissatisfaction, when he has an opportunity. The 爲 ='for,' 'for the good of.'

Par. 2 is intended to solve the question. The terms of a contract or agreement were inscribed on a slip of wood, which was then divided into two ; each party having one half of it. At the settlement, if the halves perfectly fitted to each other, it was carried through. The one who had the right in the dispute has his part of the agreement, but does not insist on it, and is forbearing ; the other insists on the conditions being even now altered in his favour. The characters by which this last case is expressed, are very enigmatical, having reference to the satisfaction of the government dues of Lâo-ʒze's time,—a subject into which it would take much space to go.

Par. 3 decides the question by the action of Heaven, which is only another name for the course of the Tâo.

80. 1. In a little state with a small population, I would so order it, that, though there were individuals with the abilities of ten or a hundred men, there should be no employment of them; I would make the people, while looking on death as a grievous thing, yet not remove elsewhere (to avoid it).

2. Though they had boats and carriages, they should have no occasion to ride in them; though they had buff coats and sharp weapons, they should have no occasion to don or use them.

3. I would make the people return to the use of knotted cords (instead of the written characters).

4. They should think their (coarse) food sweet; their (plain) clothes beautiful; their (poor) dwellings places of rest; and their common (simple) ways sources of enjoyment.

5. There should be a neighbouring state within sight, and the voices of the fowls and dogs should be heard all the way from it to us, but I would make the people to old age, even to death, not have any intercourse with it.

獨 立, 'Standing Alone.' The chapter sets forth what Lâo-ʒze conceived the ancient government of simplicity was, and what he would have government in all time to be. He does not use the personal pronoun 'I' as the subject of the thrice-recurring 使, but it is most natural to suppose that he is himself that subject; and he modestly supposes himself in charge of a little state and a small

population.   The reader can judge for himself of the consummation that would be arrived at; — a pcople rude
and uninstructed, using quippos, abstaining from war and
all travelling, kept aloof from intercourse even with their
neighbours, and without the appliances of what we call
civilisation.

The text is nearly all found in Sze-mâ *Kh*ien and
*K*wang-ʒze.   The first member of par. 1, however, is very
puzzling.   The old Jesuit translators, Julien, Chalmers,
and V. von Strauss, all differ in their views of it.   Wû
*Kh*ăng and ʒiâo Hung take what I have now rendered by
'abilities,' as meaning 'implements of agriculture,' but their
view is based on a custom of the Han dynasty, which is not
remote enough for the purpose, and on the suppression,
after Wang Pî, of a 人 in Ho ohang Kung's text.

81. 1. Sincere words are not fine; fine words are
not sincere.   Those who are skilled (in the Tâo)
do not dispute (about it); the disputatious are not
skilled in it.   Those who know (the Tâo) are not
extensively learned; the extensively learned do not
know it.

2. The sage does not accumulate (for himself).
The more that he expends for others, the more does
he possess of his own; the more that he gives to
others, the more does he have himself.

3. With all the sharpness of the Way of Heaven,
it injures not; with all the doing in the way of the
sage he does not strive.

顯 質, 'The Manifestation of Simplicity.'   The chapter
shows how quietly and effectively the Tâo proceeds, and
by contraries in a way that only the master of it can
understand.   The author, says Wû *Kh*ăng, 'sums up in
this the subject-matter of the two Parts of his Treatise,
showing that in all its five thousand characters, there is
nothing beyond what is here said.'

Par. 2 suggests to Dr. Chalmers the well-known lines of Bunyan as an analogue of it :—

'A man there was, though some did count him mad,
    The more he gave away, the more he had.'

Wû K*h*ăng brings together two sentences from *K*wang-ʒze (XXXIII, 21 b, 22 a), written evidently with the characters of this text in mind, which, as from a Tâoist mint, are a still better analogue, and I venture to put them into rhyme :—

'Amassing but to him a sense of need betrays;
    He hoards not, and thereby his affluence displays.'

I have paused long over the first pair of contraries in par. 3 (利 and 害). Those two characters primarily mean 'sharpness' and 'wounding by cutting;' they are also often used in the sense of 'being beneficial,' and 'being injurious;' — 'contraries,' both of them. Which 'contrary' had Lâo-ʒze in mind? I must think the former, though differing in this from all previous translators. The Jesuit version is, 'Celestis Tâo natura ditat omnes, nemini nocet;' Julien's, 'Il est utile aux êtres, et ne leur nuit point;' Chalmers's, 'Benefits and does not injure;' and V. von Strauss's, 'Des Himmels Weise ist wolthun und nicht beschädigen.'

THE

WRITINGS OF *K*WANG-ȜZE.

THE
WRITINGS OF *K*WANG-ЗZE.

INTRODUCTION.

BRIEF NOTICES OF THE DIFFERENT BOOKS.

BOOK I. HSIÂO-YÂO YÛ.

The three characters which form the title of this Book
have all of them the ideagram 足 (*K*o), which gives the
idea, as the Shwo Wăn explains it, of 'now walking, now
halting.' We might render the title by 'Sauntering or
Rambling at Ease;' but it is the untroubled enjoyment of
the mind which the author has in view. And this enjoyment is secured by the Tâo, though that character does
not once occur in the Book. *K*wang-ȝze illustrates his
thesis first by the cases of creatures, the largest and the
smallest, showing that however different they may be in
size, they should not pass judgment on one another, but
may equally find their happiness in the Tâo. From this
he advances to men, and from the cases of Yung-ȝze and
Lieh-ȝze proceeds to that of one who finds his enjoyment
in himself, independent of every other being or instru-
mentality; and we have the three important definitions
of the accomplished Tâoist, as 'the Perfect Man,' 'the
Spirit-like Man,' and 'the Sagely Man.' Those definitions
are then illustrated ;—the third in Yâo and Hsü Yû, and the
second in the conversation between *K*ien Wû and Lien Shû.
The description given in this conversation of the spirit-
like man is very startling, and contains statements that are
true only of Him who is a 'Spirit,' 'the Blessed and only
Potentate,' 'Who covereth Himself with light as with
a garment, Who stretcheth out the heavens as a curtain,

Who layeth the beams of His chambers in the waters, Who
maketh the clouds His chariot, Who walketh on the wings
of the wind,' 'Who rideth on a cherub,' 'Who inhabiteth
eternity.' The most imaginative and metaphorical expressions in the Tâo Teh King about the power of the
possessor of the Tâo are tame, compared with the language
of our author. I call attention to it here, as he often uses
the same extravagant style. There follows an illustration
of 'the Perfect Man,' which is comparatively feeble, and
part of it, so far as I can see, inappropriate, though Lin
Hsî-kung says that all other interpretations of the sentences are ridiculous.

In the seventh and last paragraph we have two illustrations that nothing is really useless, if only used Tâo-
istically; 'to the same effect,' says Ʒiâo Hung, 'as
Confucius in the Analects, XVII, ii.' They hang loosely,
however, from what precedes.

An old view of the Book was that Kwang-ʒze intended
himself by the great phăng, 'which,' says Lû Shû-kih,
'is wide of the mark.'

BOOK II. KHî WÛ LUN.

Mr. Balfour has translated this title by 'Essay on the
Uniformity of All Things;' and, the subject of the Book
being thus misconceived, his translation of it could not
fail to be very incorrect. The Chinese critics, I may say
without exception, construe the title as I have done. The
second and third characters, Wû Lun, are taken together,
and mean 'Discussions about Things,' equivalent to our
'Controversies.' They are under the government of the
first character Khî, used as a verb, with the signification
of 'Harmonising,' or 'Adjusting.' Let me illustrate this
by condensing a passage from the 'Supplementary Commentary of a Mr. Kang, a sub-secretary of the Imperial
Chancery,' of the Ming dynasty (張 學 士 補 註). He
says, 'What Kwang-ʒze calls "Discussions about Things"
has reference to the various branches of the numerous
schools, each of which has its own views, conflicting with

the views of the others.'   He goes on to show that if they would only adopt the method pointed out by *K*wang-ȝze, 'their controversies would be adjusted (物 論 齊),' now using the first *Kh*î in the passive voice.

This then was the theme of our author in this Book.   It must be left for the reader to discover from the translation how he pursues it.   I pointed out a peculiarity in the former Book, that though the idea of the Tâo underlies it all, the term itself is never allowed to appear.   Not only does the same idea underlie this Book, but the name is frequently employed.   The Tâo is the panacea for the evils of controversy, the solvent through the use of which the different views of men may be made to disappear.

That the Tâo is not a Personal name in the conception of *K*wang-ȝze is seen in several passages.   We have not to go beyond the phenomena of nature to discover the reason of their being what they are ; nor have we to go beyond the bigoted egoism and vaingloriousness of controversialists to find the explanation of their discussions, various as these are, and confounding like the sounds of the wind among the trees of a forest.   To man, neither in nature nor in the sphere of knowledge, is there any other 'Heaven' but what belongs to his own mind.   That is his only 'True Ruler.'   If there be any other, we do not see His form, nor any traces of His acting.   Things come about in their proper course.   We cannot advance any proof of Creation. Whether we assume that there was something 'in the beginning' or nothing, we are equally landed in contra-diction and absurdity.   Let us stop at the limit of what we know, and not try to advance a step beyond it.

Towards the end of the Book our author's agnosticism seems to reach its farthest point.   All human experience is spoken of as a dream or as 'illusion.'   He who calls another a dreamer does not know that he is not dreaming himself.   One and another commentator discover in such utterances something very like the Buddhist doctrine that all life is but so much illusion (象).   This notion has its consummation in the story with which the Book concludes.

*K*wang-ʒze had dreamt that he was a butterfly. When he awoke, and was himself again, he did not know whether he, *K*wang *K*âu, had been dreaming that he was a butterfly, or was now a butterfly dreaming that it was *K*wang *K*âu. And yet he adds that there must be a difference between *K*âu and a butterfly, but he does not say what that difference is. But had he ever dreamt that he was a butterfly, so as to lose the consciousness of his personal identity as *K*wang *K*âu? I do not think so. One may, perhaps, lose that consciousness in the state of insanity; but the language of Young is not sufficiently guarded when he writes of

'Dreams, where thought, in fancy's maze, runs mad.'

When dreaming, our thoughts are not conditioned by the categories of time and space; but the conviction of our identity is never lost.

BOOK III.   YANG SHANG *K*Û.

'The Lord of Life' is the Tâo. It is to this that we are indebted for the origin of life and for the preservation of it. Though not a Personal Being, it is here spoken of as if it were,—'the Lord of Life;' just as in the preceding Book it is made to appear as 'a True Governor,' and 'a True Ruler.' But how can we nourish the Tâo? The reply is, By avoiding all striving to do so; by a passionless, unstraining performance of what we have to do in our position in life; simply allowing the Tâo to guide and nourish us, without doing anything to please ourselves or to counteract the tendency of our being to decay and death.

Par. 1 exhibits the injury arising from not thus nourishing the life, and sets forth the rule we are to pursue.

Par. 2 illustrates the observance of the rule by the perfect skill with which the cook of the ruler Wăn-hui of Wei cut up the oxen for his employer without trouble to himself, or injury to his knife.

Par. 3 illustrates the result of a neglect of one of the cautions in par. 1 to a certain master of the Left, who had brought on himself dismemberment in the loss of one of his feet.

Par. 4 shows how even Lâo-ʒze had failed in nourishing 'the Lord of Life' by neglecting the other caution, and allowing in his good-doing an admixture of human feeling, which produced in his disciples a regard for him that was inconsistent with the nature of the Tâo, and made them wail for him excessively on his death. This is the most remarkable portion of the Book, and it is followed by a sentence which implies that the existence of man's spirit continues after death has taken place. His body is intended by the 'faggots' that are consumed by the fire. That fire represents the spirit which may be transferred elsewhere.

Some commentators dwell on the analogy between this and the Buddhistic transrotation of births; which latter teaching, however, they do not seem to understand. Others say that 'the nourishment of the Lord of Life' is simply acting as Yü did when he conveyed away the flooded waters 'by doing that which gave him no trouble;'—see Mencius, IV, ii, 26.

In Kwang-ʒze there are various other stories of the same character as that about king Wăn-hui's cook,—e. g. XIX, 3 and XXII, 9. They are instances of the dexterity acquired by habit, and should hardly be pressed into the service of the doctrine of the Tâo.

BOOK IV.   ZĂN KIEN SHIH.

A man has his place among other men in the world; he is a member, while he lives, of the body of humanity. And as he has his place in society, so also he has his special duties to discharge, according to his position, and his relation to others. Tâoist writers refer to this Book as a proof of the practical character of the writings of Kwang-ʒze.

They are right to a certain extent in doing so; but the cases of relationship which are exhibited and prescribed for are of so peculiar a character, that the Book is of little value as a directory of human conduct and duty. In the first two paragraphs we have the case of Yen Hui, who wishes to go to Wei, and try to reform the character and government of its oppressive ruler; in the third and fourth, that of the duke of Sheh, who has been entrusted by the king of *Kh*û with a difficult mission to the court of *Kh*î, which is occasioning him much anxiety and apprehension; and in the fifth, that of a Yen Ho, who is about to undertake the office of teacher to the son of duke Ling of Wei, a young man with a very bad natural disposition. The other four paragraphs do not seem to come in naturally after these three cases, being occupied with two immense and wonderful trees, the case of a poor deformed cripple, and the lecture for the benefit of Confucius by ' the madman of *Kh*û.' In all these last paragraphs, the theme is the usefulness, to the party himself at least, of being of no use.

Confucius is the principal speaker in the first four paragraphs. In what he says to Yen Hui and the duke of Sheh there is much that is shrewd and good; but we prefer the practical style of his teachings, as related by his own disciples in the Confucian Analects. Possibly, it was the object of *K*wang-ȝze to exhibit his teaching, as containing, without his being aware of it, much of the mystical character of the Tâoistic system. His conversation with the duke of Sheh, however, is less obnoxious to this charge than what he is made to say to Yen Hui. The adviser of Yen Ho is a *K*ü Po-yü, a disciple of Confucius, who still has a place in the sage's temples.

In the conclusion, the Tâoism of our author comes out in contrast with the methods of Confucius. His object in the whole treatise, perhaps, was to show how 'the doing nothing, and yet thereby doing everything,' was the method to be pursued in all the intercourses of society.

BOOK V. TEH *K*HUNG FÛ.

The fû (符) consisted in the earliest times of two slips of bamboo made with certain marks, so as to fit to each other exactly, and held by the two parties to any agreement or covenant. By the production and comparison of the slips, the parties verified their mutual relation ; and the claim of the one and the obligation of the other were sufficiently established. 'Seal' seems the best translation of the character in this title.

By 'virtue' (德) we must understand the characteristics of the Tâo. Where those existed in their full proportions in any individual, there was sure to be the evidence or proof of them in the influence which he exerted in all his intercourse with other men ; and the illustration of this is the subject of this Book, in all its five paragraphs. That influence is the 'Seal' set on him, proving him to be a true child of the Tâo.

The heroes, as I may call them, of the first three paragraphs are all men who had lost their feet, having been reduced to that condition as a punishment, just or unjust, of certain offences ; and those of the last two are distinguished by their extraordinary ugliness or disgusting deformity. But neither the loss of their feet nor their deformities trouble the serenity of their own minds, or interfere with the effects of their teaching and character upon others; so superior is their virtue to the deficiencies in their outward appearance.

Various brief descriptions of the Tâo are interspersed in the Book. The most remarkable of them are those in par. 1, where it appears as 'that in which there is no element of falsehood,' and as 'the author of all the Changes or Transformations' in the world. The sentences where these occur are thus translated by Mr. Balfour :—' He seeks to know Him in whom is nothing false. He would not be affected by the instability of creation ; even if his life were involved in the general destruction, he would yet hold firmly to his faith (in God).' And he observes in a

note, that the first short sentence ' is explained by the
commentators as referring to *K*ăn 3âi (眞 宰), the term
used by the Tâoist school for God.' But we met with
that name and synonyms of it in Book II, par. 2, as appellations of the Tâo, coupled with the denial of its personality. *K*ăn 3âi, ' the True Governor or Lord,' may
be used as a designation for god or God, but the Tâoist
school denies the existence of a Personal Being, to whom
we are accustomed to apply that name.

Hui-3ze, the sophist and friend of *K*wang-3ze, is introduced in the conclusion as disputing with him the propriety
of his representing the Master of the Tâo as being still 'a
man ;' and is beaten down by him with a repetition of his
assertions, and a reference to some of Hui-3ze's well-known
peculiarities. What would *K*wang-3ze have said, if his
opponent had affirmed that his instances were all imaginary,
and that no man had ever appeared who could appeal to
his possession of such a ' seal ' to his virtues and influence
as he described?

Lû Fang-wăng compares with the tenor of this Book
what we find in Mencius, VII, i, 21, about the nature of
the superior man. The analogy between them, however, is
very faint and incomplete.

BOOK VI. TÂ 3UNG SHIH.

So I translate the title of this Book, taking 3ung as a
verb, and 3ung Shih as =' The Master who is Honoured.'
Some critics take 3ung in the sense of ' Originator,' in
which it is employed in the Tâo Teh *K*ing, lxx, 2. Which-
ever rendering be adopted, there is no doubt that the title
is intended to be a designation of the Tâo ; and no one of
our author's Books is more important for the understanding
of his system of thought.

The key to it is found in the first of its fifteen paragraphs. There are in man two elements ;—the Heavenly
or Tâoistic, and the human. The disciple of the Tâo,
recognising them both, cultivates what he knows as a man

so as to become entirely conformed to the action of the Tâo, and submissive in all the most painful experiences in his lot, which is entirely ordered by it. A seal will be set on the wisdom of this course hereafter, when he has completed the period of his existence on earth, and returns to the state of non-existence, from which the Tâo called him to be born as a man. In the meantime he may attain to be the True man possessing the True knowledge.

Our author then proceeds to give his readers in five paragraphs his idea of the True Man. Mr. Balfour says that this name is to be understood 'in the esoteric sense, the partaking of the essence of divinity,' and he translates it by 'the Divine Man.' But we have no right to introduce here the terms 'divine' and 'divinity.' Nan-hwâi (VII, 5 b) gives a short definition of the name which is more to the point :—'What we call "the True Man" is one whose nature is in agreement with the Tâo (所 謂 眞 人 者 性 合 于 道 也;' and the commentator adds in a note, 'Such men as Fû-hsî, Hwang-Tî, and Lâo Tan.' The Khang-hsî dictionary commences its account of the character 眞 or 'True' by a definition of the True Man taken from the Shwo Wǎn as a 仙 人, 'a recluse of the mountain, whose bodily form has been changed, and who ascends to heaven;' but when that earliest dictionary was made, Tâoism had entered into a new phase, different from what it had in the time of our author. The most prominent characteristic of the True Man is that he is free from all exercise of thought and purpose, a being entirely passive in the hands of the Tâo. In par. 3 seven men are mentioned, good and worthy men, but inferior to the True.

Having said what he had to say of the True Man, *K*wang-ʒze comes in the seventh paragraph to speak directly of the Tâo itself, and describes it with many wonderful predicates which exalt it above our idea of God ;—a concept and not a personality. He concludes by mentioning a number of ancient personages who had got the Tâo, and by it wrought wonders, beginning with a Shih-wei, who preceded Fû-hsî, and ending with Fû Yüeh, the minister of

Wû-ting, in the fourteenth century B.C., and who finally became a star in the eastern portion of the zodiac. Phăng 3û
is also mentioned as living, through his possession of the Tâo,
from the twenty-third century B.C. to the seventh or later.
The sun and moon and the constellation of the Great Bear
are also mentioned as its possessors, and the fabulous Being
called the Mother of the Western King. The whole passage
is perplexing to the reader to the last degree.

The remaining paragraphs are mostly occupied with
instances of learning the Tâo, and of its effects in making
men superior to the infirmities of age and the most terrible deformities of person and calamities of penury; as
Tranquillity' under all that might seem most calculated to
disturb it. Very strange is the attempt at the conclusion of
par. 8 apparently to trace the genesis of the knowledge of
the Tâo. Confucius is introduced repeatedly as the ex-
pounder of Tâoism, and made to praise it as the ne plus
ultra of human attainment.

BOOK VII. YING TÎ WANG.

The first of the three characters in this title renders the
translation of it somewhat perplexing. Ying has different
meanings according as it is read in the first tone or in the
third. In the first tone it is the symbol of what is right,
or should be ; in the third tone of answering or responding
to. I prefer to take it here in the first tone. As Kwo
Hsiang says, ' One who is free from mind or purpose of his
own, and loves men to become transformed of themselves,
is fit to be a Ruler or a King,' and as 3hui Kwan, another
early commentator, says, ' He whose teaching is that which
is without words, and makes men in the world act as if
they were oxen or horses, is fit to be a Ruler or a King.'
This then is the object of the Book—to describe that
government which exhibits the Tâo equally in the rulers
and the ruled, the world of men all happy and good
without purpose or effort.

It consists of seven paragraphs. The first shows us the
model ruler in him of the line of Thâi, whom I have not

succeeded in identifying. The second shows us men under
such a rule, uncontrolled and safe like the bird that flies
high beyond the reach of the archer, and the mouse secure
in its deep hole from its pursuers. The teacher in this
portion is *Kh*ieh-yü, known in the Confucian school as ' the
madman of *Khû*,' and he delivers his lesson in opposition
to the heresy of a *Z*äh-*k*ung Shih, or 'Noon Beginning.'
In the third paragraph the speakers are ' a nameless man,'
and a Thien Kăn, or ' Heaven Root.' In the fourth paragraph Lâo-ʒze himself appears upon the stage, and lectures
a Yang ʒze-*k*ü, the Yang *K*û of Mencius. He concludes by
saying that ' where the intelligent kings took their stand
could not be fathomed, and they found their enjoyment in
(the realm of) nonentity.'

The fifth paragraph is longer, and tells us of the defeat
of a wizard, a physiognomist in *K*ăng, by Hû-ʒze, the
master of the philosopher Lieh-ʒze, who is thereby delivered
from the glamour which the cheat was throwing round him.
I confess to not being able to understand the various processes by which Hû-ʒze foils the wizard and makes him run
away. The whole story is told, and at greater length, in
the second book of the collection ascribed to Lieh-ʒze, and
the curious student may like to look at the translation of
that work by Mr. Ernst Faber (Der Naturalismus bei
den alten Chinesen sowohl nach der Seite des Panthe-
ismus als des Sensualismus, oder die Sämmtlichen Werke
des Philosophen Licius, 1877). The effect of the wizard's
defeat on Lieh-ʒze was great. He returned in great humility to his house, and did not go out of it for three years.
He did the cooking for his wife, and fed the pigs as if he
were feeding men. He returned to pure simplicity, and
therein continued to the end of his life. But I do not see
the connexion between this narrative and the government
of the Rulers and Kings.

The sixth paragraph is a homily by our author himself
on ' non-action.' It contains a good simile, comparing the
mind of the perfect man to a mirror, which reflects faith-
fully what comes before it, but does not retain any image
of it, when the mind is gone.

The last paragraph is an ingenious and interesting allegory relating how the gods of the southern and northern seas brought Chaos to an end by boring holes in him. Thereby they destroyed the primal simplicity, and according to Tâoism did Chaos an injury! On the whole I do not think that this Book, with which the more finished essays of *K*wang-ʒze come to an end, is so successful as those that precede it.

Book VIII. Phien Mâu.

This Book brings us to the Second Part of the writings of our author, embracing in all fifteen Books. Of the most important difference between the Books of the First and the other Parts some account has been given in the Introductory Chapter. We have here to do only with the different character of their titles. Those of the seven preceding Books are so many theses, and are believed to have been prefixed to them by *K*wang-ʒze himself; those of this Book and the others that follow are believed to have been prefixed by Kwo Hsiang, and consist of two or three characters taken from the beginning, or near the beginning of the several Books, after the fashion of the names of the Books in the Confucian Analects, in the works of Mencius, and in our Hebrew Scriptures. Books VIII to XIII are considered to be supplementary to VII by Aû-yang Hsiû.

The title of this eighth Book, Phien Mâu, has been rendered by Mr. Balfour, after Dr. Williams, 'Double Thumbs.' But the Mâu, which may mean either the Thumb or the Great Toe, must be taken in the latter sense, being distinguished in this paragraph and elsewhere from *K*ih, ' a finger,' and expressly specified also as belonging to the foot. The character phien, as used here, is defined in the Khang-hsî dictionary as ' anything additional growing out as an appendage or excrescence, a growing out at the side.' This would seem to justify the translation of it by 'double.' But in paragraph 3, while the extra finger increases the number of the fingers, this growth on the foot is represented as diminishing the number of the toes. I must consider the phien therefore as descriptive of an appendage by which the great toe was united to one or all of the other toes, and can think of no better rendering of the title than what I have given.   It is told in the 3o *K*wan (twenty-third year of duke Hsî) that the famous duke Wăn of 3in had phien hsieh, that is, that his ribs presented the appearance of forming one bone.   So much for the title.

The subject-matter of the Book seems strange to us ;— that, according to the Tâo, benevolence and righteousness are not natural growths of humanity, but excrescences on it, like the extra finger on the hand, and the membranous web of the toes.   The weakness of the Tâoistic system begins to appear.   *K*wang-3ze's arguments in support of his position must be pronounced very feeble.   The ancient Shun is introduced as the first who called in the two great virtues to distort and vex the world, keeping society for more than a thousand years in a state of uneasy excitement.   Of course he assumes that prior to Shun, he does not say for how long a time (and in other places he makes decay to have begun earlier), the world had been in a state of paradisiacal innocence and simplicity, under the guidance of the Tâo, untroubled by any consideration of what was right and what was wrong, men passively allowing their nature to have its quiet development, and happy in that condition.   All culture of art or music is wrong, and so it is wrong and injurious to be striving to manifest benevolence and to maintain righteousness.

He especially singles out two men, one of the twelfth century B.C., the famous Po-î, who died of hunger rather than acknowledge the dynasty of *K*âu ; and one of a more recent age, the robber Shih, a great leader of brigands, who brought himself by his deeds to an untimely end ; and he sees nothing to choose between them.   We must give our judgment for the teaching of Confucianism in preference to that of Tâoism, if our author can be regarded as a fair expositor of the latter.   He is ingenious in his statements and illustrations, but he was, like his master Lâo-3ze, only a dreamer.

BOOK IX. MÂ THÎ.

'Horses' and 'Hoofs' are the first two characters of the
Text, standing there in the relation of regent and regimen.
The account of the teaching of the Book given by Lin Hsî-
*k*ung is so concise that I will avail myself of it. He says :—

'Governing men is like governing horses. They may
be governed in such a way as shall be injurious to them,
just as Po-lâo governed the horse;—contrary to its true
nature. His method was not different from that of
the (first) potter and carpenter in dealing with clay and
wood ;—contrary to the nature of those substances. Notwithstanding this, one age after another has celebrated
the skill of those parties ; — not knowing what it is
that constitutes the good and skilful government of
men. Such government simply requires that men be
made to fulfil their regular constant nature,—the qualities which they all possess in common, with which they
are constituted by Heaven, and then be left to themselves.
It was this which constituted the age of perfect virtue ;
but when the sages insisted on the practice of benevolence, righteousness, ceremonies, and music, then the
people began to be without that perfect virtue. Not that
they were in themselves different from what they had been,
but those practices do not really belong to their regular
nature ; they arose from their neglecting the characteristics
of the Tâo, and abandoning their natural constitution ;—
it was the case of the skilful artisan cutting and hacking
his raw materials in order to form vessels from them.
There is no ground for doubting that Po-lâo's management
of horses gave them that knowledge with which they went
on to play the part of thieves, or that it was the sages'
government of the people which made them devote themselves to the pursuit of gain ;—it is impossible to deny the
error of those sages.

'There is but one idea in the Book from the beginning
to the end ;—it is an amplification of the expression in the
preceding Book that " all men have their regular and con-

stant constitution," and is the most easily construed of all *K*wang-ȝze's compositions. In consequence, however, of the wonderful touches of his pencil in describing the sympathy between men and other creatures in their primal state, some have imagined that there is a waste and embellishment of language, and doubted whether the Book is really his own, but thought it was written by some one in imitation of his style. I apprehend that no other hand would easily have attained to such a mastery of that style.'

There is no possibility of adjudicating definitely on the suspicion of the genuineness of the Book thus expressed in Hsî-*k*ung's concluding remarks. The same suspicion arose in my own mind in the process of translation. My surprise continues that our author did not perceive the absurdity of his notions of the primal state of men, and of his condemnation of the sages.

BOOK X. *KH*Ü *KH*IEH.

It is observed by the commentator Kwei *K*ăn-*kh*üan that one idea runs through this Book :—that the most sage and wise men have ministered to theft and robbery, and that, if there were an end of sageness and wisdom, the world would be at rest. Between it and the previous Book there is a general agreement in argument and object, but in this the author expresses himself with greater vehemence, and almost goes to excess in his denunciation of the institutions of the sages.

The reader will agree with these accounts of the Book. *K*wang-ȝze at times becomes weak in his attempts to establish his points. To my mind the most interesting portions of this Book and the last one are the full statements which we have in them of the happy state of men when the Tâo maintained its undisputed sway in the world, and the names of many of the early Tâoistic sovereigns. How can we suppose that anything would be gained by a return to the condition of primitive innocence and simplicity ? The antagonism between Tâoism and Confucianism comes out in this Book very decidedly.

The title of the Book is taken from two characters in the first clause of the first paragraph.

BOOK XI. 3âi Yû.

The two characters of the title are taken from the first sentence of the Text, but they express the subject of the Book more fully than the other titles in this Part do, and almost entitle it to a place in Part I. It is not easy to translate them, and Mr. Balfour renders them by ' Leniency towards Faults,' probably construing 3âi as equivalent to our preposition 'in,' which it often is. But *K*wang-ʒze uses both 3âi and Yû as verbs, or blends them together, the chief force of the binomial compound being derived from the significance of the 3âi. 3âi is defined by 3hun (存), which gives the idea of 'preserving' or 'keeping intact,' and Yû by Khwan (寬), 'being indulgent' or 'forbearing.' The two characters are afterwards exchanged for other two, wû wei (無 爲), 'doing nothing,' 'inaction,' a grand characteristic of the Tâo.

The following summary of the Book is taken from Hsüan Ying's explanations of our author:—'The two characters 3âi Yû express the subject-matter of the Book, and "governing" points out the opposite error as the disease into which men are prone to fall. Let men be, and the tendencies of their nature will be at rest, and there will be no necessity for governing the world. Try to govern it, and the world will be full of trouble; and men will not be able to rest in the tendencies of their nature. These are the subjects of the first two paragraphs.

' In the third paragraph we have the erroneous view of 3hui *Kh*ü that by government it was possible to make men's minds good. He did not know that governing was a disturbing meddling with the minds of men; and how Lâo-ʒze set forth the evil of such government, going on till it be irretrievable. This long paragraph vigorously attacks the injury done by governing.

' In the fourth paragraph, when Hwang-Tî questions

Kwang *K*hăng-ʒze, the latter sets aside his inquiry about the government of the world, and tells him about the government of himself; and in the fifth, when Yün *K*iang asks Hung Mung about governing men, the latter tells him about the nourishing of the heart.   These two great paragraphs set forth clearly the subtlest points in the policy of Let-a-be.   Truly it is not an empty name.

'In the two last paragraphs, *K*wang in his own words and way sets forth, now by affirmation, and now by negation, the meaning of all that precedes.'

This summary of the Book will assist the reader in understanding it.   For other remarks that will be helpful, I must refer him to the notes appended to the Text.   The Book is not easy to understand or to translate ; and a remark found in the *K*iâ-*kh*ing edition of 'the Ten Philosophers,' by Lû Hsiû-fû, who died in 1279, was welcome to me, ' If you cannot understand one or two sentences of *K*wang-ʒze, it does not matter.'

BOOK XII.   THIEN TÎ.

The first two characters of the Book are adopted as its name ;—Thien Tî, 'Heaven and Earth.'   These are employed, not so much as the two greatest material forms in the universe, but as the Great Powers whose influences extend to all below and upon them.   Silently and effectively, with entire spontaneity, their influence goes forth, and a rule and pattern is thus given to those on whom the business of the government of the world devolves.   The one character 'Heaven' is employed throughout the Book as the denomination of this purposeless spontaneity which yet is so powerful.

Lû Shû-*k*ih says :—' This Book also sets forth clearly how the rulers of the world ought simply to act in accordance with the spontaneity of the virtue of Heaven ; abjuring sageness and putting away knowledge; and doing nothing: —in this way the Tâo or proper Method of Government will be attained to.   As to the coercive methods of Mo Tî and Hui-ȝze, they only serve to distress those who follow them.'

This object of the Book appears, more or less distinctly, in most of the illustrative paragraphs; though, as has been pointed out in the notes upon it, several of them must be considered to be spurious. Paragraphs 6, 7, and 11 are thus called in question, and, as most readers will feel, with reason. From 13 to the end, the paragraphs are held to be one long paragraph where Kwang-ȝze introduces his own reflections in an unusual style; but the genuineness of the whole, so far as I have observed, has not been called in question.

Book XIII. Thien Tâo.

'Thien Tâo,' the first two characters of the first paragraph, and prefixed to the Book as the name of it, are best translated by 'The Way of Heaven,' meaning the noiseless spontaneity, which characterises all the operations of nature, proceeding silently, yet 'perfecting all things.' As the rulers of the world attain to this same way in their government, and the sages among men attain to it in their teachings, both government and doctrine arrive at a corresponding perfection. 'The joy of Heaven' and 'the joy of Men' are both realised. There ought to be no purpose or will in the universe. 'Vacancy, stillness, placidity, tastelessness, quietude, silence, and non-action; this is the perfection of the Tâo and its characteristics.'

Our author dwells especially on doing-nothing or non-action as the subject-matter of the Book. But as the world is full of doing, he endeavours to make a distinction between the Ruling Powers and those subordinate to and employed by them, to whom doing or action and purpose, though still without the thought of self, are necessary; and by this distinction he seems to me to give up the peculiarity of his system, so that some of the critics, especially Aû-yang Hsiû, are obliged to confess that these portions of the Book are unlike the writing of Kwang-ȝze. Still the antagonism of Tâoism to Confucianism is very apparent throughout.   Of the illustrative paragraphs, the seventh, relating the churlish behaviour of Lâo-ʒze to Confucius, and the way in which he subsequently argues with him and snubs him, is very amusing.   The eighth paragraph, relating the interview between Lâo and Shih-*kh*ăng *Kh*î, is very strange.   The allusions in it to certain incidents and peculiarities in Lâo's domestic life make us wish that we had fuller accounts of his history; and the way in which he rates his disciple shows him as a master of the language of abuse.

The concluding paragraph about duke Hwan of *Kh*î is interesting, but I can only dimly perceive its bearing on the argument of the Book.

Book XIV.   Thien Yün.

The contrast between the movement of the heavens (天 運), and the resting of the earth (地 處), requires the translation of the characters of the title by 'The Revolution of Heaven.'   But that idea does not enter largely into the subject-matter of the Book.   'The whole,' says Hsüan Ying, 'consists of eight paragraphs, the first three of which show that under the sky there is nothing which is not dominated by the Tâo, with which the Tîs and the Kings have only to act in accordance; while the last five set forth how the Tâo is not to be found in the material forms and changes of things, but in a spirit-like energy working imperceptibly, developing and controlling all phenomena.'

I have endeavoured in the notes on the former three paragraphs to make their meaning less obscure and unconnected than it is on a first perusal.   The five illustrative paragraphs are, we may assume, all of them factitious, and can hardly be received as genuine productions of *K*wang-ʒze.   In the sixth paragraph, or at least a part of it, Lin Hsî-*k*ung acknowledges the hand of the forger, and not less unworthy of credence are in my opinion the rest of it and much of the other four paragraphs.   If they may be taken as from the hand of our author himself, he was too much devoted to his own system to hold the balance of judgment evenly between Lâo and Khung.

BOOK XV. KHO Î.

I can think of no better translation for 刻 意, the two first characters of the Book, and which appear as its title, than our ' Ingrained Ideas;' notions, that is, held as firmly as if they were cut into the substance of the mind. They do not belong to the whole Book, however, but only to the first member of the first paragraph. That paragraph describes six classes of men, only the last of which are the right followers of the Tâo ;—the Sages, from the Tâoistic point of view, who again are in the last sentence of the last paragraph identified with ' the True Men' described at length in the sixth Book. The fifth member of this first paragraph is interesting as showing how there was a class of Tâoists who cultivated the system with a view to obtain longevity by their practices in the management of the breath ; yet our author does not accord to them his full approbation, while at the same time the higher Tâoism appears in the last paragraph, as promoting longevity without the management of the breath. *Kh*û Po-hsiû, in his commentary on *K*wang-*z*ze, which was published in 1210, gives Po-î and Shû-*kh*î as instances of the first class spoken of here ; Confucius and Mencius, of the second ; Î Yin and Fû Yüeh, of the third ; *Kh*âo Fû and Hsü Yû, as instances of the fourth. Of the fifth class he gives no example, but that of Phăng 3û mentioned in it.

That which distinguishes the genuine sage, the True Man of Tâoism, is his pure simplicity in pursuing the Way, as it is seen in the operation of Heaven and Earth, and nourishing his spirit accordingly, till there ensues an ethereal amalgamation between his Way and the orderly operation of Heaven. This subject is pursued to the end of the Book. The most remarkable predicate of the spirit so trained is that in the third paragraph,—that ' Its name is the same as Tî or God;' on which none of the critics has been able to throw any satisfactory light. Balfour's version is:—'Its name is called "One with God;"' Giles's, 'Its name is then "Of God,"' the 'then' being in consequence of his view that the subject is 'man's spiritual existence before he is born into the world of mortals.' My own view of the meaning appears in my version.

Lin Hsî-*k*ung, however, calls the genuineness of the whole Book into question, and thinks it may have proceeded from the same hand as Book XIII. They have certainly one peculiarity in common;—many references to sayings which cannot be traced, but are introduced by the formula of quotation, 'Therefore, it is said.'

BOOK XVI.   SHAN HSING.

'Rectifying or Correcting the Nature' is the meaning of the title, and expresses sufficiently well the subject matter of the Book. It was written to expose the 'vulgar' learning of the time as contrary to the principles of the true Tâoism, that learning being, according to Lû Shû-*k*ih, 'the teachings of Hui-*z*ze and Kung-sun Lung.' It is to be wished that we had fuller accounts of these. But see in Book XXXIII.

Many of the critics are fond of comparing the Book with the 21st chapter of the 7th Book of Mencius, part 1,— where that philosopher sets forth 'Man's own nature as the most important thing to him, and the source of his true enjoyment,' which no one can read without admiration. But we have more sympathy with Mencius's fundamental views about our human nature, than with those of *K*wang-*z*ze and his Tâoism. Lin Hsî-*k*ung is rather inclined to doubt the genuineness of the Book. Though he admires its composition, and admits the close and compact sequence of its sentences, there is yet something about it that does not smack of *K*wang-*z*ze's style. Rather there seems to me to underlie it the antagonism of Lâo and *K*wang to the learning of the Confucian school. The only characteristic of our author which I miss, is the illustrative stories of which he is generally so profuse. In this the Book agrees with the preceding.

BOOK XVII. *K*ẖIÛ SHUI.

*K*ẖiû Shui, or 'Autumn Waters,' the first two characters of the first paragraph of this Book, are adopted as its title. Its subject, in that paragraph, however, is not so much the waters of autumn, as the greatness of the Tâo in its spontaneity, when it has obtained complete dominion over man. No illustration of the Tâo is so great a favourite with Lâo-ʒze as water, but he loved to set it forth in its quiet, onward movement, always seeking the lowest place, and always exercising a beneficent influence.   But water is here before *K*wang-ʒze in its mightiest volume,—the inundated Ho and the all but boundless magnitude of the ocean ; and as he takes occasion from those phenomena to deliver his lessons, I translate the title by 'The Floods of Autumn.'

To adopt the account of the Book given by Lû Shû-*k*ih :—' This Book,' he says, ' shows how its spontaneity is the greatest characteristic of the Tâo, and the chief thing inculcated in it is that we must not allow the human element to extinguish in our constitution the Heavenly.

' First, using the illustrations of the Ho and the Sea, our author gives us to see the Five Tîs and the Kings of the Three dynasties as only exhibiting the Tâo in a small de-gree, while its great development is not to be found in out- ward form and appliances so that it cannot be described in words, and it is difficult to find its point of commencement, which indeed appears to be impracticable, while still by doing nothing the human may be united with the Heavenly, and men may bring back their True condition.   By means of the conversations between the guardian spirit of the Ho and Zo (the god) of the Sea this subject is exhaustively treated.'

' Next (in paragraph 8), the khwei, the millepede, and other subjects illustrate how the mind is spirit-like in its spontaneity and doing nothing.   The case of Confucius (in par. 9) shows the same spontaneity, transforming violence.

Kung-sun Lung (in par. 10), refusing to comply with that spontaneity, and seeking victory by his sophistical reasonings, shows his wisdom to be only like the folly of the frog in the well. The remaining three paragraphs bring before us *K*wang-ȝze by the spontaneity of his Tâo, now superior to the allurements of rank ; then, like the phœnix flying aloft, as enjoying himself in perfect ease; and finally, as like the fishes, in the happiness of his self-possession.' Such is a brief outline of this interesting chapter. Many of the critics would expunge the ninth and tenth paragraphs as unworthy of *K*wang-ȝze, the former as misrepresenting Confucius, the latter as extolling himself. I think they may both be allowed to stand as from his pencil.

BOOK XVIII. *K*IH LO.

The title of this Book, *K*ih Lo, or ' Perfect Enjoyment,' may also be received as describing the subject-matter of it. But the author does not tell us distinctly what he means by ' Perfect Enjoyment.' It seems to involve two elements,— freedom from trouble and distress, and freedom from the fear of death. What men seek for as their chief good would only be to him burdens. He does not indeed altogether condemn them, but his own quest is the better and more excellent way. His own enjoyment is to be obtained by means of doing nothing; that is, by the Tâo; of which passionless and purposeless action is a chief characteristic ; and is at the same time the most effective action, as is illustrated in the operation of heaven and earth.

Such is the substance of the first paragraph. The second is interesting as showing how his principle controlled *K*wang-ȝze on the death of his wife. Paragraph 3 shows us two professors of Tâoism delivered by it from the fear of their own death. Paragraph 4 brings our author before us talking to a skull, and then the skull's appearance to him in a dream and telling him of the happiness of the state after death. Paragraph 5 is occupied with Confucius and his favourite disciple Yen Hui. It stands by itself, unconnected with the rest of the Book, and its genuineness is denied by some commentators. The last paragraph, found in an enlarged form in the Books ascribed to Lieh-ȝze, has as little to do as the fifth with the general theme of the Book, and is a strange anticipation in China of the transrotation or transformation system of Buddhism.

Indeed, after reading this Book, we cease to wonder that Tâoism and Buddhism should in many practices come so near each other.

Book XIX. Tâ Shăng.

I have been inclined to translate the title of this Book by ' The Fuller Understanding of Life,' with reference to what is said in the second Book on ' The Nourishment of the Lord of Life.' There the Life before the mind of the writer is that of the Body ; here he extends his view also to the Life of the Spirit. The one subject is not kept, however, with sufficient distinctness apart from the other, and the profusion of illustrations, taken, most of them, from the works of Lieh-ȝze, is perplexing.

To use the words of Lû Shû-kih :—' This Book shows how he who would skilfully nourish his life, must maintain his spirit complete, and become one with Heaven. These two ideas preside in it throughout. In par. 2, the words of the Warden Yin show that the spirit kept complete is beyond the reach of harm. In 3, the illustration of the hunchback shows how the will must be maintained free from all confusion. In 4, that of the ferryman shows that to the completeness of the spirit there is required the dis- regard of life or death. In 5 and 6, the words of Thien Khâi-kih convey a warning against injuring the life by the indulgence of sensual desires. In 7, the sight of a sprite by duke Hwan unsettles his spirit. In 8, the gamecock is trained so as to preserve the spirit unagitated. In 9, we see the man in the water of the cataract resting calmly in his appointed lot. In 10, we have the maker of the bell- stand completing his work as he did in accordance with the mind of Heaven. All these instances show how the spirit is nourished. The reckless charioteering of Tung Yê in par. 11, not stopping when the strength of his horses was exhausted, and the false pretext of Sun Hsiû, clear as at noon-day, are instances of a different kind; while in the skilful Shui, hardly needing the application of his mind, and fully enjoying himself in all things, his movements testify of his harmony with Heaven, and his spiritual completeness.'

Book XX. Shan Mû.

It requires a little effort to perceive that Shan Mû, the title of this Book, does not belong to it as a whole, but only to the first of its nine paragraphs. That speaks of a large tree which our author once saw on a mountain. The other paragraphs have nothing to do with mountain trees, large or small. As the last Book might be considered to be supplementary to 'the Nourishment of Life,' discussed in Book III, so this is taken as having the same relation to Book IV, which treats of 'Man in the World, associated with other men.' It shows by its various narratives, some of which are full of interest, how by a strict observance of the principles and lessons of the Tâo a man may preserve his life and be happy, may do the right thing and enjoy himself and obtain the approbation of others in the various circumstances in which he may be placed. The themes both of Books I and IV blend together in it. Paragraph 8 has more the character of an apologue than most of *K*wang-𝑧ze's stories.

Book XXI. Thien 𝑧ze-fang.

Thien 𝑧ze-fang is merely the name of one of the men who appear in the first paragraph. That he was a historical character is learned from the 'Plans of the Warring States,' XIV, art. 6, where we find him at the court of the marquis Wăn of Wei (B. C. 424–387), acting as counsellor to that ruler. Thien was his surname; 𝑧ze-fang his designation, and Wû-*k*âi his name. He has nothing to do with any of the paragraphs but the first.

It is not easy to reduce all the narratives or stories in the Book to one category. The fifth, seventh, and eighth, indeed, are generally rejected as spurious, or unworthy of our author ; and the sixth and ninth are trivial, though the ninth bears all the marks of his graphic style. Paragraphs 3 and 4 are both long and important. A common idea in them and in 1, 2, and 10 seems to be that the presence and power of the Tâo cannot be communicated by words, and are independent of outward condition and circumstances.

BOOK XXII. *K*IH PEI YÛ.

With this Book the Second Part of *K*wang-ʒze's Essays or Treatises ends. ' All the Books in it,' says Lû Shû-*k*ih, ' show the opposition of Tâoism to the pursuit of know-ledge as enjoined in the Confucian and other schools ; and this Book may be regarded as the deepest, most vehement, and clearest of them all.' The concluding sentences of the last paragraph and Lâo-ʒze's advice to Confucius in par. 5, to ' sternly repress his knowledge,' may be referred to as illustrating the correctness of Lû's remark.

Book seventeenth is commonly considered to be the most eloquent of *K*wang-ʒze's Treatises, but this twenty-second Book is not inferior to it in eloquence, and it is more charac-teristic of his method of argument. The way in which he runs riot in the names with which he personifies the attri-butes of the Tâo, is a remarkable instance of the subtle manner in which he often brings out his ideas ; and in no other Book does he set forth more emphatically what his own idea of the Tâo was, though the student often fails to be certain that he has exactly caught the meaning.

The title, let it be observed, belongs only to the first paragraph. The *K*ih in it must be taken in the sense of ' knowledge,' and not of ' wisdom.'

BOOK XXIII. KĂNG-SANG *KHÛ*.

It is not at all certain that there ever was such a personage as Kăng-sang *Khû*, who gives its name to the Book.
In his brief memoir of *K*wang-ɜze, Sze-mâ *Kh*ien spells, as
we should say, the first character of the surname differently,
and for the Kăng (庚), employs Khang (亢), adding his
own opinion, that there was nothing in reality corresponding
to the account given of the characters in this and some
other Books. They would be therefore the inventions of
*K*wang-ɜze, devised by him to serve his purpose in setting
forth the teaching of Lâo-ɜze. It may have been so, but
the value of the Book would hardly be thereby affected.

Lû Shû-*k*ih gives the following very brief account of the
contents. Borrowing the language of Mencius concerning
Yen Hui and two other disciples of Confucius as compared
with the sage, he says, 'Kăng-sang *Kh*û had all the members of Lâo-ɜze, but in small proportions. To outward
appearance he was above such as abjure sagehood and put
knowledge away, but still he was unable to transform Nan-
yung *Kh*û, whom therefore he sent to Lâo-ɜze ; and he
announced to him the doctrine of the Tâo that everything
was done by doing nothing.'

The reader will see that this is a very incomplete summary of the contents of the Book. We find in it the
Tâoistic ideal of the 'Perfect Man,' and the discipline both
of body and mind through the depths of the system by
means of which it is possible for a disciple to become such.

BOOK XXIV. HSÜ WÛ-KWEI.

This Book is named from the first three characters in it,
the surname and name of Hsü Wû-kwei, who plays the
most important part in the first two paragraphs, and does
not further appear. He comes before us as a well-known
recluse of Wei, who visits the court to offer his counsels to
the marquis of the state. But whether there ever was such

a man, or whether he was only a creation of *K*wang-ʒze, we cannot, so far as I know, tell.

Scattered throughout the Book are the lessons so common with our author against sagehood and knowledge, and on the quality of doing nothing and thereby securing the doing of everything. The concluding chapter is one of the finest descriptions in the whole Work of the Tâo and of the Tâoistic idea of Heaven. 'There are in the Book,' says Lû Fang, 'many dark and mysterious expressions. It is not to be read hastily ; but the more it is studied, the more flavour will there be found in it.'

BOOK XXV. ƷEH-YANG.

This Book is named from the first two characters in it,— 'Ʒeh-yang,' which again are the designation of a gentleman of Lû, called Phăng Yang, who comes before us in *K*hû, seeking for an introduction to the king of that state, with the view, we may suppose, of giving him good counsel. Whether he ever got the introduction which he desired we do not know. The mention of him only serves to bring in three other individuals, all belonging to *K*hû, and the characters of two of them ; but we hear no more of Ʒeh-yang. The second and third paragraphs are, probably, sequels to the first, but his name does not appear.

The paragraphs from 4 to 9 have more or less interest in themselves ; but it is not easy to trace in them any sequence of thought. The tenth and eleventh are more important. The former deals with ' the Talk of the Hamlets and Villages,' the common sentiments of men, which, correct and just in themselves, are not to be accepted as a sufficient expression of the Tâo ; the latter sets forth how the name Tâo itself is only a metaphorical term, used for the purpose of description ; as if the Tâo were a thing, and not capable, therefore, from its material derivation of giving adequate expression to our highest notion of what it is.

' The Book,' says Lû Shû-*k*ih, ' illustrates how the Great Tâo cannot be described by any name ; that men ought to stop where they do not really know, and not try to find it in any phenomenon, or in any event or thing. They must forget both speech and silence, and then they may approximate to the idea of the Great Tâo.'

BOOK XXVI. WÂI WÛ.

The first two characters of the first paragraph are again adopted as the title of the Book,—Wâi Wû, 'External Things;' and the lesson supposed to be taught in it is that expressed in the first sentence, that the influence of external things on character and condition cannot be determined beforehand. It may be good, it may be evil. Mr. Balfour has translated the two characters by 'External Advantages.' Hû Wăn-ying interprets them of 'External Disadvantages.' The things may in fact be either of these. What seems useless may be productive of the greatest services ; and what men deem most advantageous may turn out to be most hurtful to them.

What really belongs to man is the Tâo. That is his own, sufficient for his happiness, and cannot be taken from him, if he prize it and cultivate it. But if he neglect it, and yield to external influences unfavourable to it, he may become bad, and suffer all that is most hateful to him and injurious.

Readers must judge for themselves of the way in which the subject is illustrated in the various paragraphs. Some of the stories are pertinent enough ; others are wide of the mark. The second, third, and fourth paragraphs are generally held to be spurious, ' poor in composition, and not at all to the point.' If my note on the ' six faculties of perception ' in par. 9 be correct, we must admit in it a Buddhistic hand, modifying the conceptions of *K*wang-ᵹze after he had passed away.

BOOK XXVII. YÜ YEN.

Yü Yen, 'Metaphorical Words,' stand at the commencement of the Book, and have been adopted as its name.

They might be employed to denote its first paragraph, but are not applicable to the Book as a whole. Nor let the reader expect to find even here any disquisition on the nature of the metaphor as a figure of speech. Translated literally, 'Yü Yen' are 'Lodged Words,' that is, Ideas that receive their meaning or character from their environment, the narrative or description in which they are deposited.

*K*wang-dze wished, I suppose, to give some description of the style in which he himself wrote :—now metaphorical, now abounding in quotations, and throughout moulded by his Tâoistic views. This last seems to be the meaning of his *K*ih Yen,—literally, 'Cup, or Goblet, Words,' that is, words, common as the water constantly supplied in the cup, but all moulded by the Tâoist principle, the element of and from Heaven blended in man's constitution and that should direct and guide his conduct. The best help in the interpretation of the paragraph is derived from a study of the difficult second Book, as suggested in the notes.

Of the five paragraphs that follow the first, the second relates to the change of views, which, it is said, took place in Confucius ; the third, to the change of feeling in Зăng-dze in his poverty and prosperity ; the fourth, to changes of character produced in his disciple by the teachings of Tung-kwo Зze-*khî* ; the fifth, to the changes in the appearance of the shadow produced by the ever-changing substance ; and the sixth, to the change of spirit and manner produced in Yang *K*û by the stern lesson of Lâo-dze.

Various other lessons, more or less appropriate and important, are interspersed.

Some critics argue that this Book must have originally been one with the thirty-second, which was made into two by the insertion between its Parts of the four spurious intervening Books, but this is uncertain and unlikely.

BOOK XXVIII. ЗANG WANG.

Зang Wang, explaining the characters as I have done,

fairly indicates the subject-matter of the Book. Not that we have a king in every illustration, but the personages adduced are always men of worth, who decline the throne, or gift, or distinction of whatever nature, proffered to them, and feel that they have something better to live for.

A persuasion, however, is widely spread, that this Book and the three that follow are all spurious. The first critic of note to challenge their genuineness was Sû Shih (better known as Sû Tung-pho, A. D. 1036–1101); and now, some of the best editors, such as Lin Hsî-kung, do not admit them into their texts, while others who are not bold enough to exclude them altogether, do not think it worth their while to discuss them seriously. Hû Wăn-ying, for instance, says, 'Their style is poor and mean, and they are, without doubt, forgeries. I will not therefore trouble myself with comments of praise or blame upon them. The reader may accept or reject them at his pleasure.'

But something may be said for them. Sze-mâ Khien seems to have been acquainted with them all. In his short biographical notice of Kwang-ȝze, he says, 'He made the Old Fisherman, the Robber Kih, and the Cutting Open Satchels, to defame and calumniate the disciples of Confucius.' Khien does not indeed mention our present Book along with XXX and XXXI, but it is less open to objection on the ground he mentions than they are. I think if it had stood alone, it would not have been condemned.

BOOK XXIX. TÂO KIH.

It has been seen above that Sze-mâ Khien expressly ascribes the Book called 'the Robber Kih' to Kwang-ȝze. Khien refers also in another place to Kih, adducing the facts of his history in contrast with those about Confucius' favourite disciple Yen Hui as inexplicable on the supposition of a just and wise Providence. We must conclude therefore that the Book existed in Khien's time, and that he had read it. On the other hand it has been shown that Confucius could not have been on terms of friendship with Liû-hsiâ *K*î, and all that is related of his brother the robber wants substantiation. That such a man ever existed appears to me very doubtful. Are we to put down the whole of the first paragraph then as a jeu d'esprit on the part of *K*wang-𝔷ze, intended to throw ridicule on Confucius and what our author considered his pedantic ways? It certainly does so, and we are amused to hear the sage outcrowed by the robber.

In the other two paragraphs we have good instances of *K*wang-𝔷ze's 'metaphorical expressions,' his coinage of names for his personages, more or less ingeniously indicating their characters; but in such cases the element of time or chronology does not enter; and it is the anachronism of the first paragraph which constitutes its chief difficulty.

The name of ' Robber *K*ih' may be said to be a coinage; and that a famous robber was popularly indicated by the name appears from its use by Mencius (III, ii, ch. 10, 3), to explain which the commentators have invented the story of a robber so-called in the time of Hwang-Tî, in the twenty-seventh century B. C.! Was there really such a legend? and did *K*wang-𝔷ze take advantage of it to apply the name to a notorious and disreputable brother of Liû-hsiâ *K*î? Still there remain the anachronisms in the paragraph which have been pointed out. On the whole we must come to a conclusion rather unfavourable to the genuineness of the Book. But it must have been forged at a very early time, and we have no idea by whom.

Book XXX. Yüeh *K*ien.

We need not suppose that anything ever occurred in *K*wang-𝔷ze's experience such as is described here. The whole narrative is metaphorical; and that he himself is made to play the part in it which he describes, only shows how the style of writing in which he indulged was ingrained into the texture of his mind. We do not know that there ever was a ruler of *K*âo who indulged in the love of the sword-fight, and kept about him a crowd of vulgar bravoes such as the story describes. We may be assured that our author never wore the bravo's dress or girt on him the bravo's sword. The whole is a metaphorical representation of the way in which a besotted ruler might be brought to a feeling of his degradation, and recalled to a sense of his duty and the way in which he might fulfil it. The narrative is full of interest and force. I do not feel any great difficulty in accepting it as the genuine composition of Kwang-ʒze. Who but himself could have composed it? Was it a good-humoured caricature of him by an able Confucian writer to repay him for the ridicule he was fond of casting on the sage?

BOOK XXXI. YÜ-FÛ.

'The Old Fisherman' is the fourth of the Books in the collection of the writings of Kwang-ʒze to which, since the time of Sû Shih, the epithet of 'spurious' has been attached by many. My own opinion, however, has been already intimated that the suspicions of the genuineness of those Books have been entertained on insufficient grounds; and so far as 'the Old Fisherman' is concerned, I am glad that it has come down to us, spurious or genuine. There may be a certain coarseness in 'the Robber Kih,' which makes us despise Confucius or laugh at him; but the satire in this Book is delicate, and we do not like the sage the less when he walks up the bank from the stream where he has been lectured by the fisherman. The pictures of him and his disciples in the forest, reading and singing on the Apricot Terrace, and of the old man slowly impelling his skiff to the land and then as quietly impelling it away till it is lost among the reeds, are delicious; there is nothing finer of its kind in the volume. What hand but that of Kwang-ʒze, so light in its touch and yet so strong, both incisive and decisive, could have delineated them?

BOOK XXXII.   LIEH YÜ-KHÂU.

Lieh Yü-khâu, the surname and name of Lieh-ȝze, with which the first paragraph commences, have become current as the name of the Book, though they have nothing to do with any but that one paragraph, which is found also in the second Book of the writings ascribed to Lieh-ȝze. There are some variations in the two Texts, but they are so slight that we cannot look on them as proofs that the two passages are narratives of independent origin.

Various difficulties surround the questions of the existence of Lieh-ȝze, and of the work which bears his name. They will be found distinctly and dispassionately stated and discussed in the 146th chapter of the Catalogue of the *K͠h*ien-lung Imperial Library. The writers seem to me to make it out that there was such a man, but they do not make it clear when he lived, or how his writings assumed their present form. There is a statement of Liû Hsiang that he lived in the time of duke Mû of *K*ăng (B.C. 627–606); but in that case he must have been earlier than Lâo-ȝze himself, whom he very frequently quotes. The writers think that Liû's 'Mû of *K*ăng' should be Mû of Lû (B.C. 4C9–377), which would make him not much anterior to Mencius and *K*wang-ȝze; but this is merely an ingenious conjecture. As to the composition of his chapters, they are evidently not at first hand from Lieh, but by some one of his disciples; whether they were current in *K*wang-ȝze's days, and he made use of various passages from them, or those passages were *K*wang-ȝze's originally, and taken from him by the followers of Lieh-ȝze and added to what fragments they had of their master's teaching;—these are points which must be left undetermined.

Whether the narrative about Lieh be from *K*wang-ȝze or not, its bearing on his character is not readily apprehended; but, as we study it, we seem to understand that his master Wû-ʓăn condemned him as not having fully attained to the Tâo, but owing his influence with others mainly to the manifestation of his merely human qualities. And this is the lesson which our author keeps before him, more or less distinctly, in all his paragraphs. As Lû Shû-*k*ih says :—

'This Book also sets forth Doing Nothing as the essential condition of the Tâo. Lieh-ȝze, frightened at the respect shown to him by the soup-vendors, and yet by his human doings drawing men to him, disowns the rule of the heavenly ; Hwan of *K*ăng, thinking himself different from other men, does not know that Heaven recompenses men according to their employment of the heavenly in them ; the resting of the sages in their proper rest shows how the ancients pursued the heavenly and not the human ; the one who learned to slay the Dragon, but afterwards did not exercise his skill, begins with the human, but afterwards goes on to the heavenly ; in those who do not rest in the heavenly, and perish by the inward war, we see how the small men do not know the secret of the Great Repose ; Ȝhâo Shang, glorying in the carriages which he had acquired, is still farther removed from the heavenly ; when Yen Ho shows that the sage, in imparting his instructions, did not follow the example of Heaven in diffusing its benefits, we learn that it is only the Doing Nothing of the True Man which is in agreement with Heaven ; the difficulty of knowing the mind of man, and the various methods required to test it, show the readiness with which, when not under the rule of Heaven, it seems to go after what is right, and the greater readiness with which it again revolts from it ; in Khao-fû, the Correct, we have one indifferent to the distinctions of rank, and from him we advance to the man who understands the great condition appointed for him, and is a follower of Heaven ; then comes he who plays the thief under the chin of the Black Dragon, running the greatest risks on a mere peradventure of success, a resolute opponent of Heaven ; and finally we have *K*wang-ȝze despising the ornaments of the sacrificial ox, looking in the same way at the worms beneath and the kites overhead, and regarding himself as quite independent

of them, thus giving us an example of the embodiment of
the spiritual, and of harmony with Heaven.'

So does this ingenious commentator endeavour to exhibit the one idea in the Book, and show the unity of its
different paragraphs.

BOOK XXXIII. THIEN HSIÂ.

The Thien Hsiâ with which this Book commences is in
regimen, and cannot be translated, so as to give an adequate
idea of the scope of the Book, or even of the first paragraph
to which it belongs. The phrase itself means literally 'under
heaven or the sky,' and is used as a denomination of 'the
kingdom,' and, even more widely, of 'the world' or 'all men.'
'Historical Phases of Tâoist Teaching' would be nearly
descriptive of the subject-matter of the Book; but may be objected to on two grounds:—first, that a chronological method
is not observed, and next, that the concluding paragraph can
hardly be said to relate to Tâoism at all, but to the sophistical teachers, which abounded in the age of *K*wang-𝑧ze.

Par. 1 sketches with a light hand the nature of Tâoism
and the forms which it assumed from the earliest times to
the era of Confucius, as imperfectly represented by him and
his school.

Par. 2 introduces us to the system of Mo Tî and his
school as an erroneous form of Tâoism, and departing, as it
continued, farther and farther from the old model.

Par. 3 deals with a modification of Mohism, advocated
by scholars who are hardly heard of elsewhere.

Par. 4 treats of a further modification of this modified
Mohism, held by scholars 'whose Tâo was not the true
Tâo, and whose "right" was really "wrong."'

Par. 5 goes back to the era of Lâo-𝑧ze, and mentions him
and Kwan Yin, as the men who gave to the system of Tâo
a grand development.

Par. 6 sets forth *K*wang-𝑧ze as following in their steps
and going beyond them, the brightest luminary of the
system.

Par. 7 leaves Tâoism, and brings up Hui Shih and other sophists.

Whether the Book should be received as from *K*wang-ʒze himself or from some early editor of his writings is 'a vexed question.' If it did come from his pencil, he certainly had a good opinion of himself. It is hard for a foreign student at this distant time to be called on for an opinion on the one side or the other.

THE
WRITINGS OF *K*WANG-3ZE.

BOOK I.

PART I. SECTION I.

Hsiâo-yâo Yû, or 'Enjoyment in Untroubled Ease[1].'

1. In the Northern Ocean there is a fish, the name of which is Khwăn[2],—I do not know how many lî in size. It changes into a bird with the name of Phăng, the back of which is (also)—I do not know how many lî in extent. When this bird rouses itself and flies, its wings are like clouds all round the sky. When the sea is moved (so as to bear it along), it prepares to remove to the Southern Ocean. The Southern Ocean is the Pool of Heaven.

---

[1] See notice on pp. 127, 128, on the Title and Subject-matter of the Book.

[2] The khwăn and the phăng are both fabulous creatures, far transcending in size the dimensions ascribed by the wildest fancy of the West to the kraken and the roc. *K*wang-ȝze represents them as so huge by way of contrast to the small creatures which he is intending to introduce ;—to show that size has nothing to do with the Tâo, and the perfect enjoyment which the possession of it affords. The passage is a good specimen of the Yü Yen (寓 言), metaphorical or parabolical narratives or stories, which are the chief characteristic of our author's writings; but the reader must keep in mind that the idea or lesson in its ' lodging' is generally of a Tâoistic nature.

There is the (book called) *K*hî Hsieh [1],—a record of marvels.   We have in it these words :—' When the phăng is removing to the Southern Ocean it flaps (its wings) on the water for 3000 lî.   Then it ascends on a whirlwind 90,000 lî, and it rests only at the end of six months.'   (But similar to this is the movement of the breezes which we call) the horses of the fields, of the dust (which quivers in the sunbeams), and of living things as they are blown against one another by the air [2].   Is its azure the proper colour of the sky ?   Or is it occasioned by its distance and illimitable extent ?   If one were looking down (from above), the very same appearance would just meet his view.

2. And moreover, (to speak of) the accumulation of water ;—if it be not great, it will not have strength to support a large boat.   Upset a cup of water in a cavity, and a straw will float on it as if it were a boat.   Place a cup in it, and it will stick fast;—the water is shallow and the boat is large.   (So it is with) the accumulation of wind; if it be not great, it will not have strength to support great wings.   Therefore (the phăng ascended to) the height of 90,000 lî, and there was such a mass of wind beneath it; thenceforth the accumulation of wind was sufficient.   As it seemed to bear the blue sky on its back, and there was nothing to obstruct or arrest its course, it could pursue its way to the South.

---

[1] There may have been a book with this title, to which *K*wang-ȝze appeals, as if feeling that what he had said needed to be substantiated.

[2] This seems to be interjected as an afterthought, suggesting to the reader that the phăng, soaring along at such a height, was only an exaggerated form of the common phenomena with which he was familiar.

A cicada and a little dove laughed at it, saying, 'We make an effort and fly towards an elm or sapan-wood tree; and sometimes before we reach it, we can do no more but drop to the ground. Of what use is it for this (creature) to rise 90,000 lî, and make for the South?' He who goes to the grassy suburbs[1], returning to the third meal (of the day), will have his belly as full as when he set out; he who goes to a distance of 100 lî will have to pound his grain where he stops for the night; he who goes a thousand lî, will have to carry with him provisions for three months. What should these two small creatures know about the matter? The knowledge of that which is small does not reach to that which is great; (the experience of) a few years does not reach to that of many. How do we know that it is so? The mushroom of a morning does not know (what takes place between) the beginning and end of a month; the short-lived cicada does not know (what takes place between) the spring and autumn. These are instances of a short term of life. In the south of *Khû*[2] there is the (tree) called Ming-ling[3], whose spring is 500 years, and its autumn the same; in high antiquity there was that called Tâ-*kh*un[4],

---

[1] In Chinese, Mang Zhang; but this is not the name of any particular place. The phrase denotes the grassy suburbs (from their green colour), not far from any city or town.

[2] The great state of the South, having its capital Ying in the present Hû-pei, and afterwards the chief competitor with *Kh*in for the sovereignty of the kingdom.

[3] Taken by some as the name of a tortoise.

[4] This and the Ming-ling tree, as well as the mushroom mentioned above, together with the khwăn and phăng, are all mentioned in the fifth Book of the writings of Lieh-ʒze, referred to in the next paragraph.

whose spring was 8000 years, and its autumn the same. And Phăng 3û[1] is the one man renowned to the present day for his length of life :—if all men were (to wish) to match him, would they not be miserable ?

3. In the questions put by Thang[2] to Kî we have similar statements :—' In the bare and barren north there is the dark and vast ocean,— the Pool of Heaven. In it there is a fish, several thousand lî in breadth, while no one knows its length. Its name is the khwăn. There is (also) a bird named the phăng ; its back is like the Thâi mountain, while its wings are like clouds all round the sky. On a whirlwind it mounts upwards as on the whorls of a goat's horn for 90,000 lî, till, far removed from the cloudy vapours, it bears on its back the blue sky, and then it shapes its course for the South, and proceeds to the ocean there.' A quail by the side of a marsh laughed at it, and said, ' Where is it going to ? I spring up with a bound, and come down again when I have reached but a few fathoms, and then fly about among the brushwood and bushes ; and

---

[1] Or 'the patriarch Phăng.' Confucius compared himself to him (Analects, VII, 1) ;—'our old Phăng ;' and Kû Hsî thinks he was a worthy officer of the Shang dynasty. Whoever he was, the legends about him are a mass of Tâoistic fables. At the end of the Shang dynasty (B.C. 1123) he was more than 767 years old, and still in unabated vigour. We read of his losing 49 wives and 54 sons ; and that he still left two sons, Wû and Î, who died in Fû-kien, and gave their names to the Wû-î, or Bû-î hills, from which we get our Bohea tea ! See Mayers' ' Chinese Reader's Manual,' p. 175.

[2] The founder of the Shang dynasty (B.C. 1766–1754). In Lieh-3ze his interlocutor is called Hsiâ Ko, and 3ze-kî.

this is the perfection of flying.   Where is that creature going to?'   This shows the difference between
the small and the great.

Thus it is that men, whose wisdom is sufficient
for the duties of some one office, or whose conduct
will secure harmony in some one district, or whose
virtue is befitting a ruler so that they could efficiently
govern some one state, are sure to look on themselves in this manner (like the quail), and yet Yung-
ʒze [1] of Sung [1] would have smiled and laughed at
them.   (This Yung-ʒze), though the whole world
should have praised him, would not for that have
stimulated himself to greater endeavour, and though
the whole world should have condemned him, would
not have exercised any more repression of his
course ; so fixed was he in the difference between
the internal (judgment of himself) and the external
(judgment of others), so distinctly had he marked
out the bounding limit of glory and disgrace.   Here,
however, he stopped.   His place in the world indeed
had become indifferent to him, but still he had not
planted himself firmly (in the right position).

There was Lieh-ʒze [2], who rode on the wind and
pursued his way, with an admirable indifference (to

---

[1] We can hardly tell who this Yung-ʒze was.   Sung was a
duchy, comprehending portions of the present provinces of Ho-
nan, An-hui, and Kiang-sû.

[2] See note on the title of Book XXXII.   Whether there ever
was a personage called Lieh-ʒze or Lieh Yü-khâu, and what is the
real character of the writings that go under his name, are questions
that cannot be more than thus alluded to in a note.   He is often
introduced by Kwang-ʒze, and many narratives are common to
their books.   Here he comes before us, not as a thinker and writer,
but as a semi-supernatural being, who has only not yet attained to
the highest consummations of the Tâo.

all external things), returning, however, after fifteen days, (to his place). In regard to the things that (are supposed to) contribute to happiness, he was free from all endeavours to obtain them; but though he had not to walk, there was still something for which he had to wait. But suppose one who mounts on (the ether of) heaven and earth in its normal operation, and drives along the six elemental energies of the changing (seasons), thus enjoying himself in the illimitable,—what has he to wait for[1]? Therefore it is said, 'The Perfect man has no (thought of) self; the Spirit-like man, none of merit; the Sagely-minded man, none of fame[1].'

4. Yâo[2], proposing to resign the throne to Hsü Yû[3], said, 'When the sun and moon have come forth, if the torches have not been put out, would it not be difficult for them to give light? When the seasonal rains are coming down, if we still keep watering the ground, will not our toil be labour lost for all the good it will do? Do you, Master, stand forth (as sovereign), and the kingdom will (at once) be well governed. If I still (continue to) preside over it, I must look on myself as vainly occupying the place;—I beg to resign the throne to you.' Hsü

---

[1] The description of a master of the Tâo, exalted by it, unless the predicates about him be nothing but the ravings of a wild extravagance, above mere mortal man. In the conclusion, however, he is presented under three different phrases, which the reader will do well to keep in mind.

[2] The great sovereign with whom the documents of the Shû King commence:—B. C. 2357–2257.

[3] A counsellor of Yâo, who is once mentioned by Sze-mâ Khien in his account of Po-î,—in the first Book of his Biographies (列 傳). Hsü Yû is here the instance of 'the Sagely man,' with whom the desire of a name or fame has no influence.

Yû said, 'You, Sir, govern the kingdom, and the
kingdom is well governed. If I in these circumstances take your place, shall I not be doing so for
the sake of the name? But the name is but the
guest of the reality;—shall I be playing the part of
the guest? The tailor-bird makes its nest in the
deep forest, but only uses a single branch ; the mole [1]
drinks from the Ho, but only takes what fills its
belly. Return and rest in being ruler,—I will have
nothing to do with the throne. Though the cook
were not attending to his kitchen, the representative
of the dead and the officer of prayer would not leave
their cups and stands to take his place.'

5. *K*ien Wû [2] asked Lien Shû [2], saying, 'I heard
*Kh*ieh-yü [3] talking words which were great, but had
nothing corresponding to them (in reality);—once
gone, they could not be brought back. I was frightened by them;—they were like the Milky Way [4]
which cannot be traced to its beginning or end.
They had no connexion with one another, and were
not akin to the experiences of men.' 'What were
his words?' asked Lien Shû, and the other replied,
(He said) that 'Far away on the hill of Kû-shih [5]
there dwelt a Spirit-like man whose flesh and skin

---

[1] Some say the tapir.

[2] Known to us only through *K*wang-₃ze.

[3] ' The madman of *Kh*û' of the Analects, XVIII, 5, who eschews
intercourse with Confucius. See Hwang-fû Mî's account of him,
under the surname and name of Lû Thung, in his Notices of Eminent Tâoists, I, 25.

[4] Literally, 'the Ho and the Han;' but the name of those
rivers combined was used to denote 'the Milky Way.'

[5] See the Khang-hsî Thesaurus under the character 射. All
which is said about the hill is that it was ' in the North Sea.'

were (smooth) as ice and (white) as snow; that his
manner was elegant and delicate as that of a virgin;
that he did not eat any of the five grains, but in-
haled the wind and drank the dew; that he mounted
on the clouds, drove along the flying dragons, rambling and enjoying himself beyond the four seas;
that by the concentration of his spirit-like powers he
could save men from disease and pestilence, and
secure every year a plentiful harvest.' These words
appeared to me wild and incoherent and I did not
believe them. 'So it is,' said Lien Shû. 'The blind
have no perception of the beauty of elegant figures,
nor the deaf of the sound of bells and drums. But
is it only the bodily senses of which deafness and
blindness can be predicated? There is also a similar defect in the intelligence; and of this your words
supply an illustration in yourself. That man, with
those attributes, though all things were one mass of
confusion, and he heard in that condition the whole
world crying out to him to be rectified, would not
have to address himself laboriously to the task, as
if it were his business to rectify the world. Nothing
could hurt that man; the greatest floods, reaching
to the sky, could not drown him, nor would he feel
the fervour of the greatest heats melting metals and
stones till they flowed, and scorching all the ground
and hills. From the dust and chaff of himself, he
could still mould and fashion Yâos and Shuns[1];—
how should he be willing to occupy himself with
things[2]?'

---

[1] Shun was the successor of Yâo in the ancient kingdom.

[2] All this description is to give us an idea of the 'Spirit-like
man.' We have in it the results of the Tâo in its fullest embodiment.

6. A man of Sung, who dealt in the ceremonial caps (of Yin)[1], went with them to Yüeh[2], the people of which cut off their hair and tattooed their bodies, so that they had no use for them. Yâo ruled the people of the kingdom, and maintained a perfect government within the four seas. Having gone to see the four (Perfect) Ones[3] on the distant hill of Kû-shih, when (he returned to his capital) on the south of the Făn water[4], his throne appeared no more to his deep-sunk oblivious eyes[5].

7. Hui-jze[6] told *K*wang-jze, saying, 'The king of Wei[7] sent me some seeds of a large calabash, which I sowed. The fruit, when fully grown, could contain five piculs (of anything). I used it to contain water,

---

[1] See the Lî *K*î, IX, iii, 3.

[2] A state, part of the present province of *K*ieh-*k*iang.

[3] Said to have been Hsü Yû mentioned above, with Nieh *Kh*üeh, Wang Î, and Phî-î, who will by and by come before us.

[4] A river in Shan-hsî, on which was the capital of Yâo ;—a tributary of the Ho.

[5] This paragraph is intended to give us an idea of ' the Perfect man,' who has no thought of himself. The description, however, is brief and tame, compared with the accounts of Hsü Yû and of ' the Spirit-like man.'

[6] Or Hui Shih, the chief minister of ' king Hui of Liang (or Wei), (B. c. 370–333),' with an interview between whom and Mencius the works of that philosopher commence. He was a friend of *K*wang-jze, and an eccentric thinker; and in Book XXXIII there is a long account of several of his views. I do not think that the conversations about ' the great calabash ' and ' the great tree ' really took place; *K*wang-jze probably invented them, to illustrate his point that size had nothing to do with the Tâo, and that things which seemed useless were not really so when rightly used.

[7] Called also Liang from the name of its capital. Wei was one of the three states (subsequently kingdoms), into which the great fief of 3in was divided about B. c. 400.

but it was so heavy that I could not lift it by myself.
I cut it in two to make the parts into drinking
vessels; but the dried shells were too wide and
unstable and would not hold (the liquor); nothing
but large useless things!   Because of their uselessness I knocked them to pieces.'   _K_wang-ȝze replied,
'You were indeed stupid, my master, in the use of
what was large.   There was a man of Sung who
was skilful at making a salve which kept the hands
from getting chapped; and (his family) for generations had made the bleaching of cocoon-silk their
business.   A stranger heard of it, and proposed to
buy the art of the preparation for a hundred ounces
of silver.   The kindred all came together, and considered the proposal.   "We have," said they, "been
bleaching cocoon-silk for generations, and have only
gained a little money.   Now in one morning we can
sell to this man our art for a hundred ounces;—let
him have it."   The stranger accordingly got it and
went away with it to give counsel to the king of
Wû[1], who was then engaged in hostilities with Yüeh.
The king gave him the command of his fleet, and
in the winter he had an engagement with that of
Yüeh, on which he inflicted a great defeat[2], and was
invested with a portion of territory taken from Yüeh.
The keeping the hands from getting chapped was
the same in both cases; but in the one case it led to
the investiture (of the possessor of the salve), and

---

[1] A great and ancient state on the sea-board, north of Yüeh.
The name remains in the district of Wû-_k_iang in the prefecture of
Sû-_k_âu.

[2] The salve gave the troops of Wû a great advantage in a war
on the _K_iang, especially in winter.

in the other it had only enabled its owners to continue their bleaching. The difference of result was
owing to the different use made of the art. Now
you, Sir, had calabashes large enough to hold five
piculs;—why did you not think of making large
bottle-gourds of them, by means of which you could
have floated over rivers and lakes, instead of giving
yourself the sorrow of finding that they were useless
for holding anything. Your mind, my master, would
seem to have been closed against all intelligence!'

Hui-𝑧ze said to *K*wang-𝑧ze, 'I have a large tree,
which men call the Ailantus[1]. Its trunk swells out
to a large size, but is not fit for a carpenter to apply
his line to it; its smaller branches are knotted and
crooked, so that the disk and square cannot be used
on them. Though planted on the wayside, a builder
would not turn his head to look at it. Now your
words, Sir, are great, but of no use;—all unite in
putting them away from them.' *K*wang-𝑧ze replied,
'Have you never seen a wild cat or a weasel? There
it lies, crouching and low, till the wanderer approaches; east and west it leaps about, avoiding
neither what is high nor what is low, till it is caught
in a trap, or dies in a net. Again there is the Yak[2],
so large that it is like a cloud hanging in the sky.
It is large indeed, but it cannot catch mice. You,
Sir, have a large tree and are troubled because it is
of no use;—why do you not plant it in a tract where
there is nothing else, or in a wide and barren wild?

---

[1] The Ailantus glandulosa, common in the north of China,
called 'the fetid tree,' from the odour of its leaves.

[2] The bos grunniens of Thibet, the long tail of which is in
great demand for making standards and chowries.

There you might saunter idly by its side, or in the enjoyment of untroubled ease sleep beneath it. Neither bill nor axe would shorten its existence; there would be nothing to injure it.   What is there in its uselessness to cause you distress?'

BOOK II.

Part I. Section II.

Khî Wû Lun, or ' The Adjustment of Controversies [1].'

1. Nan-kwo 3ze-*khî* [2] was seated, leaning forward on his stool. He was looking up to heaven and breathed gently, seeming to be in a trance, and to have lost all consciousness of any companion. (His disciple), Yen *Kh*ăng 3ze-yû [3], who was in attendance and standing before him, said, ' What is this? Can the body be made to become thus like a withered tree, and the mind to become like slaked lime? His appearance as he leans forward on the stool to-day is such as I never saw him have before in the same position.' 3ze-*khî* said, 'Yen, you do well to ask such a question, I had just now lost myself [4]; but how should you understand it? You

---

[1] See pp. 128–130.

[2] Nan-kwo, 'the southern suburb,' had probably been the quarter where 3ze-*khî* had resided, and is used as his surname. He is introduced several times by *K*wang-3ze in his writings :— Books IV, 7; XXVII, 4, and perhaps elsewhere.

[3] We have the surname of this disciple, Yen (顏); his name, Yen (偃); his honorary or posthumous epithet (*Kh*ăng); and his ordinary appellation, 3ze-yû. The use of the epithet shows that he and his master had lived before our author.

[4] ' He had lost himself;' that is, he had become unconscious of all around him, and even of himself, as if he were about to enter

may have heard the notes [1] of Man, but have not
heard those of Earth; you may have heard the notes
of Earth, but have not heard those of Heaven.'

3ze-yû said, 'I venture to ask from you a description of all these.' The reply was, 'When the breath
of the Great Mass (of nature) comes strongly, it is
called Wind. Sometimes it does not come so; but
when it does, then from a myriad apertures there
issues its excited noise;—have you not heard it in
a prolonged gale? Take the projecting bluff of a
mountain forest;—in the great trees, a hundred
spans round, the apertures and cavities are like the
nostrils, or the mouth, or the ears; now square, now
round like a cup or a mortar; here like a wet foot-
print, and there like a large puddle. (The sounds
issuing from them are like) those of fretted water, of
the arrowy whizz, of the stern command, of the inhaling of the breath, of the shout, of the gruff note,
of the deep wail, of the sad and piping note. The
first notes are slight, and those that follow deeper,
but in harmony with them. Gentle winds produce
a small response; violent winds a great one. When
the fierce gusts have passed away, all the apertures

---

into the state of 'an Immortal,' a mild form of the Buddhistic
samâdhi. But his attitude and appearance were intended by
*K*wang-ʒze to indicate what should be the mental condition in
reference to the inquiry pursued in the Book;— a condition, it
appears to me, of agnosticism. See the account of Lâo-ʒze in
a similar trance in Book XXI, par. 4.

[1] The Chinese term here (lâi) denotes a reed or pipe, with three
holes, by a combination of which there was formed the rudimentary
or reed organ. Our author uses it for the sounds or notes heard in
nature, various as the various opinions of men in their discussions
about things.

are empty (and still) ;—have you not seen this in the bending and quivering of the branches and leaves?'

3ze-yû said, 'The notes of Earth then are simply those which come from its myriad apertures; and the notes of Man may just be compared to those which (are brought from the tubes of) bamboo ;— allow me to ask about the notes of Heaven [1].' 3ze-*khî* replied, 'When (the wind) blows, (the sounds from) the myriad apertures are different, and (its cessation) makes them stop of themselves. Both of these things arise from (the wind and the apertures) themselves :—should there be any other agency that excites them?'

2. Great knowledge is wide and comprehensive ; small knowledge is partial and restricted. Great speech is exact and complete; small speech is (merely) so much talk [2]. When we sleep, the soul communicates with (what is external to us) ; when we awake, the body is set free. Our intercourse with others then leads to various activity, and daily there is the striving of mind with mind. There are hesitancies; deep difficulties; reservations; small apprehensions causing restless distress, and great

---

[1] The sounds of Earth have been described fully and graphically. Of the sounds of Man very little is said, but they form the subject of the next paragraph. Nothing is said in answer to the disciple's inquiry about the notes of Heaven. It is intimated, however, that there is no necessity to introduce any foreign Influence or Power like Heaven in connexion with the notes of Earth. The term Heaven, indeed, is about to pass with our author into a mere synonym of Tâo, the natural 'course' of the phenomena of men and things.

[2] Words are the 'sounds' of Man ; and knowledge is the 'wind' by which they are excited.

apprehensions producing endless fears. Where their
utterances are like arrows from a bow, we have
those who feel it their charge to pronounce what is
right and what is wrong.; where they are given out
like the conditions of a covenant, we have those who
maintain their views, determined to overcome. (The
weakness of their arguments), like the decay (of
things) in autumn and winter, shows the failing (of
the minds of some) from day to day; or it is like
their water which, once voided, cannot be gathered
up again. Then their ideas seem as if fast bound with
cords, showing that the mind is become like an old
and dry moat, and that it is nigh to death, and
cannot be restored to vigour and brightness.

Joy and anger, sadness and pleasure, anticipation
and regret, fickleness and fixedness, vehemence and
indolence, eagerness and tardiness;—(all these
moods), like music from an empty tube, or mush-
rooms from the warm moisture, day and night
succeed to one another and come before us, and we
do not know whence they sprout. Let us stop ! Let
us stop ! Can we expect to find out suddenly how
they are produced ?

If there were not (the views of) another, I should
not have mine; if there were not I (with my views),
his would be uncalled for :—this is nearly a true statement of the case, but we do not know what it is that
makes it be so. It might seem as if there would be
a true Governor [1] concerned in it, but we do not find

---

[1] 'A true Governor' would be a good enough translation for
'the true God.' But *K*wang-ȝze did not admit any supernatural
Power or Being as working in man. His true Governor was the
Tâo; and this will be increasingly evident as we proceed with the
study of his Books.

any trace (of his presence and acting). That such an One could act so I believe; but we do not see His form. He has affections, but He has no form.

Given the body, with its hundred parts, its nine openings, and its six viscera, all complete in their places, which do I love the most? Do you love them all equally? or do you love some more than others? Is it not the case that they all perform the part of your servants and waiting women? All of them being such, are they not incompetent to rule one another? or do they take it in turns to be now ruler and now servants? There must be a true Ruler (among them)[1] whether by searching you can find out His character or not, there is neither advantage nor hurt, so far as the truth of His operation is concerned. When once we have received the bodily form complete, its parts do not fail to perform their functions till the end comes. In conflict with things or in harmony with them, they pursue their course to the end, with the speed of a galloping horse which cannot be stopped;—is it not sad? To be constantly toiling all one's lifetime, without seeing the fruit of one's labour, and to be weary and worn out with his labour, without knowing where he is going to:—is it not a deplorable case? Men may say, 'But it is not death;' yet of what advantage is this? When the body is decomposed, the mind will be the same along with it:—must not the case be pronounced very deplorable[2]? Is the life

---

[1] The name 'Ruler' is different from 'Governor' above; but they both indicate the same concept in the author's mind.

[2] The proper reply to this would be that the mind is not dissolved with the body; and Kwang-3ze's real opinion, as we shall find, was that life and death were but phases in the phenomenal

of man indeed enveloped in such darkness? Is it I
alone to whom it appears so? And does it not
appear to be so to other men?

3. If we were to follow the judgments of the pre-
determined mind, who would be left alone and without
a teacher[1]? Not only would it be so with those who
know the sequences (of knowledge and feeling) and
make their own selection among them, but it would
be so as well with the stupid and unthinking. For
one who has not this determined mind, to have his
affirmations and negations is like the case described
in the saying, 'He went to Yüeh to-day, and arrived
at it yesterday[2].' It would be making what was not
a fact to be a fact. But even the spirit-like Yü[3]
could not have known how to do this, and how should
one like me be able to do it?

But speech is not like the blowing (of the wind);
the speaker has (a meaning in) his words. If, however, what he says, be indeterminate (as from a
mind not made up), does he then really speak or
not? He thinks that his words are different from the
chirpings of fledgelings; but is there any distinction
between them or not? But how can the Tâo be
so obscured, that there should be 'a True' and 'a
False' in it? How can speech be so obscured that
there should be 'the Right' and 'the Wrong' about
them? Where shall the Tâo go to that it will not

development. But the course of his argument suggests to us the
question here, 'Is life worth living?'

   [1] This 'teacher' is 'the Tâo.'

   [2] Expressing the absurdity of the case. This is one of the
sayings of Hui-3ze;—see Book XXXIII, par. 7.

   [3] The successor and counsellor of Shun, who coped with and
remedied the flood of Yâo.

be found ? Where shall speech be found that it
will be inappropriate? Tâo becomes obscured
through the small comprehension (of the mind), and
speech comes to be obscure through the vain-glori-
ousness (of the speaker). So it is that we have the
contentions between the Literati[1] and the Mohists[2],
the one side affirming what the other denies, and
vice versâ. If we would decide on their several
affirmations and denials, no plan is like bringing the
(proper) light (of the mind)[3] to bear on them.

All subjects may be looked at from (two points of
view),—from that and from this. If I look at a
thing from another's point of view, I do not see it;
only as I know it myself, do I know it. Hence it is
said, ' That view comes from this; and this view is
a consequence of that : '—which is the theory that
that view and this—(the opposite views)—produce
each the other[4]. Although it be so, there is affirmed
now life and now death; now death and now life;
now the admissibility of a thing and now its inadmissibility; now its inadmissibility and now its admissibility. (The disputants) now affirm and now deny;
now deny and now affirm. Therefore the sagely
man does not pursue this method, but views things
in the light of (his) Heaven[5] (-ly nature), and hence
forms his judgment of what is right.

---

[1] The followers of Confucius.

[2] The disciples of Mih-ʒze, or Mih Tî, the heresiarch, whom
Mencius attacked so fiercely ;—see Mencius, V, 1, 5, et al. His era
must be assigned between Confucius and Mencius.

[3] That is, the perfect mind, the principle of the Tâo.

[4] As taught by Hui-ʒze ;—see XXXIII, 7 ; but it is doubtful if
the quotation from Hui's teaching be complete.

[5] Equivalent to the Tâo. See on the use in Lâo-ʒze and
Kwang-ʒze of the term ' Heaven,' in the Introduction, pp. 16–18.

This view is the same as that, and that view is the same as this. But that view involves both a right and a wrong; and this view involves also a right and a wrong :—are there indeed, or are there not the two views, that and this? They have not found their point of correspondency which is called the pivot of the Tâo. As soon as one finds this pivot, he stands in the centre of the ring (of thought), where he can respond without end to the changing views ;—without end to those affirming, and without end to those denying. Therefore I said, ' There is nothing like the proper light (of the mind).'

4. By means of a finger (of my own) to illustrate that the finger (of another) is not a finger is not so good a plan as to illustrate that it is not so by means of what is (acknowledged to be) not a finger ; and by means of (what I call) a horse to illustrate that (what another calls) a horse is not so, is not so good a plan as to illustrate that it is not a horse, by means of what is (acknowledged to be) not a horse [1]. (All things in) heaven and earth may be (dealt with as) a finger ; (each of) their myriads may be (dealt with as) a horse. Does a thing seem so to me ? (I say that) it is so. Does it seem not so to me ? (I say that) it is not so. A path is formed by (constant)

[1] The language of our author here is understood to have reference to the views of Kung-sun Lung, a contemporary of Hui-ʒze, and a sophist like him. One of his treatises or arguments had the title of ' The White Horse,' and another that of 'Pointing to Things.' If these had been preserved, we might have seen more clearly the appropriateness of the text here. But the illustration of the monkeys and their actions shows us the scope of the whole paragraph to be that controversialists, whose views are substantially the same, may yet differ, and that with heat, in words.

treading on the ground. A thing is called by its name through the (constant) application of the name to it. How is it so? It is so because it is so. How is it not so? It is not so, because it is not so. Everything has its inherent character and its proper capability. There is nothing which has not these. Therefore, this being so, if we take a stalk of grain [1] and a (large) pillar, a loathsome (leper) and (a beauty like) Hsî Shih [2], things large and things insecure, things crafty and things strange;—they may in the light of the Tâo all be reduced to the same category (of opinion about them).

It was separation that led to completion; from completion ensued dissolution. But all things, without regard to their completion and dissolution, may again be comprehended in their unity;—it is only the far reaching in thought who know how to comprehend them in this unity. This being so, let us give up our devotion to our own views, and occupy ourselves with the ordinary views. These ordinary views are grounded on the use of things. (The study of that) use leads to the comprehensive judgment, and that judgment secures the success (of the inquiry). That success gained, we are near (to the object of our search), and there we stop. When we stop, and yet we do not know how it is so, we have what is called the Tâo.

When we toil our spirits and intelligence, obstin-

---

[1] The character in the text means both 'a stalk of grain' and 'a horizontal beam.' Each meaning has its advocates here.

[2] A famous beauty, a courtezan presented by the king of Yüeh to his enemy, the king of Wû, and who hastened on his progress to ruin and death, she herself perishing at the same time.

ately determined (to establish our own view), and do not know the agreement (which underlies it and the views of others), we have what is called ' In the morning three.'   What is meant by that ' In the morning three?'   A keeper of monkeys, in giving them out their acorns, (once) said, ' In the morning I will give you three (measures) and in the evening four.'   This made them all angry, and he said, 'Very well.   In the morning I will give you four and in the evening three.'   His two proposals were substantially the same, but the result of the one was to make the creatures angry, and of the other to make them pleased :—an illustration of the point I am insisting on.   Therefore the sagely man brings together a dispute in its affirmations and denials, and rests in the equal fashioning of Heaven [1].   Both sides of the question are admissible.

5. Among the men of old their knowledge reached the extreme point.   What was that extreme point?   Some held that at first there was not anything. This is the extreme point, the utmost point to which nothing can be added [2].   A second class held that there was something, but without any responsive recognition [3] of it (on the part of men).

A third class held that there was such recognition, but there had not begun to be any expression of different opinions about it.

---

[1] Literally, ' the Heaven-Mould or Moulder,'—another name for the Tâo, by which all things are fashioned.

[2] See the same passage in Book XXIII, par. 10.

[3] The ordinary reading here is fǎng (封), 'a boundary' or 'distinctive limit.'   Lin Hsî-*k*ung adopts the reading 對, ' a response,' and I have followed him.

It was through the definite expression of different opinions about it that there ensued injury to (the doctrine of) the Tâo.   It was this injury to the (doctrine of the) Tâo which led to the formation of (partial) preferences.   Was it indeed after such preferences were formed that the injury came ? or did the injury precede the rise of such preferences ?   If the injury arose after their formation, *K*âo's method of playing on the lute was natural.   If the injury arose before their formation, there would have been no such playing on the lute as *K*âo's [1].

*K*âo Wăn's playing on the lute, Shih Kwang's indicating time with his staff, and Hui-ʒze's (giving his views), while leaning against a dryandra tree (were all extraordinary).   The knowledge of the three men (in their several arts) was nearly perfect, and therefore they practised them to the end of their lives.   They loved them because they were different from those of others.   They loved them and wished to make them known to others.   But as they could not be made clear, though they tried to make them so, they ended with the obscure (discussions) about 'the hard' and 'the white.'   And their sons [2], moreover, with all the threads of their fathers' compositions, yet to the end of their lives accomplished nothing.   If they, proceeding in this way, could be said to have succeeded, then am I also successful;

---

[1] *K*âo Wăn and Shih Kwang were both musicians of the state of Ʒin.   Shih, which appears as Kwang's surname, was his denomination as 'music-master.'   It is difficult to understand the reason why *K*wang-ʒze introduces these men and their ways, or how it helps his argument.

[2] Perhaps we should read here 'son,' with special reference to the son of Hui-ʒze.

if they cannot be pronounced successful, neither I
nor any other can succeed.

Therefore the scintillations of light from the midst
of confusion and perplexity are indeed valued by
the sagely man; but not to use one's own views and
to take his position on the ordinary views is what is
called using the (proper) light.

6. But here now are some other sayings[1] :—I do
not know whether they are of the same character as
those which I have already given, or of a different
character.   Whether they be of the same character
or not when looked at along with them, they have a
character of their own, which cannot be distinguished
from the others.   But though this be the case, let
me try to explain myself.

There was a beginning.   There was a beginning
before that beginning[2].   There was a beginning
previous to that beginning before there was the
beginning.

There was existence; there had been no existence.
There was no existence before the beginning of that
no existence[2].   There was no existence previous to
the no existence before there was the beginning
of the no existence.   If suddenly there was non-
existence, we do not know whether it was really
anything existing, or really not existing.   Now
I have said what I have said, but I do not know
whether what I have said be really anything to the
point or not.

---

[1] Referring, I think, to those below commencing ' There was a
beginning.'

[2] That is, looking at things from the standpoint of an original
non-existence, and discarding all considerations of space and time.

Under heaven there is nothing greater than the
tip of an autumn down, and the Thâi mountain is
small.   There is no one more long-lived than a child
which dies prematurely, and Phăng 3û did not live
out his time.   Heaven, Earth, and I were produced
together, and all things and I are one.   Since they
are one, can there be speech about them?   But
since they are spoken of as one, must there not be
room for speech?   One and Speech are two; two
and one are three.   Going on from this (in our
enumeration), the most skilful reckoner cannot
reach (the end of the necessary numbers), and how
much less can ordinary people do so!   Therefore
from non-existence we proceed to existence till we
arrive at three; proceeding from existence to existence, to how many should we reach?   Let us
abjure such procedure, and simply rest here[1].

7. The Tâo at first met with no responsive recognition.   Speech at first had no constant forms of
expression.   Because of this there came the demarcations (of different views).   Let me describe those
demarcations :—they are the Left and the Right[2];
the Relations and their Obligations[3]; Classifications[4]

---

[1] On this concluding clause, 3iâo Hung says :—'Avoiding such
procedure, there will be no affirmations and denials (no contraries).
The phrase 因 是 己 occurs in the Book several times, and in-
terpreters have missed its meaning from not observing that 是 己
serve merely as a final particle, and often have the 因 added to
them, without affecting its meaning.'   See also Wang Yin on the
usages of 因 in the 皇 清 經 解, ch. 1208, art. 6.

[2] That is, direct opposites.

[3] Literally, ' righteousnesses; ' the proper way of dealing with the
relations.

[4] Literally, ' separations.'

and their Distinctions ; Emulations and Contentions.
These are what are called 'the Eight Qualities.'
Outside the limits of the world of men[1], the sage
occupies his thoughts, but does not discuss about
anything; inside those limits he occupies his
thoughts, but does not pass any judgments.   In the
*Kh*un *Kh*iû[2], which embraces the history of the
former kings, the sage indicates his judgments, but
does not argue (in vindication of them).   Thus it is
that he separates his characters from one another
without appearing to do so, and argues without the
form of argument.   How does he do so ?   The sage
cherishes his views in his own breast, while men
generally state theirs argumentatively, to show them
to others.   Hence we have the saying, ' Disputation
is a proof of not seeing clearly.'

   The Great Tâo[3] does not admit of being praised.
The Great Argument does not require words.
Great Benevolence is not (officiously) benevolent.
Great Disinterestedness does not vaunt its humility.
Great Courage is not seen in stubborn bravery.

   The Tâo that is displayed is not the Tâo. Words
that are argumentative do not reach the point.
Benevolence that is constantly exercised does not
accomplish its object.   Disinterestedness that vaunts
its purity is not genuine.   Courage that is most stub-

---

   [1] Literally, ' the six conjunctions,' meaning the four cardinal
points of space, with the zenith and nadir ; sometimes a name for
the universe of space.   Here we must restrict the meaning as I
have done.
   [2] ' The Spring and Autumn ;'—Confucius's Annals of Lû, here
complimented by *K*wang-ȝze.   See in Mencius, IV, ii, 21.
   [3] Compare the Tâo Teh *K*ing, ch. 25, et al.

born is ineffectual. These five seem to be round (and complete), but they tend to become square (and immovable)[1]. Therefore the knowledge that stops at what it does not know is the greatest. Who knows the argument that needs no words, and the Way that is not to be trodden[2]?

He who is able to know this has what is called 'The Heavenly Treasure-house[3].' He may pour into it without its being filled; he may pour from it without its being exhausted; and all the while he does not know whence (the supply) comes. This is what is called 'The Store of Light[3].'

Therefore of old Yâo asked Shun, saying, 'I wish to smite (the rulers of) 3ung, Kwei, and Hsü-âo[4]. Even when standing in my court, I cannot get them out of my mind. How is it so?' Shun replied, 'Those three rulers live (in their little states) as if they were among the mugwort and other brushwood; —how is it that you cannot get them out of your mind? Formerly, ten suns came out together, and all things were illuminated by them;—how much should (your) virtue exceed (all) suns!'

8. Nieh *Kh*üeh[5] asked Wang Î[5], saying, 'Do you know, Sir, what all creatures agree in approving and

---

[1] Compare the use of 方 in the Shû *K*ing, I, iii, 11.

[2] The classic of Lâo, in chaps. 1, 2.

[3] Names for the Tâo.

[4] Three small states. Is Yâo's wish to smite an instance of the 'quality' of 'emulation' or jealousy?

[5] Both Tâoistic worthies of the time of Yâo, supposed to have been two of the Perfect Ones whom Yâo visited on the distant hill of Kû-shih (I, par. 6). According to Hwang Mî, Wang Î was the teacher of Nieh *Kh*üeh, and he again of Hsü Yû.

affirming?' 'How should I know it?' was the reply.
'Do you know what it is that you do not know?'
asked the other again, and he got the same reply.
He asked a third time,—'Then are all creatures thus
without knowledge?' and Wang Î answered as before,
(adding however), 'Notwithstanding, I will try and
explain my meaning. How do you know that when
I say "I know it," I really (am showing that) I do
not know it, and that when I say "I do not know
it," I really am showing that I do know it[1].' And
let me ask you some questions :—'If a man sleep in
a damp place, he will have a pain in his loins, and
half his body will be as if it were dead; but will it
be so with an eel? If he be living in a tree, he will
be frightened and all in a tremble; but will it be so
with a monkey? And does any one of the three
know his right place? Men eat animals that have
been fed on grain and grass; deer feed on the thick-
set grass; centipedes enjoy small snakes; owls and
crows delight in mice; but does any one of the four
know the right taste? The dog-headed monkey
finds its mate in the female gibbon; the elk and the
axis deer cohabit; and the eel enjoys itself with
other fishes. Mâo 3hiang[2] and Lî *K*î[2] were accounted by men to be most beautiful, but when
fishes saw them, they dived deep in the water from
them; when birds, they flew from them aloft; and

---

[1] Compare par. 1 of Book XXII.

[2] Two famous beauties;—the former, a contemporary of Hsî
Shih (par. 4, note 2), and like her also, of the state of Yüeh; the
latter, the daughter of a barbarian chief among the Western Jung.
She was captured by duke Hsien of 3in, in B.C. 672. He subsequently made her his wife,—to the great injury of his family
and state.

when deer saw them, they separated and fled away[1]. But did any of these four know which in the world is the right female attraction? As I look at the matter, the first principles of benevolence and righteousness and the paths of approval and disapproval are inextricably mixed and confused together:—how is it possible that I should know how to discriminate among them?'

Nieh *Kh*üeh said (further), ' Since you, Sir, do not know what is advantageous and what is hurtful, is the Perfect man also in the same way without the knowledge of them?' Wang Î replied, ' The Perfect man is spirit-like. Great lakes might be boiling about him, and he would not feel their heat; the Ho and the Han might be frozen up, and he would not feel the cold; the hurrying thunderbolts might split the mountains, and the wind shake the ocean, without being able to make him afraid. Being such, he mounts on the clouds of the air, rides on the sun and moon, and rambles at ease beyond the four seas. Neither death nor life makes any change in him, and how much less should the considerations of advantage and injury do so[2]!'

9. *Kh*ü 3hiâo-ȝze[3] asked *Kh*ang-wû 3ze[3], saying,

---

[1] Not thinking them beautiful, as men did, but frightened and repelled by them.

[2] Compare Book I, pars. 3 and 5.

[3] We know nothing of the former of these men, but what is mentioned here; the other appears also in Book XXV, 6, q. v. If ' the master' that immediately follows be Confucius they must have been contemporary with him. The *Kh*iû in *Kh*ang-wû's reply would seem to make it certain ' the master' was Confucius, but the oldest critics, and some modern ones as well, think that *Kh*ang-wû's name was also *Kh*iû. But this view is attended with more

' I heard the Master (speaking of such language as the following) :—" The sagely man does not occupy himself with worldly affairs. He does not put himself in the way of what is profitable, nor try to avoid what is hurtful; he has no pleasure in seeking (for anything from any one); he does not care to be found in (any established) Way; he speaks without speaking; he does not speak when he speaks ; thus finding his enjoyment outside the dust and dirt (of the world)." The Master considered all this to be a shoreless flow of mere words, and I consider it to describe the course of the Mysterious Way.—What do you, Sir, think of it?' *K*/*h*ang-wû 3ze replied, ' The hearing of such words would have perplexed even Hwang-Tî, and how should *K*/*h*iû be competent to understand them ? And you, moreover, are too hasty in forming your estimate (of their meaning). You see the egg, and (immediately) look out for the cock (that is to be hatched from it); you see the bow, and (immediately) look out for the dove (that is to be brought down by it) being roasted. I will try to explain the thing to you in a rough way; do you in the same way listen to me.

' How could any one stand by the side of the sun and moon, and hold under his arm all space and all time ? (Such language only means that the sagely man) keeps his mouth shut, and puts aside questions that are uncertain and dark ; making his inferior capacities unite with him in honouring (the One Lord). Men in general bustle about and toil ; the

---

difficulties than the other. By the clause interjected in the translation after the first ' Master,' I have avoided the incongruity of ascribing the long description of Tâoism to Confucius.

sagely man seems stupid and to know nothing[1]. He
blends ten thousand years together in the one (conception of time); the myriad things all pursue their
spontaneous course, and they are all before him as
doing so.

'How do I know that the love of life is not a
delusion? and that the dislike of death is not like
a young person's losing his way, and not knowing
that he is (really) going home? Lî Kî[2] was a daughter of the border Warden of Âi. When (the ruler
of) the state of Zin first got possession of her, she
wept till the tears wetted all the front of her dress.
But when she came to the place of the king[3], shared
with him his luxurious couch, and ate his grain-and-
grass-fed meat, then she regretted that she had wept.
How do I know that the dead do not repent of their
former craving for life?

'Those who dream of (the pleasures of) drinking
may in the morning wail and weep; those who dream
of wailing and weeping may in the morning be going
out to hunt. When they were dreaming they did
not know it was a dream; in their dream they
may even have tried to interpret it[4]; but when
they awoke they knew that it was a dream. And

---

[1] Compare Lâo-ȝze's account of himself in his Work, ch. 20.

[2] See note 2 on page 191. The lady is there said to have
been the daughter of a barbarian chief; here she appears as the
child of the border Warden of Âi. But her maiden surname of
Kî (姬) shows her father must have been a scion of the royal
family of Kâu. Had he forsaken his wardenship, and joined one
of the Tî tribes, which had adopted him as its chief?

[3] Zin was only a marquisate. How does Kwang-ȝze speak of its
ruler as 'a king?'

[4] This could not be; a man does not come to himself in his
dream, and in that state try to interpret it.

there is the great awaking, after which we shall
know that this life was a great dream[1]. All the
while, the stupid think they are awake, and with nice
discrimination insist on their knowledge; now playing the part of rulers, and now of grooms. Bigoted
was that Khiû! He and you are both dreaming. I
who say that you are dreaming am dreaming myself.
These words seem very strange; but if after ten
thousand ages we once meet with a great sage who
knows how to explain them, it will be as if we met
him (unexpectedly) some morning or evening.

10. 'Since you made me enter into this discussion
with you, if you have got the better of me and not I
of you, are you indeed right, and I indeed wrong?
If I have got the better of you and not you of me,
am I indeed right and you indeed wrong? Is the
one of us right and the other wrong? are we both
right or both wrong? Since we cannot come to a
mutual and common understanding, men will certainly continue in darkness on the subject.

'Whom shall I employ to adjudicate in the matter?
If I employ one who agrees with you, how can he,
agreeing with you, do so correctly? And the same
may be said, if I employ one who agrees with me.
It will be the same if I employ one who differs from
us both or one who agrees with us both. In this
way I and you and those others would all not
be able to come to a mutual understanding; and
shall we then wait for that (great sage)? (We need
not do so.) To wait on others to learn how conflicting opinions are changed is simply like not so

---

[1] Compare XVIII, par. 4.

waiting at all. The harmonising of them is to be found in the invisible operation of Heaven, and by following this on into the unlimited past. It is by this method that we can complete our years (without our minds being disturbed)[1].

'What is meant by harmonising (conflicting opinions) in the invisible operation of Heaven? There is the affirmation and the denial of it; and there is the assertion of an opinion and the rejection of it. If the affirmation be according to the reality of the fact, it is certainly different from the denial of it:— there can be no dispute about that. If the assertion of an opinion be correct, it is certainly different from its rejection:—neither can there be any dispute about that. Let us forget the lapse of time; let us forget the conflict of opinions. Let us make our appeal to the Infinite, and take up our position there[2].'

11. The Penumbra asked the Shadow[3], saying, 'Formerly you were walking on, and now you have stopped; formerly you were sitting, and now you have risen up:—how is it that you are so without stability?' The Shadow replied, 'I wait for the movements of something else to do what I do, and that something else on which I wait waits further

---

[1] See this passage again in Book XXVII, par. 1, where the phrase which I have called here 'the invisible operation of Heaven,' is said to be the same as 'the Heavenly Mould or Moulder,' that is, the Heavenly Fashioner, one of the Tâoistic names for the Tâo.

[2] That is, all things being traced up to the unity of the Tâo, we have found the pivot to which all conflicting opinions, all affirmations, all denials, all positions and negatives converge, and bring to bear on them the proper light of the mind. Compare paragraph 3.

[3] A story to the same effect as this here, with some textual variations, occurs in Book XXVII, immediately after par. 1 referred to above.

on another to do as it does [1]. My waiting,—is it for
the scales of a snake, or the wings of a cicada[2]?
How should I know why I do one thing, or do not
do another [3] ?

   ' Formerly, I, *K*wang *K*âu, dreamt that I was a
butterfly, a butterfly flying about, feeling that it
was enjoying itself. I did not know that it was *K*âu.
Suddenly I awoke, and was myself again, the veri-
table *K*âu. I did not know whether it had formerly
been *K*âu dreaming that he was a butterfly, or it
was now a butterfly dreaming that it was *K*âu. But
between *K*âu and a butterfly there must be a difference [4]. This is a case of what is called the Transformation of Things [4].'

---

   [1] The mind cannot rest in second causes, and the first cause, if
there be one, is inscrutable.
   [2] Even these must wait for the will of the creature; but the case
of the shadow is still more remarkable.
   [3] I have put this interrogatively, as being more graphic, and
because of the particle 則, which is generally, though not necessarily, interrogative.
   [4] Hsüan Ying, in his remarks on these two sentences, brings
out the force of the story very successfully:—' Looking at them in
their ordinary appearance, there was necessarily a difference between
them, but in the delusion of the dream each of them appeared the
other, and they could not distinguish themselves! *K*âu could be a
butterfly, and the butterfly could be *K*âu;—we may see that in the
world all traces of that and this may pass away, as they come under
the influence of transformations.' For the phrase, ' the transformation of things,' see in Book XI, par. 5, et al. But the Tâoism here
can hardly be distinguished from the Buddhism that holds that all
human experience is merely so much mâya or illusion.

BOOK III.

Part I. Section III.

Yang Shang *K*û, or 'Nourishing the Lord of Life[1].'

1. There is a limit to our life, but to knowledge there is no limit. With what is limited to pursue after what is unlimited is a perilous thing; and when, knowing this, we still seek the increase of our knowledge, the peril cannot be averted[2]. There should not be the practice of what is good with any thought of the fame (which it will bring), nor of what is evil with any approximation to the punishment (which it will incur)[3]:—an accordance with the Central Element (of our nature)[4] is the regular way to preserve the body, to maintain the life, to nourish our parents, and to complete our term of years.

2. His cook[5] was cutting up an ox for the ruler Wăn-hui[5]. Whenever he applied his hand, leaned forward with his shoulder, planted his foot, and em-

---

[1] See pp. 130, 131.

[2] Under what is said about knowledge here there lies the objection of Tâoists to the Confucian pursuit of knowledge as the means for the right conduct of life, instead of the quiet simplicity and self-suppression of their own system.

[3] This is the key to the three paragraphs that follow. But the text of it is not easily construed. The 'doing good' and the 'doing evil' are to be lightly understood.

[4] A name for the Tâo.

[5] 'The ruler Wăn-hui' is understood to be 'king Hui of Liang (or Wei),' with the account of an interview between whom and Mencius the works of that philosopher commence.

ployed the pressure of his knee, in the audible rip-
ping off of the skin, and slicing operation of the
knife, the sounds were all in regular cadence. Movements and sounds proceeded as in the dance of ' the
Mulberry Forest [1] ' and the blended notes of ' the
*K*ing Shâu [1].' The ruler said, 'Ah! Admirable!
That your art should have become so perfect!'
(Having finished his operation), the cook laid down
his knife, and replied to the remark, 'What your
servant loves is the method of the Tâo, something
in advance of any art. When I first began to cut
up an ox, I saw nothing but the (entire) carcase.
After three years I ceased to see it as a whole. Now
I deal with it in a spirit-like manner, and do not look
at it with my eyes. The use of my senses is discarded, and my spirit acts as it wills. Observing the
natural lines, (my knife) slips through the great
crevices and slides through the great cavities, taking
advantage of the facilities thus presented. My art
avoids the membranous ligatures, and much more
the great bones.

'A good cook changes his knife every year;—(it
may have been injured) in cutting; an ordinary cook
changes his every month;—(it may have been)
broken. Now my knife has been in use for nineteen years; it has cut up several thousand oxen, and
yet its edge is as sharp as if it had newly come from
the whetstone. There are the interstices of the
joints, and the edge of the knife has no (appreciable)
thickness; when that which is so thin enters where
the interstice is, how easily it moves along! The

---

[1] Two pieces of music, ascribed to *K*hăng Thang and Hwang-
Tî.

blade has more than room enough. Nevertheless, whenever I come to a complicated joint, and see that there will be some difficulty, I proceed anxiously and with caution, not allowing my eyes to wander from the place, and moving my hand slowly. Then by a very slight movement of the knife, the part is quickly separated, and drops like (a clod of) earth to the ground. Then standing up with the knife in my hand, I look all round, and in a leisurely manner, with an air of satisfaction, wipe it clean, and put it in its sheath.' The ruler Wăn-hui said, 'Excellent! I have heard the words of my cook, and learned from them the nourishment of (our) life.'

3. When Kung-wăn Hsien[1] saw the Master of the Left, he was startled, and said, 'What sort of man is this? How is it he has but one foot? Is it from Heaven? or from Man?' Then he added[2], 'It must be from Heaven, and not from Man. Heaven's making of this man caused him to have but one foot. In the person of man, each foot has its marrow. By this I know that his peculiarity is from Heaven, and not from Man. A pheasant of the marshes has to take ten steps to pick up a mouthful of food, and thirty steps to get a drink, but it does not seek to be nourished in a coop. Though its spirit would (there) enjoy a royal abundance, it does not think (such confinement) good.'

---

[1] There was a family in Wei with the double surname Kung-wăn. This would be a scion of it.

[2] This is Hsien still speaking. We have to understand his reasoning ad sensum and not ad verbum. The master of the Left had done 'evil,' so as to incur the punishment from which he suffered; and had shown himself less wise than a pheasant.

4. When Lâo Tan died [1], *K*hin Shih [2] went to condole (with his son), but after crying out three times,
he came out. The disciples [3] said to him, 'Were
you not a friend of the Master?' 'I was,' he replied, and they said, 'Is it proper then to offer your
condolences merely as you have done?' He said,
'It is. At first I thought he was the man of men,
and now I do not think so. When I entered a little
ago and expressed my condolences, there were
the old men wailing as if they had lost a son, and
the young men wailing as if they had lost their
mother. In his attracting and uniting them to himself in such a way there must have been that which
made them involuntarily express their words (of
condolence), and involuntarily wail, as they were
doing. And this was a hiding from himself of his
Heaven (-nature), and an excessive indulgence of his
(human) feelings;—a forgetting of what he had received (in being born); what the ancients called the
punishment due to neglecting the Heaven (-nature) [4].
When the Master came [5], it was at the proper time;
when he went away, it was the simple sequence (of
his coming). Quiet acquiescence in what happens
at its proper time, and quietly submitting (to its
ceasing) afford no occasion for grief or for joy [6]. The
ancients described (death) as the loosening of the

---

[1] Then the account that Lâo-3ze went westwards, and that
nothing is known as to where he died, must be without foundation.

[2] Nothing more is known of this person.

[3] Probably the disciples of Lâo-3ze.

[4] Lâo had gone to an excess in his 'doing good,' as if he were
seeking reputation.

[5] Into the world.

[6] See *K*wang-3ze's remarks and demeanour on the death of his
wife, in Book XVIII.

cord on which God suspended (the life) ¹. What we can point to are the faggots that have been consumed; but the fire is transmitted (elsewhere), and we know not that it is over and ended ².

---

¹ This short sentence is remarkable by the use of the character Tî (帝), 'God,' in it, a usage here ascribed to the ancients.

² The concluding sentence might stand as a short paragraph by itself. The 'faggots' are understood to represent the body, and the 'fire' the animating spirit. The body perishes at death as the faggots are consumed by the fire. But the fire may be transmitted to other faggots, and so the spirit may migrate, and be existing elsewhere.

BOOK IV.

PART I. SECTION IV.

*Z*ăn *K*ien Shih, or 'Man in the World, Associated with other Men[1].'

1. Yen Hui[2] went to see *K*ung-nî[3], and asked leave to take his departure. 'Where are you going to?' asked the Master. 'I will go to Wei[4]' was the reply. 'And with what object?' 'I have heard that the ruler of Wei[5] is in the vigour of his years, and consults none but himself as to his course. He deals with his state as if it were a light matter, and has no perception of his errors. He thinks lightly of his people's dying; the dead are lying all over the country as if no smaller space could contain them; on the plains[6] and about the marshes, they are as thick as heaps of fuel. The people know not where to turn to. I have heard you, Master, say, "Leave the state that is well

---

[1] See pp. 131, 132.

[2] The favourite disciple of Confucius, styled also 3ze-yüan.

[3] Of course, Confucius;—his designation or married name.

[4] A feudal state, embracing portions of the present provinces of Ho-nan, *K*îh-lî, and Shan-tung. There was another state, which we must also call Wei in English, though the Chinese characters of them are different;—one of the fragments of the great state of 3in, more to the west.

[5] At this time the marquis Yüan, known to us by his post-humous title of duke Ling;—see Book XXV, 9.

[6] Adopting Lin's reading of 平 instead of the common 乎.

governed ; go to the state where disorder prevails [1]."
At the door of a physician there are many who are
ill.   I wish through what I have heard (from you)
to think out some methods (of dealing with Wei), if
peradventure the evils of the state may be cured.'

*K*ung-nî said, 'Alas!   The risk is that you will
go only to suffer in the punishment (of yourself)!
The right method (in such a case) will not admit
of any admixture.   With such admixture, the one
method will become many methods.   Their multiplication will embarrass you.   That embarrassment
will make you anxious.   However anxious you may
be, you will not save (yourself).   The perfect men
of old first had (what they wanted to do) in themselves, and afterwards they found (the response to
it) in others.   If what they wanted in themselves
was not fixed, what leisure had they to go and
interfere with the proceedings of any tyrannous
man ?

'Moreover, do you know how virtue is liable to
be dissipated, and how wisdom proceeds to display
itself ?   Virtue is dissipated in (the pursuit of) the
name for it, and wisdom seeks to display itself in the
striving with others.   In the pursuit of the name
men overthrow one another ;   wisdom becomes
a weapon of contention.   Both these things are
instruments of evil, and should not be allowed to
have free course in one's conduct.   Supposing one's
virtue to be great and his sincerity firm, if he do
not comprehend the spirit of those (whom he wishes
to influence) ;   and supposing he is free from the

---

[1] Compare in the Analects, VIII, xiii, 2, where a different
lesson is given ; but Confucius may at another time have spoken
as Hui says.

disposition to strive for reputation, if he do not comprehend their minds;—when in such a case he forcibly insists on benevolence and righteousness, setting them forth in the strongest and most direct language, before the tyrant, then he, hating (his reprover's) possession of those excellences, will put him down as doing him injury.   He who injures others is sure to be injured by them in return. You indeed will hardly escape being injured by the man (to whom you go)!

'Further, if perchance he takes pleasure in men of worth and hates those of an opposite character, what is the use of your seeking to make yourself out to be different (from such men about him)? Before you have begun to announce (your views), he, as king and ruler, will take advantage of you, and immediately contend with you for victory. Your eyes will be dazed and full of perplexity; you will try to look pleased with him; you will frame your words with care; your demeanour will be conformed to his; you will confirm him in his views.   In this way you will be adding fire to fire, and water to water, increasing, as we may express it, the evils (which you deplore).   To these signs of deferring to him at the first there will be no end. You will be in danger, seeing he does not believe you, of making your words more strong, and you are sure to die at the hands of such a tyrant.

'And formerly Kieh[1] killed Kwan Lung-făng[2], and Kâu[3] killed the prince Pî-kan[4].   Both of

---

[1] The tyrant with whom the dynasty of Hsiâ ended.

[2] A worthy minister of Kieh.

[3] The tyrant with whom the dynasty of Shang or Yin ended.

[4] A half-brother of Kâu, the tyrant of the Yin dynasty.

these cultivated their persons, bending down in sympathy with the lower people to comfort them suffering (as they did) from their oppressors, and on their account opposing their superiors. On this account, because they so ordered their conduct, their rulers compassed their destruction:—such regard had they for their own fame. (Again), Yâo anciently attacked (the states of) 3hung-kih [1] and Hsü-âo [1], and Yü attacked the ruler of Hû [1]. Those states were left empty, and with no one to continue their population, the people being exterminated. They had engaged in war without ceasing; their craving for whatever they could get was insatiable. And this (ruler of Wei) is, like them, one who craves after fame and greater substance;—have you not heard it? Those sages were not able to overcome the thirst for fame and substance;—how much less will you be able to do so! Nevertheless you must have some ground (for the course which you wish to take); pray try and tell it to me.'

Yen Hui said, 'May I go, doing so in uprightness and humility, using also every endeavour to be uniform (in my plans of operation)?' 'No, indeed!' was the reply. 'How can you do so? This man makes a display [2] of being filled to overflowing (with virtue), and has great self-conceit. His feelings are not to be determined from his countenance. Ordinary men do not (venture to) oppose him, and he proceeds from the way in which he affects them

---

[1] See in par. 7, Book II, where Hsü-âo is mentioned, though not 3hung-kih. See the Shû, III, ii.

[2] I take 陽 here as = 佯;—a meaning given in the Khang-hsî dictionary.

to seek still more the satisfaction of his own mind.
He may be described as unaffected by the (small
lessons of) virtue brought to bear on him from day
to day; and how much less will he be so by your
great lessons? He will be obstinate, and refuse
to be converted. He may outwardly agree with
you, but inwardly there will be no self-condemna-
tion;—how can you (go to him in this way and be
successful)?'

(Yen Hui) rejoined, 'Well then; while inwardly
maintaining my straightforward intention, I will
outwardly seem to bend to him. I will deliver (my
lessons), and substantiate them by appealing to
antiquity. Inwardly maintaining my straightforward
intention, I shall be a co-worker with Heaven.
When I thus speak of being a co-worker with
Heaven, it is because I know that (the sovereign,
whom we style) the son of Heaven, and myself, are
equally regarded by Heaven as Its sons. And
should I then, as if my words were only my own,
be seeking to find whether men approved of them,
or disapproved of them? In this way men will
pronounce me a (sincere and simple [1]) boy. This
is what is called being a co-worker with Heaven.

'Outwardly bending (to the ruler), I shall be a
co-worker with other men. To carry (the memorandum tablet to court) [2], to kneel, and to bend the
body reverentially:—these are the observances of
ministers. They all employ them, and should I
presume not to do so? Doing what other men do,
they would have no occasion to blame me. This

---

[1] Entirely unsophisticated, governed by the Tâo.
[2] See the Lî *K*î, XI, ii, 16, 17.

THE TEXTS OF TÂOISM.K. IV.

is what is called being a fellow-worker with other men.

'Fully declaring my sentiments and substantiating them by appealing to antiquity, I shall be a co-worker with the ancients. Although the words in which I convey my lessons may really be condemnatory (of the ruler), they will be those of antiquity, and not my own. In this way, though straightforward, I shall be free from blame. This is what is called being a co-worker with antiquity. May I go to Wei in this way, and be successful?' 'No indeed!' said *K*ung-nî. 'How can you do so? You have too many plans of proceeding, and have not spied out (the ruler's character). Though you firmly adhere to your plans, you may be held free from transgression, but this will be all the result. How can you (in this way) produce the transformation (which you desire)? All this only shows (in you) the mind of a teacher!'

2. Yen Hui said, 'I can go no farther; I venture to ask the method from you.' *K*ung-nî replied, 'It is fasting[1], (as) I will tell you. (But) when you have the method, will you find it easy to practise it? He who thinks it easy will be disapproved of by the bright Heaven.' Hui said, 'My family is poor. For months together we have no spirituous drink, nor do we taste the proscribed food or any strong-smelling vegetables[2];—can this be regarded as fasting?' The reply was, 'It is the fasting appropriate to sacrificing, but it is not the fasting

---

[1] The term is emphatic, as Confucius goes on to explain.

[2] Such as onions and garlic, with horse, dog, cow, goose, and pigeon.

of the mind.' 'I venture to ask what that fasting of the mind is,' said Hui, and *K*ung-nî answered, 'Maintain a perfect unity in every movement of your will. You will not wait for the hearing of your ears about it, but for the hearing of your mind. You will not wait even for the hearing of your mind, but for the hearing of the spirit[1]. Let the hearing (of the ears) rest with the ears. Let the mind rest in the verification (of the rightness of what is in the will). But the spirit is free from all pre-occupation and so waits for (the appearance of) things. Where the (proper) course is[2], there is freedom from all pre-occupation;—such freedom is the fasting of the mind.' Hui said[3], 'Before it was possible for me to employ (this method), there I was, the Hui that I am; now, that I can employ it, the Hui that I was has passed away. Can I be said to have obtained this freedom from pre-occupation?' The Master replied, 'Entirely. I tell you that you can enter and be at ease in the enclosure (where he is), and not come into collision with the reputation (which belongs to him). If he listen to your counsels, let him hear your notes; if he will not listen, be silent. Open no (other) door; employ no other medicine; dwell with him (as with a friend) in the same apartment, and as if you had no other option, and you will not be far from success in your object. Not to move a step is easy; to walk without treading on the ground is difficult. In acting after the manner of men, it is easy to fall

---

[1] The character in the text for 'spirit' here is 氣, 'the breath.'

[2] The T âo.

[3] 'Said;' probably, after having made trial of this fasting.

into hypocrisy; in acting after the manner of Heaven, it is difficult to play the hypocrite. I have heard of flying with wings; I have not heard of flying without them. I have heard of the knowledge of the wise; I have not heard of the knowledge of the unwise. Look at that aperture (left in the wall);—the empty apartment is filled with light through it. Felicitous influences rest (in the mind thus emblemed), as in their proper resting place. Even when they do not so rest, we have what is called (the body) seated and (the mind) galloping abroad. The information that comes through the ears and eyes is comprehended internally, and the knowledge of the mind becomes something external:—(when this is the case), the spiritual intelligences will come, and take up their dwelling with us, and how much more will other men do so! All things thus undergo a transforming influence. This was the hinge on which Yü and Shun moved; it was this which Fû-hsî [1] and Kî-khü [2] practised all their lives: how much more should other men follow the same rule!'

3. Ꝫze-kâo [3], duke of Sheh, being about to proceed on a mission to Khî, asked Kung-nî, saying, ' The king is sending me, Kû-liang [3], on a mission which

---

[1] Often spoken of as Fo-hî, the founder of the Chinese kingdom. His place in chronology should be assigned to him more than B.C. 3000 rather than under that date.

[2] A predecessor of Fû-hsî, a sovereign of the ancient paradisiacal time.

[3] The name of Sheh remains in Sheh-hsien, a district of the department Nan-yang, Ho-nan. Its governor, who is the subject of this narrative, was a Shăn Kû-liang, styled Ꝫze-kâo. He was

is very important. *K*hî will probably treat me as his commissioner with great respect, but it will not be in a hurry (to attend to the business). Even an ordinary man cannot be readily moved (to action), and how much less the prince of a state! I am very full of apprehension. You, Sir, once said to me that of all things, great or small, there were few which, if not conducted in the proper way[1], could be brought to a happy conclusion; that, if the thing were not successful, there was sure to be the evil of being dealt with after the manner of men[2]; that, if it were successful, there was sure to be the evil of constant anxiety[3]; and that, whether it succeeded or not, it was only the virtuous man who could secure its not being followed by evil. In my diet I take what is coarse, and do not seek delicacies,—a man whose cookery does not require him to be using cooling drinks. This morning I received my charge, and in the evening I am drinking iced water;—am I not feeling the internal heat (and discomfort)? Such is my state before I have actually engaged in the affair;—I am already suffering from conflicting anxieties. And if the thing do not succeed, (the king) is sure to deal with me after the manner of men. The evil is twofold; as a minister, I am not able to bear the burden (of the mission). Can

---

not a duke, but as the counts of *K*hû had usurped the name of king, they gave high-sounding names to all their ministers and officers.

[1] Or, 'according to the Tâo.'

[2] As a criminal; punished by his sovereign.

[3] Anxiety 'night and day,' or 'cold and hot' fits of trouble;—a peculiar usage of Yin Yang.

you, Sir, tell me something (to help me in the case)?'

*K*ung-nî replied, 'In all things under heaven there are two great cautionary considerations :—the one is the requirement implanted (in the nature)[1] ; the other is the conviction of what is right.   The love of a son for his parents is the implanted requirement, and can never be separated from his heart; the service of his ruler by a minister is what is right, and from its obligation there is no escaping anywhere between heaven and earth.   These are what are called the great cautionary considerations. Therefore a son finds his rest in serving his parents without reference to or choice of place; and this is the height of filial duty.   In the same way a subject finds his rest in serving his ruler, without reference to or choice of the business; and this is the fullest discharge of loyalty.   When men are simply obeying (the dictates of) their hearts, the considerations of grief and joy are not readily set before them.   They know that there is no alternative to their acting as they do, and rest in it as what is appointed; and this is the highest achievement of virtue.   He who is in the position of a minister or of a son has indeed to do what he cannot but do.   Occupied with the details of the business (in hand), and forgetful of his own person, what leisure has he to think of his pleasure in living or his dislike of death ?   You, my master, may well proceed on your mission.

'But let me repeat to you what I have heard :—In

---

[1] The Ming of the text here is that in the first sentence of the *K*ung Yung.

all intercourse (between states), if they are near to each other, there should be mutual friendliness, verified by deeds; if they are far apart, there must be sincere adherence to truth in their messages. Those messages will be transmitted by internuncios. But to convey messages which express the complacence or the dissatisfaction of the two parties is the most difficult thing in the world. If they be those of mutual complacence, there is sure to be an overflow of expressions of satisfaction; if of mutual dissatisfaction, an overflow of expressions of dislike. But all extravagance leads to reckless language, and such language fails to command belief. When this distrust arises, woe to the internuncio! Hence the Rules for Speech[1] say, "Transmit the message exactly as it stands; do not transmit it with any overflow of language; so is (the internuncio) likely to keep himself whole."

4. 'Moreover, skilful wrestlers begin with open trials of strength, but always end with masked attempts (to gain the victory); as their excitement grows excessive, they display much wonderful dexterity. Parties drinking according to the rules at first observe good order, but always end with disorder; as their excitement grows excessive, their fun becomes uproarious[2]. In all things it is so. People are at first sincere, but always end with becoming rude; at the commencement things are treated as trivial,

---

[1] Probably a Collection of Directions current at the time; and which led to the name of Yang Hsiung's Treatise with the same name in our first century.

[2] See the Shih, II, vii, 6.

but as the end draws near, they assume great proportions. Words are (like) the waves acted on by
the wind; the real point of the matters (discussed by
them) is lost. The wind and waves are easily set in
motion; the success of the matter of which the real
point is lost is easily put in peril. Hence quarrels
are occasioned by nothing so much as by artful words
and one-sided speeches. The breath comes angrily,
as when a beast, driven to death, wildly bellows forth
its rage. On this animosities arise on both sides.
Hasty examination (of the case) eagerly proceeds,
and revengeful thoughts arise in their minds;—they
do not know how. Since they do not know how
such thoughts arise, who knows how they will end?
Hence the Rules for Speech [1] say, "Let not an in-
ternuncius depart from his instructions. Let him
not urge on a settlement. If he go beyond the
regular rules, he will complicate matters. Departing
from his instructions and urging on a settlement im-
perils negotiations. A good settlement is proved by
its lasting long, and a bad settlement cannot be
altered;—ought he not to be careful?"

'Further still, let your mind find its enjoyment in
the circumstances of your position; nourish the central course which you pursue, by a reference to your
unavoidable obligations. This is the highest object
for you to pursue; what else can you do to fulfil the
charge (of your father and ruler) [2]. The best thing
you can do is to be prepared to sacrifice your life;
and this is the most difficult thing to do.'

---

[1] See above, on preceding page.
[2] Not meaning the king of *Khû*; but the Tâo, whose will was
to be found in his nature and the conditions of his lot.

5. Yen Ho[1], being about to undertake the office of Teacher of the eldest son of duke Ling of Wei, consulted ᴋü Po-yü[2]. 'Here,' said he, 'is this (young) man, whose natural disposition is as bad as it could be.   If I allow him to proceed in a bad way, it will be at the peril of our state ; if I insist on his proceeding in a right way, it will be at the peril of my own person.   His wisdom is just sufficient to know the errors of other men, but he does not know how he errs himself.   What am I to do in such a case ?' ᴋü Po-yü replied, 'Good indeed is your question!   Be on your guard; be careful; see that you keep yourself correct!   Your best plan will be, with your person to seek association with him, and with your mind to try to be in harmony with him; and yet there are dangers connected with both of these things.   While seeking to keep near to him, do not enter into his pursuits ; while cultivating a harmony of mind with him, do not show how superior you are to him.   If in your personal association you enter into his pursuits, you will fall with him and be ruined, you will tumble down with a crash.   If in maintaining a harmony with his mind, you show how different you are from him, he will think you do so for the reputation and the name, and regard you as a creature of evil omen[3].   If you find him to be a mere boy, be you with him as another boy ; if you find him one of those who will not have their ground marked out in the ordinary way, do you humour

---

[1] A member of the Yen family of Lû. We shall meet with him again in Books XIX, XXVIII, and XXXII.

[2] A minister of Wei ; a friend and favourite of Confucius.

[3] Compare in the ᴋung Yung, ii, ch. 24.

him in this characteristic [1]; if you find him to be free from lofty airs, show yourself to be the same;—(ever) leading him on so as to keep him free from faults.

'Do you not know (the fate of) the praying mantis? It angrily stretches out its arms, to arrest the progress of the carriage, unconscious of its inability for such a task, but showing how much it thinks of its own powers. Be on your guard; be careful. If you cherish a boastful confidence in your own excellence, and place yourself in collision with him, you are likely to incur the fate (of the mantis).

'Do you not know how those who keep tigers proceed? They do not dare to supply them with living creatures, because of the rage which their killing of them will excite. They do not (even) dare to give them their food whole, because of the rage which their rending of it will excite. They watch till their hunger is appeased, (dealing with them) from their knowledge of their natural ferocity. Tigers are different from men, but they fawn on those who feed them, and do so in accordance with their nature. When any of these are killed by them, it is because they have gone against that nature.

'Those again who are fond of horses preserve their dung in baskets, and their urine in jars. If musquitoes and gadflies light on them, and the grooms brush them suddenly away, the horses break their bits, injure (the ornaments on) their heads, and smash those on their breasts. The more care that is taken of them, the more does their fond-

---

[1] Equivalent to 'Do not cross him in his peculiarities.'

ness (for their attendants) disappear.   Ought not caution to be exercised (in the management of them)?'

6. A (master) mechanic, called Shih, on his way to *K*hî, came to *K*hü-yüan[1], where he saw an oak-tree, which was used as the altar for the spirits of the land.   It was so large that an ox standing behind it could not be seen.   It measured a hundred spans round, and rose up eighty cubits on the hill before it threw out any branches, after which there were ten or so, from each of which a boat could be hollowed out.   People came to see it in crowds as in a market place, but the mechanic did not look round at it, but held on his way without stopping.   One of his workmen, however, looked long and admiringly at it, and then ran on to his master, and said to him, ' Since I followed you with my axe and bill, I have never seen such a beautiful mass of timber as this.   Why would you, Sir, not look round at it, but went on without stopping?'   'Have done,' said Mr. Shih, ' and do not speak about it.   It is quite useless.   A boat made from its wood would sink; a coffin or shell would quickly rot; an article of furniture would soon go to pieces; a door would be covered with the exuding sap; a pillar would be riddled by insects; the material of it is good for nothing, and hence it is that it has attained to so great an age[2].'

---

[1] The name of a place; of a road; of a bend in the road; of a hill.   All these accounts of the name are found in different editions of our author, showing that the locality had not been identified.

[2] No one has thought it worth cutting down.

When Mr. Shih was returning, the altar-oak appeared to him in a dream, and said, 'What other tree will you compare with me? Will you compare me to one of your ornamental trees? There are hawthorns, pear-trees, orange-trees, pummelo-trees, gourds and other low fruit-bearing plants. When their fruits are ripe, they are knocked down from them, and thrown among the dirt[1]. The large branches are broken, and the smaller are torn away. So it is that their productive ability makes their lives bitter to them; they do not complete their natural term of existence, but come to a premature end in the middle of their time, bringing on themselves the destructive treatment which they ordinarily receive. It is so with all things. I have sought to discover how it was that I was so useless; —I had long done so, till (the effort) nearly caused my death; and now I have learned it :—it has been of the greatest use to me. Suppose that I had possessed useful properties, should I have become of the great size that I am? And moreover you and I are both things;—how should one thing thus pass its judgment on another? how is it that you a useless man know all this about me a useless tree?' When Mr. Shih awoke, he kept thinking about his dream, but the workman said, 'Being so taken with its uselessness, how is it that it yet acts here as the altar for the spirits of the land?' 'Be still,' was the master's reply, 'and do not say a word. It simply happened to grow here; and thus those who do not know it do not speak ill of it as an evil thing. If it were not used as the altar, would it be in danger of

---

[1] This is the indignity intended.

being cut down ?   Moreover, the reason of its being preserved is different from that of the preservation of things generally ; is not your explaining it from the sentiment which you have expressed wide of the mark ? '

7. Nan-po 3ze-*kh*î[1] in rambling about the Heights of Shang[2], saw a large and extraordinary tree.   The teams of a thousand chariots might be sheltered under it, and its shade would cover them all!   3ze-*kh*î said, ' What a tree is this!   It must contain an extraordinary amount of timber !   When he looked up, however, at its smaller branches, they were so twisted and crooked that they could not be made into rafters and beams ; when he looked down to its root, its stem was divided into so many rounded portions that neither coffin nor shell could be made from them.   He licked one of its leaves, and his mouth felt torn and wounded.   The smell of it would make a man frantic, as if intoxicated, for more than three whole days together.   ' This, indeed,' said he, ' is a tree good for nothing, and it is thus that it has attained to such a size.   Ah! and spirit-like men acknowledge this worthlessness (and its result)[3].'

In Sung there is the district of *K*ing-shih[4], in which catalpae, cypresses, and mulberry trees grow well.   Those of them which are a span or two or rather more in circumference[5] are cut down by persons who want to make posts to which to tie their

---

[1] Probably the Nan-kwo 3ze-*kh*î at the beginning of the second Book.

[2] In the present department of Kwei-teh, Ho-nan.

[3] A difficult sentence to construe.

[4] In what part of the duchy we do not know.

[5] See Mencius, VI, i, 13.

monkeys; those which are three or four spans
round are cut down by persons who want beams for
their lofty and famous houses; and those of seven
or eight spans are cut down by noblemen and rich
merchants who want single planks for the sides of
their coffins. The trees in consequence do not
complete their natural term of life, and come to a
premature end in the middle of their growth under
the axe and bill;—this is the evil that befalls them
from their supplying good timber.

In the same way the *K*ieh [1] (book) specifies oxen
that have white foreheads, pigs that have turned-up
snouts, and men that are suffering from piles, and
forbids their being sacrificed to the Ho. The
wizards know them by these peculiarities and consider them to be inauspicious, but spirit-like men
consider them on this account to be very fortunate.

8. There was the deformed object Shû [2]. His chin
seemed to hide his navel; his shoulders were higher
than the crown of his head; the knot of his hair
pointed to the sky; his five viscera were all com-
pressed into the upper part of his body, and his two
thigh bones were like ribs. By sharpening needles
and washing clothes he was able to make a living.
By sifting rice and cleaning it, he was able to support
ten individuals. When the government was calling
out soldiers, this poor Shû would bare his arms
among the others; when it had any great service
to be undertaken, because of his constant ailments,
none of the work was assigned to him; when it was

---

[1] Probably the name of an old work on sacrifices. But was there
ever a time in China when human sacrifices were offered to the Ho,
or on any altar?

[2] One of *K*wang-ʒze's creations.

giving out grain to the sick, he received three *k*ung, and ten bundles of firewood. If this poor man, so deformed in body, was still able to support himself, and complete his term of life, how much more may they do so, whose deformity is that of their faculties[1]!

9. When Confucius went to *K*hû[2], *K*hieh-yû, the madman of *K*hû[3], as he was wandering about, passed by his door, and said, ' O Phoenix, O Phoenix, how is your virtue degenerated! The future is not to be waited for; the past is not to be sought again! When good order prevails in the world, the sage tries to accomplish all his service; when disorder prevails, he may preserve his life; at the present time, it is enough if he simply escape being punished. Happiness is lighter than a feather, but no one knows how to support it; calamity is heavier than the earth, and yet no one knows how to avoid it. Give over! give over approaching men with the lessons of your virtue! You are in peril! you are in peril, hurrying on where you have marked out the ground against your advance! I avoid publicity, I avoid publicity, that my path may not be injured. I pursue my course, now going backwards, now crookedly, that my feet may not be hurt[4].

---

[1] The deficiency of their faculties—here mental faculties—would assimilate them to the useless trees in the last two paragraphs, whose uselessness only proved useful to them.

[2] The great state of the south, having its capital in the present Hû-pei.

[3] See the Analects, XVIII, v.

[4] The madman would seem to contrast his own course with that of Confucius; but the meaning is very uncertain, and the text cannot be discussed fully in these short notes. There is a jingle

'The mountain by its trees weakens itself [1]. The grease which ministers to the fire fries itself. The cinnamon tree can be eaten, and therefore it is cut down. The varnish tree is useful, and therefore incisions are made in it. All men know the advantage of being useful, but no one knows the advantage of being useless.'

of rhyme also in the sentence, and some critics find something like this in them:

'Ye ferns, ye thorny ferns, O injure not my way!
To save my feet, I backward turn, or winding stray!'

[1] Literally, 'robs itself;'—exhausts its moisture or productive strength.

BOOK V.

PART I. SECTION V.

Teh *Kh*ung Fû, or 'The Seal of Virtue
Complete[1].'

1. In Lû[2] there was a Wang Thâi[3] who had lost
both his feet[4]; while his disciples who followed and
went about with him were as numerous as those of
*K*ung-nî. *Kh*ang *K*î[5] asked *K*ung-nî about him,
saying, 'Though Wang Thâi is a cripple, the disciples who follow him about divide Lû equally with
you, Master. When he stands, he does not teach
them; when he sits, he does not discourse to them.
But they go to him empty, and come back full. Is
there indeed such a thing as instruction without
words[6]? and while the body is imperfect, may the
mind be complete? What sort of man is he?'

*K*ung-nî replied, 'This master is a sage. I have

---

[1] See pp. 133, 134.

[2] The native state of Confucius, part of the present Shan-tung.

[3] A Tâoist of complete virtue; but probably there was not really
such a person. Our author fabricates him according to his fashion.

[4] The character uh (*JL*) does not say that he had lost both his
feet, but I suppose that such is the meaning, because of what is
said of Toeless below that 'he walked on his heels to see Confucius.'
The feet must have been amputated, or mutilated rather (justly or
unjustly), as a punishment; but *K*wang-ȝze wished to say nothing
on that point.

[5] Perhaps a disciple of Confucius;—not elsewhere mentioned as
such.

[6] See the Tâo Teh *K*ing, ch. 2.

only been too late in going to him. I will make
him my teacher; and how much more should those
do so who are not equal to me! Why should
only the state of Lû follow him? I will lead on all
under heaven with me to do so.' *Kh*ang *Kî* rejoined, ' He is a man who has lost his feet, and yet
he is known as the venerable Wang [1];—he must be
very different from ordinary men. What is the
peculiar way in which he employs his mind?' The
reply was, ' Death and life are great considerations,
but they could work no change in him. Though
heaven and earth were to be overturned and fall,
they would occasion him no loss. His judgment is
fixed regarding that in which there is no element
of falsehood [2]; and, while other things change, he
changes not. The transformations of things are to
him the developments prescribed for them, and he
keeps fast hold of the author of them [2].'

*Kh*ang *Kî* said, ' What do you mean?'   ' When
we look at things,' said *K*ung-nî, ' as they differ, we
see them to be different, (as for instance) the liver
and the gall, or *Kh*û and Yüeh; when we look at
them, as they agree, we see them all to be a unity.
So it is with this (Wang Thâi). He takes no knowledge of the things for which his ears and eyes are
the appropriate organs, but his mind delights itself
in the harmony of (all excellent) qualities. He looks
at the unity which belongs to things, and does not
perceive where they have suffered loss. He looks

---

[1] Literally, ' the Senior;' often rendered ' Teacher.'

[2] ' That in which there is no element of falsehood' is the Tâo,
which also is the 'Author' of all the changes that take place in
time and space. See the Introductory Note on the title and subject
of the Book.

on the loss of his feet as only the loss of so much earth.'

*Kh*ang *Kî* said, ' He is entirely occupied with his (proper) self[1]. By his knowledge he has discovered (the nature of) his mind, and to that he holds as what is unchangeable[1]; but how is it that men make so much of him ?' The reply was, 'Men do not look into running water as a mirror, but into still water;—it is only the still water that can arrest them all, and keep them (in the contemplation of their real selves). Of things which are what they are by the influence of the earth, it is only the pine and cypress which are the best instances;—in winter as in summer brightly green[2]. Of those which were what they were by the influence of Heaven[3], the most correct examples were Yâo and Shun; fortunate in (thus) maintaining their own life correct, and so as to correct the lives of others.

' As a verification of the (power of) the original endowment, when it has been preserved, take the result of fearlessness,—how the heroic spirit of a single brave soldier has been thrown into an army of nine hosts[4]. If a man only seeking for fame and able in this way to secure it can produce such an effect, how much more (may we look for a greater

---

[1] Wang Thâi saw all things in the Tâo, and the Tâo in all things. Comp. Book XI, par. 7, et al.

[2] Notwithstanding his being a cripple. He forgets that circumstance himself, and all others forget it, constrained and won by his embodiment of the Tâo. What follows is an illustration of this, exaggerated indeed, but not so extravagantly as in many other passages.

[3] In the Tâoistic meaning of the term.

[4] The royal army consisted of six hosts; that of a great feudal prince of three. ' Nine hosts '=a very great army.

result) from one whose rule is over heaven and
earth, and holds all things in his treasury, who
simply has his lodging in the six members[1] of his
body, whom his ears and eyes serve but as convey-
ing emblematic images of things, who comprehends
all his knowledge in a unity, and whose mind never
dies! If such a man were to choose a day on which
he would ascend far on high, men would (seek to)
follow him there. But how should he be willing to
occupy himself with other men?'

2. Shăn-thû *K*iâ[2] was (another) man who had lost
his feet. Along with 3ze-*kh*ân[3] of *K*ăng[3] he studied
under the master Po-hwăn Wû-*z*ăn[4]. 3ze-*kh*ân said
to him (one day), 'If I go out first, do you remain
behind; and if you go out first, I will remain behind.' Next day they were again sitting together
on the same mat in the hall, when 3ze-*kh*ân spoke
the same words to him, adding, ' Now I am about to
go out; will you stay behind or not? Moreover,
when you see one of official rank (like myself), you
do not try to get out of his way;—do you consider
yourself equal to one of official rank?' Shăn-thû
*K*iâ replied, ' In our Master's school is there indeed
such recognition required of official rank? You are
one, Sir, whose pleasure is in your official rank, and
would therefore take precedence of other men. I

---

[1] The arms, legs, head, and trunk.

[2] Another cripple introduced by our author to serve his purpose.

[3] Kung-sun *Kh*iâo; a good and able minister of *K*ăng, an
earldom forming part of the present Ho-nan. He was a contemporary of Confucius, who wept when he heard of his death in
B.C. 522. He was a scion of the ruling house, which again was
a branch of the royal family of *K*âu.

[4] A Tâoist teacher. See XXI, par. 9; XXXII, par. 1.

have heard that when a mirror is bright, the dust
does not rest on it; when dust rests on it the mirror
is not bright.   When one dwells long with a man of
ability and virtue, he comes to be without error.
There now is our teacher whom you have chosen to
make you greater than you are; and when you still
talk in this way, are you not in error?' 3ze-*kh*ân
rejoined, 'A (shattered) object as you are, you would
still strive to make yourself out as good as Yâo! If
I may form an estimate of your virtue, might it not be
sufficient to lead you to the examination of yourself?'
The other said, 'Most criminals, in describing their
offences, would make it out that they ought not to
have lost (their feet) for them; few would describe
them so as to make it appear that they should not
have preserved their feet.   They are only the virtuous
who know that such a calamity was unavoidable, and
therefore rest in it as what was appointed for them.
When men stand before (an archer like) Î [1] with his
bent bow, if they are in the middle of his field, that
is the place where they should be hit; and if they
be not hit, that also was appointed.   There are
many with their feet entire who laugh at me because I have lost my feet, which makes me feel
vexed and angry.   But when I go to our teacher,
I throw off that feeling, and return (to a better
mood);—he has washed, without my knowing it, the
other from me by (his instructions in) what is good.
I have attended him now for nineteen years, and
have not known that I am without my feet.   Now,
you, Sir, and I have for the object of our study the

---

[1] A famous archer of antiquity in the twenty-second century
B.C., or perhaps earlier.

(virtue) which is internal, and not an adjunct of the body, and yet you are continually directing your attention to my external body;—are you not wrong in this?' 3ze-*kh*ân felt uneasy, altered his manner and looks, and said, 'You need not, Sir, say anything more about it.'

3. In Lû there was a cripple, called Shû-shan the Toeless[1], who came on his heels to see *K*ung-nî. *K*ung-nî said to him, ' By your want of circumspection in the past, Sir, you have incurred such a calamity;—of what use is your coming to me now?' Toeless said, 'Through my ignorance of my proper business and taking too little care of my body, I came to lose my feet. But now I am come to you, still possessing what is more honourable than my feet, and which therefore I am anxious to preserve entire. There is nothing which Heaven does not cover, and nothing which Earth does not sustain; you, Master, were regarded by me as doing the part of Heaven and Earth;—how could I know that you would receive me in such a way?' Confucius rejoined, ' I am but a poor creature. But why, my master, do you not come inside, where I will try to tell you what I have learned?' When Toeless had gone out, Confucius said, ' Be stimulated to effort, my disciples. This toeless cripple is still anxious to learn to make up for the evil of his former conduct; —how much more should those be so whose conduct has been unchallenged!'

Mr. Toeless, however, told Lâo Tan (of the inter-

---

[1] 'Toeless' is a sort of nickname. Shû-shan or Shû hill was, probably, where he dwelt :—'Toeless of Shû hill.'

view), saying, 'Khung *K*%iû, I apprehend, has not yet attained to bc a Perfect man. What has he to do with keeping a crowd of disciples around him ? He is seeking to have the reputation of being an extra-ordinary and marvellous man, and does not know that the Perfect man considers this to be as handcuffs and fetters to him.' Lâo Tan said, 'Why did you not simply lead him to see the unity of life and death, and that the admissible and inadmissible belong to one category, so freeing him from his fetters? Would this be possible?' Toeless said, 'It is the punishment inflicted on him by Heaven [1]. How can he be freed from it?'

4. Duke Âi of Lû [2] asked *K*ung-nî, saying, 'There was an ugly man in Wei, called Âi-thâi Tho [3]. His father-in-law, who lived with him, thought so much of him that he could not be away from him. His wife, when she saw him (ugly as he was), represented to her parents, saying, " I had more than ten times rather be his concubine than the wife of any other man [4]." He was never heard to take the lead in dis-cussion, but always seemed to be of the same opinion with others. He had not the position of a ruler, so as to be able to save men from death. He had no revenues, so as to bc able to satisfy men's craving for food. He was ugly enough, moreover, to scare

---

[1] 'Heaven' here is a synonym of Tâo. Perhaps the meaning is 'unavoidable ;' it is so in the Tâoistic order of things.

[2] It was in the sixteenth year of duke Âi that Confucius died. Âi was marquis of Lû from B.C. 494 to 468.

[3] The account of Âi-thâi Tho is of course *K*wang-ʒze's own fabrication. Âi-thâi is understood to be descriptive of his ugliness, and Tho to be his name.

[4] Perhaps this was spoken by his wife before their marriage.

the whole world. He agreed with men instead of trying to lead them to adopt his views; his knowledge did not go beyond his immediate neighbourhood [1]. And yet his father-in-law and his wife were of one mind about him in his presence (as I have said);—he must have been different from other men. I called him, and saw him. Certainly he was ugly enough to scare the whole world. He had not lived with me, however, for many months, when I was drawn to the man; and before he had been with me a full year, I had confidence in him. The state being without a chief minister, I (was minded) to commit the government to him. He responded to my proposal sorrowfully, and looked undecided as if he would fain have declined it. I was ashamed of myself (as inferior to him), but finally gave the government into his hands. In a little time, however, he left me and went away. I was sorry and felt that I had sustained a loss, and as if there were no other to share the pleasures of the kingdom with me. What sort of man was he?'

*K*ung-nî said, 'Once when I was sent on a mission to *Kh*û, I saw some pigs sucking at their dead mother. After a little they looked with rapid glances, when they all left her, and ran away. They felt that she did not see them, and that she was no longer like themselves. What they had loved in their mother was not her bodily figure, but what had given animation to her figure. When a man dies in battle, they do not at his interment employ the usual appendages

---

[1] One sees dimly the applicability of this illustration to the case in hand. What made Âi-thâi Tho so much esteemed was his mental power, quite independent of his ugly person.

of plumes [1] : as to supplying shoes to one who has
lost his feet, there is no reason why he should care
for them ;—in neither case is there the proper reason
for their use [1]. The members of the royal harem
do not pare their nails nor pierce their ears [2] ; when
a man is newly married, he remains (for a time)
absent from his official duties, and unoccupied with
them [2]. That their bodies might be perfect was
sufficient to make them thus dealt with ;—how
much greater results should be expected from men
whose mental gifts are perfect ! This Âi-thâi Tho
was believed by men, though he did not speak a
word ; and was loved by them, though he did no
special service for them. He made men appoint
him to the government of their states, afraid only
that he would not accept the appointment. He
must have been a man whose powers [3] were perfect,
though his realisation of them [3] was not manifested
in his person.'

Duke Âi said, ' What is meant by saying that his
powers were complete ? ' *K*ung-nî replied, ' Death
and life, preservation and ruin, failure and success,
poverty and wealth, superiority and inferiority,
blame and praise, hunger and thirst, cold and heat ;—
these are the changes of circumstances, the operation
of our appointed lot. Day and night they succeed
to one another before us, but there is no wisdom

---

[1] See the Lî *K*î, VIII, i, 7 ; but the applicability of these two
illustrations is not so clear.

[2] These two have force as in 'reasoning from the less to the
greater.' With the latter of the two compare the mosaical provision
in Deuteronomy xxiv. 5.

[3] 'Powers' are the capacities of the nature,—the gift of the Tâo.
'Virtue' is the realisation or carrying out of those capacities.

able to discover to what they owe their origination. They are not sufficient therefore to disturb the harmony (of the nature), and are not allowed to enter into the treasury of intelligence.   To cause this harmony and satisfaction ever to be diffused, while the feeling of pleasure is not lost from the mind; to allow no break to arise in this state day or night, so that it is always spring-time [1] in his relations with external things; in all his experiences to realise in his mind what is appropriate to each season (of the year) [2] :— these are the characteristics of him whose powers are perfect.'

'And what do you mean by the realisation of these powers not being manifested in the person?' (pursued further the duke).   The reply was, 'There is nothing so level as the surface of a pool of still water.   It may serve as an example of what I mean. All within its circuit is preserved (in peace), and there comes to it no agitation from without.   The virtuous efficacy is the perfect cultivation of the harmony (of the nature).   Though the realisation of this be not manifested in the person, things cannot separate themselves (from its influence).'

Some days afterwards duke Âi told this conversation to Min-ʒze [3], saying, 'Formerly it seemed to me the work of the sovereign to stand in court with his face to the south, to rule the kingdom, and to pay good heed to the accounts of the people concerned, lest any should come to a (miserable) death ;—this

---

[1] Specially the season of complacent enjoyment.

[2] So, in Lin Hsî-kung ; but the meaning has to be forced out of the text.

[3] The disciple Min Sun or Min ʒze-khien.

I considered to be the sum (of his duty). Now that I have heard that description of the Perfect man, I fear that my idea is not the real one, and that, by employing myself too lightly, I may cause the ruin of my state. I and Khung *K*ʰiû are not on the footing of ruler and subject, but on that of a virtuous friendship.'

5. A person who had no lips, whose legs were bent so that he could only walk on his toes, and who was (otherwise) deformed [1], addressed his counsels to duke Ling of Wei, who was so pleased with him, that he looked on a perfectly formed man as having a lean and small neck in comparison with him. Another who had a large goitre like an earthenware jar [1] addressed his counsels to duke Hwan of *K*ʰî [2], who was so pleased with him that he looked on a perfectly formed man as having a neck lean and small in comparison with him [3]. So it is that when one's virtue is extraordinary, (any deficiency in) his bodily form may be forgotten. When men do not forget what is (easily) forgotten, and forget what is not (easily) forgotten, we have a case of real oblivion. Therefore the sagely man has that in which his mind finds its enjoyment, and (looks on) wisdom as (but) the shoots from an old stump; agreements with others are to him but so much glue; kindnesses are

---

[1] These two men are undoubtedly inventions of *K*wang-ȝze. They are brought before us, not by surnames and names, but by their several deformities.

[2] The first of the five presiding chiefs; marquis of *K*ʰî from B.C. 685 to 643.

[3] Lin Hsî-*k*ung wonders whether the story of the man who was so taken with the charms of a one-eyed courtesan, that he thought other women all had an eye too many, was taken from this!

(but the arts of) intercourse; and great skill is (but as) merchants' wares. The sagely man lays no plans;—of what use would wisdom be to him? He has no cutting and hacking to do;—of what use would glue be to him? He has lost nothing;—of what use would arts of intercourse be to him? He has no goods to dispose of;—what need has he to play the merchant? (The want of) these four things are the nourishment of (his) Heavenly (nature); that nourishment is its Heavenly food. Since he receives this food from Heaven, what need has he for anything of man's (devising)? He has the bodily form of man, but not the passions and desires of (other) men. He has the form of man, and therefore he is a man. Being without the passions and desires of men, their approvings and disapprovings are not to be found in him. How insignificant and small is (the body) by which he belongs to humanity! How grand and great is he in the unique perfection of his Heavenly (nature)!

Hui-ʒze said to Kwang-ʒze, 'Can a man indeed be without desires and passions?' The reply was, 'He can.' 'But on what grounds do you call him a man, who is thus without passions and desires?' Kwang-ʒze said, 'The Tâo[1] gives him his personal appearance (and powers); Heaven[2] gives him his bodily form; how should we not call him a man?' Hui-ʒze rejoined, 'Since you call him a man, how

---

[1] Lû Shû-kih maintains here that 'the Tâo' and 'Heaven' have the same meaning; nor does he make any distinction between mâo (貌), 'the personal appearance,' and hsing (形), 'the figure,' or 'bodily form.'

[2] Compare in the Tâo Teh King expressions in li, 2, and lv, 5.

can he be without passions and desires?' The
reply was, 'You are misunderstanding what I mean
by passions and desires. What I mean when I say
that he is without these is, that this man does not by
his likings and dislikings do any inward harm to his
body ;—he always pursues his course without effort,
and does not (try to) increase his (store of) life.'
Hui-𝔷ze rejoined, ' If there were not that increasing
of (the amount) of life, how would he get his body[1]?'
*K*wang-𝔷ze said, ' The Tâo gives him his personal
appearance (and powers) ; Heaven gives him his
bodily form ; and he does not by his likings and dislikings do any internal harm to his body. But now
you, Sir, deal with your spirit as if it were something
external to you, and subject your vital powers to toil.
You sing (your ditties), leaning against a tree ; you
go to sleep, grasping the stump of a rotten dryandra
tree. Heaven selected for you the bodily form (of
a man), and you babble about what is strong and
what is white[2].'

---

[1] Apparently a gross meaning attached by Hui-𝔷ze to *K*wang-𝔷ze's
words.

[2] *K*wang-𝔷ze beats down his opponent, and contemptuously
refers to some of his well-known peculiarities ;—as in II, par. 5,
XXXIII, par. 7, and elsewhere.

BOOK VI.

PART I. SECTION VI.

Tâ Ꜫung Shih, or 'The Great and Most Honoured Master[1].'

1. He who knows the part which the Heavenly[2] (in him) plays, and knows (also) that which the Human[2] (in him ought to) play, has reached the perfection (of knowledge). He who knows the part which the Heavenly plays (knows) that it is naturally born with him; he who knows the part which the Human ought to play (proceeds) with the knowledge which he possesses to nourish it in the direction of what he does not (yet) know[3]:—to complete one's natural term of years and not come to an untimely end in the middle of his course is the fulness of knowledge. Although it be so, there is an evil (attending this condition). Such knowledge still awaits the confirmation of it as correct; it does so because it is not yet determined[4]. How do we know that what

---

[1] See pp. 134–136.

[2] Both 'Heaven' and 'Man' here are used in the Tâoistic sense;—the meaning which the terms commonly have both with Lâo and Kwang.

[3] The middle member of this sentence is said to be the practical outcome of all that is said in the Book; conducting the student of the Tâo to an unquestioning submission to the experiences in his lot, which are beyond his comprehension, and approaching nearly to what we understand by the Christian virtue of Faith.

[4] That is, there may be the conflict, to the end of life, between

we call the Heavenly (in us) is not the Human? and that what we call the Human is not the Heavenly? There must be the True man[1], and then there is the True knowledge.

2. What is meant by 'the True Man[2]?' The True men of old did not reject (the views of) the few; they did not seek to accomplish (their ends) like heroes (before others); they did not lay plans to attain those ends[3]. Being such, though they might make mistakes, they had no occasion for repentance; though they might succeed, they had no self-complacency. Being such, they could ascend the loftiest heights without fear; they could pass through water without being made wet by it; they could go into fire without being burnt; so it was

---

faith and fact, so graphically exhibited in the Book of Job, and compendiously described in the seventy-third Psalm.

[1] Here we meet with the True Man, a Master of the Tâo. He is the same as the Perfect Man, the Spirit-like Man, and the Sagely Man (see pp. 127, 128), and the designation is sometimes interchanged in the five paragraphs that follow with 'the Sagely Man.' Mr. Balfour says here that this name 'is used in the esoteric sense,—" partaking of the essence of divinity;"' and he accordingly translates 眞 人 by 'the divine man.' But he might as well translate any one of the other three names in the same way. The Shwo Wăn dictionary defines the name by 仙 人, 'a recluse of the mountain, whose bodily form has been changed, and who ascends to heaven;' but when this account was made, Tâoism had entered into a new phase, different from what it had in the time of our author.

[2] In this description of 'the True Man,' and in what follows, there is what is grotesque and what is exaggerated (see note on the title of the first Book, p. 127). The most prominent characteristic of him was his perfect comprehension of the Tâo and participation of it.

[3] 士 has here the sense of 事.

that by their knowledge they ascended to and reached the Tâo[1].

The True men of old did not dream when they slept, had no anxiety when they awoke, and did not care that their food should be pleasant. Their breathing came deep and silently. The breathing of the true man comes (even) from his heels, while men generally breathe (only) from their throats. When men are defeated in argument, their words come from their gullets as if they were vomiting. Where lusts and desires are deep, the springs of the Heavenly are shallow.

The True men of old knew nothing of the love of life or of the hatred of death. Entrance into life occasioned them no joy; the exit from it awakened no resistance. Composedly they went and came. They did not forget what their beginning had been, and they did not inquire into what their end would be. They accepted (their life) and rejoiced in it; they forgot (all fear of death), and returned (to their state before life)[1]. Thus there was in them what is called the want of any mind to resist the Tâo, and of all attempts by means of the Human to assist the Heavenly. Such were they who are called the True men.

3. Being such, their minds were free from all thought[2]; their demeanour was still and unmoved;

---

[1] Was not this the state of non-existence? We cannot say of Pantâoism. However we may describe that, the Tâo operates in nature, but is not identical with it.

[2] 心 忘 appears in the common editions as 心 志, which must have got into the text at a very early time. 'The mind forgetting,' or 'free from all thought and purpose,' appears every-

their foreheads beamed simplicity. Whatever coldness came from them was like that of autumn; whatever warmth came from them was like that of spring. Their joy and anger assimilated to what we see in the four seasons. They did in regard to all things what was suitable, and no one could know how far their action would go. Therefore the sagely man might, in his conduct of war, destroy a state without losing the hearts of the people [1]; his benefits and favours might extend to a myriad generations without his being a lover of men. Hence he who tries to share his joys with others is not a sagely man; he who manifests affection is not benevolent; he who observes times and seasons (to regulate his conduct) is not a man of wisdom; he to whom profit and injury are not the same is not a superior man; he who acts for the sake of the name of doing so, and loses his (proper) self is not the (right) scholar; and he who throws away his person in a way which is not the true (way) cannot command the service of others. Such men as Hû Pû-*k*ieh, Wû Kwang, Po-î, Shû-*kh*î, the count of *K*î, Hsü-yü, *K*î Thâ, and Shăn-thû Tî, all did service for other men, and sought to secure for them what they desired, not seeking their own pleasure [2].

where in the Book as a characteristic of the True Man. Not a few critics contend that it was this, and not the Tâo of which it is a quality, that *K*wang-ʒze intended by the ' Master' in the title.

[1] Such antithetic statements are startling, but they are common with both Lâo-ʒze and our author.

[2] The seven men mentioned here are all adduced, I must suppose, as instances of good and worthy men, but still inferior to the True Man. Of Hû Pû-*k*ieh all that we are told is that he was ' an ancient worthy.' One account of Wû Kwang is that he was of the time of Hwang-Tî, with ears seven inches long; another, that he

4. The True men of old presented the aspect of judging others aright, but without being partisans; of feeling their own insufficiency, but being without flattery or cringing. Their peculiarities were natural to them, but they were not obstinately attached to them; their humility was evident, but there was nothing of unreality or display about it. Their placidity and satisfaction had the appearance of joy; their every movement seemed to be a necessity to them. Their accumulated attractiveness drew men's looks to them; their blandness fixed men's attachment to their virtue. They seemed to accommodate themselves to the (manners of their age), but with a certain severity; their haughty indifference was beyond its control. Unceasing seemed their endeavours to keep (their mouths) shut; when they looked down, they had forgotten what they wished to say.

They considered punishments to be the substance (of government, and they never incurred it); ceremonies to be its supporting wings (and they always observed them); wisdom (to indicate) the time (for action, and they always selected it); and virtue to be accordance (with others), and they were all-accordant. Considering punishments to be the substance (of government), yet their generosity appeared in the (manner of their) infliction of death. Considering ceremonies to be its supporting wings, they pursued

---

was of the time of Thang, of the Shang dynasty. Po-î and Shû-*khî* are known to us from the Analects; and also the count of *Khî*, whose name, it is said, was Hsü-yü. I can find nothing about *Kî* Thâ;—his name in Ꝫiâo Hung's text is 紀 他 沱. Shăn-thû Tî was of the Yin dynasty, a contemporary of Thang. He drowned himself in the Ho. Most of these are referred to in other places.

by means of them their course in the world.   Considering wisdom to indicate the time (for action), they felt it necessary to employ it in (the direction of) affairs.   Considering virtue to be accordance (with others), they sought to ascend its height along with all who had feet (to climb it).   (Such were they), and yet men really thought that they did what they did by earnest effort [1].

5. In this way they were one and the same in all their likings and dislikings.   Where they liked, they were the same; where they did not like, they were the same.   In the former case where they liked, they were fellow workers with the Heavenly (in them); in the latter where they disliked, they were co-workers with the Human in them.   The one of these elements (in their nature) did not overcome the other.   Such were those who are called the True men.

Death and life are ordained, just as we have the constant succession of night and day;—in both cases from Heaven.   Men have no power to do anything in reference to them;—such is the constitution of things [2].   There are those who specially regard Heaven [3] as their father, and they still love It (distant as It is) [3];—how much more should they love

---

[1] All this paragraph is taken as illustrative of the True man's freedom from thought or purpose in his course.

[2] See note 3 on par. 1, p. 236.

[3] Love is due to a parent, and so such persons should love Heaven.   There is in the text here, I think, an unconscious reference to the earliest time, before the views of the earliest Chinese diverged to Theism and Tâoism.   We cannot translate the 身 here.

That which stands out (Superior and Alone)[1]! Some
specially regard their ruler as superior to themselves, and will give their bodies to die for him;—
how much more should they do so for That which
is their true (Ruler)[1]! When the springs are dried
up, the fishes collect together on the land. Than
that they should moisten one another there by the
damp about them, and keep one another wet by their
slime, it would be better for them to forget one
another in the rivers and lakes[2]. And when men
praise Yâo and condemn *K*ieh, it would be better
to forget them both, and seek the renovation of
the Tâo.

6. There is the great Mass (of nature);—I find the
support of my body on it; my life is spent in toil on
it; my old age seeks ease on it; at death I find rest
in it;—what makes my life a good makes my death
also a good[3]. If you hide away a boat in the ravine
of a hill, and hide away the hill in a lake, you will
say that (the boat) is secure; but at midnight there
shall come a strong man and carry it off on his back,
while you in the dark know nothing about it. You
may hide away anything, whether small or great, in
the most suitable place, and yet it shall disappear
from it. But if you could hide the world in the
world[4], so that there was nowhere to which it could
be removed, this would be the grand reality of the

---

[1] The great and most honoured Master,—the Tâo.

[2] This sentence contrasts the cramping effect on the mind of
Confucianism with the freedom given by the doctrine of the Tâo.

[3] The Tâo does this. The whole paragraph is an amplification
of the view given in the preceding note.

[4] The Tâo cannot be taken away. It is with its possessor, an
'ever-during thing.'

ever-during Thing [1]. When the body of man comes
from its special mould [2], there is even then occasion
for joy; but this body undergoes a myriad transformations, and does not immediately reach its perfection;—does it not thus afford occasion for joys
incalculable? Therefore the sagely man enjoys
himself in that from which there is no possibility
of separation, and by which all things are preserved.
He considers early death or old age, his beginning
and his ending, all to be good, and in this other men
imitate him;—how much more will they do so in
regard to That Itself on which all things depend,
and from which every transformation arises!

7. This is the Tâo;—there is in It emotion and
sincerity, but It does nothing and has no bodily
form [3]. It may be handed down (by the teacher),
but may not be received (by his scholars). It may
be apprehended (by the mind), but It cannot be
seen. It has Its root and ground (of existence) in
Itself. Before there were heaven and earth, from
of old, there It was, securely existing. From It
came the mysterious existences of spirits, from It the
mysterious existence of God [4]. It produced heaven;
It produced earth. It was before the Thâi-*k*î [5], and

---

[1] See p. 242, note 4.

[2] Adopting the reading of 範 for 犯, supplied by Hwâi-nan 3ze.

[3] Our author has done with ‘the True Man,’ and now brings in
the Tâo itself as his subject. Compare the predicates of It here
with Bk. II, par. 2. But there are other, and perhaps higher,
things said of it here.

[4] Men at a very early time came to believe in the existence of
their spirits after death, and in the existence of a Supreme Ruler or
God. It was to the Tâo that those concepts were owing.

[5] The primal ether out of which all things were fashioned by the
interaction of the Yin and Yang. This was something like the

yet could not be considered high [1]; It was below all space, and yet could not be considered deep.[1]. It was produced before heaven and earth, and yet could not be considered to have existed long [1]; It was older than the highest antiquity, and yet could not be considered old [1].

Shih-wei got It [2], and by It adjusted heaven and earth. Fû-hsî got It, and by It penetrated to the mystery of the maternity of the primary matter. The Wei-tâu [3] got It, and from all antiquity has made no eccentric movement. The Sun and Moon got It, and from all antiquity have not intermitted (their bright shining). Khan-pei got It, and by It became lord of Khwăn-lun [4]. Făng-î [5] got It, and by It enjoyed himself in the Great River. *K*ien Wû [6] got It, and by It dwelt on mount Thâi. Hwang-Tî [7] got It, and by It ascended the cloudy sky. *K*wan-hsü [8]

current idea of protoplasm; but while protoplasm lies down in the lower parts of the earth, the Thâi-*k*î was imagined to be in the higher regions of space.

[1] The Tâo is independent both of space and time.

[2] A prehistoric sovereign.

[3] A name for the constellation of the Great Bear.

[4] Name of the spirit of the Khwăn-lun mountains in Thibet, the fairy-land of Tâoist writers, very much in Tâoism what mount Sumêru is in Buddhism.

[5] The spirit presiding over the Yellow River;—see Mayers's Manual, pp. 54, 55.

[6] Appears here as the spirit of mount Thâi, the great eastern mountain; we met with him in I, 5, but simply as one of *K*wang-ʒze's fictitious personages.

[7] Appears before in Bk. II; the first of Sze-mâ *K*hien's 'Five Tîs;' no doubt a very early sovereign, to whom many important discoveries and inventions are ascribed; is placed by many at the head of Tâoism itself.

[8] The second of the 'Five Tîs;' a grandson of Hwang-Tî. I do not know what to say of his 'Dark Palace.'

got It, and by It dwelt in the Dark Palace. Yü-*kh*iang[1] got It, and by It was set on the North Pole. Hsî Wang-mû[2] got It, and by It had her seat in (the palace of) Shâo-kwang. No one knows Its beginning; no one knows Its end. Phăng 3û got It, and lived on from the time of the lord of Yü to that of the Five Chiefs[3]. Fû Yüeh[4] got It, and by It became chief minister to Wû-ting[4], (who thus) in a trice became master of the kingdom. (After his death), Fû Yüeh mounted to the eastern portion of the Milky Way, where, riding on Sagittarius and Scorpio, he took his place among the stars.

8. Nan-po 3ze-khwei[5] asked Nü Yü[6], saying, 'You are old, Sir, while your complexion is like that of a child;—how is it so?' The reply was, 'I have become acquainted with the Tâo.' The other said, 'Can I learn the Tâo?' Nü Yü said, 'No. How can you? You, Sir, are not the man to do so. There was Pû-liang Î[7] who had the abilities of a sagely man, but not the Tâo, while I had the Tâo, but not the abilities. I wished, however, to teach him, if, peradventure, he might

---

[1] The Spirit of the Northern regions, with a man's face, and a bird's body, &c.

[2] A queen of the Genii on mount Khwăn-lun. See Mayers's Manual, pp. 178, 179.

[3] Phăng 3û has been before us in Bk. I. Shun is intended by 'the Lord of Yü.' The five Chiefs;—see Mencius, VI, ii, 7.

[4] See the Shû, IV, viii; but we have nothing there of course about the Milky Way and the stars.—This passage certainly lessens our confidence in *K*wang-ȝze's statements.

[5] Perhaps the same as Nan-po 3ze-*kh*î in Bk. IV, par. 7.

[6] Must have been a great Tâoist. Nothing more can be said of him or her.

[7] Only mentioned here.

become the sagely man indeed. If he should not do so, it was easy (I thought) for one possessing the Tâo of the sagely man to communicate it to another possessing his abilities. Accordingly, I proceeded to do so, but with deliberation[1]. After three days, he was able to banish from his mind all worldly (matters). This accomplished, I continued my intercourse with him in the same way; and in seven days he was able to banish from his mind all thought of men and things. This accomplished, and my instructions continued, after nine days, he was able to count his life as foreign to himself. This accomplished, his mind was afterwards clear as the morning; and after this he was able to see his own individuality[2]. That individuality perceived, he was able to banish all thought of Past or Present. Freed from this, he was able to penetrate to (the truth that there is no difference between) life and death;—(how) the destruction of life is not dying, and the communication of other life is not living. (The Tâo) is a thing which accompanies all other things and meets them, which is present when they are overthrown and when they obtain their completion. Its name is Tranquillity amid all Disturbances, meaning that such Disturbances lead to Its Perfection[3].'

'And how did you, being alone (without any teacher), learn all this?' 'I learned it,' was the reply, 'from the son of Fû-mo[4]; he learned it from

---

[1] So the 守 is explained.

[2] Standing by himself, as it were face to face with the Tâo.

[3] Amid all changes, in life and death, the possessor of the Tâo has peace.

[4] Meaning writings; literally, 'the son of the assisting pigment.'

the grandson of Lo-sung; he learned it from Shan-ming; he learned it from Nieh-hsü; he, from Hsü-yî; he, from Wû-âo; he, from Hsüan-ming; he, from 3han-liâo; and he learned it from Î-shih.'

9. 3ze-sze [1], 3ze-yü [1], 3ze-lî [1], and 3ze-lâi [1], these four men, were talking together, when some one said, 'Who can suppose the head to be made from nothing, the spine from life, and the rump-bone from death? Who knows how death and birth, living on and disappearing, compose the one body? —I would be friends with him [2].' The four men looked at one another and laughed, but no one seized with his mind the drift of the questions. All, however, were friends together.

Not long after 3ze-yü fell ill, and 3ze-sze went to inquire for him. 'How great,' said (the sufferer), 'is the Creator [3]! That He should have made me the deformed object that I am!' He was a crooked hunchback; his five viscera were squeezed into the

---

We are not to suppose that by this and the other names that follow individuals are intended. Kwang-3ze seems to have wished to give, in his own fashion, some notion of the genesis of the idea of the Tâo from the first speculations about the origin of things.

[1] We need not suppose that these are the names of real men. They are brought on the stage by our author to serve his purpose. Hwâi-nan makes the name of the first to have been 3ze-shui (子 水).

[2] Compare the same representation in Bk. XXIII, par. 10. Kû Teh-kih says on it here, 'The head, the spine, the rump-bone mean simply the head and tail, the beginning and end. All things begin from nothing and end in nothing. Their birth and their death are only the creations of our thought, the going and coming of the primary ether. When we have penetrated to the non-reality of life and death, what remains of the body of so many feet?'

[3] The 'Creator' or 'Maker' (造 物 者) is the Tâo.

upper part of his body; his chin bent over his navel; his shoulder was higher than his crown; on his crown was an ulcer pointing to the sky; his breath came and went in gasps[1]:—yet he was easy in his mind, and made no trouble of his condition. He limped to a well, looked at himself in it, and said, 'Alas that the Creator should have made me the deformed object that I am!' Ʒze said, 'Do you dislike your condition?' He replied, 'No, why should I dislike it? If He were to transform my left arm into a cock, I should be watching with it the time of the night; if He were to transform my right arm into a cross-bow, I should then be looking for a hsiâo to (bring down and) roast; if He were to transform my rump-bone into a wheel, and my spirit into a horse, I should then be mounting it, and would not change it for another steed. Moreover, when we have got (what we are to do), there is the time (of life) in which to do it; when we lose that (at death), submission (is what is required). When we rest in what the time requires, and manifest that submission, neither joy nor sorrow can find entrance (to the mind)[2]. This would be what the ancients called loosing the cord by which (the life) is suspended. But one hung up cannot loose himself;—he is held fast by his bonds[3]. And that creatures cannot overcome

---

[1] Compare this description of Ʒze-yü's deformity with that of the poor Shû, in IV, 8.

[2] Such is the submission to one's lot produced by the teaching of Tâoism.

[3] Compare the same phraseology in III, par. 4, near the end. In correcting Mr. Balfour's mistranslation of the text, Mr. Giles himself falls into a mistranslation through not observing that the 解

Heaven (the inevitable) is a long-acknowledged fact;—why should I hate my condition?'

10. Before long Ȝze-lâi fell ill, and lay gasping at the point of death, while his wife and children stood around him wailing [1]. Ȝze-lî went to ask for him, and said to them, 'Hush! Get out of the way! Do not disturb him as he is passing through his change.' Then, leaning against the door, he said (to the dying man), 'Great indeed is the Creator! What will He now make you to become? Where will He take you to? Will He make you the liver of a rat, or the arm of an insect [2]?' Ȝze-lâi replied, 'Wherever a parent tells a son to go, east, west, south, or north, he simply follows the command. The Yin and Yang are more to a man than his parents are. If they are hastening my death, and I do not quietly submit to them, I shall be obstinate and rebellious. There is the great Mass (of nature);—I find the support of my body in it; my life is spent in toil on it; my old age seeks ease on it; at death I find rest on it:—what has made my life a good will make my death also a good.

'Here now is a great founder, casting his metal. If the metal were to leap up (in the pot), and say, "I must be made into a (sword like the) Mo-yeh [3],"

---

is passive, having the 懸 that precedes as its subject (observe the force of the 也 after 解 in the best editions), and not active, or governing the 懸 that follows.

[1] Compare the account of the scene at Lâo-ȝze's death, in III, par. 4.

[2] Here comes in the belief in transformation.

[3] The name of a famous sword, made for Ho-lü, the king of

the great founder would be sure to regard it as uncanny. So, again, when a form is being fashioned in the mould of the womb, if it were to say, " I must become a man; I must become a man," the Creator would be sure to regard it as uncanny. When we once understand that heaven and earth are a great melting-pot, and the Creator a great founder, where can we have to go to that shall not be right for us? We are born as from a quiet sleep, and we die to a calm awaking.'

11. 3ze-sang Hû[1], Măng 3ze-fan[1], and 3ze-*kh*in *K*ang[1], these three men, were friends together. (One of them said), 'Who can associate together without any (thought of) such association, or act together without any (evidence of) such co-operation? Who can mount up into the sky and enjoy himself amidst the mists, disporting beyond the utmost limits (of things)[2], and forgetting all others as if this were living, and would have no end?' The three men looked at one another and laughed, not perceiving the drift of the questions; and they continued to associate together as friends.

Suddenly, after a time[3], 3ze-sang Hû died. Before he was buried, Confucius heard of the event, and

---

Wû (B. C. 514–494). See the account of the forging of it in the 東周列國志, ch. 74. The mention of it would seem to indicate that 3ze-lâi and the other three men were of the time of Confucius.

[1] These three men were undoubtedly of the time of Confucius, and some would identify them with the 3ze-sang Po-3ze of Ana. VI, 1, Măng *K*ih-fan of VI, 13, and the Lâo of IX, vi, 4. This is very unlikely. They were Tâoists.

[2] Or, 'without end.'

[3] Or, ' Some time went by silently, and.'

sent 3ze-kung to go and see if he could render
any assistance.   One of the survivors had composed a ditty, and the other was playing on his
lute.   Then they sang together in unison,

'Ah! come, Sang Hû! ah! come, Sang Hû!
Your being true you've got again,
While we, as men, still here remain
                                Ohone[1]!'

3ze-kung hastened forward to them, and said,
'I venture to ask whether it be according to the
rules to be singing thus in the presence of the
corpse?' The two men looked at each other, and
laughed, saying, 'What does this man know about
the idea that underlies (our) rules?'   3ze-kung
returned to Confucius, and reported to him, saying,
'What sort of men are those? They had made
none of the usual preparations[2], and treated the
body as a thing foreign to them.   They were
singing in the presence of the corpse, and there was
no change in their countenances.   I cannot describe
them;—what sort of men are they?' Confucius
replied, 'Those men occupy and enjoy themselves
in what is outside the (common) ways (of the world),
while I occupy and enjoy myself in what lies within
those ways.   There is no common ground for those
of such different ways; and when I sent you to
condole with those men, I was acting stupidly.
They, moreover, make man to be the fellow of the

---

[1] In accordance with the ancient and modern practice in China
of calling the dead back.   But these were doing so in a song to
the lute.

[2] Or, 'they do not regulate their doings (in the usual way).'

Creator, and seek their enjoyment in the formless condition of heaven and earth. They consider life to be an appendage attached, an excrescence annexed to them, and death to be a separation of the appendage and a dispersion of the contents of the excrescence. With these views, how should they know wherein death and life are to be found, or what is first and what is last? They borrow different substances, and pretend that the common form of the body is composed of them[1]. They dismiss the thought of (its inward constituents like) the liver and gall, and (its outward constituents), the ears and eyes. Again and again they end and they begin, having no knowledge of first principles. They occupy themselves ignorantly and vaguely with what (they say) lies outside the dust and dirt (of the world), and seek their enjoyment in the business of doing nothing. How should they confusedly address themselves to the ceremonies practised by the common people, and exhibit themselves as doing so to the ears and eyes of the multitude?'

3ze-kung said, 'Yes, but why do you, Master, act according to the (common) ways (of the world)?' The reply was, 'I am in this under the condemning sentence of Heaven[2]. Nevertheless, I will share

---

[1] The idea that the body is composed of the elements of earth, wind or air, fire, and water.

[2] A strange description of himself by the sage. Literally, 'I am (one of) the people killed and exposed to public view by Heaven;' referring, perhaps, to the description of a living man as 'suspended by a string from God.' Confucius was content to accept his life, and used it in pursuing the path of duty, according to his conception of it, without aiming at the transcendental method of the Tâoists. I can attach no other or better meaning to the expression.

with you (what I have attained to).'   3ze-kung rejoined, 'I venture to ask the method which you
pursue;' and Confucius said, 'Fishes breed and grow
in the water; man developes in the Tâo.   Growing
in the water, the fishes cleave the pools, and their
nourishment is supplied to them.   Developing in
the Tâo, men do nothing, and the enjoyment of
their life is secured.   Hence it is said, " Fishes forget one another in the rivers and lakes; men forget
one another in the arts of the Tâo." '

3ze-kung said, 'I venture to ask about the man
who stands aloof from others[1].'   The reply was,
' He stands aloof from other men, but he is in accord
with Heaven!   Hence it is said, "The small man
of Heaven is the superior man among men; the
superior man among men is the small man of
Heaven[2]!" '

12. Yen Hui asked Kung-nî, saying, 'When the
mother of Măng-sun 3hâi[3] died, in all his wailing for
her he did not shed a tear; in the core of his heart
he felt no distress; during all the mourning rites, he
exhibited no sorrow.   Without these three things,
he (was considered to have) discharged his mourning well;—is it that in the state of Lû one who has
not the reality may yet get the reputation of having
it?   I think the matter very strange.'   Kung-nî

---

[1] Misled by the text of Hsüang Ying, Mr. Balfour here reads
崎 instead of 畸.

[2] Here, however, he aptly compares with the language of Christ
in Matthew vii. 28.—Kwang-3ze seems to make Confucius praise
the system of Tâoism as better than his own!

[3] Must have been a member of the Măng or Măng-sun family
of Lû, to a branch of which Mencius belonged.

said, ' That Măng-sun carried out (his views) to the utmost. He was advanced in knowledge; but (in this case) it was not possible for him to appear to be negligent (in his ceremonial observances)[1], but he succeeded in being really so to himself. Măng-sun does not know either what purposes life serves, or what death serves; he does not know which should be first sought, and which last[2]. If he is to be transformed into something else, he will simply await the transformation which he does not yet know. This is all he does. And moreover, when one is about to undergo his change, how does he know that it has not taken place? And when he is not about to undergo his change, how does he know that it has taken place[3]? Take the case of me and you :—are we in a dream from which we have not begun to awake[4]?

' Moreover, Măng-sun presented in his body the appearance of being agitated, but in his mind he was conscious of no loss. The death was to him like the issuing from one's dwelling at dawn, and no (more terrible) reality. He was more awake than others were. When they wailed, he also wailed, having in himself the reason why he did so. And we all have our individuality which makes us what we are as compared together; but how do we know that we

---

[1] The people set such store by the mourning rites, that Măng-sun felt he must present the appearance of observing them. This would seem to show that Tâoism arose after the earlier views of the Chinese.

[2] I adopt here, with many of the critics, the reading of 孰 instead of the more common 就.

[3] This is to me very obscure.

[4] Are such dreams possible? See what I have said on II, par. 9.

determine in any case correctly that individuality? Moreover you dream that you are a bird, and seem to be soaring to the sky; or that you are a fish, and seem to be diving in the deep. But you do not know whether we that are now speaking are awake or in a dream[1]. It is not the meeting with what is pleasurable that produces the smile; it is not the smile suddenly produced that produces the arrangement (of the person). When one rests in what has been arranged, and puts away all thought of the transformation, he is in unity with the mysterious Heaven.'

13. Î-*r* 3ze[2] having gone to see Hsü Yû, the latter said to him, 'What benefit have you received from Yâo?' The reply was, 'Yâo says to me, You must yourself labour at benevolence and righteousness, and be able to tell clearly which is right and which wrong (in conflicting statements).' Hsü Yû rejoined, 'Why then have you come to me? Since Yâo has put on you the brand of his benevolence and righteousness, and cut off your nose with his right and wrong[3], how will you be able to wander in the way of aimless enjoyment, of unregulated contemplation, and the ever-changing forms (of dispute)?' Î-*r* 3ze said, 'That may be; but I should

---

[1] This also is obscure; but Confucius is again made to praise the Tâoistic system.

[2] Î-*r* is said by Lî Î to have been 'a worthy scholar;' but Î-*r* is an old name for the swallow, and there is a legend of a being of this name appearing to king Mû, and then flying away as a swallow;—see the Khang-hsî Thesaurus under 鳦. The personage is entirely fabulous.

[3] Dismembered or disfigured you.

like to skirt along its hedges.' 'But,' said the other, 'it cannot be. Eyes without pupils can see nothing of the beauty of the eyebrows, eyes, and other features; the blind have nothing to do with the green, yellow, and variegated colours of the sacrificial robes.' Î-*r* 3ze rejoined, 'Yet, when Wû-*k*wang[1] lost his beauty, *K*ü-liang[1] his strength, and Hwang-Tî his wisdom, they all (recovered them)[2] under the moulding (of your system);—how do you know that the Maker will not obliterate the marks of my branding, and supply my dismemberment, so that, again perfect in my form, I may follow you as my teacher?' Hsü Yû said, 'Ah! that cannot yet be known. I will tell you the rudiments. O my Master! O my Master! He gives to all things their blended qualities, and does not count it any righteousness; His favours reach to all generations, and He does not count it any benevolence; He is more ancient than the highest antiquity, and does not count Himself old; He overspreads heaven and supports the earth; He carves and fashions all bodily forms, and does not consider it any act of skill;—this is He in whom I find my enjoyment.'

14. Yen Hui said, 'I am making progress.' *K*ung-nî replied, 'What do you mean?' 'I have ceased to think of benevolence and righteousness,' was the reply. 'Very well; but that is not enough.'

Another day, Hui again saw *K*ung-nî, and said, 'I am making progress.' 'What do you mean?'

---

[1] Names of parties, of whom we know nothing. It is implied, we must suppose, that they had suffered as is said by their own inadvertence.

[2] We must suppose that they had done so.

'I have lost all thought of ceremonies and music.'
'Very well, but that is not enough.'

A third day, Hui again saw (the Master), and
said, 'I am making progress.' 'What do you mean?'
'I sit and forget everything[1].' *K*ung-nî changed
countenance, and said, 'What do you mean by saying that you sit and forget (everything)?' Yen Hui
replied, 'My connexion with the body and its parts
is dissolved; my perceptive organs are discarded.
Thus leaving my material form, and bidding fare-
well to my knowledge, I am become one with the
Great Pervader[2]. This I call sitting and forgetting
all things.' *K*ung-nî said, 'One (with that Pervader),
you are free from all likings; so transformed, you
are become impermanent. You have, indeed, become superior to me! I must ask leave to follow
in your steps[3].'

15. 3ze-yü[4] and 3ze-sang[4] were friends. (Once),
when it had rained continuously for ten days, 3ze-yü
said, 'I fear that 3ze-sang may be in distress.' So
he wrapped up some rice, and went to give it to him
to eat. When he came to 3ze-sang's door, there
issued from it sounds between singing and wailing;

---

[1] 'I sit and forget;'—generally thus supplemented (無 所 不
忘). Hui proceeds to set forth the meaning he himself attached
to the phrase.

[2] Another denomination, I think, of the Tâo. The 大 通
is also explained as meaning, 'the great void in which there is no
obstruction (太 虛 之 無 得).'

[3] Here is another testimony, adduced by our author, of Confucius's appreciation of Tâoism; to which the sage would, no doubt,
have taken exception.

[4] Two of the men in pars. 9, 10.

a lute was struck, and there came the words, 'O
Father! O Mother! O Heaven! O Men!' The
voice could not sustain itself, and the line was hur-
riedly pronounced.   Ꝫze-yü entered and said, 'Why
are you singing, Sir, this line of poetry in such a
way?' The other replied, 'I was thinking, and thinking in vain, how it was that I was brought to such
extremity. Would my parents have wished me to be
so poor ?   Heaven overspreads all without any partial feeling, and so does Earth sustain all;—would
Heaven and Earth make me so poor with any un-
kindly feeling?   I was trying to find out who had
done it, and I could not do so. But here I am in this
extremity!—it is what was appointed for me[1]!'

---

[1] Here is the highest issue of Tâoism;—unquestioning submission to what is beyond our knowledge and control.

BOOK VII.

PART I. SECTION VII.

Ying Tî Wang[1], or 'The Normal Course for Rulers and Kings[1].'

1. Nieh *Kh*üeh[2] put four questions to Wang Î[2], not one of which did he know (how to answer). On this Nieh *Kh*üeh leaped up, and in great delight walked away and informed Phû-î-ȝze[3] of it, who said to him, 'Do you (only) now know it?' He of the line of Yü[4] was not equal to him of the line of Thâi[5]. He of Yü still kept in himself (the idea of) benevolence by which to constrain (the submission of) men ; and he did win men, but he had not begun to proceed by what did not belong to him as a man. He of the line of Thâi would sleep tranquilly, and awake in contented simplicity. He would consider himself now (merely) as a horse, and now (merely) as an ox[6]. His knowledge was real and untroubled

---

[1] See pp. 136-138.

[2] See p. 190, note 5.

[3] An ancient Tâoist, of the time of Shun. So, Hwang-fû Mî, who adds that Shun served him as his master when he was eight years old. I suppose the name indicates that his clothes were made of rushes.

[4] Shun. See p. 245, note 3.

[5] An ancient sovereign, earlier, no doubt, than Fû-hsî ; but nothing is known of him.

[6] He thought nothing about his being, as a man, superior to the lower creatures. Shun in governing employed his acquired knowledge ; Thâi had not begun to do so.

by doubts; and his virtue was very true :—he had not begun to proceed by what belonged to him as a man.

2. *K*ien Wû [1] went to see the mad (recluse), *Kh*ieh-yü [2], who said to him, 'What did *Z*ăh-*k*ung Shih [3] tell you ?' The reply was, 'He told me that when rulers gave forth their regulations according to their own views and enacted righteous measures, no one would venture not to obey them, and all would be transformed.' *Kh*ieh-yü said, 'That is but the hypocrisy of virtue. For the right ordering of the world it would be like trying to wade through the sea and dig through the Ho, or employing a musquito to carry a mountain on its back. And when a sage is governing, does he govern men's outward actions? He is (himself) correct, and so (his government) goes on ;—this is the simple and certain way by which he secures the success of his affairs. Think of the bird which flies high, to avoid being hurt by the dart on the string of the archer, and the little mouse which makes its hole deep under Shăn-*kh*iû [4] to avoid the danger of being smoked or dug out ;—are (rulers) less knowing than these two little creatures ?'

3. Thien Kăn [5], rambling on the south of (mount) Yin [6], came to the neighbourhood of the Liâo-water.

---

[1] See p. 170, note 2.

[2] See p. 170, note 3.

[3] A name ;—'a worthy,' it is said.

[4] Name of some hill, or height.

[5] A name ('Root of the sky'), but probably mythical. There is a star so called.

[6] Probably the name of. a mountain, though this meaning of Yin is not given in the dictionary.

Happening there to meet with the man whose name is not known[1], he put a question to him, saying, 'I beg to ask what should be done [2] in order to (carry on) the government of the world.'   The nameless man said, 'Go away; you are a rude borderer.   Why do you put to me a question for which you are unprepared [3] ? I would simply play the part of the Maker of (all) things [4].   When wearied, I would mount on the bird of the light and empty air, proceed beyond the six cardinal points, and wander in the region of non-entity, to dwell in the wilderness of desert space. What method have you, moreover, for the government of the world that you (thus) agitate my mind ?' (Thien Kăn), however, again asked the question, and the nameless man said, 'Let your mind find its enjoyment in pure simplicity; blend yourself with (the primary) ether in idle indifference; allow all things to take their natural course; and admit no personal or selfish consideration :—do this and the world will be governed.'

4.   Yang 3ze-_k_ü[5], having an interview with Lâo Tan, said to him, ' Here is a man, alert and vigorous

---

[1] Or, 'a nameless man.'   We cannot tell whether _K_wang-ʒze had any particular Being, so named, in view or not.

[2] The objectionable point in the question is the supposition that 'doing' was necessary in the case.

[3] Or, 'I am unprepared.'   But as Thien Kăn repeats the question, it seems better to supply the second pronoun.   He had thought on the subject.

[4] See the same phraseology in VI, par. 11.   What follows is merely our author's way of describing the non-action of the Tâo.

[5] The Yang _K_û, whom Mencius attacked so fiercely.   He was, perhaps, a contemporary and disciple of Lâo-ʒze.

in responding to all matters[1], clearsighted and widely intelligent, and an unwearied student of the Tâo;—can he be compared to one of the intelligent kings?' The reply was, 'Such a man is to one of the intelligent kings but as the bustling underling of a court who toils his body and distresses his mind with his various contrivances[2]. And moreover, it is the beauty of the skins of the tiger and leopard which makes men hunt them; the agility of the monkey, or (the sagacity of) the dog that catches the yak, which make men lead them in strings; but can one similarly endowed be compared to the intelligent kings?'

Yang Ʒze-kü looked discomposed and said, 'I venture to ask you what the government of the intelligent kings is.' Lâo Tan replied, 'In the governing of the intelligent kings, their services overspread all under the sky, but they did not seem to consider it as proceeding from themselves; their transforming influence reached to all things, but the people did not refer it to them with hope. No one could tell the name of their agency, but they made men and things be joyful in themselves. Where they took their stand could not be fathomed, and they found their enjoyment in (the realm of) nonentity.'

5. In Kăng there was a mysterious wizard[3] called

---

[1] The 嚮 may be taken as = 向, in which case we must understand a 道 as its object; or as = 響, 'an echo,' indicating the quickness of the man's response to things.

[2] Compare the language of Lâo Tan, in Bk. XII, par. 8, near the beginning.

[3] 巫 is generally feminine, meaning 'a witch.' We must take

*K*i-hsien.   He knew all about the deaths and births of men, their preservation and ruin, their misery and happiness, and whether their lives would be long or short, foretelling the year, the month, the decade and the day like a spirit.   When the people of *K*ăng saw him, they all ran out of his way.   Lieh-3ze went to see him, and was fascinated[1] by him.   Returning, he told Hû-3ze of his interview, and said, 'I considered your doctrine, my master, to be perfect, but I have found another which is superior to it.'   Hû-3ze[2] replied, 'I have communicated to you but the outward letter of my doctrine, and have not communicated its reality and spirit; and do you think that you are in possession of it?   However many hens there be, if there be not the cock among them, how should they lay (real) eggs[3]?   When you confront the world with your doctrine, you are sure to show in your countenance (all that is in your mind)[4], and so enable (this) man to succeed in interpreting your physiognomy.   Try and come to me with him, that I may show myself to him.'

On the morrow, accordingly, Lieh-3ze came with the man and saw Hû-3ze.   When they went out, the

---

it here as masculine (=覡).   The general meaning of the character is 'magical,' the antics of such performers to bring down the spirits.

[1] Literally, 'intoxicated.'

[2] The teacher in Tâoism of Lieh-3ze, called also Hû *K*hiû, with the name Lin (林).   See the remarks on the whole paragraph in the Introductory Notice of the Book.

[3] 'The hens' signify the letter of the doctrine; 'the cock,' its spirit; 'the eggs,' a real knowledge of it.

[4] 信 is here in the first tone, and read as 伸, meaning 'to stretch,' 'to set forth.'

wizard said, 'Alas! your master is a dead man. He
will not live ;—not for ten days more! I saw something strange about him ;—I saw the ashes (of his
life) all slaked with water!' When Lieh-𝔷ze re-
entered, he wept till the front of his jacket was wet
with his tears, and told Hû-𝔷ze what the man had
said. Hû-𝔷ze said, 'I showed myself to him with the
forms of (vegetation beneath) the earth. There were
the sprouts indeed, but without (any appearance of)
growth or regularity:—he seemed to see me with
the springs of my (vital) power closed up. Try and
come to me with him again.'

Next day, accordingly, Lieh-𝔷ze brought the man
again and saw Hû-𝔷ze. When they went out, the
man said, 'It is a fortunate thing for your master
that he met with me. He will get better ; he has
all the signs of living! I saw the balance (of the
springs of life) that had been stopped (inclining in
his favour).' Lieh-𝔷ze went in, and reported these
words to his master, who said, 'I showed myself to
him after the pattern of the earth (beneath the) sky.
Neither semblance nor reality entered (into my exhibition), but the springs (of life) were issuing from
beneath my feet ;—he seemed to see me with the
springs of vigorous action in full play. Try and
come with him again.'

Next day Lieh-𝔷ze came with the man again,
and again saw Hû-𝔷ze with him. When they went
out, the wizard said, 'Your master is never the
same. I cannot understand his physiognomy. Let
him try to steady himself, and I will again view him.'
Lieh-𝔷ze went in and reported this to Hû-𝔷ze, who
said, 'This time I showed myself to him after the
pattern of the grand harmony (of the two elemental

forces), with the superiority inclining to neither. He seemed to see me with the springs of (vital) power in equal balance. Where the water wheels about from (the movements of) a dugong[1], there is an abyss; where it does so from the arresting (of its course), there is an abyss; where it does so, and the water keeps flowing on, there is an abyss. There are nine abysses with their several names, and I have only exhibited three of them. Try and come with him again.'

Next day they came, and they again saw Hû-ᵹze. But before he had settled himself in his position, the wizard lost himself and ran away. ' Pursue him,' said Hû-ᵹze, and Lieh-ᵹze did so, but could not come up with him. He returned, and told Hû-ᵹze, saying, ' There is an end of him; he is lost; I could not find him.' Hû-ᵹze rejoined, ' I was showing him myself after the pattern of what was before I began to come from my author. I confronted him with pure vacancy, and an easy indifference. He did not know what I meant to represent. Now he thought it was the idea of exhausted strength, and now that of an onward flow, and therefore he ran away.'

After this, Lieh-ᵹze considered that he had not yet begun to learn (his master's doctrine). He returned to his house, and for three years did not go out. He did the cooking for his wife. He fed the pigs as if he were feeding men. He took no part

---

[1] One of the dugong. It has various names in Chinese, one being 人 魚, 'the Man-Fish,' from a fancied resemblance of its head and face to a human being;—the origin perhaps of the idea of the mermaid.

or interest in occurring affairs. He put away the carving and sculpture about him, and returned to pure simplicity. Like a clod of earth he stood there in his bodily presence. Amid all distractions he was (silent) and shut up in himself. And in this way he continued to the end of his life.

6. Non-action (makes its exemplifier) the lord of all fame; non-action (serves him as) the treasury of all plans; non-action (fits him for) the burden of all offices; non-action (makes him) the lord of all wisdom [1]. The range of his action is inexhaustible, but there is nowhere any trace of his presence. He fulfils all that he has received from Heaven [2], but he does not see that he was the recipient of anything. A pure vacancy (of all purpose) is what characterises him. When the perfect man employs his mind, it is a mirror. It conducts nothing and anticipates nothing; it responds to (what is before it), but does not retain it. Thus he is able to deal successfully with all things, and injures none.

7. The Ruler [3] of the Southern Ocean was Shû [4], the

---

[1] The four members of this sentence occasion the translator no small trouble. They are constructed on the same lines, and seem to me to be indicative and not imperative. Lin Hsî-kung observes that all the explanations that had been offered of them were inappropriate. My own version is substantially in accordance with his interpretations. The chief difficulty is with the first member, which seems anti-Tâoistic; but our author is not speaking of the purpose of any actor, but of the result of his non-action. 尸 is to be taken in the sense of 主, 'lord,' 'exercising lordship.' The 其 in the third sentence indicates a person or persons in the author's mind in what precedes.

[2] = the Heavenly or self-determining nature.

[3] Perhaps 'god' would be a better translation.

[4] Meaning 'Heedless.'

Ruler of the Northern Ocean was Hû[1], and the Ruler of the Centre was Chaos. Shû and Hû were continually meeting in the land of Chaos, who treated them very well. They consulted together how they might repay his kindness, and said, ' Men all have seven orifices for the purpose of seeing, hearing, eating, and breathing, while this (poor) Ruler alone has not one. Let us try and make them for him.' Accordingly they dug one orifice in him every day; and at the end of seven days Chaos died [2].

---

[1] Meaning ' Sudden.'

[2] The little allegory is ingenious and amusing. ' It indicates,' says Lin, ' how action (the opposite of non-inaction) injures the first condition of things.' More especially it is in harmony with the Tâoistic opposition to the use of knowledge in government. One critic says that an ' alas! ' might well follow the concluding ' died.' But surely it was better that Chaos should give place to another state. ' Heedless ' and ' Sudden' did not do a bad work.

BOOK VIII.

PART II. SECTION I.

Phien Mâu, or 'Webbed Toes[1].'

1. A ligament uniting the big toe with the other toes and an extra finger may be natural[2] growths, but they are more than is good for use. Excrescences on the person and hanging tumours are growths from the body, but they are unnatural additions to it. There are many arts of benevolence and righteousness, and the exercise of them is distributed among the five viscera[3]; but this is not the correct method according to the characteristics of the Tâo. Thus it is that the addition to the foot is but the attachment to it of so much useless flesh, and the addition to the hand is but the planting on it of a useless finger. (So it is that) the connecting (the virtues) with the five viscera renders, by excess or restraint, the action of benevolence and righteousness bad, and leads to many arts as in the employment of (great) powers of hearing or of vision.

2. Therefore an extraordinary power of vision

---

[1] See pp. 138, 139.

[2] 'Come out from the nature,' but 'nature' must be taken here as in the translation. The character is not Tâo.

[3] The five viscera are the heart, the liver, the stomach, the lungs, and the kidneys. To the liver are assigned the element 'wood,' and the virtue of benevolence; to the lungs, the element 'metal,' and the virtue of righteousness.

leads to the confusion of the five colours [1] and an excessive use of ornament. (Its possessor), in the resplendence of his green and yellow, white and black, black and green, will not stop till he has become a Lî *K*û [2]. An extraordinary power of hearing leads to a confusion of the five notes [3], and an excessive use of the six musical accords [4]. (Its possessor), in bringing out the tones from the instruments of metal, stone, silk, and bamboo, aided by the Hwang-*k*ung [4] and Tâ-lü [4] (tubes), will not stop till he has become a Shih Khwang [5]. (So), excessive benevolence eagerly brings out virtues and restrains its (proper) nature, that (its possessor) may acquire a famous reputation, and cause all the organs and drums in the world to celebrate an unattainable condition; and he will not stop till he has become a 3ăng (Shăn) [6] or a Shih (3hiû) [7]. An ex-

---

[1] Black, red, azure (green, blue, or black), white, and yellow.

[2] The same as the Lî Lâu of Mencius (IV, i, 1),—of the time of Hwang-Tî. It is not easy to construe the text here, and in the analogous sentences below. Hsüan Ying, having read on to the 煌 煌 as the uninterrupted predicate of the sharp seer, says, ' Is not this a proof of the extraordinary gift ? ' What follows would be, ' But it was exemplified in Lî *K*û.' The meaning that is given in the version was the first that occurred to myself.

[3] The five notes of the Chinese musical scale.

[4] There are twelve of these musical notes, determined by the twelve regulating tubes; six, represented here by Hwang-*k*ung, the name of the first tube, giving the sharp notes; and six, represented by Tâ-lü, giving the flat notes.

[5] See in II, par. 5.

[6] The famous 3ăng-3ze, or 3ăng Shăn, one of Confucius's ablest disciples.

[7] An officer of Wei in the sixth century B. C. He belonged to a family of historiographers, and hence the surname Shih (史). Confucius mentions him in the most honourable terms in the

traordinary faculty in debating leads to the piling up of arguments like a builder with his bricks, or a net-maker with his string. (Its possessor) cunningly contrives his sentences and enjoys himself in discussing what hardness is and what whiteness is, where views agree and where they differ, and pressing on, though weary, with short steps, with (a multitude of) useless words to make good his opinion; nor will he stop till he has become a Yang (Kû)[1] or Mo (Tî)[1]. But in all these cases the parties, with their redundant and divergent methods, do not proceed by that which is the correct path for all under the sky. That which is the perfectly correct path is not to lose the real character of the nature with which we are endowed. Hence the union (of parts) should not be considered redundance, nor their divergence superfluity; what is long should not be considered too long, nor what is short too short. A duck's legs, for instance, are short, but if we try to lengthen them, it occasions pain; and a crane's legs are long, but if we try to cut off a portion of them, it produces grief. Where a part is by nature long, we are not to amputate, or where it is by nature short, we are not to lengthen it. There is no occasion to try to remove any trouble that it may cause.

3. The presumption is that benevolence and righteousness are not constituents of humanity; for to how much anxiety does the exercise of them give rise! Moreover when another toe is united to the

---

Analect XV, vi, by the name Shih Yü. 'Righteousness' was his great attribute.

[1] The two heresiarchs so much denounced by Mencius. Both have appeared in previous Books.

great toe, to divide the membrane makes you weep; and when there is an extra finger, to gnaw it off makes you cry out.   In the one case there is a member too many, and in the other a member too few; but the anxiety and pain which they cause is the same.   The benevolent men of the present age look at the evils of the world, as with eyes full of dust, and are filled with sorrow by them, while those who are not benevolent, having violently altered the character of their proper nature, greedily pursue after riches and honours.   The presumption therefore is that benevolence and righteousness are contrary to the nature of man :—how full of trouble and contention has the world been ever since the three dynasties [1] began !

And moreover, in employing the hook and line, the compass and square, to give things their correct form you must cut away portions of what naturally belongs to them; in employing strings and fastenings, glue and varnish to make things firm, you must violently interfere with their qualities.   The bendings and stoppings in ceremonies and music, and the factitious expression in the countenance of benevolence and righteousness, in order to comfort the minds of men :—these all show a failure in observing the regular principles (of the human constitution).   All men are furnished with such regular principles; and according to them what is bent is not made so by the hook, nor what is straight by the line, nor what is round by the compass, nor what is square by the carpenter's square.   Nor is adhesion effected by

---

[1] Those of Hsiâ, Shang, and *K*âu ;—from the twenty-third century B. C. to our author's own time.

the use of glue and varnish, nor are things bound together by means of strings and bands. Thus it is that all in the world are produced what they are by a certain guidance, while they do not know how they are produced so; and they equally attain their several ends while they do not know how it is that they do so. Anciently it was so, and it is so now; and this constitution of things should not be made of none effect. Why then should benevolence and righteousness be employed as connecting (links), or as glue and varnish, strings and bands, and the enjoyment arising from the Tâo and its characteristics be attributed to them?—it is a deception practised upon the world. Where the deception is small, there will be a change in the direction (of the objects pursued); where it is great, there will be a change of the nature itself. How do I know that it is so? Since he of the line of Yü called in his benevolence and righteousness to distort and vex the world, the world has not ceased to hurry about to execute their commands;—has not this been by means of benevolence and righteousness to change (men's views) of their nature?

4. I will therefore try and discuss this matter. From the commencement of the three dynasties downwards, nowhere has there been a man who has not under (the influence of external) things altered (the course of) his nature. Small men for the sake of gain have sacrificed their persons; scholars for the sake of fame have done so; great officers, for the sake of their families; and sagely men, for the sake of the kingdom. These several classes, with different occupations, and different repu-

tations, have agreed in doing injury to their nature and sacrificing their persons.   Take the case of a male and female slave[1];—they have to feed the sheep together, but they both lose their sheep.   Ask the one what he was doing, and you will find that he was holding his bamboo tablets and reading.   Ask the other, and you will find that she was amusing herself with some game[2].   They were differently occupied, but they equally lose their sheep.   (So), Po-î[3] died at the foot of Shâu-yang[4] to maintain his fame, and the robber *K*ih[5] died on the top of Tung-ling[6] in his eagerness for gain.   Their deaths were occasioned by different causes, but they equally shortened their lives and did violence to their nature ;—why must we approve of Po-î, and condemn the robber *K*ih ?   In cases of such sacrifice all over the world, when one makes it for the sake of bene-volence and righteousness, the common people style him 'a superior man,' but when another does it for the sake of goods and riches, they style him ' a small man.'   The action of sacrificing is the same, and yet we have 'the superior man ' and 'the small man ! ' In the matter of destroying his life, and doing injury to his nature, the robber *K*ih simply did the same as Po-î ; —why must we make the distinction of 'superior man ' and 'small man ' between them ?

---

[1] See the Khang-hsî dictionary under the character 臧.

[2] Playing at some game with dice.   [3] See VI, par. 3.

[4] A mountain in the present Shan-hsî, probably in the depart-ment of Phû-*k*âu.

[5] A strange character, but not historical, represented as a brother of Liû-hsiâ Hui.   See Bk. XXIX.

[6] ' The Eastern Height,'= the Thâi mountain in the present Shan-tung.

5. Moreover, those who devote their nature to
(the pursuit) of benevolence and righteousness,
though they should attain to be like Ȝăng (Shăn)
and Shih (Ȝhiû), I do not pronounce to be good;
those who devote it to (the study of) the five
flavours, though they attain to be like Shû-*r* [1], I do
not pronounce to be good; those who devote it to
the (discrimination of the) five notes, though they
attain to be like Shih Khwang, I do not pronounce
to be quick of hearing; those who devote it to
the (appreciation of the) five colours, though they
attain to be like Lî *K*û, I do not pronounce to be
clear of vision.   When I pronounce men to be good,
I am not speaking of their benevolence and righteousness;—the goodness is simply (their possession
of) the qualities (of the Tâo).   When I pronounce
them to be good, I am not speaking of what are
called benevolence and righteousness; but simply
of their allowing the nature with which they are
endowed to have its free course.   When I pronounce
men to be quick of hearing, I do not mean that they
hearken to anything else, but that they hearken to
themselves; when I pronounce them to be clear of
vision, I do not mean that they look to anything
else, but that they look to themselves.   Now those
who do not see themselves but see other things,
who do not get possession of themselves but get
possession of other things, get possession of what
belongs to others, and not of what is their own; and
they reach forth to what attracts others, and not to
that in themselves which should attract them.   But

---

[1] Different from Yîh-ya, the famous cook of duke Hwan of *K*hî.
This is said to have been of the time of Hwang-Tî.   But there are
different readings of the name.

thus reaching forth to what attracts others and not to what should attract them in themselves, be they like the robber *K*ih or like Po-î, they equally err in the way of excess or of perversity. What I am ashamed of is erring in the characteristics of the Tâo, and therefore, in the higher sphere, I do not dare to insist on the practice of benevolence and righteousness, and, in the lower, I do not dare to allow myself either in the exercise of excess or perversity.

BOOK IX.

PART II. SECTION II.

Mâ Thî, or 'Horses's Hoofs[1].'

1. Horses can with their hoofs tread on the hoar-frost and snow, and with their hair withstand the wind and cold; they feed on the grass and drink water; they prance with their legs and leap:—this is the true nature of horses. Though there were made for them grand towers[2] and large dormitories, they would prefer not to use them. But when Po-lâo[3] (arose and) said, 'I know well how to manage horses,' (men proceeded)[4] to singe and mark them, to clip their hair, to pare their hoofs, to halter their heads, to bridle them and hobble them, and to confine them in stables and corrals. (When subjected to this treatment), two or three in every ten of them died. (Men proceeded further) to subject them to hunger and thirst, to gallop them and race them,

---

[1] See pp. 140, 141.

[2] Literally, 'righteous towers;' but 羲 is very variously applied, and there are other readings. Compare the name of ling thâi, given by the people to the tower built by king Wăn; Shih, III, i, 8.

[3] A mythical being, the first tamer of horses. The name is given to a star, where he is supposed to have his seat as superintendent of the horses of heaven. It became a designation of Sun Yang, a famous charioteer of the later period of the Kâu dynasty, but it could not be he whom Kwang-ʒze had in view.

[4] Po-lâo set the example of dealing ·with horses as now described; but the supplement which I have introduced seems to bring out better our author's meaning.

and to make them go together in regular order.   In front were the evils of the bit and ornamented breast-bands, and behind were the terrors of the whip and switch.   (When so treated), more than half of them died.

The (first) potter said, ' I know well how to deal with clay;' and (men proceeded) to mould it into circles as exact as if made by the compass, and into squares as exact as if formed by the measuring square.   The (first) carpenter said, ' I know well how to deal with wood;' and (men proceeded) to make it bent as if by the application of the hook, and straight as if by the application of the plumb-line. But is it the nature of clay and wood to require the application of the compass and square, of the hook and line ?   And yet age after age men have praised Po-lâo, saying, ' He knew well how to manage horses,' and also the (first) potter and carpenter, saying, ' They knew well how to deal with clay and wood.'   This is just the error committed by the governors of the world.

2. According to my idea, those who know well to govern mankind would not act so.   The people had their regular and constant nature [1] :—they wove and made themselves clothes ; they tilled the ground and got food [2].   This was their common faculty.   They were all one in this, and did not form themselves into separate .classes ; so were they constituted and left to their natural tendencies [3].   Therefore in the

---

[1] Compare the same language in the previous Book, par. 3.

[2] But the weaver's or agriculturist's art has no more title to be called primitive than the potter's or carpenter's.

[3] A difficult expression ; but the translation, probably, gives its

age of perfect virtue men walked along with slow and grave step, and with their looks steadily directed forwards. At that time, on the hills there were no foot-paths, nor excavated passages; on the lakes there were no boats nor dams; all creatures lived in companies; and the places of their settlement were made close to one another. Birds and beasts multiplied to flocks and herds; the grass and trees grew luxuriant and long. In this condition the birds and beasts might be led about without feeling the constraint; the nest of the magpie might be climbed to, and peeped into. Yes, in the age of perfect virtue, men lived in common with birds and beasts, and were on terms of equality with all creatures, as forming one family;—how could they know among themselves the distinctions of superior men and small men? Equally without knowledge, they did not leave (the path of) their natural virtue; equally free from desires, they were in the state of pure simplicity. In that state of pure simplicity, the nature of the people was what it ought to be. But when the sagely men appeared, limping and wheeling about in (the exercise of) benevolence, pressing along and standing on tiptoe in the doing of righteousness, then men universally began to be perplexed. (Those sages also) went to excess in their performances of music, and in their gesticulations in the practice of ceremonies, and then men began to be separated from one another. If the raw materials

---

true significance. 'Heaven' here is synonymous with 'the Tâo;' but its use shows how readily the minds, even of Lâo and *K*wang, had recourse to the earliest term by which the Chinese fathers had expressed their recognition of a Supreme and Controlling Power and Government.

had not been cut and hacked, who could have made
a sacrificial vase from them? If the natural jade
had not been broken and injured, who could have
made the handles for the libation-cups from it? If
the attributes of the Tâo had not been disallowed,
how should they have preferred benevolence and
righteousness? If the instincts of the nature had
not been departed from, how should ceremonies and
music have come into use? If the five colours had
not been confused, how should the ornamental figures
have been formed? If the five notes had not been
confused, how should they have supplemented
them by the musical accords? The cutting and
hacking of the raw materials to form vessels was the
crime of the skilful workman; the injury done to the
characteristics of the Tâo in order to the practice of
benevolence and righteousness was the error of the
sagely men.

3. Horses, when living in the open country, eat
the grass, and drink water; when pleased, they
intertwine their necks and rub one another; when
enraged, they turn back to back and kick one
another;—this is all that they know to do. But
if we put the yoke on their necks, with the moon-
like frontlet displayed on all their foreheads, then
they know to look slily askance, to curve their necks,
to rush viciously, trying to get the bit out of their
mouths, and to filch the reins (from their driver);—
this knowledge of the horse and its ability thus to
act the part of a thief is the crime of Po-lâo. In
the time of (the Tî) Ho-hsü [1], the people occupied

_____

[1] An ancient sovereign; but nothing more definite can be said
about him. Most of the critics identify him with Shǎn-nǎng, the

their dwellings without knowing what they were doing, and walked out without knowing where they were going. They filled their mouths with food and were glad; they slapped their stomachs to express their satisfaction. This was all the ability which they possessed. But when the sagely men appeared, with their bendings and stoppings in ceremonies and music to adjust the persons of all, and hanging up their benevolence and righteousness to excite the endeavours of all to reach them, in order to comfort their minds, then the people began to stump and limp about in their love of knowledge, and strove with one another in their pursuit of gain, so that there was no stopping them:—this was the error of those sagely men.

Father of Husbandry, who occupies the place in chronological tables after Fû-hsî, between him and Hwang-Tî. In the Tables of the Dynastic Histories, published in 1817, he is placed seventh in the list of fifteen reigns, which are placed without any specification of their length between Fû-hsî and Shăn-năng. The name is written as 合胥 and 赫胥.

BOOK X.

PART II.   SECTION III.

*K*h*ü* *K*h*i*eh, or 'Cutting open Satchels[1].'

1. In taking precautions against thieves who cut open satchels, search bags, and break open boxes, people are sure to cord and fasten them well, and to employ strong bonds and clasps; and in this they are ordinarily said to show their wisdom. When a great thief comes, however, he shoulders the box, lifts up the satchel, carries off the bag, and runs away with them, afraid only that the cords, bonds, and clasps may not be secure; and in this case what was called the wisdom (of the owners) proves to be nothing but a collecting of the things for the great thief. Let me try and set this matter forth. Do not those who are vulgarly called wise prove to be collectors for the great thieves? And do not those who are called sages prove to be but guardians in the interest of the great thieves?

How do I know that the case is so? Formerly, in the state of *K*h*î*, the neighbouring towns could see one another; their cocks and dogs never ceased to answer the crowing and barking of other cocks and dogs (between them). The nets were set (in the water and on the land); and the ploughs and hoes were employed over more than a space of two thousand l*î* square. All within its four boundaries, the

---

[1] See pp. 141, 142.

establishment of the ancestral temples and of the
altars of the land and grain, and the ordering of the
hamlets and houses, and of every corner in the
districts, large, medium, and small, were in all particulars according to the rules of the sages[1]. So it
was; but yet one morning, Thien *Kh*ăng-ɀze[2] killed
the ruler of *Kh*î, and stole his state. And was it
only the state that he stole? Along with it he stole
also the regulations of the sages and wise men
(observed in it). And so, though he got the name
of being a thief and a robber, yet he himself continued to live as securely as Yâo and Shun had done.
Small states did not dare to find fault with him;
great states did not dare to take him off; for twelve
generations (his descendants) have possessed the
state of *Kh*î[3]. Thus do we not have a case in
which not only did (the party) steal the state of *Kh*î,

---

[1] The meaning is plain; but to introduce the various geograph-
ical terms would make the translation cumbrous. The concluding
冊 is perplexing.

[2] This event is mentioned in the Analects, XIV, xxii, where the
perpetrator of the murder is called *Kh*ăn *Kh*ăng-ɀze, and *Kh*ăn
Hăng. Hăng was his name, and *Kh*ăng the honorary title given to
him after his death. The family to which he belonged had originally taken refuge in *Kh*î from the state of *Kh*ăn in b.c. 672. Why
and when its chiefs adopted the surname Thien instead of *Kh*ăn is
not well known. The murder took place in 482. Hăng did not
immediately usurp the marquisate; but he and his successors disposed of it at their pleasure among the representatives of the old
House till 386, when Thien Ho was recognised by the king of
*K*âu as the marquis; and his next successor but one took the title
of king.

[3] The kingdom of *Kh*î came to an end in b.c. 221, the first
year of the dynasty of *Kh*in, after it had lasted through five
reigns. How *K*wang-ɀze made out his 'twelve generations' we
cannot tell. There may be an interpolation in his text made in
the time of *Kh*in, or subsequently.

but at the same time the regulations of its sages and wise men, which thereby served to guard the person of him, thief and robber as he was?

2. Let me try to set forth this subject (still further). Have not there been among those vulgarly styled the wisest, such as have collected (their wealth) for the great chief? and among those styled the most sage such as have guarded it for him? How do I know that it has been so? Formerly, Lung-făng[1] was beheaded; Pî-kan[2] had his heart torn out; Khang Hung[3] was ripped open; and 3ze-hsü[4] was reduced to pulp (in the Kiang). Worthy as those four men were, they did not escape such dreadful deaths. The followers of the robber Kih[5] asked him, saying, 'Has the robber also any method or principle (in his proceedings)?' He replied, 'What profession is there which has not its principles? That the robber in his recklessness comes to the conclusion that there are valuable deposits in an apartment shows his sageness; that he is the first to enter it shows his bravery; that he is the last to quit it shows his righteousness; that he knows whether (the robbery) may be attempted or not shows his wisdom; and that he makes an equal

---

[1] See on Book IV, par. 1.

[2] See on Book IV, par. 1.

[3] A historiographer of Kâu, with whom Confucius is said to have studied music. He was weakly and unjustly put to death, as here described by king Kăng, in B. C. 492.

[4] Wû 3ze-hsü, the hero of revenge, who fled from Khû to Wû, which he long served. He was driven at last to commit suicide, and his body was then put into a leathern wine-sack, and thrown into the Kiang near the present Sû-kâu;—about B. C. 475.

[5] See on Book VIII, par. 4.

division of the plunder shows his benevolence. Without all these five qualities no one in the world has
ever attained to become a great robber.' Looking
at the subject in this way, we see that good men do
not arise without having the principles of the sages,
and that Kih could not have pursued his course
without the same principles. But the good men in
the world are few, and those who are not good are
many;—it follows that the sages benefit the world
in a few instances and injure it in many. Hence it is
that we have the sayings, 'When the lips are gone
the teeth are cold[1];' 'The poor wine of Lû gave occasion to the siege of Han-tan[2];' 'When sages are born
great robbers arise[3].' When the stream is dried,
the valley is empty; when the mound is levelled,
the deep pool (beside it) is filled up. When the
sages have died, the great robbers will not arise;
the world would be at peace, and there would be no
more troubles. While the sagely men have not
died, great robbers will not cease to appear. The
more right that is attached to (the views of) the
sagely men for the government of the world, the
more advantage will accrue to (such men as) the
robber Kih. If we make for men pecks and bushels

---

[1] This is an instance of cause and effect naturally happening.

[2] At a meeting of the princes, presided over by king Hsüan of
Khû (B. C. 369–340), the ruler of Lû brought very poor wine for
the king, which was presented to him as wine of Kâo, in consequence of a grudge against that kingdom by his officer of wines.
In consequence of this king Hsüan ordered siege to be laid to
Han-tan, the capital of Kâo. This is an instance of cause and
effect occurring irregularly.

[3] There seems to be no connexion of cause and effect here;
but Kwang-3ze goes on in his own way to make out that there is
such a connexion.

to measure (their wares), even by means of those pecks and bushels should we be teaching them to steal[1]; if we make for them weights and steelyards to weigh (their wares), even by means of those weights and steelyards shall we be teaching them to steal. If we make for them tallies and seals to secure their good faith, even by means of those tallies and seals shall we be teaching them to steal. If we make for them benevolence and righteousness to make their doings correct, even by means of benevolence and righteousness shall we be teaching them to steal. How do I know that it is so? Here is one who steals a hook (for his girdle);—he is put to death for it: here is another who steals a state;—he becomes its prince. But it is at the gates of the princes that we find benevolence and righteousness (most strongly) professed;—is not this stealing benevolence and righteousness, sageness and wisdom? Thus they hasten to become great robbers, carry off princedoms, and steal benevolence and righteousness, with all the gains springing from the use of pecks and bushels, weights and steelyards, tallies and seals:—even the rewards of carriages and coronets have no power to influence (to a different course), and the terrors of the axe have no power to restrain in such cases. The giving of so great gain to robbers (like) Kih, and making it impossible to restrain them;—this is the error committed by the sages.

3. In accordance with this it is said, 'Fish should

---

[1] The verb 'to steal' is here used transitively, and with a hiphil force.

not be taken from (the protection of) the deep
waters; the agencies for the profit of a state should
not be shown to men[1].' But those sages (and their
teachings) are the agencies for the profit of the
world, and should not be exhibited to it. Therefore
if an end were put to sageness and wisdom put away,
the great robbers would cease to arise. If jade were
put away and pearls broken to bits, the small thieves
would not appear. If tallies were burned and seals
broken in pieces, the people would become simple
and unsophisticated. If pecks were destroyed and
steelyards snapped in two, the people would have no
wrangling. If the rules of the sages were entirely
set aside in the world, a beginning might be made
of reasoning with the people. If the six musical
accords were reduced to a state of utter confusion,
organs and lutes all burned, and the ears of the
(musicians like the) blind Khwang[2] stopped up, all
men would begin to possess and employ their
(natural) power of hearing. If elegant ornaments
were abolished, the five embellishing colours disused,
and the eyes of (men like) Lî Kû[3] glued up, all
men would begin to possess and employ their
(natural) power of vision. If the hook and line were
destroyed, the compass and square thrown away, and
the fingers of men (like) the artful Khui[4] smashed,
all men would begin to possess and employ their
(natural) skill;—as it is said, 'The greatest art is

---

[1] See the Tâo Teh King, ch. 36. Our author's use of it
throws light on its meaning.

[2] Note 1, p. 186.

[3] Note 2, p. 269.

[4] A skilful maker of arrows of the time of Yâo,—the Kung-
kung of the Shû, II, i, 21; V, xxii, 19.

like stupidity[1].' If conduct such as that of 3ăng (Shăn)[2] and Shih (*Kh*iû)[3] were discarded, the mouths of Yang (*K*û)[4] and Mo (Tî) gagged, and benevolence and righteousness seized and thrown aside, the virtue of all men would begin to display its mysterious excellence. When men possessed and employed their (natural) power of vision, there would be no distortion in the world. When they possessed and employed their (natural) power of hearing, there would be no distractions in the world. When they possessed and employed their (natural) faculty of knowledge, there would be no delusions in the world. When they possessed and employed their (natural) virtue, there would be no depravity in the world. Men like 3ăng (Shăn), Shih (*Kh*iû), Yang (*K*û), Mo (Tî), Shih Khwang (the musician), the artist *Kh*ui, and Lî *K*û, all display their qualities outwardly, and set the world in a blaze (of admiration) and confound it;—a method which is of no use!

4. Are you, Sir, unacquainted with the age of perfect virtue? Anciently there were Yung-*kh*ăng, Tâ-thing, Po-hwang, *K*ang-yang, Lî-lû, Lî-*kh*û, Hsien-yüan, Ho-hsü, 3un-lû, *K*û-yung, Fû-hsî, and Shăn-năng[5]. In their times the people made

---

[1] The Tâo Teh *K*ing, ch. 45.
[2] Note 6, p. 269.
[3] Note 7, p. 269.
[4] Note 5, p. 261.
[5] Of the twelve names mentioned here the reader is probably familiar with those of Fû-hsî and Shăn-năng, the first and second of the Tî in chronology. Hsien-yüan is another name for Hwang-Tî, the third of them. *K*û-yung was, perhaps, a minister of Hwang-Tî. Ho-hsü has occurred before in Book IV. Of the other seven, five occur among the fifteen sovereigns placed in the 'Compendium

knots on cords in carrying on their affairs. They
thought their (simple) food pleasant, and their
(plain) clothing beautiful. They were happy in
their (simple) manners, and felt at rest in their
(poor) dwellings. (The people of) neighbouring
states might be able to descry one another; the
voices of their cocks and dogs might be heard (all
the way) from one to the other; they might not die
till they were old; and yet all their life they would
have no communication together [1]. In those times
perfect good order prevailed.

Now-a-days, however, such is the state of things
that you shall see the people stretching out their
necks, and standing on tiptoe, while they say, 'In
such and such a place there is a wise and able
man.' Then they carry with them whatever dry
provisions they may have left, and hurry towards
it, abandoning their parents in their homes, and
neglecting the service of their rulers abroad. Their
footsteps may be traced in lines from one state
to another, and the ruts of their chariot-wheels also
for more than a thousand lî. This is owing to the
error of their superiors in their (inordinate) fondness
for knowledge. When those superiors do really love
knowledge, but do not follow the (proper) course,
the whole world is thrown into great confusion.

How do I know that the case is so? The knowledge shown in the (making of) bows, cross-bows,
hand-nets, stringed arrows, and contrivances with
springs is great, but the birds are troubled by them

---

of History' between Fû-hsî and Shăn-năng. The remaining two
may be found, I suppose, in the Lû Shih of Lo Pî.
   [1] See the eightieth chapter of the Tâo Teh *K*ing.

above; the knowledge shown in the hooks, baits, various kinds of nets, and bamboo traps is great, but the fishes arc disturbed by them in the waters; the knowledge shown in the arrangements for setting nets, and the nets and snares themselves, is great, but the animals are disturbed by them in the marshy grounds. (So), the versatility shown in artful deceptions becoming more and more pernicious, in ingenious discussions as to what is hard and what is white, and in attempts to disperse the dust and reconcile different views, is great, but the common people are perplexed by all the sophistry. Hence there is great disorder continually in the world, and the guilt of it is due to that fondness for knowledge. Thus it is that all men know to seek for the knowledge that they have not attained to ; and do not know to seek for that which they already have (in themselves); and that they know to condemn what they do not approve (in others), and do not know to condemn what they have allowed in themselves ;—it is this which occasions the great confusion and disorder. It is just as if, above, the brightness of the sun and moon were darkened; as if, beneath, the productive vigour of the hills and streams were dried up; and as if, between, the operation of the four seasons were brought to an end :—in which case there would not be a single weak and wriggling insect, nor any plant that grows up, which would not lose its proper nature. Great indeed is the disorder produced in the world by the love of knowledge. From the time of the three dynasties downwards it has been so. The plain and honest-minded people are neglected, and the plausible representations of restless spirits received with pleasure; the quiet and unexciting method of non-action is put away, and pleasure taken in ideas garrulously expressed. It is this garrulity of speech which puts the world in disorder.

BOOK XI.

PART II. SECTION IV,

3âi Yû, or 'Letting Be, and Exercising For-
bearance[1].'

1. I have heard of letting the world be, and exercising forbearance; I have not heard of governing the world. Letting be is from the fear that men, (when interfered with), will carry their nature beyond its normal condition; exercising forbearance is from the fear that men, (when not so dealt with), will alter the characteristics of their nature. When all men do not carry their nature beyond its normal condition, nor alter its characteristics, the good government of the world is secured.

Formerly, Yâo's government of the world made men look joyful; but when they have this joy in their nature, there is a want of its (proper) placidity. The government of the world by *K*ieh, (on the contrary), made men look distressed; but when their nature shows the symptoms of distress, there is a want of its (proper) contentment. The want of placidity and the want of contentment are contrary to the character (of the nature); and where this obtains, it is impossible that any man or state should anywhere abide long. Are men exceedingly joyful?—the Yang or element of expansion in them is too much developed. Are they exceedingly

---

[1] See pp. 142, 143.

irritated?—the Yin or opposite element is too much developed. When those elements thus predominate in men, (it is as if[1]) the four seasons were not to come (at their proper times), and the harmony of cold and heat were not to be maintained;—would there not result injury to the bodies of men? Men's joy and dissatisfaction are made to arise where they ought not to do so; their movements are all uncertain; they lose the mastery of their thoughts; they stop short midway, and do not finish what they have begun. In this state of things the world begins to have lofty aims, and jealous dislikes, ambitious courses, and fierce animosities, and then we have actions like those of the robber *K*ih, or of 3ăng (Shăn) and Shih (3hiû)[2]. If now the whole world were taken to reward the good it would not suffice, nor would it be possible with it to punish the bad. Thus the world, great as it is, not sufficing for rewards and punishments, from the time of the three dynasties downwards, there has been nothing but bustle and excitement. Always occupied with rewards and punishments, what leisure have men had to rest in the instincts of the nature with which they are endowed?

2. Moreover, delight in the power of vision leads

---

[1] I supply the ' it is as if,' after the example of the critic Lû Shû-*k*ih, who here introduces a 猶 in his commentary (猶 四 時 之 氣 乖 其 序 云 云). What the text seems to state as a fact is only an illustration. Compare the concluding paragraphs in all the Sections and Parts of the fourth Book of the Lî *K*î.

[2] Our moral instincts protest against Tâoism which thus places in the same category such sovereigns as Yâo and *K*ieh, and such men as the brigand *K*ih and 3ăng and Shih.

to excess in the pursuit of (ornamental) colours; delight in the power of hearing, to excess in seeking (the pleasures of) sound; delight in benevolence tends to disorder that virtue (as proper to the nature); delight in righteousness sets the man in opposition to what is right in reason; delight in (the practice of) ceremonies is helpful to artful forms; delight in music leads to voluptuous airs; delight in sageness is helpful to ingenious contrivances; delight in knowledge contributes to fault-finding. If all men were to rest in the instincts of their nature, to keep or to extinguish these eight delights might be a matter of indifference; but if they will not rest in those instincts, then those eight delights begin to be imperfectly and unevenly developed or violently suppressed, and the world is thrown into disorder. But when men begin to honour them, and to long for them, how great is the deception practised on the world! And not only, when (a performance of them) is once over, do they not have done with them, but they prepare themselves (as) with fasting to describe them, they seem to kneel reverentially when they bring them forward, and they go through them with the excitements of music and singing; and then what can be done (to remedy the evil of them)? Therefore the superior man, who feels himself constrained to engage in the administration of the world will find it his best way to do nothing[1]. In (that policy of) doing nothing, he can rest in the instincts of the nature with which he is endowed. Hence he who will administer (the government of) the world

---

[1] Here is the Tâoistic meaning of the title of this Book.

honouring it as he honours his own person, may have that government committed to him, and he who will administer it loving it as he loves his own person, may have it entrusted to him [1]. Therefore, if the superior man will keep (the faculties lodged in) his five viscera unemployed, and not display his powers of seeing and hearing, while he is motionless as a representative of the dead, his dragon-like presence will be seen; while he is profoundly silent, the thunder (of his words) will resound; while his movements are (unseen) like those of a spirit, all heavenly influences will follow them; while he is (thus) unconcerned and does nothing, his genial influence will attract and gather all things round him:—what leisure has he to do anything more for the government of the world?

3. 3hui *Khü* [2] asked Lâo Tan, saying, 'If you do not govern the world, how can you make men's minds good?' The reply was, 'Take care how you meddle with and disturb men's minds. The mind, if pushed about, gets depressed; if helped forward, it gets exalted. Now exalted, now depressed, here it appears as a prisoner, and there as a wrathful fury. (At one time) it becomes pliable and soft, yielding to what is hard and strong; (at another), it is sharp as the sharpest corner, fit to carve or chisel (stone or jade). Now it is hot as a scorching fire, and anon it is cold as ice. It is so swift that while one is bending down and lifting up his head, it shall twice

---

[1] A quotation, but without any indication that it is so, from the Tâo Teh *K*ing, ch. 13.

[2] Probably an imaginary personage.

have put forth a soothing hand beyond the four seas. Resting, it is still as a deep abyss; moving, it is like one of the bodies in the sky; in its resolute haughtiness, it refuses to be bound;—such is the mind of man [1]!'

Anciently, Hwang-Tî was the first to meddle with and disturb the mind of man with his benevolence and righteousness [2]. After him, Yâo and Shun wore their thighs bare and the hair off the calves of their legs, in their labours to nourish the bodies of the people. They toiled painfully with all the powers in their five viscera at the practice of their benevolence and righteousness; they tasked their blood and breath to make out a code of laws;—and after all they were unsuccessful. On this Yâo sent away Hwan Tâu to Khung hill, and (the Chiefs of) the Three Miâo to San-wei, and banished the Minister of Works to the Dark Capital; so unequal had they been to cope with the world [3]. Then we are carried on to the kings of the Three (dynasties), when the world was in a state of great distraction. Of the lowest type of character there were Kieh and Kih; of a higher type there were Ȝăng (Shăn) and Shih (Ȝhiû). At the same time there arose the classes of

---

[1] I must suppose that the words of Lâo-ȝze stop here, and that what follows is from Kwang-ȝze himself, down to the end of the paragraph. We cannot have Lâo-ȝze referring to men later than himself, and quoting from his own Book.

[2] Hitherto Yâo and Shun have appeared as the first disturbers of the rule of the Tâo by their benevolence and righteousness. Here that innovation is carried further back to Hwang-Tî.

[3] See these parties, and the way they were dealt with, in the Shû King, Part II, Book I, 3. The punishment of them is there ascribed to Shun; but Yâo was still alive, and Shun was acting as his viceroy.

the Literati and the Mohists. Hereupon, complacency in, and hatred of, one another produced mutual
suspicions; the stupid and the wise imposed on one
another; the good and the bad condemned one
another; the boastful and the sincere interchanged
their recriminations;—and the world fell into decay.
Views as to what was greatly virtuous did not agree,
and the nature with its endowments became as if
shrivelled by fire or carried away by a flood. All were
eager for knowledge, and the people were exhausted
with their searchings (after what was good). On
this the axe and the saw were brought into play;
guilt was determined as by the plumb-line and death
inflicted; the hammer and gouge did their work.
The world fell into great disorder, and presented the
appearance of a jagged mountain ridge. The crime
to which all was due was the meddling with and
disturbing men's minds. The effect was that men
of ability and worth lay concealed at the foot of the
crags of mount Thâi, and princes of ten thousand
chariots were anxious and terrified in their ancestral
temples. In the present age those who have been
put to death in various ways lie thick as if pillowed on
each other; those who are wearing the cangue press
on each other (on the roads); those who are suffering the bastinado can see each other (all over the
land). And now the Literati and the Mohists begin
to stand, on tiptoe and with bare arms, among the
fettered and manacled crowd! Ah! extreme is their
shamelessness, and their failure to see the disgrace!
Strange that we should be slow to recognise their
sageness and wisdom in the bars of the cangue, and
their benevolence and righteousness in the rivets of
the fetters and handcuffs! How do we know that

3ăng and Shih are not the whizzing arrows of *K*ieh and *K*ih [1] ?   Therefore it is said, 'Abolish sageness and cast away knowledge, and the world will be brought to a state of great order [2].'

4. Hwang-Tî had been on the throne for nineteen years [3], and his ordinances were in operation all through the kingdom, when he heard that Kwang *K*hăng-3ze [4] was living on the summit of Khung-thung [5], and went to see him.   'I have heard,' he said, 'that you, Sir, are well acquainted with the perfect Tâo.   I venture to ask you what is the essential thing in it.   I wish to take the subtlest influences of heaven and earth, and assist with them the (growth of the) five cereals for the (better) nourishment of the people.   I also wish to direct the (operation of the) Yin and Yang, so as to secure the comfort of all living beings.   How shall I proceed to accomplish those objects ?'   Kwang *K*hăng-3ze replied, 'What you wish to ask about is the original substance of all things [6]; what you

---

[1] Compare this picture of the times after Yâo and Shun with that given by Mencius in III, ii, ch. 9 et al.   But the conclusions arrived at as to the causes and cure of their evils by him and our author are very different.

[2] A quotation, with the regular formula, from the Tâo Teh *K*ing, ch. 19, with some variation of the text.

[3] ? in B.C. 2678.

[4] Another imaginary personage; apparently, a personification of the Tâo.   Some say he was Lâo-3ze,—in one of his early states of existence; others that he was 'a True Man,' the teacher of Hwang-Tî.   See Ko Hung's 'Immortals,' I, i.

[5] Equally imaginary is the mountain Khung-thung.   Some critics find a place for it in the province of Ho-nan; the majority say it is the highest point in the constellation of the Great Bear.

[6] The original ether, undivided, out of which all things were formed.

wish to have the direction of is that substance as it was shattered and divided[1]. According to your government of the world, the vapours of the clouds, before they were collected, would descend in rain; the herbs and trees would shed their leaves before they became yellow; and the light of the sun and moon would hasten to extinction. Your mind is that of a flatterer with his plausible words;—it is not fit that I should tell you the perfect Tâo.'

Hwang-Tî withdrew, gave up (his government of) the kingdom, built himself a solitary apartment, spread in it a mat of the white mâo grass, dwelt in it unoccupied for three months, and then went again to seek an interview with (the recluse). Kwang *Kh*ăng-ʒze was then lying down with his head to the south. Hwang-Tî, with an air of deferential submission, went forward on his knees, twice bowed low with his face to the ground, and asked him, saying, ' I have heard that you, Sir, are well acquainted with the perfect Tâo;—I venture to ask how I should rule my body, in order that it may continue for a long time.' Kwang *Kh*ăng-ʒze hastily rose, and said, ' A good question! Come and I will tell you the perfect Tâo. Its essence is (surrounded with) the deepest obscurity; its highest reach is in darkness and silence. There is nothing to be seen; nothing to be heard. When it holds the spirit in its arms in stillness, then the bodily form of itself will become correct. You must be still; you must be pure; not subjecting your body to toil, not agitating your vital force;—then you may live for long. When

---

[1] The same ether, now in motion, now at rest, divided into the Yin and Yang.

your eyes see nothing, your ears hear nothing, and your mind knows nothing, your spirit will keep your body, and the body will live long.   Watch over what is within you, shut up the avenues that connect you with what is external;—much knowledge is pernicious.   I (will) proceed with you to the summit of the Grand Brilliance, where we come to the source of the bright and expanding (element); I will enter with you the gate of the Deepest Obscurity, where we come to the source of the dark and repressing (element).   There heaven and earth have their controllers; there the Yin and Yang have their Repositories.   Watch over and keep your body, and all things will of themselves give it vigour.   I maintain the (original) unity (of these elements), and dwell in the harmony of them.   In this way I have cultivated myself for one thousand and two hundred years, and my bodily form has undergone no decay [1].'

Hwang-Tî twice bowed low with his head to the ground, and said, ' In Kwang Khăng-ȝze we have an example of what is called Heaven [2].'   The other said, ' Come, and I will tell you :—(The perfect Tâo) is something inexhaustible, and yet men all think it has an end; it is something unfathomable, and yet men all think its extreme limit can be reached.   He who attains to my Tâo, if he be in a high position, will be one of the August ones, and in a low position, will be a king.   He who fails in attaining it, in his highest attainment will see the light, but will

---

[1] It seems very clear here that the earliest Tâoism taught that the cultivation of the Tâo tended to prolong and preserve the bodily life.

[2] A remarkable, but not a singular, instance of Kwang-ȝze's application of the name ' Heaven.'

descend and be of the Earth. At present all things are produced from the Earth and return to the Earth. Therefore I will leave you, and enter the gate of the Unending, to enjoy myself in the fields of the Illimitable. I will blend my light with that of the sun and moon, and will endure while heaven and earth endure. If men agree with my views, I will be unconscious of it; if they keep far apart from them, I will be unconscious of it; they may all die, and I will abide alone [1]!'

5. Yün *K*iang [2], rambling to the east, having been borne along on a gentle breeze [3], suddenly encountered Hung Mung [2], who was rambling about, slapping his buttocks [4] and hopping like a bird. Amazed at the sight, Yün *K*iang stood reverentially, and said to the other, 'Venerable Sir, who are you? and why are you doing this?' Hung Mung went on slapping his buttocks and hopping like a bird, but replied, 'I am enjoying myself.' Yün *K*iang said, 'I

---

[1] A very difficult sentence, in interpreting which there are great differences among the critics.

[2] I have preferred to retain Yün *K*iang and Hung Mung as if they were the surnames and names of two personages here introduced. Mr. Balfour renders them by 'The Spirit of the Clouds,' and 'Mists of Chaos.' The Spirits of heaven or the sky have still their place in the Sacrificial Canon of China, as 'the Cloud-Master, the Rain-Master, the Baron of the Winds, and the Thunder Master.' Hung Mung, again, is a name for 'the Great Ether,' or, as Dr. Medhurst calls it, 'the Primitive Chaos.'

[3] Literally, 'passing by a branch of Fû-yâo;' but we find fû-yâo in Book I, meaning 'a whirlwind.' The term 'branch' has made some critics explain it here as 'the name of a tree,' which is inadmissible. I have translated according to the view of Lû Shû-*k*ih.

[4] Or 'stomach,'—according to another reading.

wish to ask you a question.' Hung Mung lifted up his head, looked at the stranger, and said, 'Pooh!' Yün Kiang, however, continued, 'The breath of heaven is out of harmony; the breath of earth is bound up; the six elemental influences [1] do not act in concord; the four seasons do not observe their proper times. Now I wish to blend together the essential qualities of those six influences in order to nourish all living things;—how shall I go about it?' Hung Mung slapped his buttocks, hopped about, and shook his head, saying, 'I do not know; I do not know!'

Yün Kiang could not pursue his question; but three years afterwards, when (again) rambling in the east, as he was passing by the wild of Sung, he happened to meet Hung Mung. Delighted with the rencontre, he hastened to him, and said, 'Have you forgotten me, O Heaven? Have you forgotten me, O Heaven[2]?' At the same time, he bowed twice with his head to the ground, wishing to receive his instructions. Hung Mung said, 'Wandering listlessly about, I know not what I seek; carried on by a wild impulse, I know not where I am going. I wander about in the strange manner (which you have seen), and see that nothing proceeds without method and order[3];—what more should I know?' Yün Kiang replied, 'I also seem carried on by an aimless influence, and yet the people follow me wherever I go. I cannot help their doing so. But now as they thus

---

[1] Probably, the yin, the yang, wind, rain, darkness, and light;—see Mayers, p. 323.

[2] See Introduction, pp. 17, 18.

[3] Compare in Book XXIII, par. 1.

imitate me, I wish to hear a word from you (in the case).' The other said, 'What disturbs the regular method of Heaven, comes into collision with the nature of things, prevents the accomplishment of the mysterious (operation of) Heaven, scatters the herds of animals, makes the birds all sing at night, is calamitous to vegetation, and disastrous to all insects;—all this is owing, I conceive, to the error of governing men.' 'What then,' said Yün *K*iang, 'shall I do?' 'Ah,' said the other, 'you will only injure them! I will leave you in my dancing way, and return to my place.' Yün *K*iang rejoined, 'It has been a difficult thing to get this meeting with you, O Heaven! I should like to hear from you a word (more).' Hung Mung said, 'Ah! your mind (needs to be) nourished. Do you only take the position of doing nothing, and things will of themselves become transformed. Neglect your body; cast out from you your power of hearing and sight; forget what you have in common with things; cultivate a grand similarity with the chaos of the plastic ether; unloose your mind; set your spirit free; be still as if you had no soul. Of all the multitude of things every one returns to its root. Every one returns to its root, and does not know (that it is doing so). They all are as in the state of chaos, and during all their existence they do not leave it[1]. If

---

[1] They never show any will of their own.—On the names Yün *K*iang and Hung Mung, Lû Shû-*k*ih makes the following remarks:—'These were not men, and yet they are introduced here as questioning and answering each other; showing us that our author frames and employs his surnames and names to serve his own purpose. Those names and the speeches made by the parties are all from him. We must believe that he introduces Confucius, Yâo, and Shun just in the same way.'

they knew (that they were returning to their root), they would be (consciously) leaving it. They do not ask its name; they do not seek to spy out their nature; and thus it is that things come to life of themselves.'

Yün *K*iang said, ' Heaven, you have conferred on me (the knowledge of) your operation, and revealed to me the mystery of it. All my life I had been seeking for it, and now I have obtained it.' He then bowed twice, with his head to the ground, arose, took his leave, and walked away.

6. The ordinary men of the world [1] all rejoice in men's agreeing with themselves, and dislike men's being different from themselves. This rejoicing and this dislike arise from their being bent on making themselves distinguished above all others. But have they who have this object at heart so risen out above all others? They depend on them to rest quietly (in the position which they desire), and their knowledge is not equal to the multitude of the arts of all those others [2]! When they wish again to administer a state for its ruler, they proceed to employ all the methods which the kings of the three dynasties considered profitable without seeing the evils of such a course. This is to make the state depend on the peradventure of their luck. But how seldom it is that that peradventure does not issue in the ruin of the state! Not once in ten thousand instances will such men preserve a state. Not once will they succeed, and in more than ten thousand cases will they

---

[1] Meaning eccentric thinkers not Tâoists, like Hui-ȝze, Kung-sun Lung, and others.

[2] The construing and connexion of this sentence are puzzling.

ruin it.   Alas that the possessors of territory,—(the rulers of states),—should not know the danger (of employing such men)!   Now the possessors of territory possess the greatest of (all) things.   Possessing the greatest of all things,—(possessing, that is, men), —they should not try to deal with them as (simply) things.   And it is he who is not a thing (himself) that is therefore able to deal with (all) things as they severally require.   When (a ruler) clearly understands that he who should so deal with all things is not a thing himself, will he only rule the kingdom ? He will go out and in throughout the universe (at his pleasure) ; he will roam over the nine regions [1], alone in going, alone in coming.   Him we call the sole possessor (of this ability); and the sole possessor (of this ability) is what is called the noblest of all.

The teaching of (this) great man goes forth as the shadow from the substance, as the echo responds to the sound.   When questioned, he responds, exhausting (from his own stores) all that is in the (enquirer's) mind, as if front to front with all under heaven.   His resting-place gives forth no sound ; his sphere of activity has no restriction of place. He conducts every one to his proper goal, proceeding to it and bringing him back to it as by his own movement.   His movements have no trace ; his going forth and his re-enterings have no deviation ; his course is like that of the sun without beginning (or ending).

---

[1] 'The nine regions' generally means the nine provinces into which the Great Yü divided the kingdom.   As our author is here describing the grand Tâoist ruler after his fashion in his relation to the universe, we must give the phrase a wider meaning ; but I have not met with any attempt to define it.

If you would praise or discourse about his personality, he is united with the great community of existences. He belongs to that great community, and has no individual self. Having no individual self, how should he have anything that can be called his ? If you look at those who have what they call their own, they are the superior men of former times ; if you look at him who has nothing of the kind, he is the friend of heaven and earth.

7. Mean, and yet demanding to be allowed their free course ;—such are Things. Low, and yet requiring to be relied on ;—such are the People. Hidden (as to their issues), and yet requiring to be done ;—such are Affairs. Coarse, and yet necessary to be set forth ;—such are Laws. Remote, and yet necessary to have dwelling (in one's self) ;—such is Righteousness. Near, and yet necessary to be widely extended ;—such is Benevolence. Restrictive, and yet necessary to be multiplied ;—such are Ceremonies. Lodged in the centre, and yet requiring to be exalted ;—such is Virtue. Always One, and yet requiring to be modified ;—such is the Tâo. Spirit-like, and yet requiring to be exercised ;—such is Heaven [1].

Therefore the sages contemplated Heaven, but did not assist It. They tried to perfect their virtue, but did not allow it to embarrass them. They proceeded according to the Tâo, but did not lay any plans. They associated benevolence (with all their doings), but did not rely on it. They pursued right-

---

[1] All these sentences are understood to show that even in the non-action of the Master of the Tâo there are still things he must do.

eousness extensively, but did not try to accumulate it. They responded to ceremonies, but did not conceal (their opinion as to the troublesomeness of them). They engaged in affairs as they occurred, and did not decline them. They strove to render their laws uniform, but (feared that confusion) might arise from them. They relied upon the people, and did not set light by them. They depended on things as their instruments, and did not discard them [1].

They did not think things equal to what they employed them for, but yet they did not see that they could do without employing them. Those who do not understand Heaven are not pure in their virtue. Those who do not comprehend the Tâo have no course which they can pursue successfully. Alas for them who do not clearly understand the Tâo!

What is it that we call the Tâo [2]? There is the Tâo, or Way of Heaven; and there is the Tâo, or Way of Man. Doing nothing and yet attracting all honour is the Way of Heaven; Doing and being embarrassed thereby is the Way of Man. It is the Way of Heaven that plays the part of the Lord; it is the Way of Man that plays the part of the Servant. The Way of Heaven and the Way of Man are far apart. They should be clearly distinguished from each other.

---

[1] Antithetic to the previous sentences, and showing that what such a Master does does not interfere with his non-action.

[2] This question and what follows shows clearly enough that, even with *K*wang-ʒze, the character Tâo (道) retained its proper meaning of the Way or Course.

BOOK XII.

PART II.   SECTION V.

Thien Tî, or 'Heaven and Earth[1].'

1. Notwithstanding the greatness of heaven and earth, their transforming power proceeds from one lathe; notwithstanding the number of the myriad things, the government of them is one and the same; notwithstanding the multitude of mankind, the lord of them is their (one) ruler[2]. The ruler's (course) should proceed from the qualities (of the Tâo) and be perfected by Heaven[3], when it is so, it is called 'Mysterious and Sublime.' The ancients ruled the world by doing nothing;—simply by this attribute of Heaven[4].

If we look at their words[5] in the light of the Tâo, (we see that) the appellation for the ruler of the

---

[1] See pp. 143, 144.

[2] Implying that that ruler, 'the Son of Heaven,' is only one.

[3] 'Heaven' is here defined as meaning 'Non-action, what is of itself (無爲自然);' the teh (德) is the virtue, or qualities of the Tâo;—see the first paragraph of the next Book.

[4] This sentence gives the thesis, or subject-matter of the whole Book, which the author never loses sight of.

[5] Perhaps we should translate here, 'They looked at their words,' referring to 'the ancient rulers.'   So Gabelentz construes :—'Dem Tâo gemäss betrachteten sie die reden.'   The meaning that I have given is substantially the same.   The term 'words' occasions a difficulty.   I understand it here, with most of the critics, as 稱 名之言, 'the words of appellation.'

world [1] was correctly assigned; if we look in the same light at the distinctions which they instituted, (we see that) the separation of ruler and ministers was right; if we look at the abilities which they called forth in the same light, (we see that the duties of) all the offices were well performed; and if we look generally in the same way at all things, (we see that) their response (to this rule) was complete [2]. Therefore that which pervades (the action of) Heaven and Earth is (this one) attribute; that which operates in all things is (this one) course; that by which their superiors govern the people is the business (of the various departments); and that by which aptitude is given to ability is skill. The skill was manifested in all the (departments of) business; those departments were all administered in righteousness; the righteousness was (the outflow of) the natural virtue; the virtue was manifested according to the Tâo; and the Tâo was according to (the pattern of) Heaven.

Hence it is said [3], 'The ancients who had the nourishment of the world wished for nothing and the world had enough; they did nothing and all things were transformed; their stillness was abysmal, and the people were all composed.' The Record says [4], 'When the one (Tâo) pervades it, all business

---

[1] Meaning, probably, his appellation as Thien 3ze, 'the Son of Heaven.'

[2] That is, 'they responded to the Tâo,' without any constraint but the example of their rulers.

[3] Here there would seem to be a quotation which I have not been able to trace to its source.

[4] This 'Record' is attributed to Lâo-3ze; but we know nothing of it. In illustration of the sentiment in the sentence, the critics

is completed.   When the mind gets to be free from
all aim, even the Spirits submit.'

2.   The Master said[1], 'It is the Tâo that overspreads and sustains all things.   How great It is in
Its overflowing influence!   The Superior man ought
by all means to remove from his mind (all that is contrary to It).   Acting without action is what is called
Heaven(-like).   Speech coming forth of itself is
what is called (a mark of) the (true) Virtue.   Loving
men and benefiting things is what is called Benevolence.   Seeing wherein things that are different yet
agree is what is called being Great.   Conduct free
from the ambition of being distinguished above
others is what is called being Generous.   The possession in himself of a myriad points of difference
is what is called being Rich.   Therefore to hold
fast the natural attributes is what is called the
Guiding Line (of government)[2];   the perfecting of
those attributes is what is called its Establishment;
accordance with the Tâo is what is called being
Complete;   and not allowing anything external to
affect the will is what is called being Perfect.   When
the Superior man understands these ten things,
he keeps all matters as it were sheathed in himself,
showing the greatness of his mind;   and through
the outflow of his doings, all things move (and come
to him).   Being such, he lets the gold lie hid in the
hill, and the pearls in the deep;   he considers not

---

refer to par. 34 in the fourth Appendix to the Yî King; but it is
not to the point.

[1] Who is 'the Master' here? Confucius? or Lâo-ʒze?   I think
the latter, though sometimes even our author thus denominates
Confucius;—see par. 9.

[2] ? the Tâo.

property or money to be any gain; he keeps aloof
from riches and honours; he rejoices not in long life,
and grieves not for early death; he does not account
prosperity a glory, nor is ashamed of indigence; he
would not grasp at the gain of the whole world
to be held as his own private portion; he would
not desire to rule over the whole world as his own
private distinction. His distinction is in understanding that all things belong to the one treasury,
and that death and life should be viewed in the
same way[1].'

3. The Master said, ' How still and deep is the
place where the Tâo resides! How limpid is its
purity! Metal and stone without It would give
forth no sound. They have indeed the (power of)
sound (in them), but if they be not struck, they do
not emit it. Who can determine (the qualities that
are in) all things ?

'The man of kingly qualities holds on his way
unoccupied, and is ashamed to busy himself with
(the conduct of) affairs. He establishes himself in
(what is) the root and source (of his capacity), and
his wisdom grows to be spirit-like. In this way his
attributes become more and more great, and when
his mind goes forth, whatever things come in his
way, it lays hold of them (and deals with them).
Thus, if there were not the Tâo, the bodily form
would not have life, and its life, without the attributes (of the Tâo), would not be manifested. Is
not he who preserves the body and gives the fullest
development to the life, who establishes the attri-

---

[1] Balfour :—' The difference between life and death exists no
more ; ' Gabelentz :—' Sterben und Leben haben gleiche Ersch-
einung.'

butes of the Tâo and clearly displays It, possessed
of kingly qualities? How majestic is he in his
sudden issuings forth, and in his unexpected movements, when all things follow him!—This we call
the man whose qualities fit him to rule.

' He sees where there is the deepest obscurity; he
hears where there is no sound. In the midst of the
deepest obscurity, he alone sees and can distinguish
(various objects); in the midst of a soundless
(abyss), he alone can hear a harmony (of notes).
Therefore where one deep is succeeded by a greater,
he can people all with things; where one mysterious
range is followed by another that is more so, he
can lay hold of the subtlest character of each. In
this way in his intercourse with all things, while he
is farthest from having anything, he can yet give
to them what they seek; while he is always hurrying
forth, he yet returns to his resting-place; now large,
now small; now long, now short; now distant, now
near [1].'

4. Hwang-Tî, enjoying himself on the north of
the Red-water, ascended to the height of the
Khwăn-lun (mountain), and having looked towards
the south, was returning home, when he lost his
dark-coloured pearl [2]. He employed Wisdom to
search for it, but he could not find it. He employed
(the clear-sighted) Lî *K*û to search for it, but he

---

[1] I can hardly follow the reasoning of *K*wang-ʒze here. The whole
of the paragraph is obscure. I have translated the two concluding
characters 修 遠, as if they were 遠 近, after the example of Lin
Hsî-yî, whose edition of *K*wang-ʒze was first published in 1261.

[2] Meaning the Tâo. This is not to be got or learned by
wisdom, or perspicacity, or man's reasoning. It is instinctive to
man, as the Heavenly gift or Truth (天 眞).

could not find it. He employed (the vehement debater) *Kh*ieh *Kh*âu[1] to search for it, but he could not find it. He then employed Purposeless[1], who found it; on which Hwang-Tî said, 'How strange that it was Purposeless who was able to find it!'

5. The teacher of Yâo was Hsü Yû[2]; of Hsü Yû, Nieh *Kh*üeh[2]; of Nieh *Kh*üeh, Wang Î[2]; of Wang Î, Pheî-î[2]. Yâo asked Hsü Yû, saying, 'Is Nieh *Kh*üeh fit to be the correlate of Heaven[3]? (If you think he is), I will avail myself of the services of Wang Î to constrain him (to take my place).' Hsü Yû replied, 'Such a measure would be hazardous, and full of peril to the kingdom! The character of Nieh *Kh*üeh is this;—he is acute, perspicacious, shrewd and knowing, ready in reply, sharp in retort, and hasty; his natural (endowments) surpass those of other men, but by his human qualities he seeks to obtain the Heavenly gift; he exercises his discrimination in suppressing his errors, but he does not know what is the source from which his errors arise. Make him the correlate of Heaven! He would employ the human qualities, so that no regard would be paid to the Heavenly gift. Moreover, he would assign different functions to the different parts of the one person[4].

---

[1] The meaning of the characters shows what is the idea emblemed by this name; and so with Hsiang Wang,—'a Semblance,' and 'Nonentity;'='Mindless,' 'Purposeless.'

[2] All these names have occurred, excepting that of Pheî-î, who heads Hwang-fû Mî's list of eminent Tâoists. We shall meet with him again. He is to be distinguished from Phû-î.

[3] 'Match Heaven;' that is, be sovereign below, as Heaven above ruled all.

[4] We are referred for the meaning of this characteristic to 肝膽 楚越, in Bk. V, par. 1.

Moreover, honour would be given to knowledge, and he would have his plans take effect with the speed of fire. Moreover, he would be the slave of everything he initiated. Moreover, he would be embarrassed by things. Moreover, he would be looking all round for the response of things (to his measures). Moreover, he would be responding to the opinion of the multitude as to what was right. Moreover, he would be changing as things changed, and would not begin to have any principle of constancy. How can such a man be fit to be the correlate of Heaven? Nevertheless, as there are the smaller branches of a family and the common ancestor of all its branches, he might be the father of a branch, but not the father of the fathers of all the branches[1]. Such government (as he would conduct) would lead to disorder. It would be calamity in one in the position of a minister, and ruin if he were in the position of the sovereign.'

6. Yâo was looking about him at Hwâ[2], the border-warden of which said, 'Ha! the sage! Let me ask blessings on the sage! May he live long!'

---

[1] That is, Nieh might be a minister, but could not be the sovereign. The phraseology is based on the rules for the rise of sub-surnames in the same clan, and the consequent division of clans under different ancestors;—see the Lî *K*î, Bk. XIII, i, 10–14, and XIV, 8.

[2] 'Hwâ' is evidently intended for the name of a place, but where it was can hardly be determined. The genuineness of the whole paragraph is called in question; and I pass it by, merely calling attention to what the border-warden is made to say about the close of the life of the sage (Tâoist), who after living a thousand years, ascends among the Immortals (僊 = 仙), and arrives at the place of God, and is free from the three evils of disease, old age, and death; or as some say, after the Buddhists, water, fire, and wind!

Yâo said, 'Hush!' but the other went on, 'May the sage become rich!' Yâo (again) said, 'Hush!' but (the warden) continued, 'May the sage have many sons!' When Yâo repeated his 'Hush,' the warden said, 'Long life, riches, and many sons are what men wish for;—how is it that you alone do not wish for them?' Yâo replied, 'Many sons bring many fears; riches bring many troubles; and long life gives rise to many obloquies. These three things do not help to nourish virtue; and therefore I wish to decline them.' The warden rejoined, 'At first I considered you to be a sage; now I see in you only a Superior man. Heaven, in producing the myriads of the people, is sure to have appointed for them their several offices. If you had many sons, and gave them (all their) offices, what would you have to fear? If you had riches, and made other men share them with you, what trouble would you have? The sage finds his dwelling like the quail (without any choice of its own), and is fed like the fledgling; he is like the bird which passes on (through the air), and leaves no trace (of its flight). When good order prevails in the world, he shares in the general prosperity. When there is no such order, he cultivates his virtue, and seeks to be unoccupied. After a thousand years, tired of the world, he leaves it, and ascends among the immortals. He mounts on the white clouds, and arrives at the place of God. The three forms of evil do not reach him, his person is always free from misfortune;—what obloquy has he to incur?'

With this the border-warden left him. Yâo followed him, saying, 'I beg to ask—;' but the other said, 'Begone!'

7. When Yâo was ruling the world, Po-*kh*ăng 3ze-
kâo[1] was appointed by him prince of one of the
states. From Yâo (afterwards) the throne passed to
Shun, and from Shun (again) to Yü; and (then) Po-
*kh*ăng 3ze-kâo resigned his principality and began
to cultivate the ground. Yü went to see him, and
found him ploughing in the open country. Hurrying to him, and bowing low in acknowledgment of
his superiority, Yü then stood up, and asked him,
saying, ' Formerly, when Yâo was ruling the world,
you, Sir, were appointed prince of a state. He
gave his sovereignty to Shun, and Shun gave his to
me, when you, Sir, resigned your dignity, and are
(now) ploughing (here);—I venture to ask the reason of your conduct.' 3ze-kâo said, ' When Yâo
ruled the world, the people stimulated one another
(to what was right) without his offering them rewards, and stood in awe (of doing wrong) without
his threatening them with punishments. Now you
employ both rewards and punishments, and the
people notwithstanding are not good. Their virtue
will from this time decay; punishments will from this
time prevail; the disorder of future ages will from
this time begin. Why do you, my master, not go
away, and not interrupt my work?' With this he
resumed his ploughing with his head bent down, and
did not (again) look round.

8. In the Grand Beginning (of all things) there
was nothing in all the vacancy of space; there was
nothing that could be named[2]. It was in this state

---

[1] Some legends say that this Po-*kh*ăng 3ze-kâo was a pre-incar-
nation of Lâo-3ze; but this paragraph is like the last, and cannot
be received as genuine.

[2] This sentence is differently understood, according as it is

that there arose the first existence [1] ;—the first existence, but still without bodily shape. From this
things could then be produced, (receiving) what we
call their proper character [2]. That which had no
bodily shape was divided [3]; and then without intermission there was what we call the process of conferring [4]. (The two processes) continuing in operation, things were produced. As things were completed, there were produced the distinguishing lines
of each, which we call the bodily shape. That shape
was the body preserving in it the spirit [5], and each
had its peculiar manifestation, which we call its
Nature. When the Nature has been cultivated, it
returns to its proper character; and when that has
been fully reached, there is the same condition as at
the Beginning. That sameness is pure vacancy,
and the vacancy is great. It is like the closing of
the beak and silencing the singing (of a bird). That
closing and silencing is like the union of heaven and
earth (at the beginning) [6]. The union, effected, as it

---

punctuated;—有 無 無, 有 無 名, or 有 無, 無 有 無
名. Each punctuation has its advocates. For myself, I can only
adopt the former; the other is contrary to my idea of Chinese
composition. If the author had wished to be understood so, he
would have written differently, as, for instance, 無 未 有 名.

[1] Probably, the primary ether, what is called the Thâi Kih.

[2] This sentence is anticipatory.

[3] Into what we call the yin and the yang;—the same ether,
now at rest, now in motion.

[4] The conferring of something more than what was material.
By whom or what? By Heaven; the Tâoist understanding by
that term the Tâo.

[5] So then, man consists of the material body and the immaterial
spirit.

[6] The potential heaven and earth, not yet fashioned from the
primal ether.

is, might seem to indicate stupidity or darkness, but
it is what we call the ' mysterious quality' (existing
at the beginning); it is the same as the Grand Submission (to the Natural Course).

9. The Master [1] asked Lâo Tan, saying, ' Some
men regulate the Tâo (as by a law), which they have
only to follow ;—(a thing, they say,) is admissible or
it is inadmissible; it is so, or it is not so. (They
are like) the sophists who say that they can distinguish what is hard and what is white as clearly
as if the objects were houses suspended in the sky.
Can such men be said to be sages [2] ?' The reply was,
' They are like the busy underlings of a court, who
toil their bodies and distress their minds with their
various artifices ;—dogs, (employed) to their sorrow
to catch the yak, or monkeys [3] that are brought
from their forests (for their tricksiness).   Khiû, I
tell you this ;—it is what you cannot hear, and what
you cannot speak of :—Of those who have their
heads and feet, and yet have neither minds nor ears,
there are multitudes; while of those who have their
bodies, and at the same time preserve that which
has no bodily form or shape, there are really none.
It is not in their movements or stoppages, their
dying or living, their falling and rising again, that
this is to be found.   The regulation of the course
lies in (their dealing with) the human element in
them.   When they have forgotten external things,

----

[1] This ' Master' is without doubt Confucius.
[2] The meaning and point of Confucius's question are not clear.
Did he mean to object to Lâo-ʒze that all his disquisitions about
the Tâo as the one thing to be studied and followed were
unnecessary ?
[3] Compare in Bk. VII, par. 4.

and have also forgotten the heavenly element in them, they may be named men who have forgotten themselves. The man who has forgotten himself is he of whom it is said that he has become identified with Heaven[1].'

10. At an interview with *Kî Khêh*[2], *K*iang-lü Mien[2] said to him, 'Our ruler of Lû asked to receive my instructions. I declined, on the ground that I had not received any message[3] for him. Afterwards, however, I told him (my thoughts). I do not know whether (what I said) was right or not, and I beg to repeat it to you. I said to him, "You must strive to be courteous and to exercise self-restraint; you must distinguish the public-spirited and loyal, and repress the cringing and selfish;—who among the people will in that case dare not to be in harmony with you?"' *Kî Khê*h laughed quietly and said, 'Your words, my master, as a description of the right course for a Tî or King, were like the threatening movement of its arms by a mantis which would thereby stop the advance of a carriage;—inadequate to accomplish your object. And moreover, if he guided himself by your directions, it would be as if he were to increase the dangerous height of his towers

---

[1] Their action is like that of Heaven, silent but most effective, without motive from within or without, simply from the impulse of the Tâo.

[2] These two men are only known by the mention of them here. They must have been officers of Lû, *Kî Khê*h a member of the great *Kî* or *K*î-sun family of that state. He would appear also to have been the teacher of the other; if, indeed, they were real personages, and not merely the production of *K*wang-ȝze's imagination.

[3] That is any lessons or instructions from you, my master, which I should communicate to him.

and add to the number of his valuables collected in them;—the multitudes (of the people) would leave their (old) ways, and bend their steps in the same direction.'

Kiang-lü Mien was awe-struck, and said in his fright, 'I am startled by your words, Master, nevertheless, I should like to hear you describe the influence (which a ruler should exert).' The other said, 'If a great sage ruled the kingdom, he would stimulate the minds of the people, and cause them to carry out his instructions fully, and change their manners ; he would take their minds which had become evil and violent and extinguish them, carrying them all forward to act in accordance with the (good) will belonging to them as individuals, as if they did it of themselves from their nature, while they knew not what it was that made them do so.   Would such an one be willing to look up to Yâo and Shun in their instruction of the people as his elder brothers ?   He would treat them as his juniors, belonging himself to the period of the original plastic ether [1].   His wish would be that all should agree with the virtue (of that early period), and quietly rest in it.'

11. 3ze-kung had been rambling in the south in Khû, and was returning to 3in.   As he passed (a place) on the north of the Han, he saw an old man who was going to work on his vegetable garden. He had dug his channels, gone to the well, and was bringing from it in his arms a jar of water to pour into them.   Toiling away, he expended a great deal

---

[1] The Chinese phrase here is explained by Dr. Williams :—
'A vivifying influence, a vapour or aura producing things.'

of strength, but the result which he accomplished was very small. 3ze-kung said to him, ' There is a contrivance here, by means of which a hundred plots of ground may be irrigated in one day. With the expenditure of a very little strength, the result accomplished is great. Would you, Master, not like (to try it) ? ' The gardener looked up at him, and said, ' How does it work ? ' 3ze-kung said, ' It is a lever made of wood, heavy behind, and light in front. It raises the water as quickly as you could do with your hand, or as it bubbles over from a boiler. Its name is a shadoof.' The gardener put on an angry look, laughed, and said, ' I have heard from my teacher that, where there are ingenious contrivances, there are sure to be subtle doings ; and that, where there are subtle doings, there is sure to be a scheming mind. But, when there is a scheming mind in the breast, its pure simplicity is impaired. When this pure simplicity is impaired, the spirit becomes unsettled, and the unsettled spirit is not the proper residence of the Tâo. It is not that I do not know (the contrivance which you mention), but I should be ashamed to use it.'

(At these words) 3ze-kung looked blank and ashamed ; he hung down his head, and made no reply. After an interval, the gardener said to him, ' Who are you, Sir ? ' ' A disciple of Khung *Kh*iû,' was the reply. The other continued, ' Are you not the scholar whose great learning makes you comparable to a sage, who make it your boast that you surpass all others, who sing melancholy ditties all by yourself, thus purchasing a famous reputation throughout the kingdom ? If you would (only) forget the energy of your spirit, and neglect the care of

your body, you might approximate (to the Tâo).
But while you cannot regulate yourself, what leisure
have you to be regulating the world ? Go on your
way, Sir, and do not interrupt my work.'

ȝze-kung shrunk back abashed, and turned pale.
He was perturbed, and lost his self-possession, nor did
he recover it, till he had walked a distance of thirty
lî. His disciples then said, 'Who was that man ?
Why, Master, when you saw him, did you change
your bearing, and become pale, so that you have
been all day without returning to yourself ? ' He
replied to them, ' Formerly I thought that there was
but one man [1] in the world, and did not know that
there was this man. I have heard the Master say
that to seek for the means of conducting his undertakings so that his success in carrying them out may
be complete, and how by the employment of a little
strength great results may be obtained, is the way
of the sage. Now (I perceive that) it is not so at
all. They who hold fast and cleave to the Tâo
are complete in the qualities belonging to it. Complete in those qualities, they are complete in their
bodies. Complete in their bodies, they are complete in their spirits. To be complete in spirit is
the way of the sage. (Such men) live in the world
in closest union with the people, going along with
them, but they do not know where they are going.
Vast and complete is their simplicity ! Success,
gain, and ingenious contrivances, and artful clever-
ness, indicate (in their opinion) a forgetfulness of the
(proper) mind of man. These men will not go
where their mind does not carry them, and will do

---

[1] Confucius.

nothing of which their mind does not approve. Though all the world should praise them, they would (only) get what they think should be loftily disregarded ; and though all the world should blame them, they would but lose (what they think) fortuitous and not to be received ;—the world's blame and praise can do them neither benefit nor injury.   Such men may be described as possessing all the attributes (of the Tâo), while I can only be called one of those who are like the waves carried about by the wind.'   When he returned to Lû, (3ze-kung) reported the interview and conversation to Confucius, who said, ' The man makes a pretence of cultivating the arts of the Embryonic Age[1].   He knows the first thing, but not the sequel to it.   He regulates what is internal in himself, but not what is external to himself.   If he had intelligence enough to be entirely unsophisticated, and by doing nothing to seek to return to the normal simplicity, embodying (the instincts of) his nature, and keeping his spirit (as it were) in his arms, so enjoying himself in the common ways, you might then indeed be afraid of him !   But what should you and I find in the arts of the embryonic time, worth our knowing?'

12. Kun Mâng[2], on his way to the ocean, met with Yüan Fung[2] on the shore of the eastern sea, and

---

[1] The 'arts of the Embryonic Age' suggests the idea of the earliest men in their struggles for support; not the Tâo of Heaven in its formation of the universe.   But the whole of the paragraph, not in itself uninteresting, is believed to be a spurious introduction, and not the production of Kwang-3ze.

[2] These are not names of men, but like Yün Kiang and Hung Mung in the fifth paragraph of the last Book.   By Kun Mâng, it is said, we are to understand ' the great primal ether,' and by Yüan

was asked by him where he was going. 'I am
going,' he replied, 'to the ocean;' and the other
again asked, 'What for?' Kun Mâng said, 'Such
is the nature of the ocean that the waters which
flow into it can never fill it, nor those which flow
from it exhaust it. I will enjoy myself, rambling by
it.' Yüan Fung replied, 'Have you no thoughts
about mankind[1]? I should like to hear from you
about sagely government.' Kun Mâng said, 'Under
the government of sages, all offices are distributed
according to the fitness of their nature; all appoint-
ments are made according to the ability of the men;
whatever is done is after a complete survey of all
circumstances; actions and words proceed from the
inner impulse, and the whole world is transformed.
Wherever their hands are pointed and their looks
directed, from all quarters the people arc all sure to
come (to do what they desire):—this is what is
called government by sages.'

'I should like to hear about (the government of)
the kindly, virtuous men[2],' (continued Yüan Fung).
The reply was, 'Under the government of the virtuous, when quietly occupying (their place), they
have no thought, and, when they act, they have no
anxiety; they do not keep stored (in their minds)
what is right and what is wrong, what is good and

Fung, 'the east wind.' Why these should discourse together as
they are here made to do, only Kwang-3ze himself could tell.

[1] Literally, 'men with their cross eyes;' an appellation for mankind, men having their eyes set across their face more on the same
plane than other animals;—'an extraordinary application of the
characters,' says Lin Hsî-kung.

[2] The text is simply 'virtuous men;' but the reply justifies us
in giving the meaning as 'kindly' as well. 德 has often this
signification.

what is bad. They share their benefits among all within the four seas, and this produces what is called (the state of) satisfaction; they dispense their gifts to all, and this produces what is called (the state of) rest. (The people) grieve (on their death) like babies who have lost their mothers, and are perplexed like travellers who have lost their way. They have a superabundance of wealth and all necessaries, and they know not whence it comes; they have a sufficiency of food and drink, and they know not from whom they get it:—such are the appearances (under the government) of the kindly and virtuous.'

'I should like to hear about (the government of) the spirit-like men,' (continued Yüan Fung once more).

The reply was, ' Men of the highest spirit-like qualities mount up on the light, and (the limitations of) the body vanish. This we call being bright and ethereal. They carry out to the utmost the powers with which they are endowed, and have not a single attribute unexhausted. Their joy is that of heaven and earth, and all embarrassments of affairs melt away and disappear; all things return to their proper nature:—and this is what is called (the state of) chaotic obscurity[1].'

13. Măn Wû-kwei[2] and *Kh*ih-*k*ang Man-*kh*î[2] had been looking at the army of king Wû, when the latter said, ' It is because he was not born in the time of the Lord of Yü[3], that therefore he is in-

---

[1] When no human element had come in to mar the development of the Tâo.

[2] If these be the names of real personages, they must have been of the time of king Wû, about B.C. 1122.

[3] Generally understood to mean ' He is not equal to the Lord of

volved in this trouble (of war).' Mǎn Wû-kwei replied, 'Was it when the kingdom was in good order, that the Lord of Yü governed it? or was it after it had become disordered that he governed it?' The other said, 'That the kingdom be in a condition of good order, is what (all) desire, and (in that case) what necessity would there be to say anything about the Lord of Yü? He had medicine for sores; false hair for the bald; and healing for those who were ill:—he was like the filial son carrying in the medicine to cure his kind father, with every sign of distress in his countenance. A sage would be ashamed (of such a thing)[1].

'In the age of perfect virtue they attached no value to wisdom, nor employed men of ability. Superiors were (but) as the higher branches of a tree; and the people were like the deer of the wild. They were upright and correct, without knowing that to be so was Righteousness; they loved one another, without knowing that to do so was Benevolence; they were honest and leal-hearted, without knowing that it was Loyalty; they fulfilled their engagements, without knowing that to do so was Good Faith; in their simple movements they employed the services of one another, without thinking that they were conferring or receiving any gift. Therefore their actions left no trace, and there was no record of their affairs.'

14. The filial son who does not flatter his father,

Yü,' or Shun. The meaning which I have given is that propounded by Hû Wan-ying, and seems to agree better with the general purport of the paragraph.

[1] Ashamed that he had not been able to keep his father from getting sick, and requiring to be thus attended to.

and the loyal minister who does not fawn on his ruler, are the highest examples of a minister and a son. When a son assents to all that his father says, and approves of all that his father does, common opinion pronounces him an unworthy son; when a minister assents to all that his ruler says, and approves of all that his ruler does, common opinion pronounces him an unworthy minister. Nor does any one reflect that this view is necessarily correct [1]. But when common opinion (itself) affirms anything and men therefore assent to it, or counts anything good and men also approve of it, then it is not said that they are mere consenters and flatterers;—is common opinion then more authoritative than a father, or more to be honoured than a ruler? Tell a man that he is merely following (the opinions) of another, or that he is a flatterer of others, and at once he flushes with anger. And yet all his life he is merely following others, and flattering them. His illustrations are made to agree with theirs; his phrases are glossed:—to win the approbation of the multitudes. From first to last, from beginning to end, he finds no fault with their views. He will let his robes hang down [2], display the colours on them, and arrange his movements and bearing, so as to win the favour of his age, and yet not call himself a flatterer. He is but a follower of those others, approving and dis-

---

[1] We can hardly tell whether this paragraph should be understood as a continuation of Khih-kang's remarks, or as from Kwang-ze himself. The meaning here is that every one feels that this opinion is right, without pausing to reason about it.

[2] See the Yî King, Appendix III, ii, 15, where this letting his robes hang down is attributed to Shun. Ought we to infer from this that in this paragraph we have Khih-kang still speaking about and against the common opinion of Shun's superiority to king Wû?

approving as they do, and yet he will not say that
he is one of them.   This is the height of stupidity.

He who knows his stupidity is not very stupid ;
he who knows that he is under a delusion is not
greatly deluded.   He who is greatly deluded will
never shake the delusion off; he who is very stupid
will all his life not become intelligent.   If three men
be walking together, and (only) one of them be
under a delusion (as to their way), they may yet
reach their goal, the deluded being the fewer; but
if two of them be under the delusion, they will not
do so, the deluded being the majority.   At the present time, when the whole world is under a delusion,
though I pray men to go in the right direction, I
cannot make them do so ;—is it not a sad case ?

Grand music does not penetrate the ears of vil-
lagers ; but if they hear 'The Breaking of the Wil-
low,' or 'The Bright Flowers [1],' they will roar with
laughter.   So it is that lofty words do not remain in
the minds of the multitude, and that perfect words
are not heard, because the vulgar words predominate.   By two earthenware instruments the (music of)
a bell will be confused, and the pleasure that it would
afford cannot be obtained.   At the present time the
whole world is under a delusion, and though I wish
to go in a certain direction, how can I succeed in
doing so ?   Knowing that I cannot do so, if I were
to try to force my way, that would be another delusion.   Therefore my best course is to let my purpose go, and no more pursue it.   If I do not pursue
it, whom shall I have to share in my sorrow [2] ?

---

[1] The names of two songs, favourites with the common people.

[2] I shall only feel the more that I am alone without any to sym-
pathise with me, and be the more sad.

If an ugly man [1] have a son born to him at midnight, he hastens with a light to look at it. Very eagerly he does so, only afraid that it may be like himself.

15 [2]. From a tree a hundred years old a portion shall be cut and fashioned into a sacrificial vase, with the bull figured on it, which is ornamented further with green and yellow, while the rest (of that portion) is cut away and thrown into a ditch. If now we compare the sacrificial vase with what was thrown into the ditch, there will be a difference between them as respects their beauty and ugliness; but they both agree in having lost the (proper) nature of the wood. So in respect of their practice of righteousness there is a difference between (the robber) *K*ih on the one hand, and 3ăng (Shăn) or Shih (3hiû) on the other; but they all agree in having lost (the proper qualities of) their nature.

Now there are five things which produce (in men) the loss of their (proper) nature. The first is (their fondness for) the five colours which disorder the eye, and take from it its (proper) clearness of vision; the second is (their fondness for) the five notes (of music), which disorder the ear and take from it its

---

[1] 厲人 should perhaps be translated 'a leper.' The illustration is edited by *K*iâo Hung and others as a paragraph by itself. They cannot tell whether it be intended to end the paragraph that precedes or to introduce the one that follows.

[2] This paragraph must be our author's own. *Kh*ih-*k*ang, of the time of king Wû, could not be criticising the schemes of life propounded by Mo and Yang, whose views were so much later in time. It breathes the animosity of Lâo and *K*wang against all schemes of learning and culture, as contrary to the simplicity of life according to the Tâo.

(proper) power of hearing; the third is (their fondness for) the five odours which penetrate the nostrils, and produce a feeling of distress all over the
forehead ; the fourth is (their fondness for) the five
flavours, which deaden the mouth, and pervert its
sense of taste ; the fifth is their preferences and
dislikes, which unsettle the mind, and cause the
nature to go flying about.   These five things are all
injurious to the life ; and now Yang and Mo begin
to stretch forward from their different standpoints,
each thinking that he has hit on (the proper course
for men).

   But the courses they have hit on are not what I
call the proper course.   What they have hit on (only)
leads to distress ;—can they have hit on what is
the right thing ?   If they have, we may say that the
dove in a cage has found the right thing for it.
Moreover, those preferences and dislikes, that (fondness for) music and colours, serve but to pile up fuel
(in their breasts) ; while their caps of leather, the
bonnet with kingfishers' plumes, the memorandum
tablets which they carry, and their long girdles,
serve but as restraints on their persons.   Thus inwardly stuffed full as a hole for fuel, and outwardly
fast bound with cords, when they look quietly round
from out of their bondage, and think they have got
all they could desire, they are no better than criminals
whose arms are tied together, and their fingers subjected to the screw, or than tigers and leopards in
sacks or cages, and yet thinking that they have got
(all they could wish).

BOOK XIII.

PART II. SECTION VI.

Thien Tâo, or ' The Way of Heaven[1].'

1. The Way of Heaven operates (unceasingly), and leaves no accumulation [2] (of its influence) in any particular place, so that all things are brought to perfection by it; so does the Way of the Tîs operate, and all under the sky turn to them (as their directors); so also does the Way of the Sages operate, and all within the seas submit to them. Those who clearly understand (the Way of) Heaven, who are in sympathy with (that of) the sages, and familiar through the universe and in the four quarters (of the earth) with the work of the Tîs and the kings, yet act spontaneously from themselves:—with the appearance of being ignorant they are yet entirely still.

The stillness of the sages does not belong to them as a consequence of their skilful ability [3]; all things are not able to disturb their minds;—it is on this account that they are still. When water is still, its clearness shows the beard and eyebrows (of him

---

[1] See pp. 144, 145.

[2] That is, its operation is universal. The Chinese critics generally explain ' accumulation' here by ' rest,' which is not quite the idea.

[3] Such is the meaning here of the 善, as in the Tâo Teh King, chaps. 2, 8, and often.

who looks into it). It is a perfect Level[1], and the greatest artificer takes his rule from it. Such is the clearness of still water, and how much greater is that of the human Spirit! The still mind of the sage is the mirror of heaven and earth, the glass of all things.

Vacancy, stillness, placidity, tastelessness, quietude, silence, and non-action ;—this is the Level of heaven and earth, and the perfection of the Tâo and its characteristics[2]. Therefore the Tîs, Kings, and Sages found in this their resting-place[3]. Resting here, they were vacant; from their vacancy came fullness ; from their fullness came the nice distinctions (of things). From their vacancy came stillness ; that stillness was followed by movement ; their movements were successful. From their stillness came their non-action. Doing-nothing, they devolved the cares of office on their employés. Doing-nothing was accompanied by the feeling of satisfaction. Where there is that feeling of satisfaction, anxieties and troubles find no place; and the years of life are many.

Vacancy, stillness, placidity, tastelessness, quietude, silence, and doing-nothing are the root of all things. When this is understood, we find such a ruler on the throne as Yâo, and such a minister as Shun. When with this a high position is occupied, we find the attributes of the Tîs and kings,—the sons of Heaven ; with this in a low position, we find the mysterious

---

[1] 準 here, is contracted in many editions into 准, which some have mistaken for 准.

[2] Such are the natural characteristics of the Tâoistic mind.

[3] Implying cessation from all thought and purpose.

sages, the uncrowned kings, with their ways. With this retiring (from public life), and enjoying themselves at leisure, we find the scholars who dwell by the rivers and seas, among the hills and forests, all submissive to it; with this coming forward to active life and comforting their age, their merit is great, and their fame is distinguished;—and all the world becomes united in one.

2. (Such men) by their stillness become sages; and by their movement, kings. Doing-nothing, they are honoured; in their plain simplicity, no one in the world can strive with them (for the palm of) excellence. The clear understanding of the virtue of Heaven and Earth is what is called 'The Great Root,' and 'The Great Origin;'—they who have it are in harmony with Heaven, and so they produce all equable arrangements in the world;—they are those who are in harmony with men. Being in harmony with men is called the Joy of men; being in harmony with Heaven is called the Joy of Heaven. _K_wang-_ʒ_ze said, 'My Master! my Master! He shall hash and blend all things in mass without being cruel; he shall dispense his favours to all ages without being benevolent. He is older than the highest antiquity, and yet is not old. He overspreads the heavens and sustains the earth; from him is the carving of all forms without any artful skill [1]! This is what is called the Joy of Heaven. Hence it is said, "Those who know the Joy of Heaven during their life, act like Heaven, and at death undergo transformation like (other) things [2]; in their stillness

---

[1] Compare in Bk. VI, pars. 13 and 7.

[2] They do not cease to be, but only become transformed or changed.

they possess the quality of the Yin, and in their movement they flow abroad as the Yang. Therefore he who knows the Joy of Heaven has no murmuring against Heaven, nor any fault-finding with men; and suffers no embarrassment from things, nor any reproof from ghosts. Hence it is said, ' His movements are those of Heaven ; his stillness is that of Earth ; his whole mind is fixed, and he rules over the world. The spirits of his dead do not come to scare him ; he is not worn out by their souls. His words proceeding from his vacancy and stillness, yet reach to heaven and earth, and show a communication with all things :—this is what is called the Joy of Heaven. This Joy of Heaven forms the mind of the sage whereby he nurtures all under the sky [1].' " '

3. It was the Way [2] of the Tîs and Kings to regard Heaven and Earth as their Author, the Tâo and its characteristics as their Lord, and Doing-nothing as their constant rule. Doing-nothing, they could use the whole world in their service and might have done more ; acting, they were not sufficient for the service required of them by the world. Hence the men of old held non-inaction in honour. When superiors do nothing and their inferiors also do nothing, inferiors and superiors possess the same virtue ; and when inferiors and superiors possess the same virtue, there are none to act as ministers. When inferiors act, and their superiors also act, then superiors and inferiors possess the same Tâo ; and when superiors and inferiors possess the same

---

[1] I suppose that from 'It is said' to this is all quotation, but from what book we do not know.

[2] 'The virtue,' or attribute ;=the way.

Tâo, there is none to preside as Lord. But that the superiors do nothing and yet thereby use the world in their service, and that the inferiors, while acting, be employed in the service of the world, is an unchangeable principle. Therefore the ancient kings who presided over the world, though their knowledge embraced (all the operations of) Heaven and Earth, took no thought of their own about them; though their nice discrimination appreciated the fine fashioning of all things, they said not a word about it; though their power comprehended all within the seas, they did nothing themselves. Heaven produces nothing, yet all things experience their transformations; Earth effects no growth, yet all things receive their nurture; the Tîs and Kings did nothing, yet all the world testified their effective services. Hence it is said, 'There is nothing more spirit-like than Heaven; there is nothing richer than Earth; there are none greater than the Tîs and Kings.' Hence it is said (further), ' The attributes of the Tîs and kings corresponded to those of Heaven and Earth.' It was thus that they availed themselves of (the operations of) Heaven and Earth, carried all things on unceasingly (in their courses), and employed the various classes of men in their service.

4. Originating belongs to those in the higher position; details (of work) to those who are in the lower. The compendious decision belongs to the lord; the minutiae of execution, to his ministers. The direction of the three hosts [1] and their men with the five weapons [2] is but a trifling quality; rewards

---

[1] 'Three hosts' constituted the military force of one of the largest states.

[2] The bow, the club, the spear, the lance, the javelin. Other

and penalties with their advantages and sufferings, and the inflictions of the five punishments [1] are but trivial elements of instruction; ceremonies, laws, measures, and numbers, with all the minutiae of jurisprudence [2], are small matters in government; the notes of bells and drums, and the display of plumes and flags are the slightest things in music, and the various grades of the mourning garments are the most unimportant manifestations of grief. These five unimportant adjuncts required the operation of the excited spirit and the employment of the arts of the mind, to bring them into use. The men of old had them indeed, but they did not give them the first place.

The ruler precedes, and the minister follows; the father precedes, and the son follows; the elder brother precedes, and the younger follows; the senior precedes, and the junior follows; the male precedes, and the female follows; the husband precedes, and the wife follows.

This precedence of the more honourable and sequence of the meaner is seen in the (relative) action of heaven and earth, and hence the sages took them as their pattern. The more honourable position of heaven and the lower one of earth are equivalent to a designation of their spirit-like and intelligent qualities. The precedence of spring and summer and the sequence of autumn and winter mark the

---

enumerations of them are given.   See the 'Officers of *K*âu,' Bk. XXXII.

[1] Branding, cutting off the nose, cutting off the feet, castration, death.

[2] I read here 刑 (not 形) 名.

order of the four seasons.   In the transformations
and growth of all things, every bud and feature has
its proper form ; and in this we have their gradual
maturing and decay, the constant flow of transformation and change.   Thus since Heaven and Earth,
which are most spirit-like, are distinguished as more
honourable and less, and by precedence and sequence,
how much more must we look for this in the ways
of men !   In the ancestral temple it is to kinship that
honour is given ; in court, to rank ; in the neigh-
bourhoods and districts, to age ; in the conduct of
affairs, to wisdom ; such is the order in those great
ways.   If we speak of the course (to be pursued in
them), and do not observe their order, we violate
their course.   If we speak of the course, and do not
observe it, why do we apply that name to it ?

5. Therefore the ancients who clearly understood
the great Tâo first sought to apprehend what was
meant by Heaven [1], and the Tâo and its characteristics came next.   When this was apprehended, then
came Benevolence and Righteousness.   When these
were apprehended, then came the Distinction of duties
and the observance of them.   This accomplished,
there came objects and their names.   After objects
and their names, came the employment of men
according to their qualities: on this there followed
the examination of the men and of their work.   This
led to the approval or disapproval of them, which
again was succeeded by the apportioning of rewards
and penalties.   After this the stupid and the intelligent understood what was required of them, and the
honourable and the mean occupied their several posi-

---

[1] The meaning, probably, is ' spontaneity.'

tions. The good and the able, and those inferior
to them, sincerely did their best. Their ability
was distributed ; the duties implied in their official
names were fulfilled. In this way did they serve
their superiors, nourish their inferiors, regulate
things, and cultivate their persons. They did not call
their knowledge and schemes into requisition ; they
were required to fall back upon (the method of)
Heaven :—this was what is called the Perfection of
the Rule of Great Peace. Hence it is said in the
Book [1], 'There are objects and there are their names.'
Objects and their names the ancients had ; but they
did not put them in the foremost place.

When the ancients spoke of the Great Tâo, it
was only after four other steps that they gave a
place to 'Objects and their Names,' and after eight
steps that they gave a place to 'Rewards and
Penalties.' If they had all at once spoken of
'Objects and their Names,' they would have shown
an ignorance of what is the Root (of government) ; if
they had all at once spoken of 'Rewards and Penalties,'
they would have shown an ignorance of the first
steps of it. Those whose words are thus an in-
version of the (proper) course, or in opposition to it,
are (only fit to be) ruled by others ;—how can they
rule others ? To speak all at once of 'Objects and
their Names,' and of 'Rewards and Penalties,' only
shows that the speaker knows the instruments of
government, but does not know the method of it,
is fit to be used as an instrument in the world, but
not fit to use others as his instruments :—he is what
we call a mere sophist, a man of one small idea.

---

[1] We cannot tell what book or books.

Ceremonies, laws, numbers, measures, with all the minutiae of jurisprudence, the ancients had; but it is by these that inferiors serve their superiors; it is not by them that those superiors nourish the world.

6. Anciently, Shun asked Yâo, saying, 'In what way does your Majesty by the Grace of Heaven[1] exercise your mind?' The reply was, 'I simply show no arrogance towards the helpless; I do not neglect the poor people; I grieve for those who die; I love their infant children; and I compassionate their widows.' Shun rejoined, 'Admirable, as far as it goes; but it is not what is Great.' 'How then,' asked Yâo, 'do you think I should do?' Shun replied, 'When (a sovereign) possesses the virtue of Heaven, then when he shows himself in action, it is in stillness. The sun and moon (simply) shine, and the four seasons pursue their courses. So it is with the regular phenomena of day and night, and with the movement of the clouds by which the rain is distributed.' Yâo said, 'Then I have only been persistently troubling myself! What you wish is to be in harmony with Heaven, while I wish to be in harmony with men.' Now (the Way of) Heaven and Earth was much thought of of old, and Hwang-Tî, Yâo, and Shun united in admiring it. Hence the kings of the world of old did nothing, but tried to imitate that Way.

7. Confucius went to the west to deposit (some) writings in the library of _K_âu[2], when _3_ze-lû coun-

---

[1] So, in the 'Spring and Autumn' Chronicle, the rightful reigning sovereign is ordinarily designated, 'Heaven's King.' It is not a Tâoistic mode of speaking of him.

[2] It is supposed that Confucius, disappointed by his want of

selled him, saying, ' I have heard that the officer in charge of this *K*ăng[1] Repository of *K*âu was one Lâo Tan, who has given up his office, and is living in his own house.   As you, Master, wish to deposit these writings here, why not go to him, and obtain his help (to accomplish your object)[2].'   Confucius said, ' Good;' and he went and saw Lâo Tan, who refused his assistance.   On this he proceeded to give an abstract of the Twelve Classics[3] to bring the other over to his views[4].   Lâo Tan, however, interrupted him while he was speaking, and said, ' This is too vague; let me hear the substance of them in brief.'   Confucius said, ' The substance of them is occupied with Benevolence and Righteousness.'   The other said, ' Let me ask whether you consider Benevolence and Righteousness to constitute the nature of man ?'   ' I do,' was the answer. ' If the superior man be not benevolent, he will not fulfil his character; if he be not righteous, he might as well not have been born.   Benevolence and Righteousness are truly the nature of man.'   Lâo Tan continued, ' Let me ask you what you mean by Benevolence and Righteousness.'   Confucius said, ' To be in one's inmost heart in kindly sympathy

---

success, wished to deposit the writings or books which he prized so much in the Royal Library, that they might not be lost, and be available for some future teacher, more fortunate than himself.

[1] The name of the Royal Library (徵); meaning, perhaps, ' Approved.'

[2] That is, help him to get his books deposited in the Library.

[3] Meaning, perhaps, the ' Spring and Autumn,' containing a chronicle of twelve marquises of Lû.   We know of no collection in the time of Confucius which could be styled the ' Twelve Classics.'

[4] 說 is to be read shui.

with all things; to love all men; and to allow no
selfish thoughts;—this is the nature of Benevolence
and Righteousness.' Lâo Tan exclaimed, 'Ah! you
almost show your inferiority by such words! "To
love all men!" is not that vague and extravagant?
"To be seeking to allow no selfish thoughts!"—that
is selfishness[1]! If you, Master, wish men not to be
without their (proper) shepherding, think of Heaven
and Earth, which certainly pursue their invariable
course; think of the sun and moon, which surely
maintain their brightness; think of the stars in the
zodiac, which preserve their order and courses;
think of birds and beasts, which do not fail to collect
together in their flocks and herds; and think of
the trees, which do not fail to stand up (in their
places). Do you, Master, imitate this way and carry
it into practice; hurry on, following this course, and
you will reach your end. Why must you further be
vehement in putting forward your Benevolence and
Righteousness, as if you were beating a drum, and
seeking a fugitive son, (only making him run away
the more)? Ah! Master, you are introducing disorder into the nature of man!'

8. Shih-*kh*ăng *Kh*î[2], having an interview with
Lâo-𝔧ze, asked him, saying, 'I heard, Master, that
you were a sage, and I came here, wishing to see
you, without grudging the length of the journey.
During the stages of the hundred days, the soles
of my feet became quite callous, but I did not dare
to stop and rest. Now I perceive that you are not

---

[1] The unselfishness was not spontaneous.

[2] We know nothing of this personage, but what is related here;
nor does the whole paragraph serve to advance the argument of
the Book.

a sage. Because there was some rice left about the holes of the rats, you sent away your younger sister, which was unkind; when your food, whether raw or cooked, remains before you not all consumed, you keep on hoarding it up to any extent[1].' Lâo-ȝze looked indifferent, and gave him no answer.

Next day *K*hî again saw Lâo-ȝze, and said, 'Yesterday I taunted you; but to-day I have gone back to a better mood of mind. What is the cause (of the change)[2]?' Lâo-ȝze replied, ' I consider that I have freed myself from the trammels of claiming to be artfully knowing, spirit-like, and sage. Yesterday if you had called me an ox, you might have done so; or if you had called me a horse, you might have done so[3]. If there be a reality (corresponding to men's ideas), and men give it a name, which another will not receive, he will in the sequel suffer the more. My manner was what I constantly observe;—I did not put it on for the occasion.'

Shih-*kh*ăng *K*hî sidled away out of Lâo's shadow; then he retraced his steps, advanced forward, and asked how he should cultivate himself. The reply was, 'Your demeanour is repelling; you stare with your eyes; your forehead is broad and yet tapering; you bark and growl with your mouth; your appearance is severe and pretentious; you are like a horse held by its tether, you would move, but are restrained, and (if let go) would start off like an

---

[1] These seem strange charges to bring against Lâo-ȝze, and no light is thrown on them from other sources.

[2] The change had been produced by the demeanour of Lâo-ȝze; the other could not tell how. Other explanations of the question are given by some of the critics.

[3] Compare in the first paragraph of Book VII.

arrow from a bow; you examine all the minutiae of
a thing; your wisdom is artful, and yet you try to
look at ease. All these are to be considered proofs
of your want of sincerity. If on the borders one
were to be found with them, he would be named a
Thief.'

9. The Master [1] said, 'The Tâo does not exhaust
itself in what is greatest, nor is it ever absent from
what is least; and therefore it is to be found complete and diffused in all things. How wide is its
universal comprehension! How deep is its un-
fathomableness! The embodiment of its attributes
in benevolence and righteousness is but a small
result of its spirit-like (working); but it is only the
perfect man who can determine this. The perfect
man has (the charge of) the world;—is not the
charge great? and yet it is not sufficient to embarrass him. He wields the handle of power over
the whole world, and yet it is nothing to him. His
discrimination detects everything false, and no consideration of gain moves him. He penetrates to
the truth of things, and can guard that which is
fundamental. So it is that heaven and earth are external to him, and he views all things with indifference,
and his spirit is never straitened by them. He has
comprehended the Tâo, and is in harmony with its
characteristics; he pushes back benevolence and
righteousness (into their proper place), and deals
with ceremonies and music as (simply) guests:—
yes, the mind of the perfect man determines all
things aright.'

---

[1] No doubt, Lâo-ʒze. In the 'Complete Works of the Ten
Philosophers,' the text is 老子 and not 夫子.

10. What the world thinks the most valuable exhibition of the T â o is to be found in books. But books are only a collection of words. Words have what is valuable in them;—what is valuable in words is the ideas they convey. But those ideas are a sequence of something else;—and what that something else is cannot be conveyed by words. When the world, because of the value which it attaches to words, commits them to books, that for which it so values them may not deserve to be valued;—because that which it values is not what is really valuable.

Thus it is that what we look at and can see is (only) the outward form and colour, and what we listen to and can hear is (only) names and sounds. Alas! that men of the world should think that form and colour, name and sound, should be sufficient to give them the real nature of the T â o. The form and colour, the name and sound, are certainly not sufficient to convey its real nature; and so it is that ' the wise do not speak and those who do speak are not wise.' How should the world know that real nature?

Duke Hwan[1], seated above in his hall, was (once) reading a book, and the wheelwright Phien was making a wheel below it[2]. Laying aside his hammer and chisel, Phien went up the steps, and said, ' I venture to ask your Grace what words you are reading?' The duke said, ' The words of the sages.' 'Are those sages alive?' Phien con-

---

[1] No doubt, duke Hwan of *K*hî, the first of the five presiding chiefs of the *K*âu dynasty.

[2] See in Mencius I, i, vii, 4 a similar reference to the hall and the courtyard below it.

tinued. 'They are dead,' was the reply. 'Then,' said the other, 'what you, my Ruler, are reading are only the dregs and sediments of those old men.' The duke said, 'How should you, a wheelwright, have anything to say about the book which I am reading? If you can explain yourself, very well; if you cannot, you shall die!' The wheelwright said, 'Your servant will look at the thing from the point of view of his own art. In making a wheel, if I proceed gently, that is pleasant enough, but the workmanship is not strong; if I proceed violently, that is toilsome and the joinings do not fit. If the movements of my hand are neither (too) gentle nor (too) violent, the idea in my mind is realised. But I cannot tell (how to do this) by word of mouth;— there is a knack in it. I cannot teach the knack to my son, nor can my son learn it from me. Thus it is that I am in my seventieth year, and am (still) making wheels in my old age [1]. But these ancients, and what it was not possible for them to convey, are dead and gone :—so then what you, my Ruler, are reading is but their dregs and sediments!'

---

[1] Compare the story in Book III about the ruler Wăn-hui and his butcher; and other passages.

BOOK XIV.

Part II. Section VII.

Thien Yün, or ' The Revolution of Heaven[1].'

1. How (ceaselessly) heaven revolves! How (constantly) earth abides at rest! And do the sun and moon contend about their (respective) places? Who presides over and directs these (things)? Who binds and connects them together? Who is it that, without trouble or exertion on his part, causes and maintains them? Is it, perhaps, that there is some secret spring, in consequence of which they cannot be but as they are? Or is it, perhaps, that they move and turn as they do, and cannot stop of themselves?

(Then) how the clouds become rain! And how the rain again forms the clouds! Who diffuses them so abundantly? Who is it that, without trouble or exertion on his part, produces this elemental enjoyment, and seems to stimulate it?

The winds rise in the north; one blows to the west, and another to the east; while some rise upwards, uncertain in their direction. By whose breathing are they produced? Who is it that, without any trouble and exertion of his own, effects all their undulations? I venture to ask their cause[2].

---

[1] See pp. 145, 146.

[2] Down to this we have a description of the phenomena of heaven and earth and of nature generally as proceeding regularly

Wû-hsien Thiâo[1] said, 'Come, and I will tell you. To heaven there belong the six Extreme Points, and the five Elements[2]. When the Tîs and Kings acted in accordance with them, there was good government; when they acted contrary to them, there was evil. Observing the things (described) in the nine divisions (of the writing) of Lo[3], their government was perfected and their virtue was complete. They inspected and enlightened the kingdom beneath them, and all under the sky acknowledged and sustained them. Such was the condition under the august (sovereigns[4]) and those before them.'

2. Tang[5], the chief administrator of Shang[5], asked *K*wang-ȝze about Benevolence[6], and the answer was, 'Wolves and tigers are benevolent.' 'What do you mean?' said Tang. *K*wang-ȝze replied, 'Father and son (among them) are affectionate to one another. Why should they be considered as not bene-

---

and noiselessly, without any apparent cause; which is the chief subject of the Book. As the description is not assigned to any one, we must suppose it to be from *K*wang-ȝze himself; and that it is he who asks the question in the last three characters.

[1] This is said by the critics to have been a minister of the Shang dynasty, under Thâi-mâu in the seventeenth century B.C.; but even *K*wang-ȝze would hardly so violate the unity of time.

[2] Generally means 'the Five Regular Virtues;' supposed to mean here 'the Five Elements.'

[3] Probably the 'Nine Divisions of the Great Plan,' in the Shû King, V, iv, fancied to be derived from the writing, which a tortoise from the Lo river exhibited to the great Yü.

[4] Possibly Fû-hsî, Shăn Năng, and Hwang-Tî.

[5] 'Shang' must be taken as the duchy of Sung, assigned by king Wû to the representative of the kings of the dynasty of Shang. 'Tang' would be a principal minister of it in the time of *K*wang-ȝze.

[6] The chief of all the virtues according to Confucianism.

volent ?' 'Allow me to ask about perfect benevolence,' pursued the other. *K*wang-ʒze said, 'Perfect
benevolence [1] does not admit (the feeling) of affection.' The minister said, 'I have heard that, without (the feeling of) affection there is no love, and
without love there is not filial duty;—is it permissible to say that the perfectly benevolent are not
filial?' *K*wang-ʒze rejoined, 'That is not the way
to put the case. Perfect Benevolence is the very
highest thing;—filial duty is by no means sufficient
to describe it. The saying which you quote is not to
the effect that (such benevolence) transcends filial
duty;—it does not refer to such duty at all. One,
travelling to the south, comes (at last) to Ying [2], and
there, standing with his face to the north, he does not
see mount Ming [3]. Why does he not see it? Because
he is so far from it. Hence it is said, "Filial duty
as a part of reverence is easy, but filial duty as a
part of love is difficult. If it be easy as a part of
love, yet it is difficult to forget [4] one's parents. It
may be easy for me to forget my parents, but it is
difficult to make my parents forget me. If it were
easy to make my parents forget me, it is difficult for
me to forget all men in the world. If it were easy
to forget all men in the world, it is difficult to make
them all forget me."

'This virtue might make one think light of Yâo
and Shun, and not wish to be they [5]. The profit

---

[1] A denomination here for the Tâo, employed by *K*wang-ʒze for
the purpose of his argument.

[2] The capital of the state of *Kh*û in the south.

[3] Name of a hill in the extreme north.

[4] The Tâo requires such forgetfulness on the part of both giver
and receiver; it is a part of its 'doing-nothing.'

[5] I think this is the meaning.

and beneficial influences of it extend to a myriad ages, and no one in the world knows whence they come. How can you simply heave a great sigh, and speak (as you do) of benevolence and filial duty? Filial duty, fraternal respect, benevolence, righteousness, loyalty, sincerity, firmness, and purity;—all these may be pressed into the service of this virtue, but they are far from sufficient to come up to it. Therefore it is said, " To him who has what is most noble[1], all the dignities of a state are as nothing[2]; to him who has what is the greatest riches, all the wealth of a state is as nothing; to him who has all that he could wish, fame and praise are as nothing." It is thus that the Tâo admits of no substitute.'

3. Pei-măn *Kh*ăng[3] asked Hwang-Tî, saying, ' You were celebrating, O Tî, a performance of the music of the Hsien-*kh*ih[4], in the open country near the Thung-thing lake. When I heard the first part of it, I was afraid; the next made me weary; and the last perplexed me. I became agitated and unable to speak, and lost my self-possession.' The Tî said, ' It was likely that it should so affect you! It was performed with (the instruments of) men, and all attuned according to (the influences of) Heaven. It

---

[1] The Tâo.

[2] This free version takes 并 as = 屏. So the Khang-hsî dictionary explains it.

[3] Only heard of, so far as I know, in this passage.

[4] The name of Hwang-Tî's music; I do not venture to translate it. In his elaborate description of it, our author intended to give an idea of the Tâo, and the effect which the study of it was calculated to produce on the mind; as appears from the concluding sentence of the paragraph.

proceeded according to (the principles of) propriety and righteousness, and was pervaded by (the idea of) the Grand Purity.

'The Perfect Music first had its response in the affairs of men, and was conformed to the principles of Heaven; it indicated the action of the five virtues, and corresponded to the spontaneity (apparent in nature). After this it showed the blended distinctions of the four seasons, and the grand harmony of all things;—the succession of those seasons one after another, and the production of things in their proper order. Now it swelled, and now it died away, its peaceful and military strains clearly distinguished and given forth. Now it was clear, and now rough, as if the contracting and expanding of the elemental processes blended harmoniously (in its notes). Those notes then flowed away in waves of light, till, as when the hibernating insects first begin to move, I commanded the terrifying crash of thunder. Its end was marked by no formal conclusion, and it began again without any prelude. It seemed to die away, and then it burst into life; it came to a close, and then it rose again. So it went on regularly and inexhaustibly, and without the intervention of any pause:—it was this which made you afraid.

'In the second part (of the performance), I made it describe the harmony of the Yin and Yang, and threw round it the brilliance of the sun and moon. Its notes were now short and now long, now soft and now hard. Their changes, however, were marked by an unbroken unity, though not dominated by a fixed regularity. They filled every valley and ravine; you might shut up every crevice, and guard your spirit (against their entrance), yet there was nothing but gave admission to them. Yea, those notes resounded slowly, and might have been pronounced high and clear. Hence the shades of the dead kept in their obscurity; the sun and moon, and all the stars of the zodiac, pursued their several courses. I made (my instruments) leave off, when (the performance) came to an end, and their (echoes) flowed on without stopping. You thought anxiously about it, and were not able to understand it; you looked for it, and were not able to see it; you pursued it, and were not able to reach it. All-amazed, you stood in the way all open around you, and then you leant against an old rotten dryandra-tree and hummed. The power of your eyes was exhausted by what you wished to see; your strength failed in your desire to pursue it, while I myself could not reach it. Your body was but so much empty vacancy while you endeavoured to retain your self-possession [1] :—it was that endeavour which made you weary.

'In the last part (of the performance), I employed notes which did not have that wearying effect. I blended them together as at the command of spontaneity. Hence they came as if following one another in confusion, like a clump of plants springing from one root, or like the music of a forest produced by no visible form. They spread themselves all around without leaving a trace (of their cause); and seemed to issue from deep obscurity where there was no sound. Their movements came from nowhere; their home was in the deep darkness;—

---

[1] See the usage of the two characters 委 蛇 in the Shih King, I, ii, Ode 3.

conditions which some would call death, and some life ; some, the fruit, and some, (merely) the flower. Those notes, moving and flowing on, separating and shifting, and not following any regular sounds, the world might well have doubts about them, and refer them to the judgment of a sage, for the sages understand the nature of this music, and judge in accordance with the prescribed (spontaneity). While the spring of that spontaneity has not been touched, and yet the regulators of the five notes are all prepared ;— this is what is called the music of Heaven, delighting the mind without the use of words. Hence it is said in the eulogy of the Lord of Piâo [1], "You listen for it, and do not hear its sound ; you look for it, and do not perceive its form ; it fills heaven and earth ; it envelopes all within the universe." You wished to hear it, but could not take it in ; and therefore you were perplexed.

' I performed first the music calculated to awe ; and you were frightened as if by a ghostly visitation. I followed it with that calculated to weary ; and in your weariness you would have withdrawn. I concluded with that calculated to perplex ; and in your perplexity you felt your stupidity. But that stupidity is akin to the Tâo ; you may with it convey the Tâo in your person, and have it (ever) with you.'

4. When Confucius was travelling in the west in Wei, Yen Yüan asked the music-master *K*in [2], say-

---

[1] Some sovereign of antiquity, of whom it is difficult to find any other mention but this. Even in the Lû Shih I have not discovered him. The name is said to be pronounced Piâo ; in which case it should consist of three 犬, and not of three 火.

[2] Only heard of here.

ing, ' How is it, do you think, with the course of the
Master ? ' The music-master replied, 'Alas! it is all
over with your Master!' ' How so ? ' asked Yen
Yüan ; and the other said, ' Before the grass-dogs[1]
are set forth (at the sacrifice), they are deposited in
a box or basket, and wrapt up with elegantly
embroidered cloths, while the representative of the
dead and the officer of prayer prepare themselves
by fasting to present them. After they have been
set forth, however, passers-by trample on their heads
and backs, and the grass-cutters take and burn them
in cooking. That is all they are good for. If one
should again take them, replace them in the box or
basket, wrap them up with embroidered cloths, and
then in rambling, or abiding at the spot, should go
to sleep under them, if he do not get (evil) dreams,
he is sure to be often troubled with the nightmare.
Now here is your Master in the same way taking the
grass-dogs, presented by the ancient kings, and leading his disciples to wander or abide and sleep under
them. Owing to this, the tree (beneath which they
were practising ceremonies) in Sung was cut down[2];
he was obliged to leave Wei[3]; he was reduced to
extremities in Shang[3] and Kâu[4]:—were not those
experiences like having (evil) dreams ? He was kept
in a state of siege between Khăn and 3hâi[5], so that
for seven days he had no cooked food to eat, and
was in a situation between life and death :—were
not those experiences like the nightmare ?

---

[1] See the Tâo Teh King, ch. 5.   [2] Analects III, xxii.
[3] In consequence of the dissoluteness of the court; Analects
VI, xxvi; IX, 17.
[4] Meaning Sung and Wei.   [5] Analects XI, ii, 1.

' If you are travelling by water, your best plan is
to use a boat; if by land, a carriage. Take a boat,
which will go (easily) along on the water, and try
to push it along on the land, and all your lifetime it
will not go so much as a fathom or two :—are not
ancient time and the present time like the water
and the dry land? and are not *K*âu and Lû like the
boat and the carriage? To seek now to practise
(the old ways of) *K*âu in Lû is like pushing along a
boat on the dry land. It is only a toilsome labour,
and has no success ; he who does so is sure to meet
with calamity. He has not learned that in handing
down the arts (of one time) he is sure to be reduced
to extremity in endeavouring to adapt them to the
conditions (of another).

'And have you not seen the working of a shadoof?
When (the rope of) it is pulled, it bends down; and
when it is let go, it rises up. It is pulled by a man,
and does not pull the man ; and so, whether it bends
down or rises up, it commits no offence against the
man. In the same way the rules of propriety,
righteousness, laws, and measures of the three
Hwangs [1] and five Tîs [1] derived their excellence,
not from their being the same as those of the present day, but from their (aptitude for) government.
We may compare them to haws [2], pears, oranges,

---

[1] It is impossible to speak definitely of who these three Hwangs
(Augustuses) and five Tîs were, or whom the speaker intended
by them. The former would seem to lead us to the purely
fàbulous ages, when twelve (or thirteen) Heavenly Hwangs, eleven
Earthly, and nine Human ruled over the young world, for a period
of 576,000 years. There is a general agreement of opinion that
the five Tîs ended with Yâo and Shun.

[2] See Williams's Dictionary, sub voc. He says it is the Cra-

and pummeloes, which are different in flavour, but all suitable to be eaten. Just so it is that the rules of propriety, righteousness, laws, and measures, change according to the time.

'If now you take a monkey, and dress it in the robes of the duke of *K*âu, it will bite and tear them, and will not be satisfied till it has got rid of them altogether. And if you look at the difference between antiquity and the present time it is as great as that between the monkey and the duke of *K*âu. In the same way, when Hsî Shih[1] was troubled in mind, she would knit her brows and frown on all in her neighbourhood. An ugly woman of the neighbourhood, seeing and admiring her beauty, went home, and also laying her hands on her heart proceeded to stare and frown on all around her. When the rich people of the village saw her, they shut fast their doors and would not go out; when the poor people saw her, they took their wives and children and ran away from her. The woman knew how to admire the frowning beauty, but she did not know how it was that she, though frowning, was beautiful. Alas! it is indeed all over with your Master[2]!'

5. When Confucius was in his fifty-first year[3], he had not heard of the Tâo, and went south to Phei[4]

taegus cuneata and pinnatifida, common in China, and much esteemed for its acidity.

[1] A famous beauty,—the concubine of king Fû-*kh*âi of Wû.

[2] The comparisons in this paragraph are not complimentary to Confucius. Of course the conversation never took place, and must have been made up to ridicule the views of the sage.

[3] This would be in B.C. 503 or 502, and Lâo-ʒze would be more than a hundred years old.

[4] Probably in what is now the district of Phei, department of Hsü-*k*âu, *K*iang-sû.

to see Lâo Tan, who said to him, 'You have come,
Sir; have you? I have heard that you are the
wisest man of the North; have you also got the
Tâo?' 'Not yet,' was the reply; and the other
went on, 'How have you sought it?' Confucius
said, 'I sought it in measures and numbers, and
after five years I had not got it.' 'And how
then did you seek it?' 'I sought it in the Yin
and Yang, and after twelve years I have not found
it.' Lâo-3ze said, 'Just so! If the Tâo could be
presented (to another), men would all present it to
their rulers; if it could be served up (to others),
men would all serve it up to their parents; if it
could be told (to others), men would all tell it to
their brothers; if it could be given to others, men
would all give it to their sons and grandsons. The
reason why it cannot be transmitted is no other but
this,—that if, within, there be not the presiding principle, it will not remain there, and if, outwardly, there
be not the correct obedience, it will not be carried
out. When that which is given out from the mind
(in possession of it) is not received by the mind
without, the sage will not give it out; and when,
entering in from without, there is no power in the
receiving mind to entertain it, the sage will not
permit it to lie hid there[1]. Fame is a possession
common to all; we should not seek to have much
of it. Benevolence and righteousness were as the
lodging-houses of the former kings; we should only
rest in them for a night, and not occupy them for

---

[1] That is, the sage will not deposit it, where it will lie hidden;—
compare Analects XVI, vi.

long.   If men see us doing so, they will have much
to say against us.

'The perfect men of old trod the path of benevolence as a path which they borrowed for the occasion,
and dwelt in Righteousness as in a lodging which they
used for a night.   Thus they rambled in the vacancy
of Untroubled Ease, found their food in the fields of
Indifference, and stood in the gardens which they had
not borrowed.   Untroubled Ease requires the doing of
nothing; Indifference is easily supplied with nourishment; not borrowing needs no outlay.   The ancients
called this the Enjoyment that Collects the True.

'Those who think that wealth is the proper thing
for them cannot give up their revenues ; those who
seek distinction cannot give up the thought of fame ;
those who cleave to power cannot give the handle of
it to others.   While they hold their grasp of those
things, they are afraid (of losing them).   When they
let them go, they are grieved; and they will not look
at a single example, from which they might perceive
the (folly) of their restless pursuits :—such men are
under the doom of Heaven [1].

'Hatred and kindness; taking and giving; reproof
and instruction ; death and life :—these eight things
are instruments of rectification, but only those are
able to use them who do not obstinately refuse to
comply with their great changes.   Hence it is said,
"Correction is Rectification."   When the minds of

[1] See the same expression used in Book VI, par. 11, used
by Confucius of himself.   Comparing the two passages together,
I must doubt the correctness of my note there (2, p. 252), that
'Heaven' is used in the Confucian sense of Tî, or God.   The
men here pursued and toiled after the pleasures of the world, rather
than the quiet satisfactions of the Tâo.

some do not acknowledge this, it is because the gate of Heaven[1] (in them) has not been opened.'

6. At an interview with Lâo Tan, Confucius spoke to him of benevolence and righteousness. Lâo Tan said, 'If you winnow chaff, and the dust gets into your eyes, then the places of heaven and earth and of the four cardinal points are all changed to you. If musquitoes or gadflies puncture your skin, it will keep you all the night[2] from sleeping. But this painful iteration of benevolence and righteousness excites my mind and produces in it the greatest confusion. If you, Sir, would cause men not to lose their natural simplicity, and if you would also imitate the wind in its (unconstrained) movements, and stand forth in all the natural attributes belonging to you! —why must you use so much energy, and carry a great drum to seek for the son whom you have lost[3]? The snow-goose does not bathe every day to make itself white, nor the crow blacken itself every day to make itself black. The natural simplicity of their black and white does not afford any ground for controversy; and the fame and praise which men like to contemplate do not make them greater than they naturally are. When the springs (supplying the pools) are dried up, the fishes huddle together on the dry land. Than that they should moisten one another there by their gasping, and keep one another wet by their milt, it would be better for them to forget one another in the rivers and lakes[4].'

---

[1] See Book XXIII, par. 9.   The phrase = 靈 府.

[2] The common reading 昔 is a mistake for 夕.

[3] Compare the same illustration in the preceding Book, par. 7.

[4] This illustration is from Book VI, par. 5.

From this interview with Lâo Tan, Confucius returned home, and for three days did not speak. His disciples (then) asked him, saying, ' Master, you have seen Lâo Tan; in what way might you admonish and correct him?' Confucius said, ' In him (I may say) that I have now seen the dragon. The dragon coils itself up, and there is its body; it unfolds itself and becomes the dragon complete. It rides on the cloudy air, and is nourished by the Yin and Yang. I kept my mouth open, and was unable to shut it;—how could I admonish and correct Lâo Tan?'

7. Ȝze-kung[1] said, ' So then, can (this) man indeed sit still as a representative of the dead, and then appear as the dragon? Can his voice resound as thunder, when he is profoundly still? Can he exhibit himself in his movements like heaven and earth? May I, Ȝhze, also get to see him?' Accordingly with a message from Confucius he went to see Lâo Tan.

Lâo Tan was then about to answer (his salutation) haughtily in the hall, but he said in a low voice, ' My years have rolled on and are passing away, what do you, Sir, wish to admonish me about?' Ȝze-kung replied, 'The Three Kings and Five Tîs[2] ruled

---

[1] Ȝze-kung would seem to have undertaken this expedition to maintain the reputation of the Master and his school;—only to be defeated by Lâo-ȝze more signally than Confucius had been.

[2] These are different probably, though the text is not quite certain, from the three Hwangs and five Tîs of par. 3. The Hwangs (or August Sovereigns) preceded the Tîs; the Kings (Wangs) came after them. The Three Kings are the three lines of kings commencing with the dynasty of Hsiâ, and following Shun. From the names mentioned by Ȝze-kung, we ought certainly so to understand the designation here.

the world not in the ṣame way, but the fame that has
accrued to them is the same.   How is it that you
alone consider that they were not sages?'   'Come
forward a little, my son.   Why do you say that (their
government) was not the same?'   'Yâo,' was the
reply, 'gave the kingdom to Shun, and Shun gave
it to Yü.   Yü had recourse to his strength, and
Thang to the force of arms.   King Wăn was
obedient to Kâu (-hsin), and did not dare to rebel;
king Wû rebelled against Kâu, and would not
submit to him.   And I say that their methods were
not the same.'   Lâo Tan said, 'Come a little more
forward, my son, and I will tell you how the Three
Hwangs and the Five Tîs [1] ruled the world.   Hwang-
Tî ruled it, so as to make the minds of the people
all conformed to the One (simplicity).   If the parents
of one of them died, and he did not wail, no one
blamed him.   Yâo ruled it so as to cause the hearts
of the people to cherish relative affection.   If any,
however, made the observances on the death of
other members of their kindred less than those for
their parents, no one blamed them [2].   Shun ruled it,
so as to produce a feeling of rivalry in the minds
of the people.   Their wives gave birth to their
children in the tenth month of their pregnancy, but
those children could speak at five months; and
before they were three years old, they began to call
people by their surnames and names.   Then it was
that men began to die prematurely.   Yü ruled it,
so as to cause the minds of the people to become
changed.   Men's minds became scheming, and they

---

[1] See note 2, preceding page.
[2] Referring to some abuses, contrary to the doctrine of relationship.

used their weapons as if they might legitimately do
so, (saying that they were) killing thieves and not
killing other men. The people formed themselves
into different combinations;—so it was throughout
the kingdom. Everywhere there was great con-
sternation, and then arose the Literati and (the
followers of) Mo (Tî). From them came first the
doctrine of the relationships (of society); and what
can be said of the now prevailing customs (in the
marrying of) wives and daughters? I tell you
that the rule of the Three Kings and Five Tîs may
be called by that name, but nothing can be greater
than the disorder which it produced. The wisdom
of the Three Kings was opposed to the brightness
of the sun and moon above, contrary to the exquisite
purity of the hills and streams below, and subversive
of the beneficent gifts of the four seasons between.
Their wisdom has been more fatal than the sting of
a scorpion or the bite of a dangerous beast [1]. Unable
to rest in the true attributes of their nature and constitution, they still regarded themselves as sages :—
was it not a thing to be ashamed of? But they were
shameless.' Ʒze-kung stood quite disconcerted and
ill at ease.

8. Confucius said to Lâo Tan, 'I have occupied
myself with the Shih, the Shû, the Lî, the Yo, the
Yî, and the *Kh*un *Kh*iû, those six Books, for what I
myself consider a long time [2], and am thoroughly

---

[1] What beast is meant here cannot be ascertained from the
characters in the text,—鮮 規 之 獸.

[2] But with the preparation of the *Kh*un *Kh*iû Confucius's life
ended ;—it is very plain that no conversation such as *K*wang-ʒze has
fabricated here could ever have taken place.

acquainted with their contents. With seventy-two rulers, all offenders against the right, I have discoursed about the ways of the former kings, and set forth the examples of (the dukes of) *K*âu and Shâo ; and not one of them has adopted (my views) and put them in practice :—how very difficult it is to prevail on such men, and to make clear the path to be pursued ! '

Lâo-ȝze replied, ' It is fortunate that you have not met with a ruler fitted to rule the age. Those six writings are a description of the vestiges left by the former kings, but do not tell how they made such vestiges ; and what you, Sir, speak about are still only the vestiges. But vestiges are the prints left by the shoes ;—are they the shoes that produced them ? A pair of white herons look at each other with pupils that do not move, and impregnation takes place ; the male insect emits its buzzing sound in the air above, and the female responds from the air below, and impregnation takes place ; the creatures called lêi are both male and female, and each individual breeds of itself [1]. The nature cannot be altered ; the conferred constitution cannot be changed ; the march of the seasons cannot be arrested ; the Tâo cannot be stopped. If you get the Tâo, there is no effect that cannot be produced ; if you miss it, there is no effect that can.'

Confucius (after this) did not go out, till at the end of three months he went again to see Lâo Tan, and said, ' I have got it. Ravens produce their young by hatching ; fishes by the communication of their milt ; the small-waisted wasp by transforma-

---

[1] Where had Lâo-ȝze or his author learned his zoology ?

tion [1]; when a younger brother comes, the elder weeps [2]. Long is it that I have not played my part in harmony with these processes of transformation. But as I did not play my part in harmony with such transformation, how could I transform men?' Lâo-ƺze said, 'You will do. *Kh*iû, you have found the Tâo.'

---

[1] See the Shih King, II, v, Ode II, 3, about the sphex.
[2] Because, as we say, 'his nose is put out.' But the sentiment, though it is ascribed to Confucius, is rarely according to the fact of the case.

BOOK XV.

PART II. SECTION VIII.

Kho Î, or ' Ingrained Ideas [1].'

1. Ingrained ideas and a high estimate of their own conduct; leaving the world, and pursuing uncommon ways; talking loftily and in resentful disparagement of others ;—all this is simply symptomatic of arrogance. This is what scholars who betake themselves to the hills and valleys, who are always blaming the world, and who stand aloof like withered trees, or throw themselves into deep pools [2], are fond of.

Discoursing of benevolence, righteousness, loyalty, and good faith ; being humble and frugal, self-forgetful and courteous ;—all this is simply symptomatic of (self-)cultivation. This is what scholars who wish to tranquillise the world, teachers and instructors, men who pursue their studies at home and abroad, are fond of.

Discoursing of their great merit and making a great name for themselves ; insisting on the ceremonies between ruler and minister ; and rectifying the relations between high and low ;—all this shows their one object to be the promotion of government. This is what officers of the court, men who honour their lord and would strengthen the state and who

---

[1] See pp. 146, 147.
[2] As did Shăn-thû Tî. See in Book VI, par. 3.

would do their utmost to incorporate other states with their own, are fond of.

Resorting to marshes and lakes ; dwelling in solitary places; occupying themselves with angling and living at ease ;—all this shows their one object to be to do nothing. This is what gentlemen of the rivers and seas, men who avoid the society of the world and desire to live at leisure, are fond of.

Blowing and breathing with open mouth ; inhaling and exhaling the breath ; expelling the old breath and taking in new ; passing their time like the (dormant) bear [1], and stretching and twisting (the neck) like a bird [1];—all this simply shows the desire for longevity. This is what the scholars who manipulate their breath, and the men who nourish the body and wish to live as long as Păng 3û, are fond of.

As to those who have a lofty character without any ingrained ideas ; who pursue the path of self-cultivation without benevolence and righteousness; who succeed in government without great services or fame ; who enjoy their ease without resorting to the rivers and seas ; who attain to longevity without the management (of the breath) ; who forget all things and yet possess all things; whose placidity is unlimited, while all things to be valued attend them :— such men pursue the way of heaven and earth, and display the characteristics of the sages. Hence it is said [2], ' Placidity, indifference, silence, quietude,

---

[1] This is probably the meaning. The text is simply :—' Bear-passing, bird-stretching.'

[2] 'It is said :'—where? and by whom? These questions we cannot answer. We have met indeed already with the same characteristics of the Tâo; but *K*wang-3ze is not likely to be quoting

absolute vacancy, and non-action:—these are the
qualities which maintain the level of heaven and
earth and are the substance of the Tâo and its
characteristics.'

2. In accordance with this it is said, ' The sage is
entirely restful, and so (his mind) is evenly balanced
and at ease. This even balance and ease appears
in his placidity and indifference. In this state of
even balance and ease, of placidity and indifference,
anxieties and evils do not find access to him, no
depraving influence can take him by surprise;
his virtue is complete, and his spirit continues
unimpaired.'

Therefore it is (also) said, ' The life of the sage is
(like) the action of Heaven; and his death is the
transformation common to (all) things. In his stillness his virtue is the same as that of the Y in, and
in movement his diffusiveness is like that of the
Yang. He does not take the initiative in producing either happiness or calamity. He responds to
the influence acting on him, and moves as he feels
the pressure. He rises to act only when he is obliged
to do so. He discards wisdom and the memories
of the past; he follows the lines of his Heaven
(-given nature); and therefore he suffers no calamity
from Heaven, no involvement from things, no
blame from men, and no reproof from the spirits of
the dead [1]. His life seems to float along; his death
seems to be a resting. He does not indulge any

---

himself. On the ' It is said,' and the five recurrences of the phrase
below, Lû Shû-*k*ih says that *K*wang-ȝze is quoting from sentences
current among the adherents of Tâoism,—the sentence-makers
often drawn on by Lâo-ȝze; compare the Tâo Teh *K*ing, ch. xli.

[1] See Book XIII, par. 2.

anxious doubts; he does not lay plans beforehand. His light is without display; his good faith is without previous arrangement. His sleep is untroubled by dreams; his waking is followed by no sorrows. His spirit is guileless and pure; his soul is not subject to weariness. Vacant and without self-assertion, placid and indifferent, he agrees with the virtue of Heaven.'

Therefore it is said (further), 'Sadness and pleasure show a depraving element in the virtue (of those who feel them); joy and anger show some error in their course; love and hatred show a failure of their virtue. Hence for the mind to be free from sorrow and pleasure is the perfection of virtue; to be of one mind that does not change is the perfection of quietude; to be conscious of no opposition is the perfection of vacancy; to have no intercourse with (external) things is the perfection of indifference; and to have no rebellious dissatisfactions is the perfection of purity.'

3. Therefore it is said (still further), 'If the body be toiled, and does not rest, it becomes worn out; if the spirit be used without cessation, it becomes toiled; and when toiled, it becomes exhausted. It is the nature of water, when free from admixture, to be clear, and, when not agitated, to be level; while if obstructed and not allowed to flow, it cannot preserve its clearness;—being an image of the virtue of Heaven.' Hence it is said (once again), 'To be guileless and pure, and free from all admixture; to be still and uniform, without undergoing any change; to be indifferent and do nothing; to move and yet to act like Heaven:—this is the way to nourish the spirit. Now he who possesses a

sword made at Kan-yüeh [1] preserves it carefully in a box, and does not dare to use it ;—it is considered the perfection of valuable swords. But the human spirit [2] goes forth in all directions, flowing on without limit, reaching to heaven above, and wreathing round the earth beneath. It transforms and nourishes all things, and cannot be represented by any form. Its name is " the Divinity (in man) [3]." It is only the path of pure simplicity which guards and preserves the Spirit. When this path is preserved and not lost, it becomes one with the Spirit ; and in this ethereal amalgamation, it acts in harmony with the orderly operation of Heaven.'

There is the vulgar saying, ' The multitude of men consider gain to be the most important thing ; pure scholars, fame ; those who are wise and able value their ambition ; the sage prizes essential purity.' Therefore simplicity is the denomination of that in which there is no admixture ; purity of that in which the spirit is not impaired. It is he who can embody simplicity and purity whom we call the True Man [4].

---

[1] Both of the seaboard states of Wû and Yüeh were famous for the swords produced in them. Kan-yüeh appears to have been the name of a valley or place in Wû, famous for the weapons made in it; unless indeed we should read 于 越, instead of 干 越, and take 于 越 as equivalent to 於 越, which is found in the 3o Khwan as the name of Yüeh.

[2] Might be translated ' the subtle spirit.'

[3] A very remarkable use of Tî (帝) for the human spirit in the sense of God. The subject of the clause, let the reader observe, is that spirit, and not the Tâo. See pp. 146, 147, where I have said something about it.

[4] See the full account of ' the True Man ' in Book VI.

BOOK XVI.

Part II. Section IX.

Shan Hsing, or 'Correcting the Nature[1].'

1. Those who would correct their nature by means of the vulgar learning[2], seeking to restore it to its original condition, and those who would regulate[3] their desires, by the vulgar ways of thinking, seeking thereby to carry their intelligence to perfection, must be pronounced to be deluded and ignorant people. The ancients who regulated the Tâo nourished their faculty of knowledge by their placidity, and all through life abstained from employing that faculty in action;—they must be pronounced to have (thus also) nourished their placidity by their knowledge[4].

When the faculty of knowledge and the placidity

---

[1] See pp. 147, 148.

[2] 'Vulgar' must mean 'common,' and 'the vulgar learning' is the teaching popular in the time of our author, and which he regarded as contrary to the principles of Tâoism, of which he was an adherent. The Chinese critics say that 'vulgar' here is used as the opposite of 'true.'

[3] 滑 is generally explained by 亂, 'to confuse,' but I cannot construe the sentence with that meaning of the term. In the Khang-hsî dictionary which I have followed, the character is defined by 治 with special reference to this passage.

[4] This sentence is the clue to the author's aim in the whole Book. The 'knowledge' is defined by 覺 生, 'the faculty of perception and apprehension.'

(thus) blend together, and they nourish each other, then from the nature there come forth harmony and orderly method. The attributes (of the Tâo) constitute the harmony; the Tâo (itself) secures the orderly method. When the attributes appear in a universal practice of forbearance, we have Benevolence; when the path is all marked by orderly method, we have Righteousness; when the righteousness is clearly manifested, and (all) things are regarded with affection, we have Leal-heartedness; when the (heart's) core is thus (pure) and real, and carried back to its (proper) qualities, we have Music; when this sincerity appears in all the range of the capacity, and its demonstrations are in accordance with what is elegant, we have Ceremony. If Ceremonies and Music are carried out in an imperfect and one-sided manner, the world is thrown into confusion. When men would rectify others, and their own virtue is beclouded, it is not sufficient to extend itself to them. If an attempt be made so to extend it, they also will lose their (proper) nature.

2. The men of old, while the chaotic condition was yet undeveloped [1], shared the placid tranquillity which belonged to the whole world. At that time the Yin and Yang were harmonious and still; their resting and movement proceeded without any disturbance; the four seasons had their definite times; not a single thing received any injury, and no living being came to a premature end. Men might be

---

[1] These 'men of old' were what we may call 'primeval men;'— men in the lowest stage of development; but which our author considered to be the highest or paradisiacal condition of their nature.

possessed of (the faculty of) knowledge, but they had no occasion for its use. This was what is called the state of Perfect Unity. At this time, there was no action on the part of any one, but a constant manifestation of spontaneity.

This condition (of excellence) deteriorated and decayed, till Sui-ẓăn and Fû-hsî arose and commenced their administration of the world[1]; on which came a compliance (with their methods), but the state of unity was lost. The condition going on to deteriorate and decay, Shăn Năng and Hwang-Tî arose, and took the administration of the world, on which (the people) rested (in their methods), but did not themselves comply with them. Still the deterioration and deçay continued till the lords of Thang and Yü[2] began to administer the world. These introduced the method of governing by transformation, resorting to the stream (instead of to the spring)[3], thus vitiating the purity and destroying the simplicity (of the nature). They left the Tâo, and substituted the Good for it, and pursued the course of Haphazard Virtue. After this they forsook their nature and followed (the promptings of) their minds. One mind and another associated their knowledge, but were unable to give rest to the world. Then they added to this knowledge (ex-

---

[1] Kwang-ẓze gives no hint of how long he considered this highest condition to have lasted. Sui-ẓăn, 'the man of the Burning Speculum,' 'the Fire-producer,' whom Williams calls 'the Prometheus of China,' appears before Fû-hsî, as the first in the line of the Rulers of the world, who broke up the Primal Unity.

[2] These were Yâo and Shun, named from the principalities over which their fathers ruled.

[3] 'The streams' were the methods of culture that arose after the simple virtues and spontaneity of the Tâo were lost.

ternal and) elegant forms, and went on to make these more and more numerous. The forms extinguished the (primal) simplicity, till the mind was drowned by their multiplicity. After this the people began to be perplexed and disordered, and had no way by which they might return to their true nature, and bring back their original condition.

3. Looking at the subject from this point of view, we see how the world lost[1] the (proper) course, and how the course (which it took) only led it further astray[1]. The world and the Way, when they came together, being (thus) lost to each other, how could the men of the Way make themselves conspicuous in the world? and how could the world rise to an appreciation of the Way? Since the Way had no means to make itself conspicuous in the world, and the world had no means of rising to an appreciation of the Way, though sagely men might not keep among the hills and forests, their virtue was hidden ;—hidden, but not because they themselves sought to hide it.

Those whom the ancients called 'Retired Scholars' did not conceal their persons, and not allow themselves to be seen ; they did not shut up their words, and refuse to give utterance to them ; they did not hide away their knowledge, and refuse to bring it forth. The conditions laid on them by the times were very much awry. If the conditions of the times had allowed them to act in the world on a great scale, they would have brought back the state of unity without any trace being perceived (of how

---

[1] It is the same character in the text which I have been obliged to translate thus differently,— 喪.

they did so). When those conditions shut them up entirely from such action, they struck their roots deeper (in themselves), were perfectly still and waited. It was thus that they preserved (the Way in) their own persons.

4. The ancients who preserved (the Way in) their own persons did not try by sophistical reasonings to gloss over their knowledge; they did not seek to embrace (everything in) the world in their knowledge, nor to comprehend all the virtues in it. Solitary and trembling they remained where they were, and sought the restoration of their nature. What had they to do with any further action? The Way indeed is not to be pursued, nor (all) its characteristics to be known on a small scale. A little knowledge is injurious to those characteristics; small doings are injurious to the Way;—hence it is said, 'They simply rectified themselves.' Complete enjoyment is what is meant by 'the Attainment of the Aim.'

What was anciently called 'the Attainment of the Aim' did not mean the getting of carriages and coronets [1]; it simply meant that nothing more was needed for their enjoyment. Now-a-days what is called 'the Attainment of the Aim' means the getting of carriages and coronets. But carriages and coronets belong to the body; they do not affect the nature as it is constituted. When such things happen to come, it is but for a time; being but for a time, their coming cannot be obstructed and their going cannot be stopped [2]. Therefore we should not

---

[1] That is, worldly distinction.

[2] Because they depend on others. Compare Mencius VI, i, ch. 17, 2.

because of carriages and coronets indulge our aims, nor because of distress and straitness resort to the vulgar (learning and thinking); the one of these conditions and the other may equally conduce to our enjoyment, which is simply to be free from anxiety. If now the departure of what is transient takes away one's enjoyment, this view shows that what enjoyment it had given was worthless. Hence it is said, 'They who lose themselves in their pursuit of things, and lose their nature in their study of what is vulgar, must be pronounced people who turn things upside down.'

BOOK XVII.

Part II. Section X.

*Kh*iû Shui, or 'The Floods of Autumn [1].'

1. The time of the autumnal floods was come, and the hundred streams were all discharging themselves into the Ho. Its current was greatly swollen [2], so that across its channel from bank to bank one could not distinguish an ox from a horse. On this the (Spirit-) earl of the Ho [3] laughed with delight, thinking that all the beauty of the world was to be found in his charge. Along the course of the river he walked east till he came to the North Sea, over which he looked, with his face to the east, without being able to see where its waters began. Then he began to turn his face round, looked across the expanse, (as if he were) confronting Zo [3], and said with a sigh, 'What the vulgar saying expresses about him who has learned a hundred points (of the Tâo), and thinks that there is no one equal to himself, was surely spoken of me. And moreover, I have heard

---

[1] See pp. 148, 149.

[2] 涇 here perhaps means 'turbid.' It has nothing to do with the river *K*ing.

[3] See Mayers's Manual, p. 54. Our author adopts the common beliefs or superstitions of his time, and after his fashion puts his own reasonings into the mouths of these mythological personages. It is more difficult to collect the legends about Zo of the sea, or of the Northern Sea. See the Khang-hsî Thesaurus under 海若.

parties making little of the knowledge of *K*ung-nî and the righteousness of Po-î, and at first I did not believe them. Now I behold the all-but-boundless extent (of your realms). If I had not come to your gate, I should have been in danger (of continuing in my ignorance), and been laughed at for long in the schools of our great System[1].'

*Z*o, (the Spirit-lord) of the Northern Sea, said, 'A frog in a well cannot be talked with about the sea;—he is confined to the limits of his hole. An insect of the summer cannot be talked with about ice;—it knows nothing beyond its own season. A scholar of limited views cannot be talked with about the Tâo;—he is bound by the teaching (which he has received). Now you have come forth from between your banks, and beheld the great sea. You have come to know your own ignorance and inferiority, and are in the way of being fitted to be talked with about great principles. Of all the waters under heaven there are none so great as the sea. A myriad streams flow into it without ceasing, and yet it is not filled; and afterwards[2] it discharges them (also) without ceasing, and yet it is not emptied. In spring and in autumn it undergoes no change; it takes no notice of floods or of drought. Its superiority over such streams even as the *K*iang and the

---

[1] Thus the Confucian learning and its worthies were to the system of the Tâo only as the waters of the Ho to the great sea.

[2] I have translated here as if the reading were 尾 閭, which is given by Lin Hsî-*k*ung. The correct reading, however, so far as depends on editions and dictionaries, is 尾 閫; which is explained in the Khang-hsî dictionary as 'a great Rock in Fû-sang on the East,' against which the water of the sea collects, and is all evaporated!

Ho cannot be told by measures or numbers; and
that I have never, notwithstanding this, made much
of myself, is because I compare my own bodily form
with (the greatness of) heaven and earth, and (re-
member that) I have received my breath from the
Yin and Yang. Between heaven and earth I am
but as a small stone or a small tree on a great hill.
So long as I see myself to be thus small, how should
I make much of myself? I estimate all within the
four seas, compared with the space between heaven
and earth, to be not so large as that occupied by
a pile of stones in a large marsh! I estimate our
Middle States, compared with the space between the
four seas, to be smaller than a single little grain of
rice in a great granary! When we would set forth
the number of things (in existence), we speak of them
as myriads; and man is only one of them. Men
occupy all the nine provinces; but of all whose life
is maintained by grain-food, wherever boats and
carriages reach, men form only one portion. Thus,
compared with the myriads of things, they are not
equal to a single fine hair on the body of a horse.
Within this range are comprehended all (the territories) which the five Tîs received in succession
from one another; all which the royal founders of
the three dynasties contended for; all which excited
the anxiety of Benevolent men; and all which men
in office have toiled for. Po-î was accounted famous
for declining (to share in its government), and *K*ung-
nî was accounted great because of the lessons which
he addressed to it. They acted as they did, making
much of themselves;—therein like you who a little
time ago did so of yourself because of your (volume
of) water!'

2. The earl of the Ho said, 'Well then, may I consider heaven and earth as (the ideal of) what is great, and the point of a hair as that of what is small ?' *Z*o of the Northern Sea replied, 'No. The (different) capacities of things are illimitable; time never stops, (but is always moving on); man's lot is ever changing; the end and the beginning of things never occur (twice) in the same way. Therefore men of great wisdom, looking at things far off or near at hand, do not think them insignificant for being small, nor much of them for being great:—knowing how capacities differ illimitably. They appeal with intelligence to things of ancient and recent occurrence, without being troubled by the remoteness of the former, or standing on tiptoe to lay hold of the latter :—knowing that time never stops in its course. They examine with discrimination (cases of) fulness and of want, not overjoyed by success, nor disheartened by failure :—knowing the inconstancy of man's lot. They know the plain and quiet path (in which things proceed), therefore they are not overjoyed to live, nor count it a calamity to die:—the end and the beginning of things never occurring (twice) in the same way.

'We must reckon that what men know is not so much as what they do not know, and that the time since they were born is not so long as that which elapsed before they were born. When they take that which is most small and try to fill with it the dimensions of what is most great, this leads to error and confusion, and they cannot attain their end. Looking at the subject in this way, how can you know that the point of a hair is sufficient to determine the minuteness of what is most small, or that heaven and earth are sufficient to complete the dimensions of what is most large?'

3. The earl of the Ho said, 'The disputers of the world all say, "That which is most minute has no bodily form; and that which is most great cannot be encompassed;"—is this really the truth?' Zo of the Northern Sea replied, 'When from the standpoint of what is small we look at what is great, we do not take it all in; when from the standpoint of what is great we look at what is small, we do not see it clearly. Now the subtile essence is smallness in its extreme degree; and the vast mass is greatness in its largest form. Different as they are, each has its suitability,—according to their several conditions. But the subtile and the gross both presuppose that they have a bodily form. Where there is no bodily form, there is no longer a possibility of numerical division; where it is not possible to encompass a mass, there is no longer a possibility of numerical estimate. What can be discoursed about in words is the grossness of things; what can be reached in idea is the subtilty of things. What cannot be discoursed about in words, and what cannot be reached by nice discrimination of thought, has nothing to do either with subtilty or grossness.

'Therefore while the actions of the Great Man are not directed to injure men, he does not plume himself on his benevolence and kindness; while his movements are not made with a view to gain, he does not consider the menials of a family as mean; while he does not strive after property and wealth, he does not plume himself on declining them; while he does not borrow the help of others to accomplish his affairs, he does not plume himself on supporting

himself by his own strength, nor does he despise
those who in their greed do what is mean; while
he differs in his conduct from the vulgar, he does
not plume himself on being so different from them;
while it is his desire to follow the multitude, he does
not despise the glib-tongued flatterers. The rank
and emoluments of the world furnish no stimulus to
him, nor does he reckon its punishments and shame
to be a disgrace. He knows that the right and the
wrong can (often) not be distinguished, and that
what is small and what is great can (often) not be
defined. I have heard it said, " The Man of Tâo
does not become distinguished; the greatest virtue
is unsuccessful; the Great Man has no thought
of self;"—to so great a degree may the lot be
restricted.'

4. The earl of the Ho said, 'Whether the subject
be what is external in things, or what is internal,
how do we come to make a distinction between them
as noble and mean, and as great or small?' *Zo* of
the Northern Sea replied, 'When we look at them
in the light of the Tâo, they are neither noble
nor mean. Looking at them in themselves, each
thinks itself noble, and despises others. Looking
at them in the light of common opinion, their being
noble or mean does not depend on themselves.
Looking at them in their differences from one
another, if we call those great which are greater
than others, there is nothing that is not great, and
in the same way there is nothing that is not small.
We shall (thus) know that heaven and earth is but
(as) a grain of the smallest rice, and that the point
of a hair is (as) a mound or a mountain;—such is
the view given of them by their relative size. Look-

ing at them from the services they render, allowing
to everything the service which it does, there is not
one which is not serviceable; and, extending the
consideration to what it does not do, there is not
one which is not unserviceable. We know (for instance) that East and West are opposed to each
other, and yet that the one cannot be without
(suggesting the idea of) the other;—(thus) their
share of mutual service is determined. Looking at
them with respect to their tendencies, if we approve
of what they approve, then there is no one who may
not be approved of; and, if we condemn what they
condemn, there is no one who may not be condemned. There are the cases of Yâo and *K*ieh,
each of whom approved of his own course, and
condemned the other;—such is the view arising
from the consideration of tendency and aim.

'Formerly Yâo and Shun resigned (their thrones),
and yet each continued to be Tî; *K*ih-khwâi[1] resigned (his marquisate) which led to his ruin. Thang
and Wû contended (for the sovereignty), and each
became king; the duke of Pâi[2] contended (for
*Kh*û), which led to his extinction. Looking at
the subject from these examples of striving by force and
of resigning, and from the conduct of Yâo (on the
one hand) and of *K*ieh (on the other), we see that
there is a time for noble acting, and a time for

---

[1] See Mencius II, ii, ch. 8, and I, ii, chaps. 10, 11, with the
notes. 之 is probably a mistake for 予.

[2] See the last narrative but one in the *Zo Kh*wan, under the
sixteenth year of duke Âi of Lû,—the year in which Confucius died.
'The duke of Pâi' was merely the chief of a district of *Kh*û; but
rebelling against the Ruler of the State, he was defeated, and
strangled himself.

mean;—these characteristics are subject to no regular rule.

5. 'A battering ram may be used against the wall of a city, but it cannot be employed to stop up a hole;—the uses of implements are different. The (horses) *K*ih-*k*î and Hwâ-liû[1] could in one day gallop 1000 lî, but for catching rats they were not equal to a wild dog or a weasel;—the gifts of creatures are different. The white horned owl collects its fleas in the night-time, and can discern the point of a hair, but in bright day it stares with its eyes and cannot see a mound or a hill;—the natures of creatures are different.

'Hence the sayings, "Shall we not follow and honour the right, and have nothing to do with the wrong? shall we not follow and honour those who secure good government, and have nothing to do with those who produce disorder?" show a want of acquaintance with the principles of Heaven and Earth, and with the different qualities of things. It is like following and honouring Heaven and taking no account of Earth; it is like following and honouring the Yin and taking no account of the Yang. It is clear that such a course cannot be pursued. Yet notwithstanding they go on talking so:—if they are not stupid, they are visionaries. The Tî sovereigns resigned their thrones to others in one way, and the rulers of the three dynasties transmitted their thrones to their successors in another. He who acts differently from the requirements of his time and contrary to its custom is called an usurper; he who complies with the time

---

[1] Two of king Mu's team of eight famous steeds.

and follows the common practice is said to be righteous. Hold your peace, O earl of the Ho. How
should you know what constitutes being noble and
being mean, or who are the small and who the great?'

6. The earl of the Ho said, 'Very well. But
what am I to do? and what am I not to do? How
am I to be guided after all in regard to what I
accept or reject, and what I pursue or put away
from me?' Zo of the Northern Sea replied, 'From
the standpoint of the Tâo, what is noble? and what
is mean? These expressions are but the different
extremes of the average level. Do not keep per-
tinaciously to your own ideas, which put you in
such opposition to the Tâo. What are few? and
what are many? These are denominations which
we employ in thanking (donors) and dispensing
gifts. Do not study to be uniform in doing so;—
it only shows how different you are from the Tâo.
Be severe and strict, like the ruler of a state who
does not selfishly bestow his favours. Be scrupu-
lous, yet gentle, like the tutelary spirit of the land,
when sacrifice is offered to him who does not
bestow his blessing selfishly. Be large-minded
like space, whose four terminating points are illimitable, and form no particular enclosures. Hold all
things in your love, favouring and supporting none
specially. This is called being without any local
or partial regard; all things are equally regarded;
there is no long or short among them.

'There is no end or beginning to the Tâo. Things
indeed die and are born, not reaching a perfect state
which can be relied on. Now there is emptiness,
and now fulness;—they do not continue in one
form. The years cannot be reproduced; time

cannot be arrested. Decay and growth, fulness
and emptiness, when they end, begin again. It is
thus that we describe the method of great righteousness, and discourse about the principle pervading
all things. The life of things is like the hurrying
and galloping along of a horse. With every movement there is a change; with every moment there
is an alteration. What should you be doing? what
should you not be doing? You have only to be
allowing this course of natural transformation to
be going on.'

7. The earl of the Ho said, 'What then is there
so valuable in the Tâo?' Zo of the Northern Sea
replied, 'He who knows the Tâo is sure to be well
acquainted with the principles (that appear in the
procedures of things). Acquainted with (those)
principles, he is sure to understand how to regulate
his conduct in all varying circumstances. Having
that understanding, he will not allow things to
injure himself. Fire cannot burn him who is (so)
perfect in virtue, nor water drown him; neither cold
nor heat can affect him injuriously; neither bird nor
beast can hurt him. This does not mean that he is
indifferent to these things; it means that he dis-
criminates between where he may safely rest and
where he will be in peril; that he is tranquil equally
in calamity and happiness; that he is careful what
he avoids and what he approaches;—so that nothing
can injure him. Hence it is said, "What is heavenly
is internal; what is human is external." The virtue
(of man) is in what is Heavenly. If you know the
operation of what is Heavenly and what is Human,
you will have your root in what is Heavenly and
your position in Virtue. You will bend or stretch

(only) after the (necessary) hesitation; you will have returned to the essential, and may be pronounced to have reached perfection.'

'What do you mean,' pursued the earl, 'by the Heavenly, and by the Human?' *Zo* replied, 'Oxen and horses have four feet;—that is what I call their Heavenly (constitution). When horses' heads are haltered, and the noses of oxen are pierced, that is what I call (the doing of) Man. Hence it is said, "Do not by the Human (doing) extinguish the Heavenly (constitution); do not for your (Human) purpose extinguish the appointment (of Heaven); do not bury your (proper) fame in (such) a pursuit of it; carefully guard (the Way) and do not lose it:—this is what I call reverting to your True (Nature)."'

8. The khwei[1] desires to be like[2] the millipede[1]; the millipede to be like the serpent; the serpent like the wind; the wind to be like the eye; and the eye to be like the mind[3].

The khwei said to the millipede, 'With my one leg I hop about, and can hardly manage to go along. Now you have a myriad feet which you can employ; how is it that you are so abundantly furnished?' The millipede said, 'It is not so. Have you not seen one ejecting saliva? The largest portion of it is like a pearl, while the smaller portions fall down like a shower of mist in innumer-

---

[1] The khwei is 'a sort of dragon (it may be, a worm) with one foot.' The hsien has many feet; one account calls it 'a centipede.'

[2] Such is the meaning of the lin or lien. The best commentators explain it by hsien (羨), 'to covet and desire.'

[3] Compare Book I, par. 3, towards the end.

able drops.   Now I put in motion the springs set in me by Heaven, without knowing how I do so.'

The millipede said to the serpent, 'I go along by means of my multitude of feet; and yet how is it that I do not go so fast as you who have no feet at all?' The serpent replied, 'How can the method of moving by the springs set in us by Heaven be changed?   How could I make use of feet?'

The serpent said to the wind, 'I get along by moving my backbone and ribs, thus appearing to have some (bodily) means of progression.   But now you, Sir, rise with a blustering force in the North Sea, and go on in the same way to the South Sea; —seemingly without any such means.   How does it take place?'   The wind said, 'Yes.   With such a blustering force I rise in the North Sea and go on to the South Sea.   But you can point to me, and therein are superior to me, as you are also in treading on me.   Yet notwithstanding, it is only I who can break great trees, and blow down great houses.   Therefore he whom all that are small cannot overcome is a great overcomer.   But it is only he who is the sagely man [1] that is the Great Conqueror (of all).'

9. When Confucius was travelling in Khwang [2],

---

[1] The sagely man is 'the True man,' who embodies the Tâo. The Tâo has given to the khwei, the millipede, the serpent, and it may be said also to the wind, their means of progression and action. Nothing is said of the eye and the mind;—it was not necessary to dwell on the Tâo in them.

[2] See Confucian Analects, IX, v and XI, xxii.   Our author's account of this event is his own, constructed by him to convey his own Tâoistic lessons.

some people of Sung (once) surrounded him (with a hostile intention) several ranks deep; but he kept singing to his lute without stopping. 3ze-lû came in, and saw him, and said, 'How is it, Master, that you are so pleased?' Confucius said, 'Come here, and I will tell you. I have tried to avoid being reduced to such a strait for a long time; and that I have not escaped shows that it was so appointed for me. I have sought to find a ruler that would employ me for a long time, and that I have not found one, shows the character of the time. Under Yâo and Shun there was no one in the kingdom reduced to straits like mine; and it was not by their sagacity that men succeeded as they did. Under *K*ieh and *K*âu no (good and able man) in the kingdom found his way to employment; and it was not for (want of) sagacity that they failed to do so. It was simply owing to the times and their character.

'People that do business on the water do not shrink from meeting iguanodons and dragons;—that is the courage of fishermen. Those who do business on land do not shrink from meeting rhinoceroses and tigers;—that is the courage of hunters. When men see the sharp weapons crossed before them, and look on death as going home;—that is the courage of the determined soldier. When he knows that his strait is determined for him, and that the employment of him by a ruler depends on the character of the time, and then meeting with great distress is yet not afraid;—that is the courage of the sagely man. Wait, my good Yû, and you will see what there is determined for me in my lot.' A little afterwards, the leader of the armed men approached and took his leave, saying, 'We thought you were

Yang Hû[1], and therefore surrounded you.   Now
we see our mistake.'   (With this) he begged to take
his leave, and withdrew.

10. Kung-sun Lung[2] asked Mâu of Wei[3], saying,
' When I was young, I learned the teachings of the
former kings; and when I was grown up, I became
proficient in the practice of benevolence and righteousness.   I brought together the views that agreed
and disagreed; I considered the questions about
hardness and whiteness[4]; I set forth what was to be
affirmed and what was not, and what was allowable
and what was not; I studied painfully the various
schools of thought, and made myself master of the
reasonings of all their masters.   I thought that I
had reached a good understanding of every subject;
but now that I have heard the words of *K*wang-3ze,
they throw me into a flutter of surprise.   I do not
know whether it be that I do not come up to him in
the power of discussion, or that my knowledge is not
equal to his.   But now I do not feel able to open my
mouth, and venture to ask you what course I should
pursue.'   Kung-3ze Mâu leant forward on his stool,
drew a long breath, looked up to heaven, smiled, and

---

[1] No doubt the Yang Ho of Analects XVII, i.

[2] The grandson (Kung-sun) of one of the rulers of *K*âo (one of
the three states into which the great state of 3in had been broken
up).   He has come down to us as a philosophic sophist, whose
views it is not easy to define.   See Mayers's Manual, p. 288, and
Book XXXIII, par. 7.

[3] Wei was another of the divisions of 3in, and Mâu was one of
the sons of its ruler at this time, a great admirer, evidently, of
*K*wang-3ze, and more than a match for the sophist Lung.

[4] Holding, it is supposed, that ' the attributes of material objects,
such as hardness and colour, are separate existences : '—so Mayers,
after Wylie.

said, ' Have you not heard of the frog of the dilapidated well, and how it said to the turtle of the Eastern Sea, " How I enjoy myself? I leap upon the parapet of this well. I enter, and having by means of the projections formed by the fragments of the broken tiles of the lining proceeded to the water, I draw my legs together, keep my chin up, (and strike out). When I have got to the mud, I dive till my feet are lost in it. Then turning round, I see that of the shrimps, crabs, and tadpoles there is not one that can do like me. Moreover, when one has entire command of all the water in the gully, and hesitates to go forward, it is the greatest pleasure to enjoy one's self here in this dilapidated well [1] ;—why do not you, Master, often come and enter, and see it for yourself?" The turtle of the Eastern Sea (was then proceeding to go forward), but before he had put in his left foot, he found his right knee caught and held fast. On this he hesitated, drew back, and told (the frog) all about the sea, saying, " A distance of a thousand lî is not sufficient to express its extent, nor would (a line of) eight thousand cubits be equal to sound its depth. In the time of Yü, for nine years out of ten the flooded land (all drained into it), and its water was not sensibly increased ; and in the time of Thang for seven years out of eight there was a drought, but the rocks on the shore (saw) no diminution of the water because of it. Thus it is that no change is produced in its waters by any cause operating for a short time or a long, and that they do not advance nor recede for any addition or subtraction, whether great or small ; and this is the great pleasure afforded by the Eastern Sea." When

---

[1] A passage difficult to construe.

the frog of the dilapidated well heard this, he was amazed and terror-struck, and lost himself in surprise.

'And moreover, when you, who have not wisdom enough to know where the discussions about what is right and what is wrong should end, still desire to see through the words of *K*wang-ȝze, that is like employing a mosquito to carry a mountain on its back, or a millipede [1] to gallop as fast as the Ho runs; —tasks to which both the insects are sure to be unequal. Still further, when you, who have not wisdom enough to know the words employed in discussing very mysterious subjects, yet hasten to show your sharpness of speech on any occasion that may occur, is not this being like the frog of the dilapidated well?

'And that (*K*wang-ȝze) now plants his foot on the Yellow Springs (below the earth), and anon rises to the height of the Empyrean. Without any regard to south and north, with freedom he launches out in every direction, and is lost in the unfathomable. Without any regard to east and west, starting from what is abysmally obscure, he comes back to what is grandly intelligible. (All the while), you, Sir, in amazement, search for his views to examine them, and grope among them for matter for discussion; —this is just like peeping at the heavens through a tube, or aiming at the earth with an awl; are not both the implements too small for the purpose? Go your ways, Sir.

'And have you not heard of the young learners of

---

[1] A different character from that for a millipede in the last paragraph;—a Shang *K*ü, evidently some small insect, but we cannot tell what.

Shâu-ling [1], and how they did in Han-tan? Before they had acquired what they might have done in that capital, they had forgotten what they had learned to do in their old city, and were marched back to it on their hands and knees. If now you do not go away, you will forget your old acquirements, and fail in your profession.'

Kung-sun Lung gaped on the speaker, and could not shut his mouth, and his tongue clave to its roof. He slank away and ran off.

11. Kwang-jze was (once) fishing in the river Phû [2], when the king of Khû [3] sent two great officers to him, with the message, 'I wish to trouble you with the charge of all within my territories.' Kwang-jze kept on holding his rod without looking round, and said, 'I have heard that in Khû there is a spirit-like tortoise-shell, the wearer of which died 3000 years ago [4], and which the king keeps, in his ancestral temple, in a hamper covered with a cloth. Was it better for the tortoise to die, and leave its shell to be thus honoured? Or would it have been better for it to live, and keep on dragging its tail through the mud?' The two officers said, 'It would have been better for it to live, and draw its tail after it over the mud [5].' 'Go your ways. I will keep on drawing my tail after me through the mud.'

---

[1] A city of Kâo, as Han-tan was its capital. Of the incident referred to, I have not been able to learn anything. The 'were marched' gives my idea of what it may have been.

[2] A river, which still gives its name to Phû-kâu, department Khao-kâu, Shan-tung.

[3] Probably king Wei, B.C. 339–330.

[4] A good antiquity for Khû!

[5] ? A species of Testudo Serpentina, such as is often seen on pieces of Japanese lacquer-ware.

12. Hui-ʒze being a minister of state in Liang[1], *K*wang-ʒze went to see him.   Some one had told Hui-ʒze that *K*wang-ʒze was come with a wish to supersede him in his office, on which he was afraid, and instituted a search for the stranger all over the kingdom for three days and three nights.   (After this) *K*wang-ʒze went and saw him, and said, 'There is in the south a bird, called " the Young Phoenix[2];" —do you know it ?   Starting from the South Sea, it flies to the Northern ; never resting but on the bignonia[3], never eating but the fruit of the melia azederach[4], and never drinking but from the purest springs.   An owl, which had got a putrid rat, (once), when a phoenix went passing overhead, looked up to it and gave an angry scream.   Do you wish now, in your possession of the kingdom of Liang, to frighten me with a similar scream ?'

13. *K*wang-ʒze and Hui-ʒze were walking on the dam over the Hâo[5], when the former said, 'These thryssas come out, and play about at their ease ;—that is the enjoyment of fishes.'   The other said, 'You are not a fish ; how do you know what

---

[1] Another name for Wei, so called from its capital ;—in the present department of Khâi-fâng.

[2] So the critics explain the name.   Williams thinks the bird may be 'the argus pheasant,' or 'a variety of the peacock.'   But what the bird was does not affect the meaning of our author's reference to it.

[3] One of the Eleococceae, the Dryandra Cordifolia of Thunberg.

[4] All the editions I have seen give 練 here, which makes no sense.   The character should doubtless be 棟, with the meaning which I have given ; and not 'bamboo,' which is found in the critics.   It is also called 'the Pride of India.'

[5] A river in the department and district of Fung-yang, An-hui.

constitutes the enjoyment of fishes[1] ?' _K_wang-ɜze rejoined, 'You are not I. How do you know that I do not know what constitutes the enjoyment of fishes ?' Hui-ɜze said, ' I am not you ; and though indeed I do not fully know you, you certainly are not a fish, and (the argument) is complete against your knowing what constitutes the happiness of fishes.' _K_wang-ɜze replied, ' Let us keep to your original question. You said to me, " How do you know what constitutes the enjoyment of fishes ? " You knew that I knew it, and yet you put your question to me ;—well, I know it (from our enjoying ourselves together) over the Hâo.'

---

[1] Surely a captious question. We infer the feelings of other creatures from their demonstrations.

TRANSLITERATION OF ORIENTAL ALPHABETS ADOPTED FOR THE TRANSLATIONS OF THE SACRED BOOKS OF THE EAST.

CONSONANTS.	MISSIONARY ALPHABET.			Sanskrit.	Zend.	Pehlevi.	Persian.	Arabic.	Hebrew.	Chinese.
	I Class.	II Class.	III Class.							
Gutturales.										
1 Tenuis	k	·	·	क	9	૭	ك	ك	כ	k
2 „ aspirata	kh	·	·	ख	δ	ﺯ	·	·	ח	kh
3 Media	g	·	·	ग	૭	૧	·	·	ד	·
4 „ aspirata	gh	·	·	घ	൨	൨	·	·	ד	·
5 Gutturo-labialis	q	·	·	·	·	·	ڨ	ڨ	ק	·
6 Nasalis	ṅ (ng)	·	·	ङ	ˊ (ng)	·	·	·	·	h, hs
7 Spiritus asper	h	·	·	ह	൚(ɴ)	ᴐ	ه	ه	ה	·
8 „ lenis	'	·	·	·	ൗ(ɷho)	·	ا	ا	א	·
9 „ asper faucalis	ʻh	·	·	·	·	·	ح	ح	ח	·
10 „ lenis faucalis	ʼh	·	·	·	·	·	ع	ع	ע	·
11 „ asper fricatus	·	ʻh	·	·	·	·	·	·	·	·
12 „ lenis fricatus	·	ʼh	·	·	·	·	·	·	·	·
Gutturales modificatae (palatales, &c.)										
13 Tenuis	·	k	·	च	౿	ل	چ	چ	·	k
14 „ aspirata	·	kh	·	छ	·	ٚ	·	·	·	kh
15 Media	·	g	·	ज	స	૭	ج	ج	·	·
16 „ aspirata	·	gh	·	झ	·	·	·	·	·	·
17 „ Nasalis	·	ñ	·	ञ	·	·	·	·	·	·

CONSONANTS (continued).	MISSIONARY ALPHABET.			Sanskrit.	Zend.	Pehlevi.	Persian.	Arabic.	Hebrew.	Chinese.
	I Class.	II Class.	III Class.							
18 Semivocalis	y			य	ز, ﺵ (init.)	و	ى	ى	י	y
19 Spiritus asper		(ẏ)								
20 ,, lenis		(j̇)								
21 ,, asper assibilatus		s					ﺝ	ﺝ		z
22 ,, lenis assibilatus		z								
23 Tenuis *(Dentales.)*	t			त ट	ﻭ	ﻭ	د	د	ת ד	t
24 ,, aspirata	th		TH	त ट		ﻭ	ﻭ	ﻭ	ת ד	th
25 ,, assibilata										
26 Media	d			द ड	द ड	ﻭ	ﻭ	ﻭ	נ ן	
27 ,, aspirata	dh		DH							
28 ,, assibilata										
29 Nasalis	n			न	ﻭ	ﻭ ,ﻭ	ﻭ	ﻭ	מ ם	n
30 Semivocalis	l	l	L							1
31 ,, mollis 1		l	L							
32 ,, mollis 2										
33 Spiritus asper 1	s		s (∫)	स	ﻭ	ﻭ	ﻭ	ﻭ	שׁ ס	s
34 ,, asper 2								ﺝ (ﺝ)		
35 ,, lenis	z		z (ʒ)		ﻭ	ﻭ	ز (ز)	ز	ז	z
36 ,, asperrimus 1			ž (ʒ)				ﺝ	ﺝ	צ	
37 ,, asperrimus 2			ž (ʒ)							š, žh

Dentales modificatae (linguales, &c.)		
38 Tenuis	t	
39 „ aspirata	th	
40 Media	d	
41 „ aspirata	dh	
42 Nasalis	n	
43 Semivocalis	r	r
44 „ fricata		
45 „ diacritica		
46 Spiritus asper		sh
47 „ lenis		zh
Labiales.		
48 Tenuis	p	p
49 „ aspirata	ph	ph
50 Media		b
51 „ aspirata		bh
52 Tenuissima		
53 Nasalis	m	m
54 Semivocalis	w	w
55 „ aspirata		hw
56 Spiritus asper	f	f
57 „ lenis		v
58 Anusvâra	m	
59 Visarga	h	

VOWELS.	MISSIONARY ALPHABET. I Class	II Class	III Class	Sanskrit.	Zend.	Pehlevi.	Persian.	Arabic.	Hebrew.	Chinese.
1 Neutralis	O								⁚	ǎ
2 Laryngo-palatalis	ă				ⵕ	) fin. ꝝ init.	ꭒ	ꭒ		
3 „ labialis	ŏ				ꝟ					a
4 Gutturalis brevis	a	(a)		ꢰ	ꝯ	ꝝ	ꭒ	ꭒ		â
5 „ longa	â			ꣃ	ꝕ		ꭒ	ꭒ	ꭒ	î
6 Palatalis brevis	i	(ĕ)		ꣳ			ꭒ	ꭒ		
7 „ longa	î			ꣳ						
8 Dentalis brevis	li			ꢷ						
9 „ longa	lí			ꢸ						u
10 Lingualis brevis	rĭ			꣟						ö
11 „ longa	rí			꣡						e
12 Labialis brevis	u	(u)		ꢼ	ꝯ	ꝝ	ꭒ	ꭒ	ꭒ	ê
13 „ longa	û			ꢵ						âi
14 Gutturo-palatalis brevis	e	(e)			ꜱ(e) ꜱ(e)	ꝝ				ei, ĕi
15 „ longa	ê (ai)	(ai)		Ꝓ Ꝓ	ꝟ					
16 Diphthongus gutturo-palatalis	âi									
17 „	ei (ĕi)									o
18 „	oi (ŏu)									âu
19 Gutturo-labialis brevis	o	(o)		Ꝓ Ꝓ	ꝕ(au)	ꝝ	ꭒ	ꭒ	ꭒ	
20 „ longa	ô (au)	(au)								
21 Diphthongus gutturo-labialis	âu									
22 „	eu (ĕu)									
23 „	ou (ŏu)									
24 Gutturalis fracta	ä									ü
25 Palatalis fracta	ï									
26 Labialis fracta	ü									
27 Gutturo-labialis fracta	ö									

A CATALOGUE OF
SELECTED DOVER BOOKS
IN ALL FIELDS OF INTEREST

A CATALOGUE OF SELECTED DOVER
BOOKS IN ALL FIELDS OF INTEREST

RACKHAM'S COLOR ILLUSTRATIONS FOR WAGNER'S RING. Rackham's finest mature work—all 64 full-color watercolors in a faithful and lush interpretation of the *Ring*. Full-sized plates on coated stock of the paintings used by opera companies for authentic staging of Wagner. Captions aid in following complete Ring cycle. Introduction. 64 illustrations plus vignettes. 72pp. 8⅝ x 11¼. 23779-6 Pa. $6.00

CONTEMPORARY POLISH POSTERS IN FULL COLOR, edited by Joseph Czestochowski. 46 full-color examples of brilliant school of Polish graphic design, selected from world's first museum (near Warsaw) dedicated to poster art. Posters on circuses, films, plays, concerts all show cosmopolitan influences, free imagination. Introduction. 48pp. 9⅜ x 12¼. 23780-X Pa. $6.00

GRAPHIC WORKS OF EDVARD MUNCH, Edvard Munch. 90 haunting, evocative prints by first major Expressionist artist and one of the greatest graphic artists of his time: *The Scream, Anxiety, Death Chamber, The Kiss, Madonna,* etc. Introduction by Alfred Werner. 90pp. 9 x 12. 23765-6 Pa. $5.00

THE GOLDEN AGE OF THE POSTER, Hayward and Blanche Cirker. 70 extraordinary posters in full colors, from Maitres de l'Affiche, Mucha, Lautrec, Bradley, Cheret, Beardsley, many others. Total of 78pp. 9⅜ x 12¼. 22753-7 Pa. $6.95

THE NOTEBOOKS OF LEONARDO DA VINCI, edited by J. P. Richter. Extracts from manuscripts reveal great genius; on painting, sculpture, anatomy, sciences, geography, etc. Both Italian and English. 186 ms. pages reproduced, plus 500 additional drawings, including studies for *Last Supper,* Sforza monument, etc. 860pp. 7⅞ x 10¾. (Available in U.S. only) 22572-0, 22573-9 Pa., Two-vol. set $19.90

THE CODEX NUTTALL, as first edited by Zelia Nuttall. Only inexpensive edition, in full color, of a pre-Columbian Mexican (Mixtec) book. 88 color plates show kings, gods, heroes, temples, sacrifices. New explanatory, historical introduction by Arthur G. Miller. 96pp. 11⅜ x 8½. (Available in U.S. only) 23168-2 Pa. $7.95

UNE SEMAINE DE BONTÉ, A SURREALISTIC NOVEL IN COLLAGE, Max Ernst. Masterpiece created out of 19th-century periodical illustrations, explores worlds of terror and surprise. Some consider this Ernst's greatest work. 208pp. 8⅛ x 11. 23252-2 Pa. $6.00

DRAWINGS OF WILLIAM BLAKE, William Blake. 92 plates from Book of Job, *Divine Comedy, Paradise Lost,* visionary heads, mythological figures, Laocoon, etc. Selection, introduction, commentary by Sir Geoffrey Keynes. 178pp. 8⅛ x 11. 22303-5 Pa. $5.00

ENGRAVINGS OF HOGARTH, William Hogarth. 101 of Hogarth's greatest works: *Rake's Progress, Harlot's Progress, Illustrations for Hudibras, Before and After, Beer Street and Gin Lane,* many more. Full commentary. 256pp. 11 x 13¾. 22479-1 Pa. $12.95

DAUMIER: 120 GREAT LITHOGRAPHS, Honore Daumier. Wide-ranging collection of lithographs by the greatest caricaturist of the 19th century. Concentrates on eternally popular series on lawyers, on married life, on liberated women, etc. Selection, introduction, and notes on plates by Charles F. Ramus. Total of 158pp. 9⅜ x 12¼. 23512-2 Pa. $6.00

DRAWINGS OF MUCHA, Alphonse Maria Mucha. Work reveals draftsman of highest caliber: studies for famous posters and paintings, renderings for book illustrations and ads, etc. 70 works, 9 in color; including 6 items not drawings. Introduction. List of illustrations. 72pp. 9⅜ x 12¼. (Available in U.S. only) 23672-2 Pa. $4.50

GIOVANNI BATTISTA PIRANESI: DRAWINGS IN THE PIERPONT MORGAN LIBRARY, Giovanni Battista Piranesi. For first time ever all of Morgan Library's collection, world's largest. 167 illustrations of rare Piranesi drawings—archeological, architectural, decorative and visionary. Essay, detailed list of drawings, chronology, captions. Edited by Felice Stampfle. 144pp. 9⅜ x 12¼. 23714-1 Pa. $7.50

NEW YORK ETCHINGS (1905-1949), John Sloan. All of important American artist's N.Y. life etchings. 67 works include some of his best art; also lively historical record—Greenwich Village, tenement scenes. Edited by Sloan's widow. Introduction and captions. 79pp. 8⅜ x 11¼. 23651-X Pa. $5.00

CHINESE PAINTING AND CALLIGRAPHY: A PICTORIAL SURVEY, Wan-go Weng. 69 fine examples from John M. Crawford's matchless private collection: landscapes, birds, flowers, human figures, etc., plus calligraphy. Every basic form included: hanging scrolls, handscrolls, album leaves, fans, etc. 109 illustrations. Introduction. Captions. 192pp. 8⅞ x 11¾. 23707-9 Pa. $7.95

DRAWINGS OF REMBRANDT, edited by Seymour Slive. Updated Lippmann, Hofstede de Groot edition, with definitive scholarly apparatus. All portraits, biblical sketches, landscapes, nudes, Oriental figures, classical studies, together with selection of work by followers. 550 illustrations. Total of 630pp. 9⅛ x 12¼. 21485-0, 21486-9 Pa., Two-vol. set $17.90

THE DISASTERS OF WAR, Francisco Goya. 83 etchings record horrors of Napoleonic wars in Spain and war in general. Reprint of 1st edition, plus 3 additional plates. Introduction by Philip Hofer. 97pp. 9⅜ x 8¼. 21872-4 Pa. $4.50

CATALOGUE OF DOVER BOOKS

THE EARLY WORK OF AUBREY BEARDSLEY, Aubrey Beardsley. 157 plates, 2 in color: *Manon Lescaut, Madame Bovary, Morte Darthur, Salome,* other. Introduction by H. Marillier. 182pp. 8⅛ x 11. 21816-3 Pa. $6.50

THE LATER WORK OF AUBREY BEARDSLEY, Aubrey Beardsley. Exotic masterpieces of full maturity: *Venus and Tannhauser, Lysistrata, Rape of the Lock, Volpone,* Savoy material, etc. 174 plates, 2 in color. 186pp. 8⅛ x 11. 21817-1 Pa. $5.95

THOMAS NAST'S CHRISTMAS DRAWINGS, Thomas Nast. Almost all Christmas drawings by creator of image of Santa Claus as we know it, and one of America's foremost illustrators and political cartoonists. 66 illustrations. 3 illustrations in color on covers. 96pp. 8⅜ x 11¼. 23660-9 Pa. $3.50

THE DORÉ ILLUSTRATIONS FOR DANTE'S DIVINE COMEDY, Gustave Doré. All 135 plates from Inferno, Purgatory, Paradise; fantastic tortures, infernal landscapes, celestial wonders. Each plate with appropriate (translated) verses. 141pp. 9 x 12. 23231-X Pa. $5.00

DORÉ'S ILLUSTRATIONS FOR RABELAIS, Gustave Doré. 252 striking illustrations of *Gargantua and Pantagruel* books by foremost 19th-century illustrator. Including 60 plates, 192 delightful smaller illustrations. 153pp. 9 x 12. 23656-0 Pa. $6.00

LONDON: A PILGRIMAGE, Gustave Doré, Blanchard Jerrold. Squalor, riches, misery, beauty of mid-Victorian metropolis; 55 wonderful plates, 125 other illustrations, full social, cultural text by Jerrold. 191pp. of text. 9⅜ x 12¼. 22306-X Pa. $7.00

THE RIME OF THE ANCIENT MARINER, Gustave Doré, S. T. Coleridge. Dore's finest work, 34 plates capture moods, subtleties of poem. Full text. Introduction by Millicent Rose. 77pp. 9¼ x 12. 22305-1 Pa. $4.50

THE DORE BIBLE ILLUSTRATIONS, Gustave Doré. All wonderful, detailed plates: Adam and Eve, Flood, Babylon, Life of Jesus, etc. Brief King James text with each plate. Introduction by Millicent Rose. 241 plates. 241pp. 9 x 12. 23004-X Pa. $6.95

THE COMPLETE ENGRAVINGS, ETCHINGS AND DRYPOINTS OF ALBRECHT DURER. "Knight, Death and Devil"; "Melencolia," and more—all Dürer's known works in all three media, including 6 works formerly attributed to him. 120 plates. 235pp. 8⅜ x 11¼. 22851-7 Pa. $7.50

MECHANICK EXERCISES ON THE WHOLE ART OF PRINTING, Joseph Moxon. First complete book (1683-4) ever written about typography, a compendium of everything known about printing at the latter part of 17th century. Reprint of 2nd (1962) Oxford Univ. Press edition. 74 illustrations. Total of 550pp. 6⅛ x 9¼. 23617-X Pa. $7.95

THE COMPLETE WOODCUTS OF ALBRECHT DURER, edited by Dr. W. Kurth. 346 in all: "Old Testament," "St. Jerome," "Passion," "Life of Virgin," Apocalypse," many others. Introduction by Campbell Dodgson. 285pp. 8½ x 12¼. 21097-9 Pa. $7.50

DRAWINGS OF ALBRECHT DURER, edited by Heinrich Wolfflin. 81 plates show development from youth to full style. Many favorites; many new. Introduction by Alfred Werner. 96pp. 8⅛ x 11. 22352-3 Pa. $6.00

THE HUMAN FIGURE, Albrecht Dürer. Experiments in various techniques—stereometric, progressive proportional, and others. Also life studies that rank among finest ever done. Complete reprinting of *Dresden Sketchbook*. 170 plates. 355pp. 8⅜ x 11¼. 21042-1 Pa. $7.95

OF THE JUST SHAPING OF LETTERS, Albrecht Dürer. Renaissance artist explains design of Roman majuscules by geometry, also Gothic lower and capitals. Grolier Club edition. 43pp. 7⅞ x 10¾ 21306-4 Pa. $3.00

TEN BOOKS ON ARCHITECTURE, Vitruvius. The most important book ever written on architecture. Early Roman aesthetics, technology, classical orders, site selection, all other aspects. Stands behind everything since. Morgan translation. 331pp. 5⅜ x 8½. 20645-9 Pa. $5.00

THE FOUR BOOKS OF ARCHITECTURE, Andrea Palladio. 16th-century classic responsible for Palladian movement and style. Covers classical architectural remains, Renaissance revivals, classical orders, etc. 1738 Ware English edition. Introduction by A. Placzek. 216 plates. 110pp. of text. 9½ x 12¾. 21308-0 Pa. $10.00

HORIZONS, Norman Bel Geddes. Great industrialist stage designer, "father of streamlining," on application of aesthetics to transportation, amusement, architecture, etc. 1932 prophetic account; function, theory, specific projects. 222 illustrations. 312pp. 7⅞ x 10¾. 23514-9 Pa. $6.95

FRANK LLOYD WRIGHT'S FALLINGWATER, Donald Hoffmann. Full, illustrated story of conception and building of Wright's masterwork at Bear Run, Pa. 100 photographs of site, construction, and details of completed structure. 112pp. 9¼ x 10. 23671-4 Pa. $5.95

THE ELEMENTS OF DRAWING, John Ruskin. Timeless classic by great Viltorian; starts with basic ideas, works through more difficult. Many practical exercises. 48 illustrations. Introduction by Lawrence Campbell. 228pp. 5⅜ x 8½. 22730-8 Pa. $3.75

GIST OF ART, John Sloan. Greatest modern American teacher, Art Students League, offers innumerable hints, instructions, guided comments to help you in painting. Not a formal course. 46 illustrations. Introduction by Helen Sloan. 200pp. 5⅜ x 8½. 23435-5 Pa. $4.00

CATALOGUE OF DOVER BOOKS

THE ANATOMY OF THE HORSE, George Stubbs. Often considered the great masterpiece of animal anatomy. Full reproduction of 1766 edition, plus prospectus; original text and modernized text. 36 plates. Introduction by Eleanor Garvey. 121pp. 11 x 14¾. 23402-9 Pa. $8.95

BRIDGMAN'S LIFE DRAWING, George B. Bridgman. More than 500 illustrative drawings and text teach you to abstract the body into its major masses, use light and shade, proportion; as well as specific areas of anatomy, of which Bridgman is master. 192pp. 6½ x 9¼. (Available in U.S. only) 22710-3 Pa. $4.50

ART NOUVEAU DESIGNS IN COLOR, Alphonse Mucha, Maurice Verneuil, Georges Auriol. Full-color reproduction of *Combinaisons ornementales* (c. 1900) by Art Nouveau masters. Floral, animal, geometric, interlacings, swashes—borders, frames, spots—all incredibly beautiful. 60 plates, hundreds of designs. 9⅜ x 8-1/16. 22885-1 Pa. $4.50

FULL-COLOR FLORAL DESIGNS IN THE ART NOUVEAU STYLE, E. A. Seguy. 166 motifs, on 40 plates, from *Les fleurs et leurs applications decoratives* (1902): borders, circular designs, repeats, allovers, "spots." All in authentic Art Nouveau colors. 48pp. 9⅜ x 12¼. 23439-8 Pa. $5.00

A DIDEROT PICTORIAL ENCYCLOPEDIA OF TRADES AND INDUSTRY, edited by Charles C. Gillispie. 485 most interesting plates from the great French Encyclopedia of the 18th century show hundreds of working figures, artifacts, process, land and cityscapes; glassmaking, papermaking, metal extraction, construction, weaving, making furniture, clothing, wigs, dozens of other activities. Plates fully explained. 920pp. 9 x 12. 22284-5, 22285-3 Clothbd., Two-vol. set $40.00

HANDBOOK OF EARLY ADVERTISING ART, Clarence P. Hornung. Largest collection of copyright-free early and antique advertising art ever compiled. Over 6,000 illustrations, from Franklin's time to the 1890's for special effects, novelty. Valuable source, almost inexhaustible.
Pictorial Volume. Agriculture, the zodiac, animals, autos, birds, Christmas, fire engines, flowers, trees, musical instruments, ships, games and sports, much more. Arranged by subject matter and use. 237 plates. 288pp. 9 x 12. 20122-8 Clothbd. $15.00

Typographical Volume. Roman and Gothic faces ranging from 10 point to 300 point, "Barnum," German and Old English faces, script, logotypes, scrolls and flourishes, 1115 ornamental initials, 67 complete alphabets, more. 310 plates. 320pp. 9 x 12. 20123-6 Clothbd. $15.00

CALLIGRAPHY (CALLIGRAPHIA LATINA), J. G. Schwandner. High point of 18th-century ornamental calligraphy. Very ornate initials, scrolls, borders, cherubs, birds, lettered examples. 172pp. 9 x 13. 20475-8 Pa. $7.95

ART FORMS IN NATURE, Ernst Haeckel. Multitude of strangely beautiful natural forms: Radiolaria, Foraminifera, jellyfishes, fungi, turtles, bats, etc. All 100 plates of the 19th-century evolutionist's *Kunstformen der Natur* (1904). 100pp. 9⅜ x 12¼. 22987-4 Pa. $5.00

CHILDREN: A PICTORIAL ARCHIVE FROM NINETEENTH-CENTURY SOURCES, edited by Carol Belanger Grafton. 242 rare, copyright-free wood engravings for artists and designers. Widest such selection available. All illustrations in line. 119pp. 8⅜ x 11¼. 23694-3 Pa. $4.00

WOMEN: A PICTORIAL ARCHIVE FROM NINETEENTH-CENTURY SOURCES, edited by Jim Harter. 391 copyright-free wood engravings for artists and designers selected from rare periodicals. Most extensive such collection available. All illustrations in line. 128pp. 9 x 12. 23703-6 Pa. $4.95

ARABIC ART IN COLOR, Prisse d'Avennes. From the greatest ornamentalists of all time—50 plates in color, rarely seen outside the Near East, rich in suggestion and stimulus. Includes 4 plates on covers. 46pp. 9⅜ x 12¼. 23658-7 Pa. $6.00

AUTHENTIC ALGERIAN CARPET DESIGNS AND MOTIFS, edited by June Beveridge. Algerian carpets are world famous. Dozens of geometrical motifs are charted on grids, color-coded, for weavers, needleworkers, craftsmen, designers. 53 illustrations plus 4 in color. 48pp. 8¼ x 11. (Available in U.S. only) 23650-1 Pa. $1.75

DICTIONARY OF AMERICAN PORTRAITS, edited by Hayward and Blanche Cirker. 4000 important Americans, earliest times to 1905, mostly in clear line. Politicians, writers, soldiers, scientists, inventors, industrialists, Indians, Blacks, women, outlaws, etc. Identificatory information. 756pp. 9¼ x 12¾. 21823-6 Clothbd. $65.00

HOW THE OTHER HALF LIVES, Jacob A. Riis. Journalistic record of filth, degradation, upward drive in New York immigrant slums, shops, around 1900. New edition includes 100 original Riis photos, monuments of early photography. 233pp. 10 x 7⅞. 22012-5 Pa. $7.00

NEW YORK IN THE THIRTIES, Berenice Abbott. Noted photographer's fascinating study of city shows new buildings that have become famous and old sights that have disappeared forever. Insightful commentary. 97 photographs. 97pp. 11⅜ x 10. 22967-X Pa. $6.00

MEN AT WORK, Lewis W. Hine. Famous photographic studies of construction workers, railroad men, factory workers and coal miners. New supplement of 18 photos on Empire State building construction. New introduction by Jonathan L. Doherty. Total of 69 photos. 63pp. 8 x 10¾. 23475-4 Pa. $4.00

CATALOGUE OF DOVER BOOKS

THE DEPRESSION YEARS AS PHOTOGRAPHED BY ARTHUR ROTH-STEIN, Arthur Rothstein. First collection devoted entirely to the work of outstanding 1930s photographer: famous dust storm photo, ragged children, unemployed, etc. 120 photographs. Captions. 119pp. 9¼ x 10¾.
23590-4 Pa. $5.95

CAMERA WORK: A PICTORIAL GUIDE, Alfred Stieglitz. All 559 illustrations and plates from the most important periodical in the history of art photography, Camera Work (1903-17). Presented four to a page, reduced in size but still clear, in strict chronological order, with complete captions. Three indexes. Glossary. Bibliography. 176pp. 8⅜ x 11¼.
23591-2 Pa. $6.95

ALVIN LANGDON COBURN, PHOTOGRAPHER, Alvin L. Coburn. Revealing autobiography by one of greatest photographers of 20th century gives insider's version of Photo-Secession, plus comments on his own work. 77 photographs by Coburn. Edited by Helmut and Alison Gernsheim. 160pp. 8⅛ x 11.
23685-4 Pa. $6.00

NEW YORK IN THE FORTIES, Andreas Feininger. 162 brilliant photographs by the well-known photographer, formerly with Life magazine, show commuters, shoppers, Times Square at night, Harlem nightclub, Lower East Side, etc. Introduction and full captions by John von Hartz. 181pp. 9¼ x 10¾.
23585-8 Pa. $6.95

GREAT NEWS PHOTOS AND THE STORIES BEHIND THEM, John Faber. Dramatic volume of 140 great news photos, 1855 through 1976, and revealing stories behind them, with both historical and technical information. Hindenburg disaster, shooting of Oswald, nomination of Jimmy Carter, etc. 160pp. 8¼ x 11.
23667-6 Pa. $6.00

THE ART OF THE CINEMATOGRAPHER, Leonard Maltin. Survey of American cinematography history and anecdotal interviews with 5 masters—Arthur Miller, Hal Mohr, Hal Rosson, Lucien Ballard, and Conrad Hall. Very large selection of behind-the-scenes production photos. 105 photographs. Filmographies. Index. Originally Behind the Camera. 144pp. 8¼ x 11.
23686-2 Pa. $5.00

DESIGNS FOR THE THREE-CORNERED HAT (LE TRICORNE), Pablo Picasso. 32 fabulously rare drawings—including 31 color illustrations of costumes and accessories—for 1919 production of famous ballet. Edited by Parmenia Migel, who has written new introduction. 48pp. 9⅜ x 12¼. (Available in U.S. only)
23709-5 Pa. $5.00

NOTES OF A FILM DIRECTOR, Sergei Eisenstein. Greatest Russian filmmaker explains montage, making of Alexander Nevsky, aesthetics; comments on self, associates, great rivals (Chaplin), similar material. 78 illustrations. 240pp. 5⅜ x 8½.
22392-2 Pa. $7.00

CATALOGUE OF DOVER BOOKS

HOLLYWOOD GLAMOUR PORTRAITS, edited by John Kobal. 145 photos capture the stars from 1926-49, the high point in portrait photography. Gable, Harlow, Bogart, Bacall, Hedy Lamarr, Marlene Dietrich, Robert Montgomery, Marlon Brando, Veronica Lake; 94 stars in all. Full background on photographers, technical aspects, much more. Total of 160pp. 8⅜ x 11¼. 23352-9 Pa. $6.95

THE NEW YORK STAGE: FAMOUS PRODUCTIONS IN PHOTO-GRAPHS, edited by Stanley Appelbaum. 148 photographs from Museum of City of New York show 142 plays, 1883-1939. *Peter Pan, The Front Page, Dead End, Our Town,* O'Neill, hundreds of actors and actresses, etc. Full indexes. 154pp. 9½ x 10. 23241-7 Pa. $6.00

DIALOGUES CONCERNING TWO NEW SCIENCES, Galileo Galilei. Encompassing 30 years of experiment and thought, these dialogues deal with geometric demonstrations of fracture of solid bodies, cohesion, leverage, speed of light and sound, pendulums, falling bodies, accelerated motion, etc. 300pp. 5⅜ x 8½. 60099-8 Pa. $5.50

THE GREAT OPERA STARS IN HISTORIC PHOTOGRAPHS, edited by James Camner. 343 portraits from the 1850s to the 1940s: Tamburini, Mario, Caliapin, Jeritza, Melchior, Melba, Patti, Pinza, Schipa, Caruso, Farrar, Steber, Gobbi, and many more—270 performers in all. Index. 199pp. 8⅜ x 11¼. 23575-0 Pa. $7.50

J. S. BACH, Albert Schweitzer. Great full-length study of Bach, life, background to music, music, by foremost modern scholar. Ernest Newman translation. 650 musical examples. Total of 928pp. 5⅜ x 8½. (Available in U.S. only) 21631-4, 21632-2 Pa., Two-vol. set $12.00

COMPLETE PIANO SONATAS, Ludwig van Beethoven. All sonatas in the fine Schenker edition, with fingering, analytical material. One of best modern editions. Total of 615pp. 9 x 12. (Available in U.S. only) 23134-8, 23135-6 Pa., Two-vol. set $17.90

KEYBOARD MUSIC, J. S. Bach. Bach-Gesellschaft edition. For harpsichord, piano, other keyboard instruments. English Suites, French Suites, Six Partitas, Goldberg Variations, Two-Part Inventions, Three-Part Sinfonias. 312pp. 8⅛ x 11. (Available in U.S. only) 22360-4 Pa. $7.95

FOUR SYMPHONIES IN FULL SCORE, Franz Schubert. Schubert's four most popular symphonies: No. 4 in C Minor ("Tragic"); No. 5 in B-flat Major; No. 8 in B Minor ("Unfinished"); No. 9 in C Major ("Great"). Breitkopf & Hartel edition. Study score. 261pp. 9⅜ x 12¼. 23681-1 Pa. $8.95

THE AUTHENTIC GILBERT & SULLIVAN SONGBOOK, W. S. Gilbert, A. S. Sullivan. Largest selection available; 92 songs, uncut, original keys, in piano rendering approved by Sullivan. Favorites and lesser-known fine numbers. Edited with plot synopses by James Spero. 3 illustrations. 399pp. 9 x 12. 23482-7 Pa.$10.95

CATALOGUE OF DOVER BOOKS

PRINCIPLES OF ORCHESTRATION, Nikolay Rimsky-Korsakov. Great classical orchestrator provides fundamentals of tonal resonance, progression of parts, voice and orchestra, tutti effects, much else in major document. 330pp. of musical excerpts. 489pp. 6½ x 9¼.   21266-1 Pa. $7.50

TRISTAN UND ISOLDE, Richard Wagner. Full orchestral score with complete instrumentation. Do not confuse with piano reduction. Commentary by Felix Mottl, great Wagnerian conductor and scholar. Study score. 655pp. 8⅛ x 11.   22915-7 Pa. $13.95

REQUIEM IN FULL SCORE, Giuseppe Verdi. Immensely popular with choral groups and music lovers. Republication of edition published by C. F. Peters, Leipzig, n. d. German frontmaker in English translation. Glossary. Text in Latin. Study score. 204pp. 9⅜ x 12¼.
23682-X Pa. $6.50

COMPLETE CHAMBER MUSIC FOR STRINGS, Felix Mendelssohn. All of Mendelssohn's chamber music: Octet, 2 Quintets, 6 Quartets, and Four Pieces for String Quartet. (Nothing with piano is included). Complete works edition (1874-7). Study score. 283 pp. 9⅜ x 12¼.
23679-X Pa. $7.50

POPULAR SONGS OF NINETEENTH-CENTURY AMERICA, edited by Richard Jackson. 64 most important songs: "Old Oaken Bucket," "Arkansas Traveler," "Yellow Rose of Texas," etc. Authentic original sheet music, full introduction and commentaries. 290pp. 9 x 12.   23270-0 Pa. $7.95

COLLECTED PIANO WORKS, Scott Joplin. Edited by Vera Brodsky Lawrence. Practically all of Joplin's piano works—rags, two-steps, marches, waltzes, etc., 51 works in all. Extensive introduction by Rudi Blesh. Total of 345pp. 9 x 12.   23106-2 Pa. $15.95

BASIC PRINCIPLES OF CLASSICAL BALLET, Agrippina Vaganova. Great Russian theoretician, teacher explains methods for teaching classical ballet; incorporates best from French, Italian, Russian schools. 118 illustrations. 175pp. 5⅜ x 8½.   22036-2 Pa. $2.75

CHINESE CHARACTERS, L. Wieger. Rich analysis of 2300 characters according to traditional systems into primitives. Historical-semantic analysis to phonetics (Classical Mandarin) and radicals. 820pp. 6⅛ x 9¼.
21321-8 Pa. $12.50

THE WARES OF THE MING DYNASTY, R. L. Hobson. Foremost scholar examines and illustrates many varieties of Ming (1368-1644). Famous blue and white, polychrome, lesser-known styles and shapes. 117 illustrations, 9 full color, of outstanding pieces. Total of 263pp. 6⅛ x 9¼. (Available in U.S. only)   23652-8 Pa. $6.00

AN ETYMOLOGICAL DICTIONARY OF MODERN ENGLISH, Ernest Weekley. Richest, fullest work, by foremost British lexicographer. Detailed word histories. Inexhaustible. Do not confuse this with Concise Etymological Dictionary, which is abridged. Total of 856pp. 6½ x 9¼.
21873-2, 21874-0 Pa., Two-vol. set $13.00

A MAYA GRAMMAR, Alfred M. Tozzer. Practical, useful English-language grammar by the Harvard anthropologist who was one of the three greatest American scholars in the area of Maya culture. Phonetics, grammatical processes, syntax, more. 301pp. 5⅜ x 8½.   23465-7 Pa. $4.00

THE JOURNAL OF HENRY D. THOREAU, edited by Bradford Torrey, F. H. Allen. Complete reprinting of 14 volumes, 1837-61, over two million words; the sourcebooks for *Walden*, etc. Definitive. All original sketches, plus 75 photographs. Introduction by Walter Harding. Total of 1804pp. 8½ x 12¼.   20312-3, 20313-1 Clothbd., Two-vol. set $80.00

CLASSIC GHOST STORIES, Charles Dickens and others. 18 wonderful stories you've wanted to reread: "The Monkey's Paw," "The House and the Brain," "The Upper Berth," "The Signalman," "Dracula's Guest," "The Tapestried Chamber," etc. Dickens, Scott, Mary Shelley, Stoker, etc. 330pp. 5⅜ x 8½.   20735-8 Pa. $4.50

SEVEN SCIENCE FICTION NOVELS, H. G. Wells. Full novels. *First Men in the Moon, Island of Dr. Moreau, War of the Worlds, Food of the Gods, Invisible Man, Time Machine, In the Days of the Comet.* A basic science-fiction library. 1015pp. 5⅜ x 8½. (Available in U.S. only)
     20264-X Clothbd. $15.00

ARMADALE, Wilkie Collins. Third great mystery novel by the author of *The Woman in White* and *The Moonstone.* Ingeniously plotted narrative shows an exceptional command of character, incident and mood. Original magazine version with 40 illustrations. 597pp. 5⅜ x 8½.
     23429-0 Pa. $7.95

FLATLAND, E. A. Abbott. Science-fiction classic explores life of 2-D being in 3-D world. Read also as introduction to thought about hyperspace. Introduction by Banesh Hoffmann. 16 illustrations. 103pp. 5⅜ x 8½.
     20001-9 Pa. $2.75

AYESHA: THE RETURN OF "SHE," H. Rider Haggard. Virtuoso sequel featuring the great mythic creation, Ayesha, in an adventure that is fully as good as the first book, *She.* Original magazine version, with 47 original illustrations by Maurice Greiffenhagen. 189pp. 6½ x 9¼.
     23649-8 Pa. $3.50

ORIENTAL RUGS, ANTIQUE AND MODERN, Walter A. Hawley. Persia, Turkey, Caucasus, Central Asia, China, other traditions. Best general survey of all aspects: styles and periods, manufacture, uses, symbols and their interpretation, and identification. 96 illustrations, 11 in color. 320pp. 6⅛ x 9¼.   22366-3 Pa. $6.95

CHINESE POTTERY AND PORCELAIN, R. L. Hobson. Detailed descriptions and analyses by former Keeper of the Department of Oriental Antiquities and Ethnography at the British Museum. Covers hundreds of pieces from primitive times to 1915. Still the standard text for most periods. 136 plates, 40 in full color. Total of 750pp. 5⅜ x 8½.
     23253-0 Pa. $10.00

UNCLE SILAS, J. Sheridan LeFanu. Victorian Gothic mystery novel, considered by many best of period, even better than Collins or Dickens. Wonderful psychological terror. Introduction by Frederick Shroyer. 436pp. 5⅜ x 8½.   21715-9 Pa. $6.95

JURGEN, James Branch Cabell. The great erotic fantasy of the 1920's that delighted thousands, shocked thousands more. Full final text, Lane edition with 13 plates by Frank Pape. 346pp. 5⅜ x 8½.
                                                  23507-6 Pa. $4.50

THE CLAVERINGS, Anthony Trollope. Major novel, chronicling aspects of British Victorian society, personalities. Reprint of Cornhill serialization, 16 plates by M. Edwards; first reprint of full text. Introduction by Norman Donaldson. 412pp. 5⅜ x 8½.   23464-9 Pa. $5.00

KEPT IN THE DARK, Anthony Trollope. Unusual short novel about Victorian morality and abnormal psychology by the great English author. Probably the first American publication. Frontispiece by Sir John Millais. 92pp. 6½ x 9¼.   23609-9 Pa. $2.50

RALPH THE HEIR, Anthony Trollope. Forgotten tale of illegitimacy, inheritance. Master novel of Trollope's later years. Victorian country estates, clubs, Parliament, fox hunting, world of fully realized characters. Reprint of 1871 edition. 12 illustrations by F. A. Faser. 434pp. of text. 5⅜ x 8½.   23642-0 Pa. $6.50

YEKL and THE IMPORTED BRIDEGROOM AND OTHER STORIES OF THE NEW YORK GHETTO, Abraham Cahan. Film *Hester Street* based on *Yekl* (1896). Novel, other stories among first about Jewish immigrants of N.Y.'s East Side. Highly praised by W. D. Howells—Cahan "a new star of realism." New introduction by Bernard G. Richards. 240pp. 5⅜ x 8½.   22427-9 Pa. $3.50

THE HIGH PLACE, James Branch Cabell. Great fantasy writer's enchanting comedy of disenchantment set in 18th-century France. Considered by some critics to be even better than his famous *Jurgen*. 10 illustrations and numerous vignettes by noted fantasy artist Frank C. Pape. 320pp. 5⅜ x 8½.   23670-6 Pa. $4.00

ALICE'S ADVENTURES UNDER GROUND, Lewis Carroll. Facsimile of ms. Carroll gave Alice Liddell in 1864. Different in many ways from final Alice. Handlettered, illustrated by Carroll. Introduction by Martin Gardner. 128pp. 5⅜ x 8½.   21482-6 Pa. $2.50

FAVORITE ANDREW LANG FAIRY TALE BOOKS IN MANY COLORS, Andrew Lang. The four Lang favorites in a boxed set—the complete *Red, Green, Yellow* and *Blue* Fairy Books. 164 stories; 439 illustrations by Lancelot Speed, Henry Ford and G. P. Jacomb Hood. Total of about 1500pp. 5⅜ x 8½.   23407-X Boxed set, Pa. $16.95

HOUSEHOLD STORIES BY THE BROTHERS GRIMM. All the great Grimm stories: "Rumpelstiltskin," "Snow White," "Hansel and Gretel," etc., with 114 illustrations by Walter Crane. 269pp. 5⅜ x 8½.
21080-4 Pa. $3.50

SLEEPING BEAUTY, illustrated by Arthur Rackham. Perhaps the fullest, most delightful version ever, told by C. S. Evans. Rackham's best work. 49 illustrations. 110pp. 7⅞ x 10¾. 22756-1 Pa. $2.95

AMERICAN FAIRY TALES, L. Frank Baum. Young cowboy lassoes Father Time; dummy in Mr. Floman's department store window comes to life; and 10 other fairy tales. 41 illustrations by N. P. Hall, Harry Kennedy, Ike Morgan, and Ralph Gardner. 209pp. 5⅜ x 8½. 23643-9 Pa. $3.00

THE WONDERFUL WIZARD OF OZ, L. Frank Baum. Facsimile in full color of America's finest children's classic. Introduction by Martin Gardner. 143 illustrations by W. W. Denslow. 267pp. 5⅜ x 8½.
20691-2 Pa. $4.50

THE TALE OF PETER RABBIT, Beatrix Potter. The inimitable Peter's terrifying adventure in Mr. McGregor's garden, with all 27 wonderful, full-color Potter illustrations. 55pp. 4¼ x 5½. (Available in U.S. only)
22827-4 Pa. $1.50

THE STORY OF KING ARTHUR AND HIS KNIGHTS, Howard Pyle. Finest children's version of life of King Arthur. 48 illustrations by Pyle. 131pp. 6⅛ x 9¼. 21445-1 Pa. $5.95

CARUSO'S CARICATURES, Enrico Caruso. Great tenor's remarkable caricatures of self, fellow musicians, composers, others. Toscanini, Puccini, Farrar, etc. Impish, cutting, insightful. 473 illustrations. Preface by M. Sisca. 217pp. 8⅜ x 11¼. 23528-9 Pa. $6.95

PERSONAL NARRATIVE OF A PILGRIMAGE TO ALMADINAH AND MECCAH, Richard Burton. Great travel classic by remarkably colorful personality. Burton, disguised as a Moroccan, visited sacred shrines of Islam, narrowly escaping death. Wonderful observations of Islamic life, customs, personalities. 47 illustrations. Total of 959pp. 5⅜ x 8½.
21217-3, 21218-1 Pa., Two-vol. set $14.00

INCIDENTS OF TRAVEL IN YUCATAN, John L. Stephens. Classic (1843) exploration of jungles of Yucatan, looking for evidences of Maya civilization. Travel adventures, Mexican and Indian culture, etc. Total of 669pp. 5⅜ x 8½. 20926-1, 20927-X Pa., Two-vol. set $7.90

AMERICAN LITERARY AUTOGRAPHS FROM WASHINGTON IRVING TO HENRY JAMES, Herbert Cahoon, et al. Letters, poems, manuscripts of Hawthorne, Thoreau, Twain, Alcott, Whitman, 67 other prominent American authors. Reproductions, full transcripts and commentary. Plus checklist of all American Literary Autographs in The Pierpont Morgan Library. Printed on exceptionally high-quality paper. 136 illustrations. 212pp. 9⅛ x 12¼. 23548-3 Pa. $12.50

AN AUTOBIOGRAPHY, Margaret Sanger. Exciting personal account of hard-fought battle for woman's right to birth control, against prejudice, church, law. Foremost feminist document. 504pp. 5⅜ x 8½.

20470-7 Pa. $7.50

MY BONDAGE AND MY FREEDOM, Frederick Douglass. Born as a slave, Douglass became outspoken force in antislavery movement. The best of Douglass's autobiographies. Graphic description of slave life. Introduction by P. Foner. 464pp. 5⅜ x 8½. 22457-0 Pa. $6.50

LIVING MY LIFE, Emma Goldman. Candid, no holds barred account by foremost American anarchist: her own life, anarchist movement, famous contemporaries, ideas and their impact. Struggles and confrontations in America, plus deportation to U.S.S.R. Shocking inside account of persecution of anarchists under Lenin. 13 plates. Total of 944pp. 5⅜ x 8½.

22543-7, 22544-5 Pa., Two-vol. set $12.00

LETTERS AND NOTES ON THE MANNERS, CUSTOMS AND CONDITIONS OF THE NORTH AMERICAN INDIANS, George Catlin. Classic account of life among Plains Indians: ceremonies, hunt, warfare, etc. Dover edition reproduces for first time all original paintings. 312 plates. 572pp. of text. 6⅛ x 9¼. 22118-0, 22119-9 Pa.. Two-vol. set $12.00

THE MAYA AND THEIR NEIGHBORS, edited by Clarence L. Hay, others. Synoptic view of Maya civilization in broadest sense, together with Northern, Southern neighbors. Integrates much background, valuable detail not elsewhere. Prepared by greatest scholars: Kroeber, Morley, Thompson, Spinden, Vaillant, many others. Sometimes called Tozzer Memorial Volume. 60 illustrations, linguistic map. 634pp. 5⅜ x 8½.

23510-6 Pa. $10.00

HANDBOOK OF THE INDIANS OF CALIFORNIA, A. L. Kroeber. Foremost American anthropologist offers complete ethnographic study of each group. Monumental classic. 459 illustrations, maps. 995pp. 5⅜ x 8½.

23368-5 Pa. $13.00

SHAKTI AND SHAKTA, Arthur Avalon. First book to give clear, cohesive analysis of Shakta doctrine, Shakta ritual and Kundalini Shakti (yoga). Important work by one of world's foremost students of Shaktic and Tantric thought. 732pp. 5⅜ x 8½. (Available in U.S. only)

23645-5 Pa. $7.95

AN INTRODUCTION TO THE STUDY OF THE MAYA HIEROGLYPHS, Syvanus Griswold Morley. Classic study by one of the truly great figures in hieroglyph research. Still the best introduction for the student for reading Maya hieroglyphs. New introduction by J. Eric S. Thompson. 117 illustrations. 284pp. 5⅜ x 8½. 23108-9 Pa. $4.00

A STUDY OF MAYA ART, Herbert J. Spinden. Landmark classic interprets Maya symbolism, estimates styles, covers ceramics, architecture, murals, stone carvings as artforms. Still a basic book in area. New introduction by J. Eric Thompson. Over 750 illustrations. 341pp. 8⅜ x 11¼.

21235-1 Pa. $6.95

GEOMETRY, RELATIVITY AND THE FOURTH DIMENSION, Rudolf Rucker. Exposition of fourth dimension, means of visualization, concepts of relativity as Flatland characters continue adventures. Popular, easily followed yet accurate, profound. 141 illustrations. 133pp. 5⅜ x 8½.
23400-2 Pa. $2.75

THE ORIGIN OF LIFE, A. I. Oparin. Modern classic in biochemistry, the first rigorous examination of possible evolution of life from nitrocarbon compounds. Non-technical, easily followed. Total of 295pp. 5⅜ x 8½.
60213-3 Pa. $5.95

PLANETS, STARS AND GALAXIES, A. E. Fanning. Comprehensive introductory survey: the sun, solar system, stars, galaxies, universe, cosmology; quasars, radio stars, etc. 24pp. of photographs. 189pp. 5⅜ x 8½. (Available in U.S. only)
21680-2 Pa. $3.75

THE THIRTEEN BOOKS OF EUCLID'S ELEMENTS, translated with introduction and commentary by Sir Thomas L. Heath. Definitive edition. Textual and linguistic notes, mathematical analysis, 2500 years of critical commentary. Do not confuse with abridged school editions. Total of 1414pp. 5⅜ x 8½.   60088-2, 60089-0, 60090-4 Pa., Three-vol. set $19.50

Prices subject to change without notice.

Available at your book dealer or write for free catalogue to Dept. GI, Dover Publications, Inc., 180 Varick St., N.Y., N.Y. 10014. Dover publishes more than 175 books each year on science, elementary and advanced mathematics, biology, music, art, literary history, social sciences and other areas.